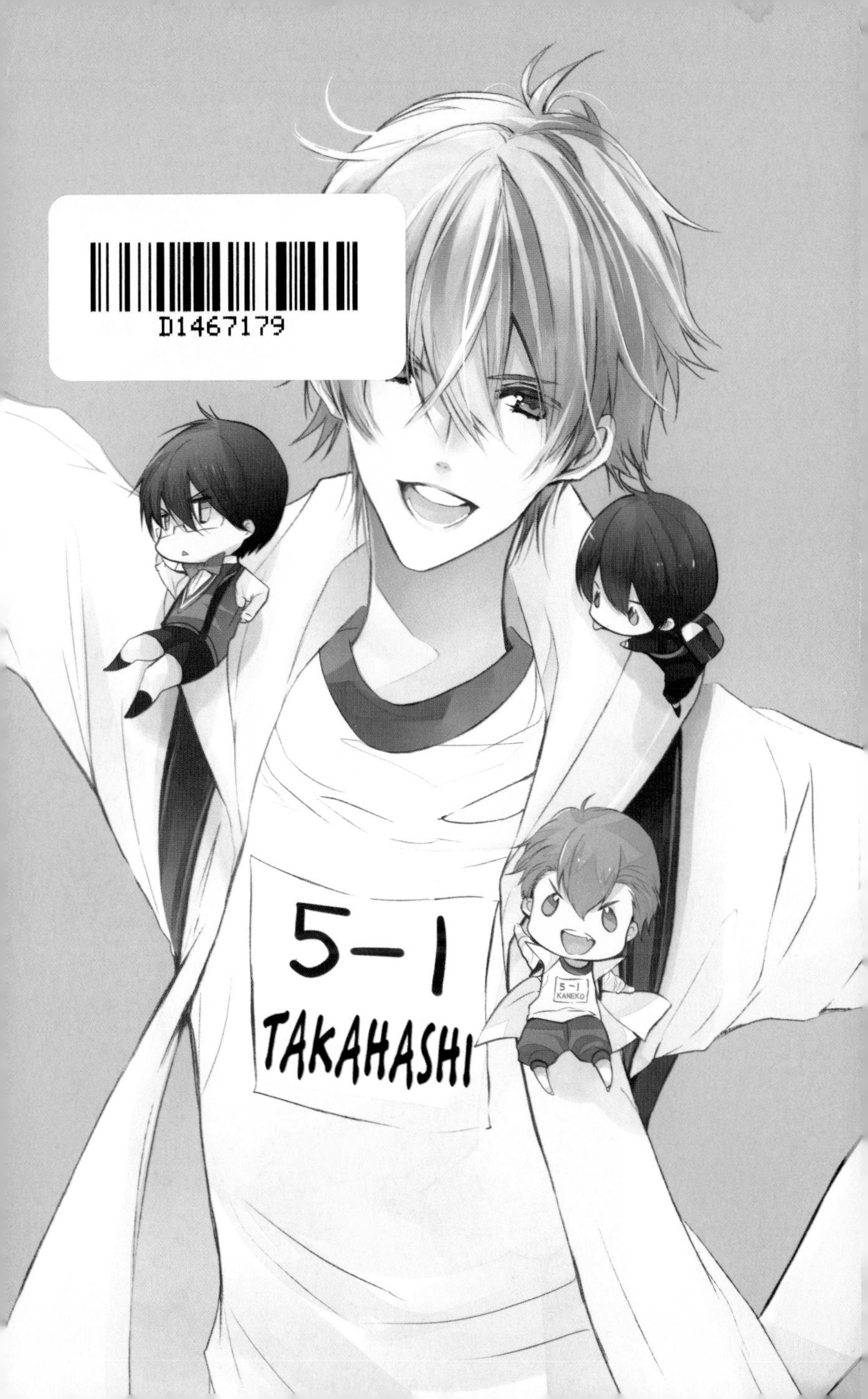
5-1
TAKAHASHI
5-1
KANEKO

CONTENTS

PACHIMON

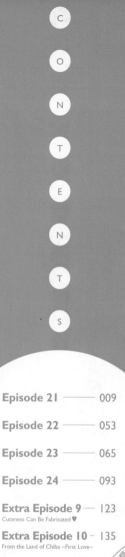

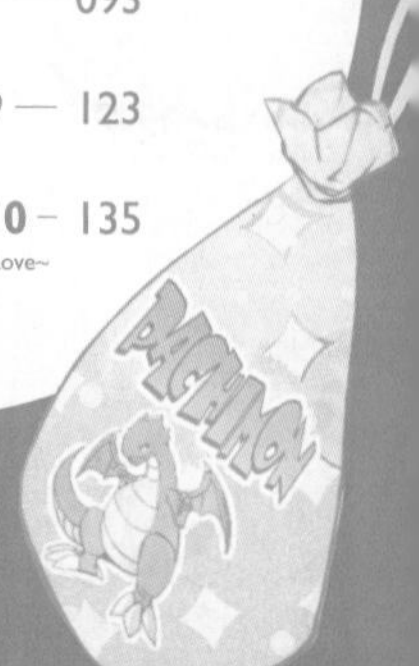

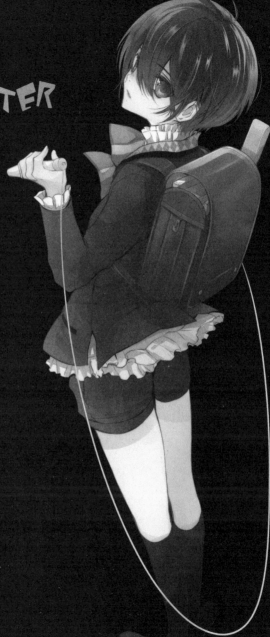

FiRST
LOVE
MONSTER

6

Akira
Hiyoshimaru

FIRST LOVE MONSTER

Character Introductions

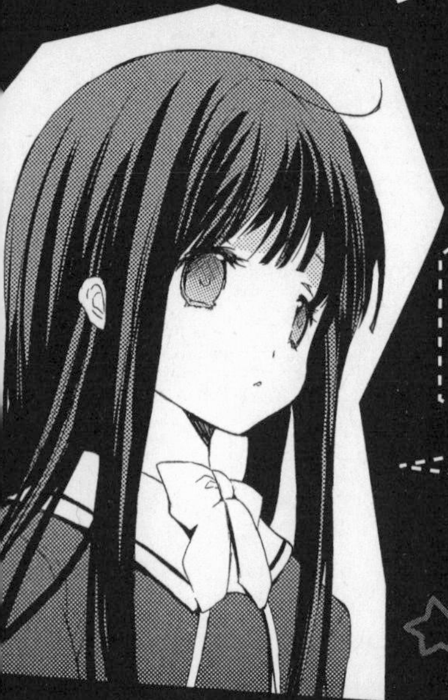

KASUMI RESIDENCY, ROOM #7
KAHO NIKAIDOU
(H.S. FIRST-YEAR)

Our heroine. A sheltered little rich girl who tends to dwell on the negative. She's living on her own for the first time at Kasumi Residency.

KASUMI RESIDENCY, LANDLORD'S ROOM
KANADE TAKAHASHI
(ELEMENTARY SCH. FIFTH-YEAR)

A hot guy on the outside, a child on the inside. His behavior charms and sometimes bewilders Kaho.

On the day she moves in, Kaho is nearly hit by a truck but is rescued at the last moment by a hot guy and instantly falls in love. They start dating, but it turns out that her boyfriend, Kanade Takahashi, is in the fifth grade!

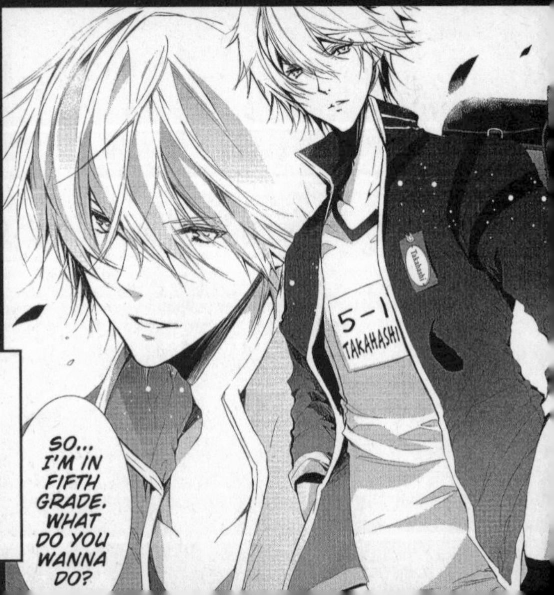
5-1 TAKAHASHI
SO... I'M IN FIFTH GRADE. WHAT DO YOU WANNA DO?

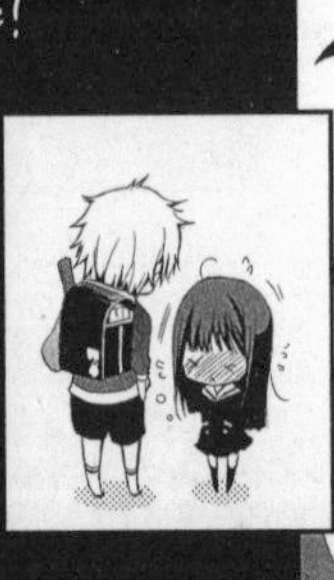

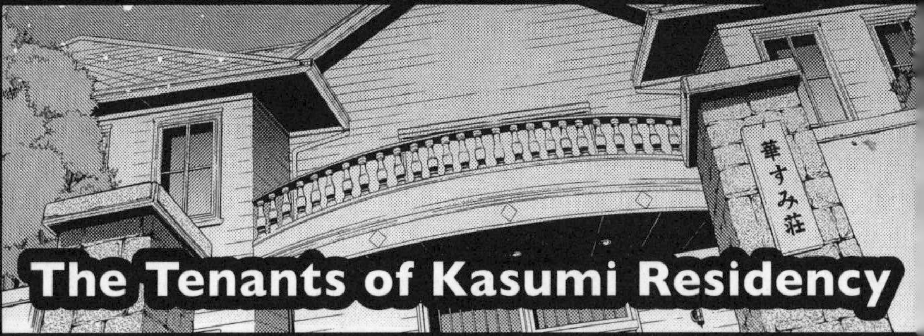
華すみ荘

The Tenants of Kasumi Residency

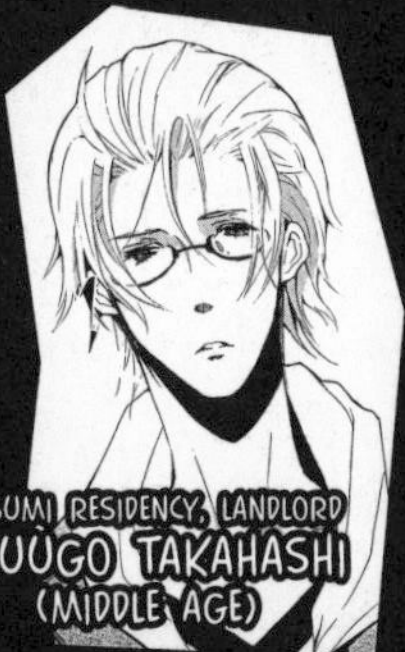

KASUMI RESIDENCY, LANDLORD
SHUUGO TAKAHASHI
(MIDDLE AGE)

Kanade's father. After the passing of his wife two years ago, he has been raising Kanade as a single father. Sometimes he has a hard time taking hints, apparently...

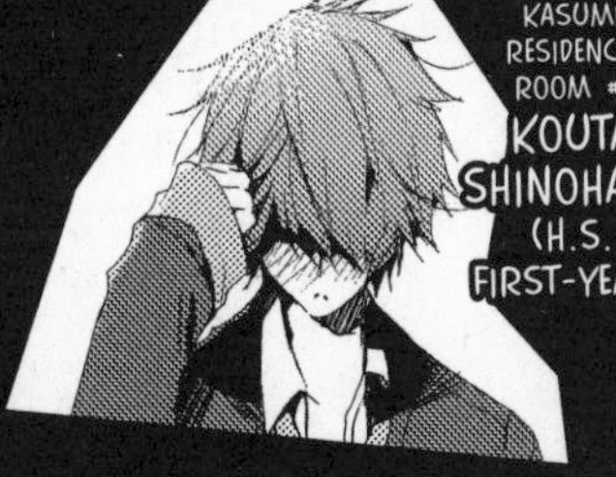

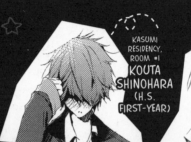

KASUMI RESIDENCY, ROOM #1
KOUTA SHINOHARA
(H.S. FIRST-YEAR)

A chaste and shy weakling, the same age as Kaho. Behind his bangs is the face of a beautiful young girl. As someone who can sympathize with Kaho, he couldn't help falling in love.

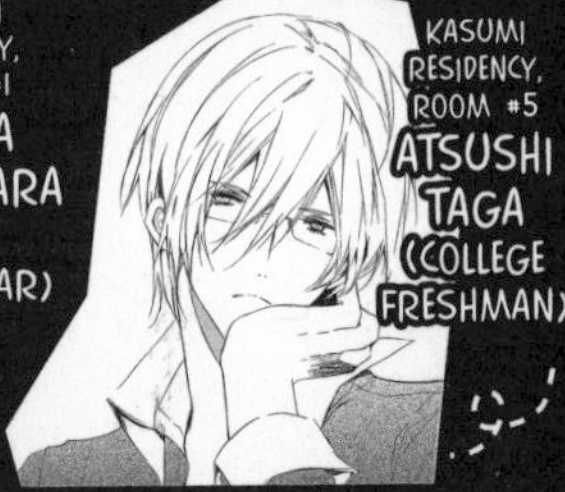

KASUMI RESIDENCY, ROOM #5
ATSUSHI TAGA
(COLLEGE FRESHMAN)

A heartless, bespectacled beast who pretends to be nice to Kaho, then tricks and bullies her. Apparently he hates her so much he doesn't know what to do with himself, but...

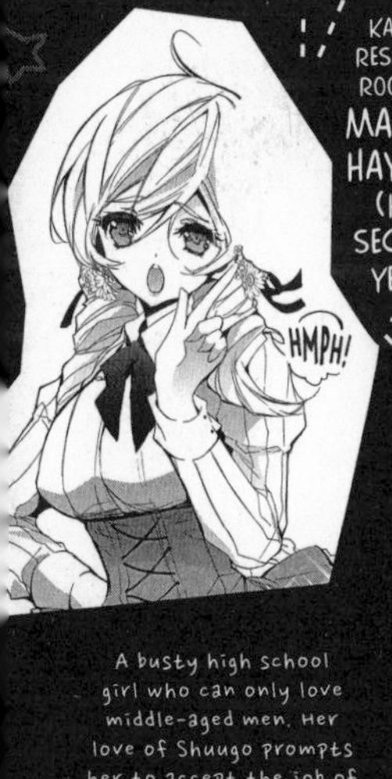
HMPH!

KASUMI RESIDENCY, ROOM #6
MAFUYU HAYASHI
(H.S. SECOND-YEAR)

A busty high school girl who can only love middle-aged men. Her love of Shuugo prompts her to accept the job of tutoring Kanade.

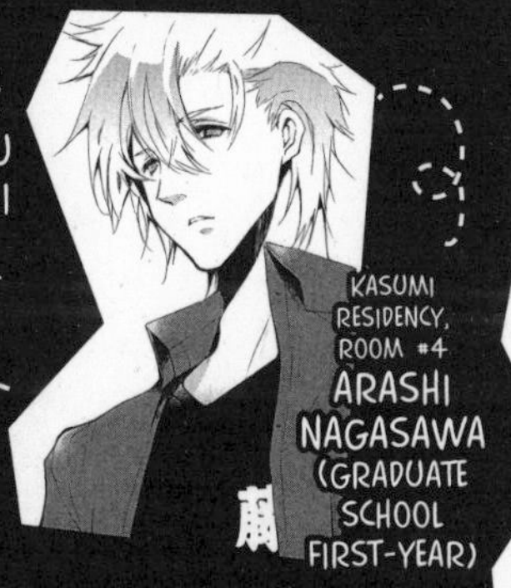

KASUMI RESIDENCY, ROOM #4
ARASHI NAGASAWA
(GRADUATE SCHOOL FIRST-YEAR)

Obsessed with figurines and lady boys, he is Chiaki's disappointing boyfriend. A caring man who lends a listening ear to Kaho.

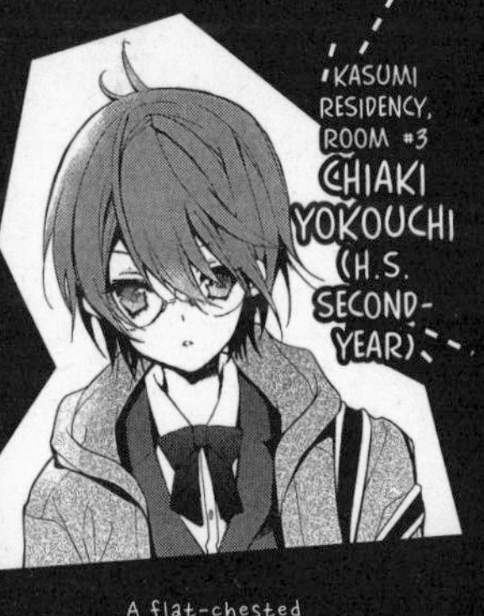

KASUMI RESIDENCY, ROOM #3
CHIAKI YOKOUCHI
(H.S. SECOND-YEAR)

A flat-chested upperclassman who is fundamentally a sadist but occasionally shows her tsundere side. Is dating Arashi.

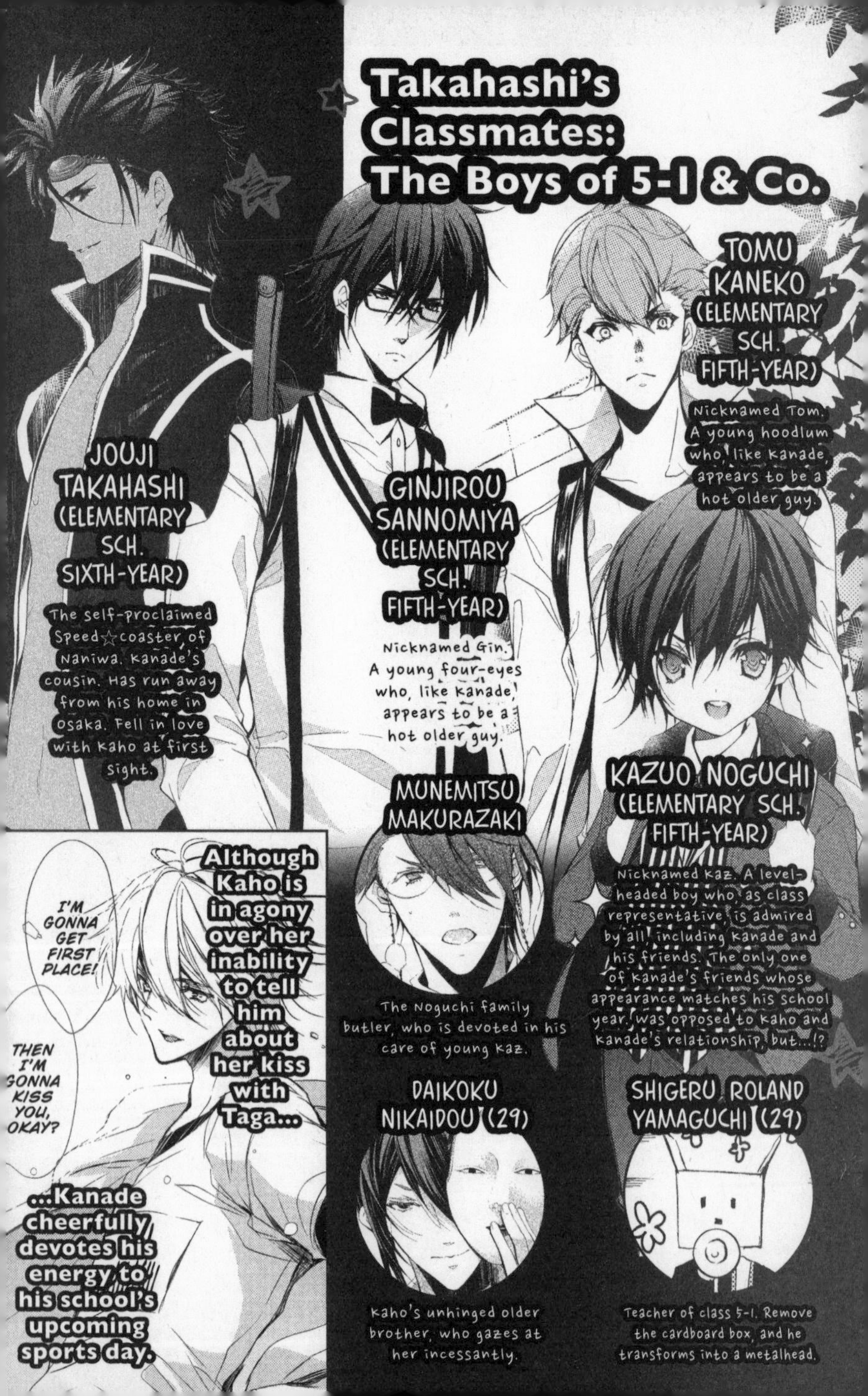
Takahashi's Classmates: The Boys of 5-1 & Co.
TOMU KANEKO (ELEMENTARY SCH. FIFTH-YEAR)
Nicknamed Tom. A young hoodlum who, like Kanade, appears to be a hot older guy.
GINJIROU SANNOMIYA (ELEMENTARY SCH. FIFTH-YEAR)
Nicknamed Gin. A young four-eyes who, like Kanade, appears to be a hot older guy.
JOUJI TAKAHASHI (ELEMENTARY SCH. SIXTH-YEAR)
The self-proclaimed Speed☆coaster of Naniwa. Kanade's cousin. Has run away from his home in Osaka. Fell in love with Kaho at first sight.
KAZUO NOGUCHI (ELEMENTARY SCH. FIFTH-YEAR)
Nicknamed Kaz. A level-headed boy who, as class representative, is admired by all, including Kanade and his friends. The only one of Kanade's friends whose appearance matches his school year. Was opposed to Kaho and Kanade's relationship, but...!?
MUNEMITSU MAKURAZAKI
The Noguchi family butler, who is devoted in his care of young Kaz.
Although Kaho is in agony over her inability to tell him about her kiss with Taga...
I'M GONNA GET FIRST PLACE!
THEN I'M GONNA KISS YOU, OKAY?
...Kanade cheerfully devotes his energy to his school's upcoming sports day.
SHIGERU ROLAND YAMAGUCHI (29)
Teacher of class 5-1. Remove the cardboard box, and he transforms into a metalhead.
DAIKOKU NIKAIDOU (29)
Kaho's unhinged older brother, who gazes at her incessantly.

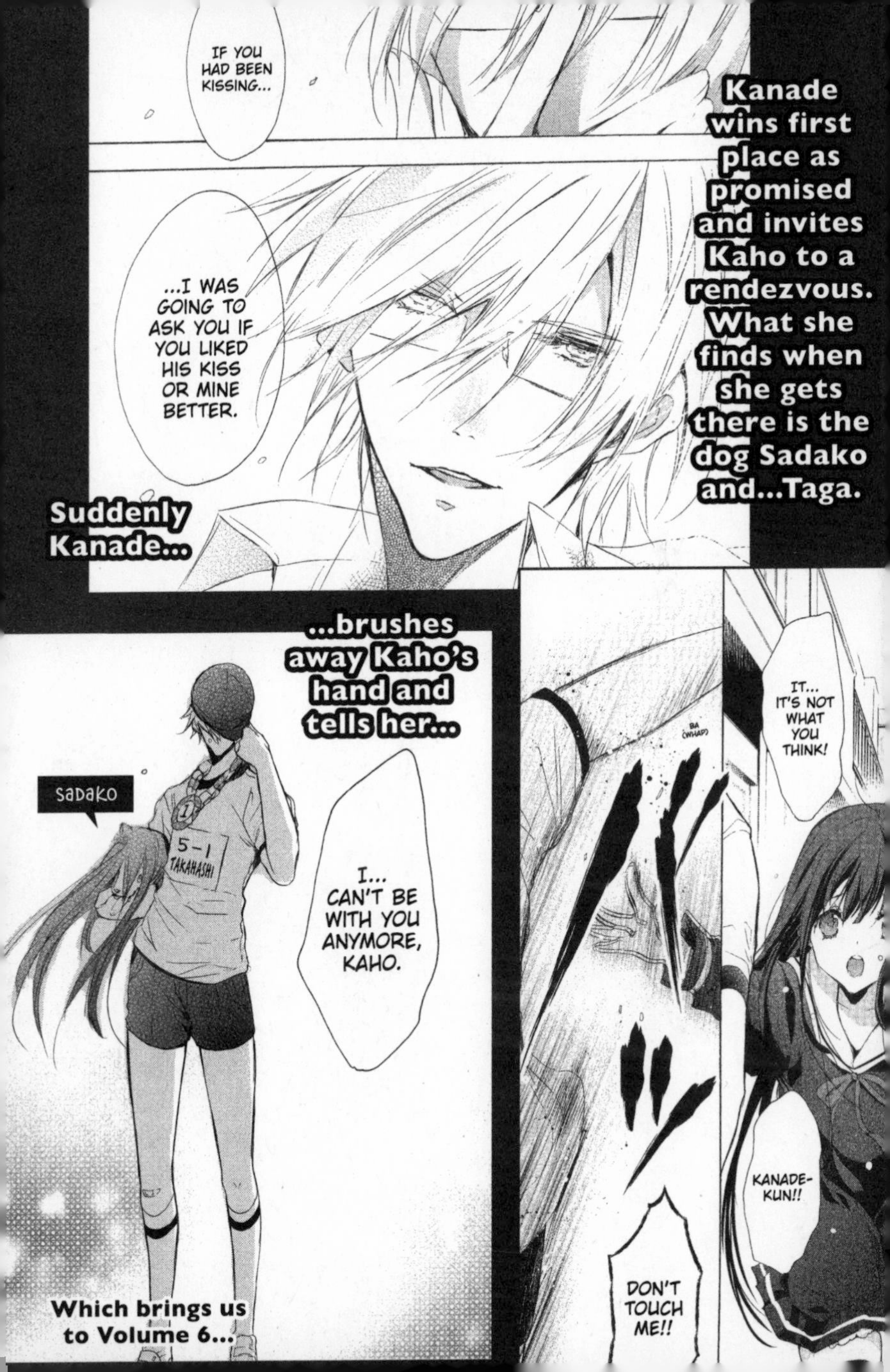
Kanade wins first place as promised and invites Kaho to a rendezvous. What she finds when she gets there is the dog Sadako and...Taga.
IF YOU HAD BEEN KISSING...
...I WAS GOING TO ASK YOU IF YOU LIKED HIS KISS OR MINE BETTER.
Suddenly Kanade...
IT... IT'S NOT WHAT YOU THINK!
BA (WHAP)
KANADE-KUN!!
DON'T TOUCH ME!!
...brushes away Kaho's hand and tells her...
SADAKO
5-1 TAKAHASHI
I... CAN'T BE WITH YOU ANYMORE, KAHO.
Which brings us to Volume 6...

first love monster

Episode 21

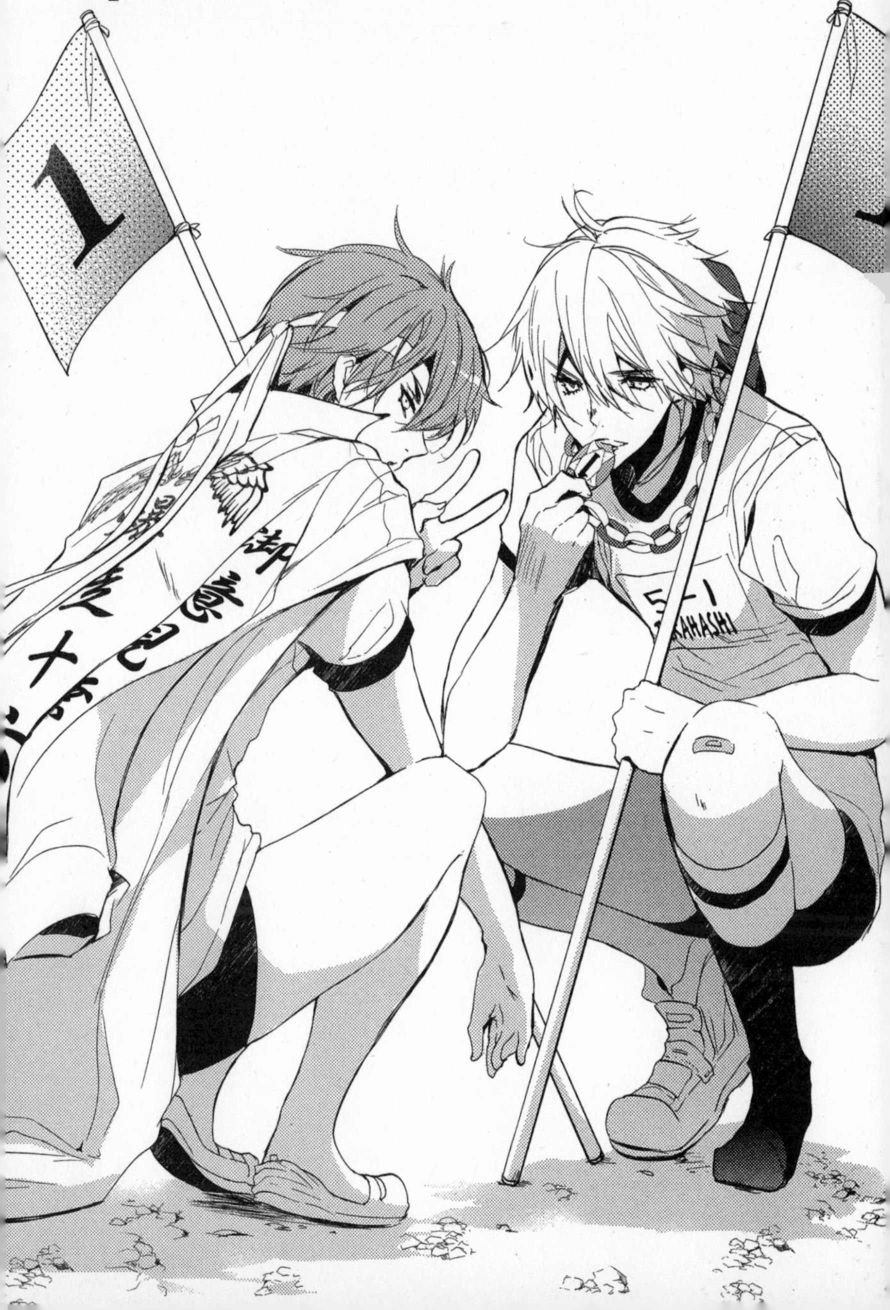
5-1

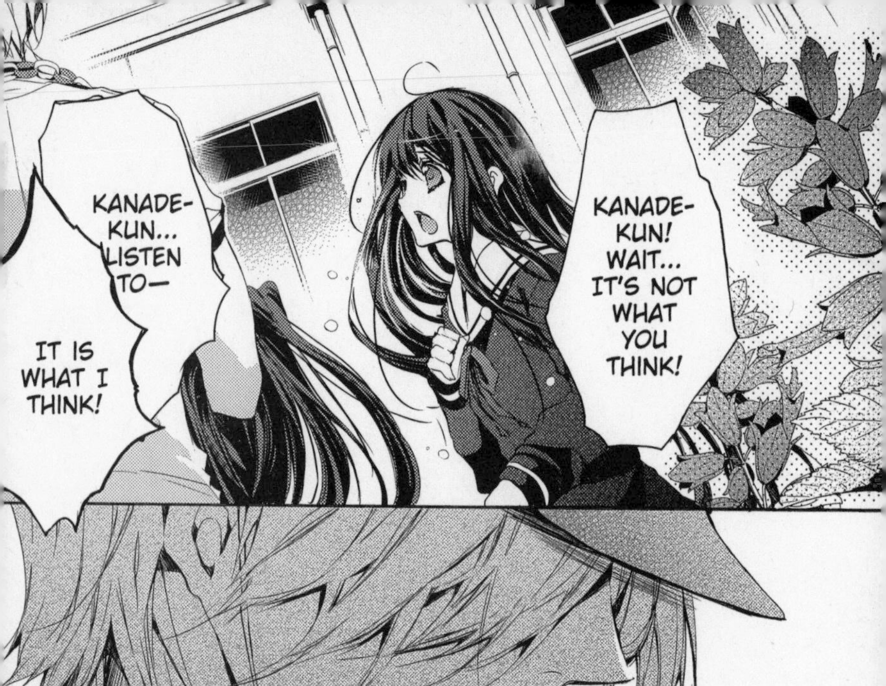
KANADE-KUN! WAIT... IT'S NOT WHAT YOU THINK!
KANADE-KUN... LISTEN TO—
IT IS WHAT I THINK!
IT'S... TOO LATE.

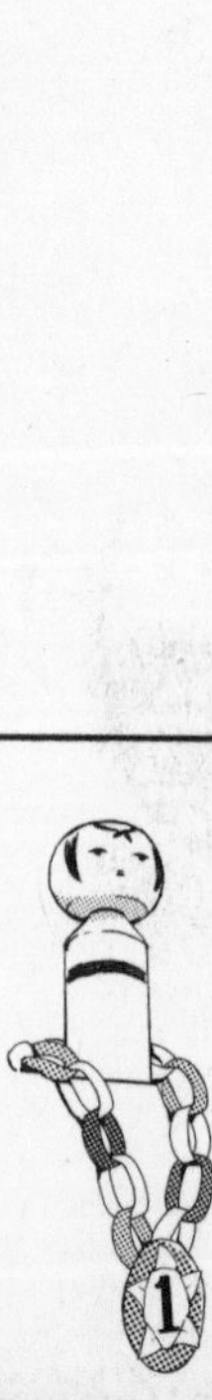
1

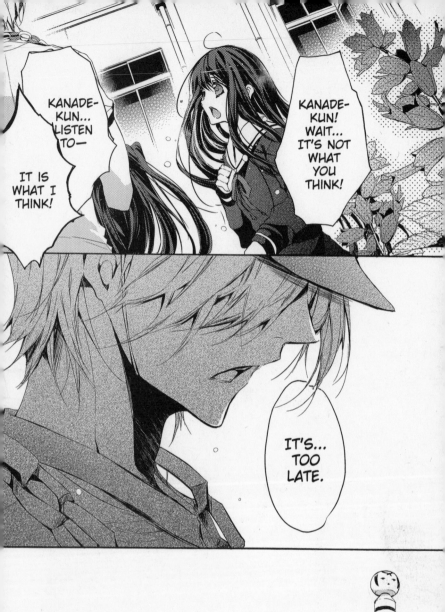

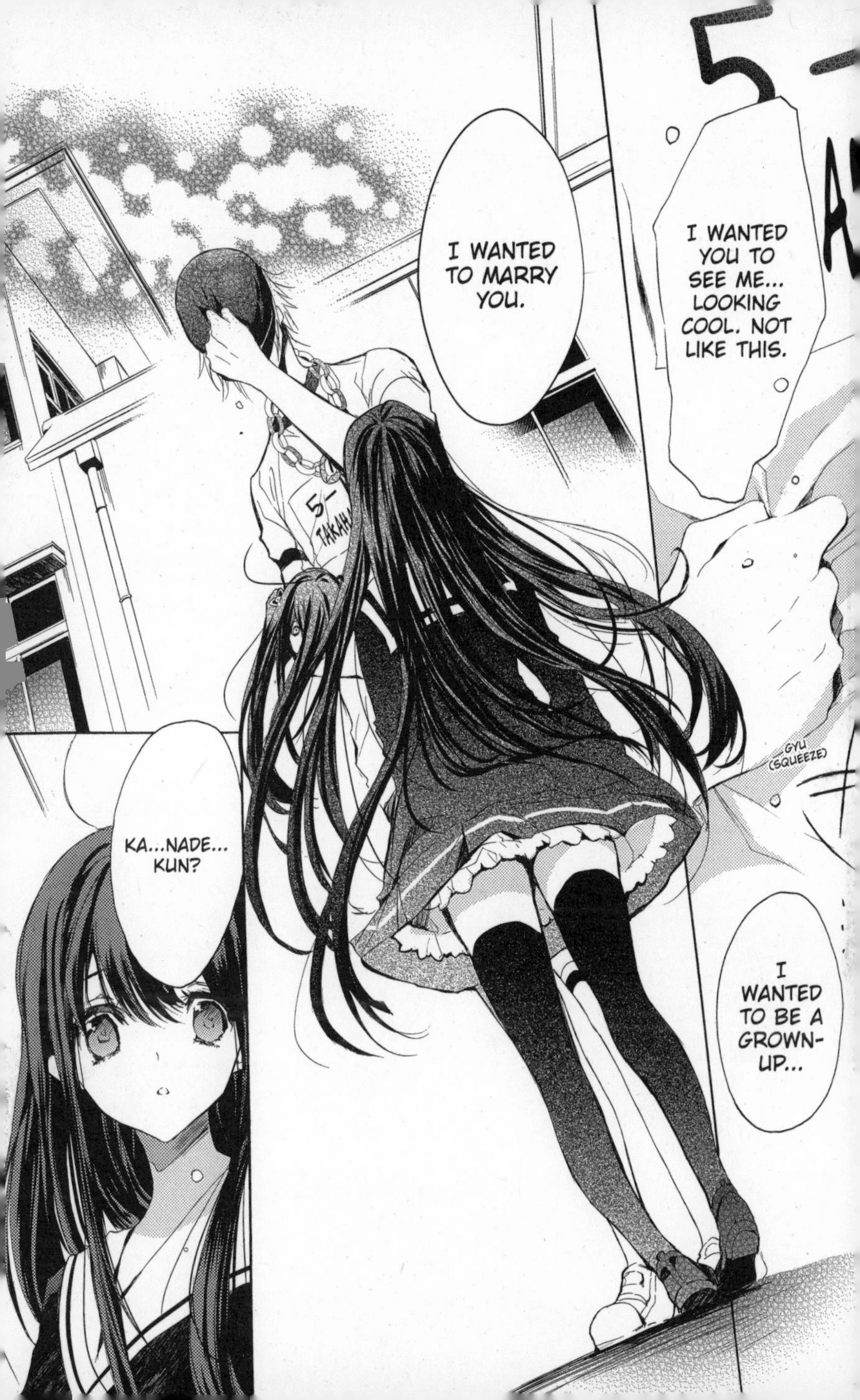

I WANTED YOU TO SEE ME... LOOKING COOL. NOT LIKE THIS.
I WANTED TO MARRY YOU.
GYU (SQUEEZE)
I WANTED TO BE A GROWN-UP...
KA...NADE... KUN?

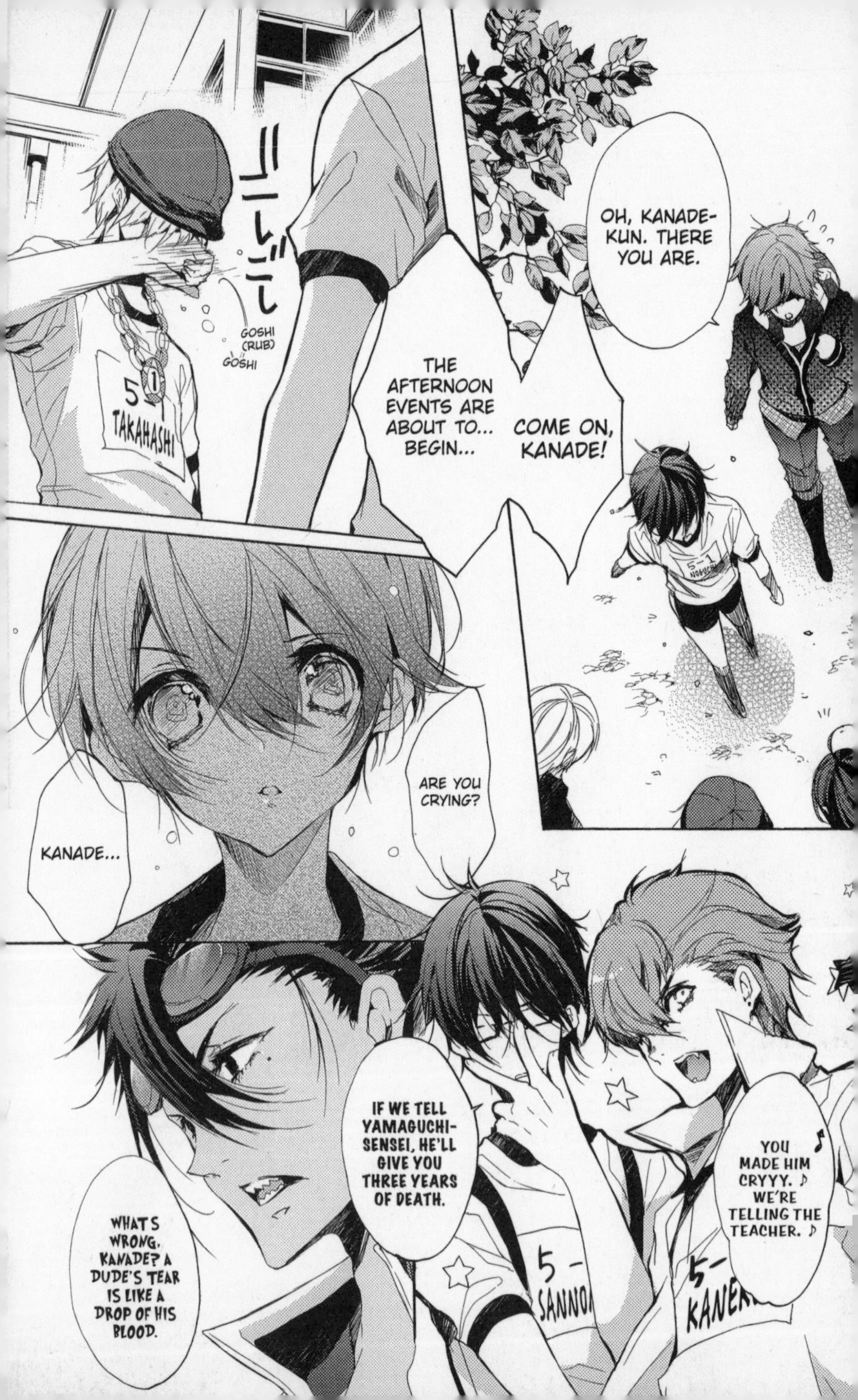
OH, KANADE-KUN. THERE YOU ARE.
THE AFTERNOON EVENTS ARE ABOUT TO... BEGIN...
COME ON, KANADE!
5-1 TAKAHASHI
GOSHI (RUB) GOSHI
ARE YOU CRYING?
KANADE...
YOU MADE HIM CRYYY. ♪ WE'RE TELLING THE TEACHER. ♪
IF WE TELL YAMAGUCHI-SENSEI, HE'LL GIVE YOU THREE YEARS OF DEATH.
WHAT'S WRONG, KANADE? A DUDE'S TEAR IS LIKE A DROP OF HIS BLOOD.

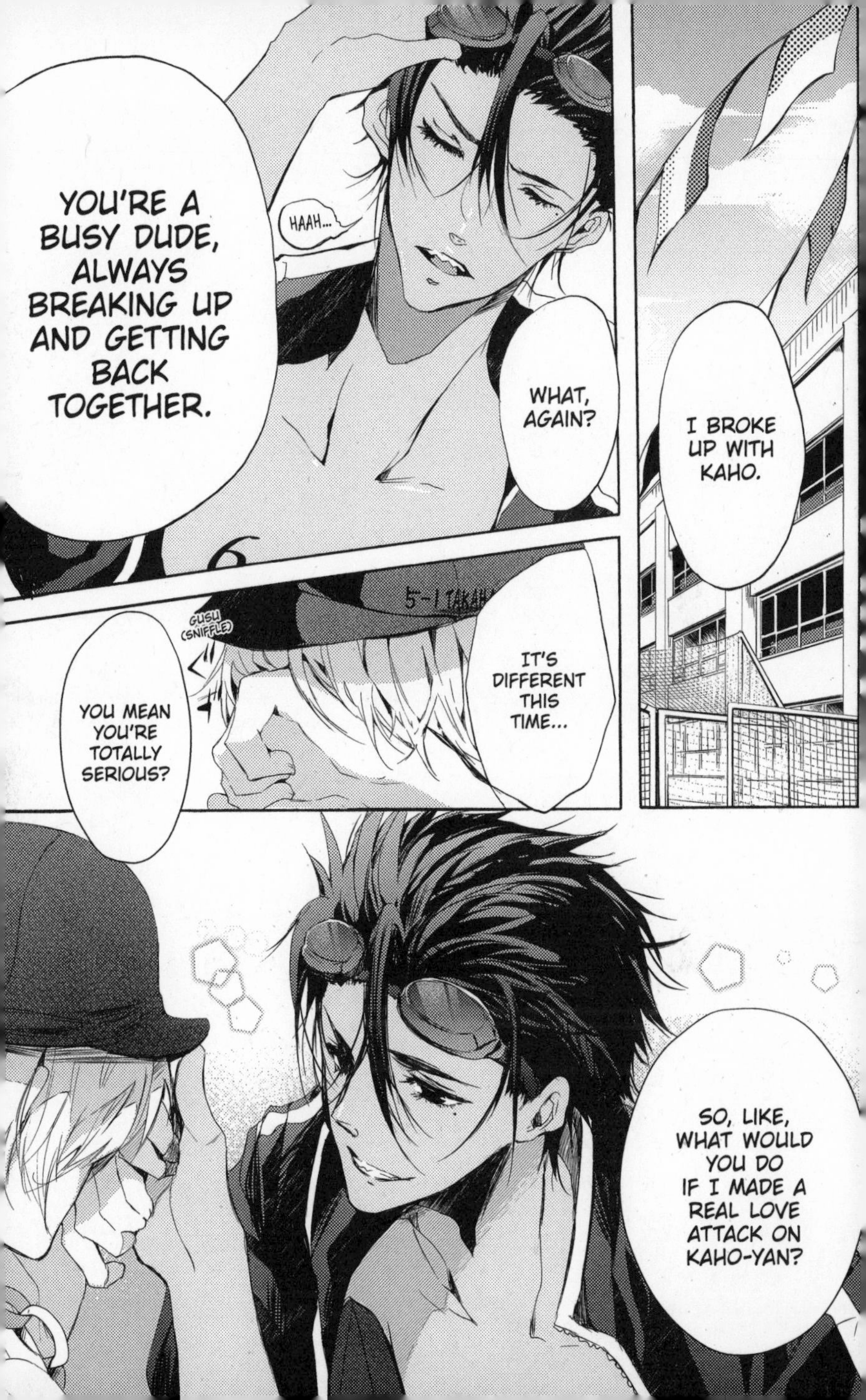
I BROKE UP WITH KAHO.
WHAT, AGAIN?
HAAH...
YOU'RE A BUSY DUDE, ALWAYS BREAKING UP AND GETTING BACK TOGETHER.
5-1 TAKAHA
IT'S DIFFERENT THIS TIME...
GUSU (SNIFFLE)
YOU MEAN YOU'RE TOTALLY SERIOUS?
SO, LIKE, WHAT WOULD YOU DO IF I MADE A REAL LOVE ATTACK ON KAHO-YAN?

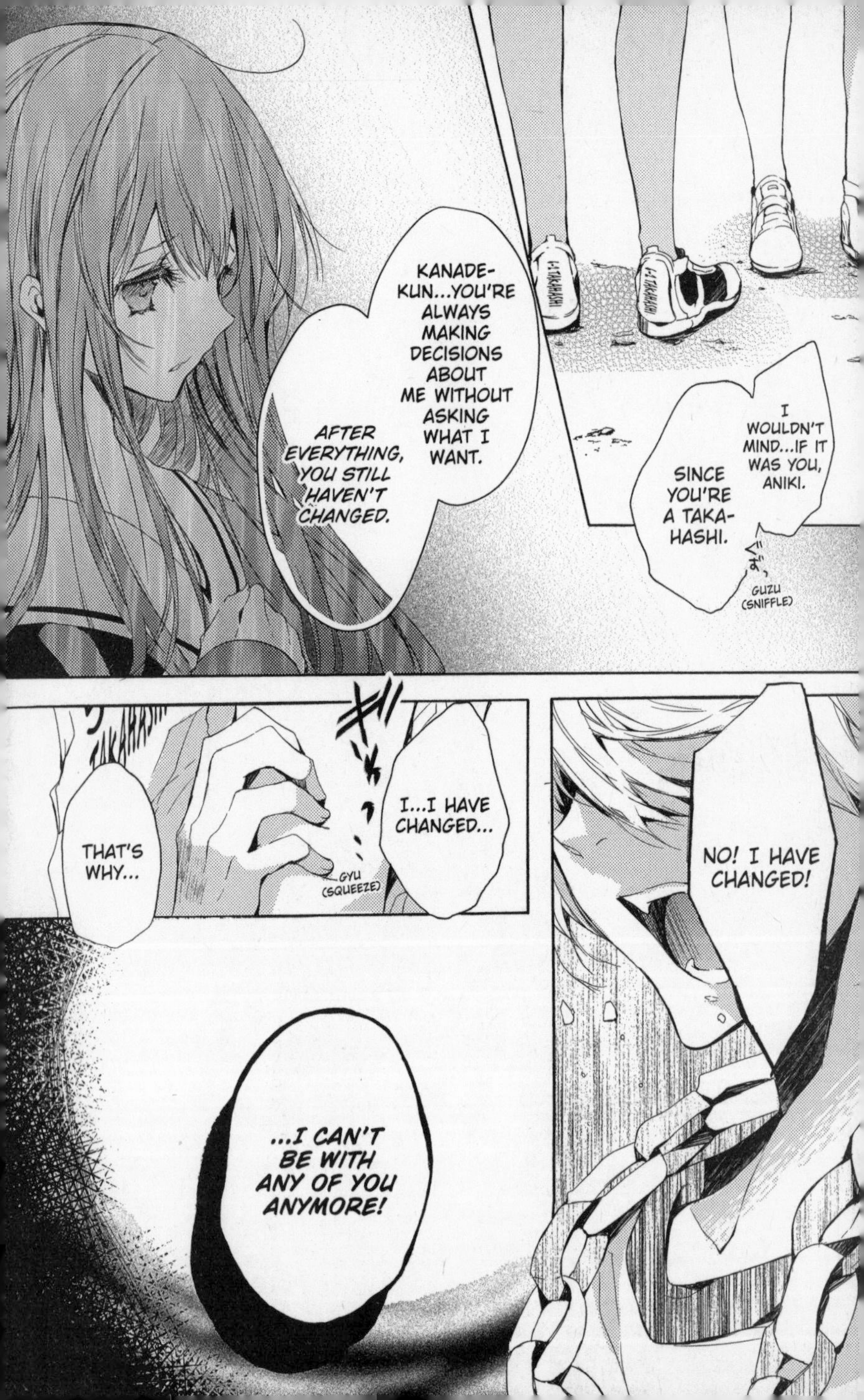
I WOULDN'T MIND...IF IT WAS YOU, ANIKI.
SINCE YOU'RE A TAKA-HASHI.
GUZU (SNIFFLE)
KANADE-KUN...YOU'RE ALWAYS MAKING DECISIONS ABOUT ME WITHOUT ASKING WHAT I WANT.
AFTER EVERYTHING, YOU STILL HAVEN'T CHANGED.
NO! I HAVE CHANGED!
I...I HAVE CHANGED...
GYU (SQUEEZE)
THAT'S WHY...
...I CAN'T BE WITH ANY OF YOU ANYMORE!

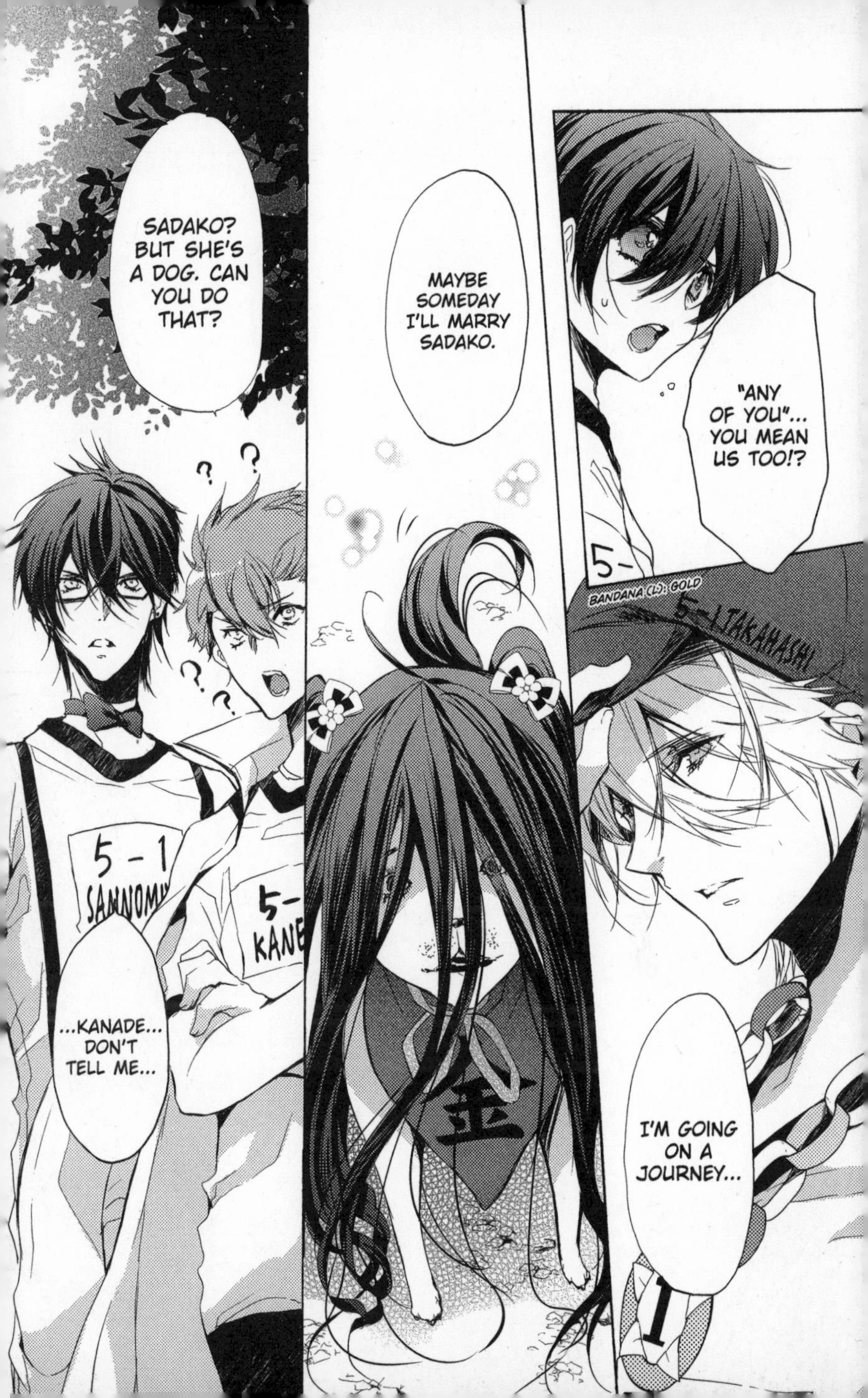
"ANY OF YOU"... YOU MEAN US TOO!?
BANDANA (L): GOLD
5-1 TAKAHASHI
I'M GOING ON A JOURNEY...
MAYBE SOMEDAY I'LL MARRY SADAKO.
SADAKO? BUT SHE'S A DOG. CAN YOU DO THAT?
5-1 SANNOMI
...KANADE... DON'T TELL ME...

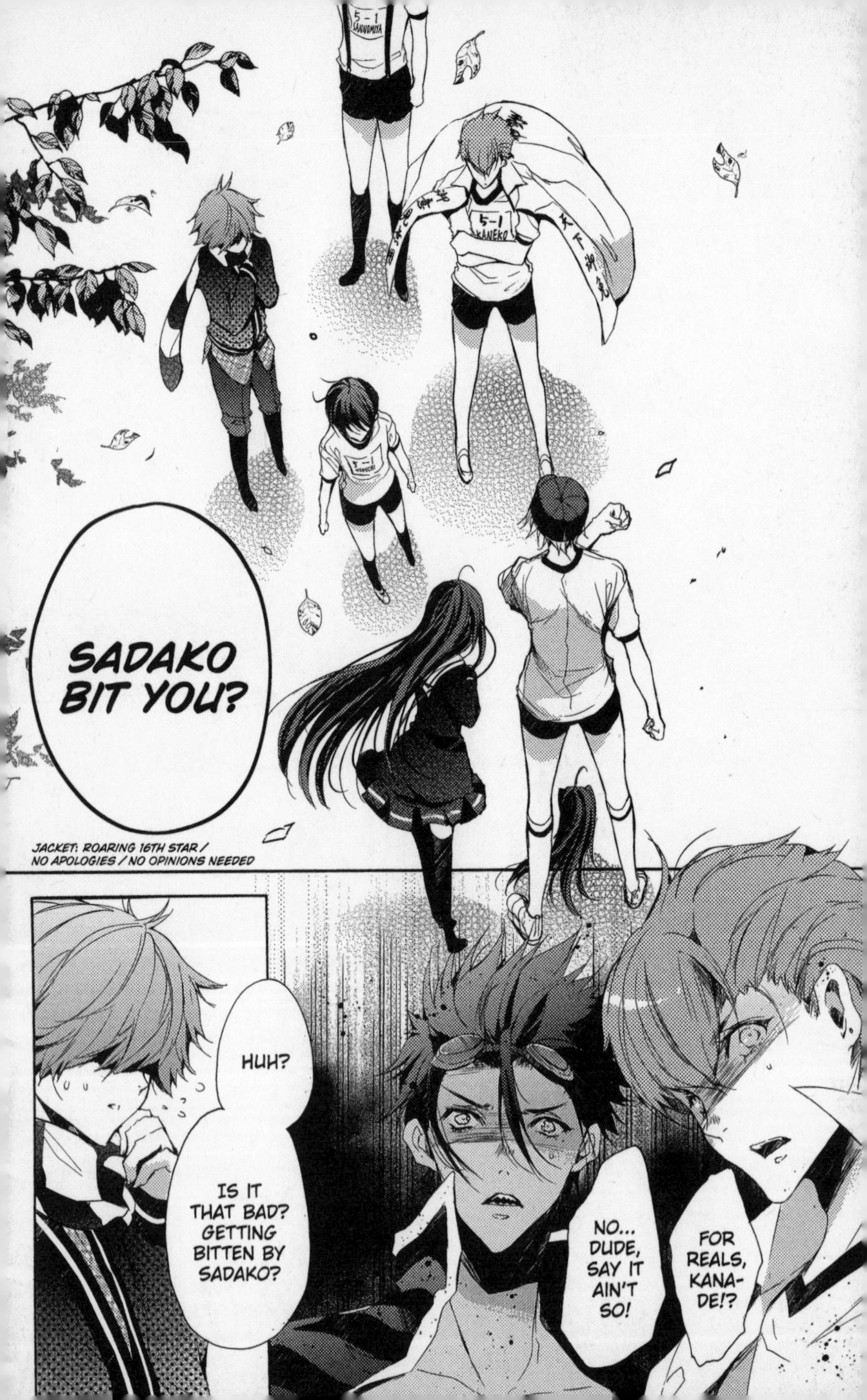
5-1 SANNOMIYA
5-1 KANEKO
SADAKO BIT YOU?
JACKET: ROARING 16TH STAR / NO APOLOGIES / NO OPINIONS NEEDED
FOR REALS, KANADE!?
NO... DUDE, SAY IT AIN'T SO!
HUH?
IS IT THAT BAD? GETTING BITTEN BY SADAKO?

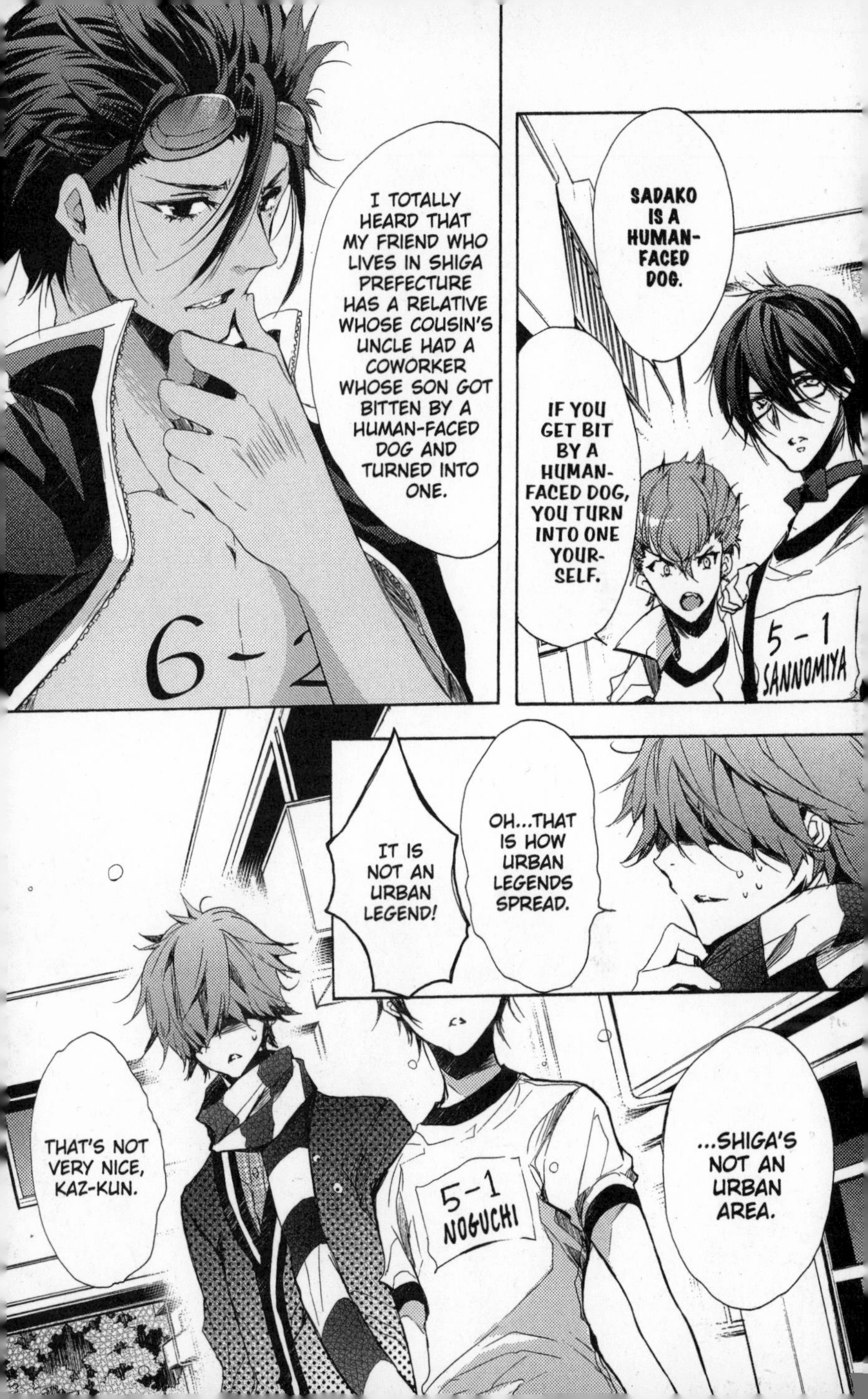
SADAKO IS A HUMAN-FACED DOG.
IF YOU GET BIT BY A HUMAN-FACED DOG, YOU TURN INTO ONE YOURSELF.
5-1 SANNOMIYA
I TOTALLY HEARD THAT MY FRIEND WHO LIVES IN SHIGA PREFECTURE HAS A RELATIVE WHOSE COUSIN'S UNCLE HAD A COWORKER WHOSE SON GOT BITTEN BY A HUMAN-FACED DOG AND TURNED INTO ONE.
OH...THAT IS HOW URBAN LEGENDS SPREAD.
IT IS NOT AN URBAN LEGEND!
...SHIGA'S NOT AN URBAN AREA.
5-1 NOGUCHI
THAT'S NOT VERY NICE, KAZ-KUN.

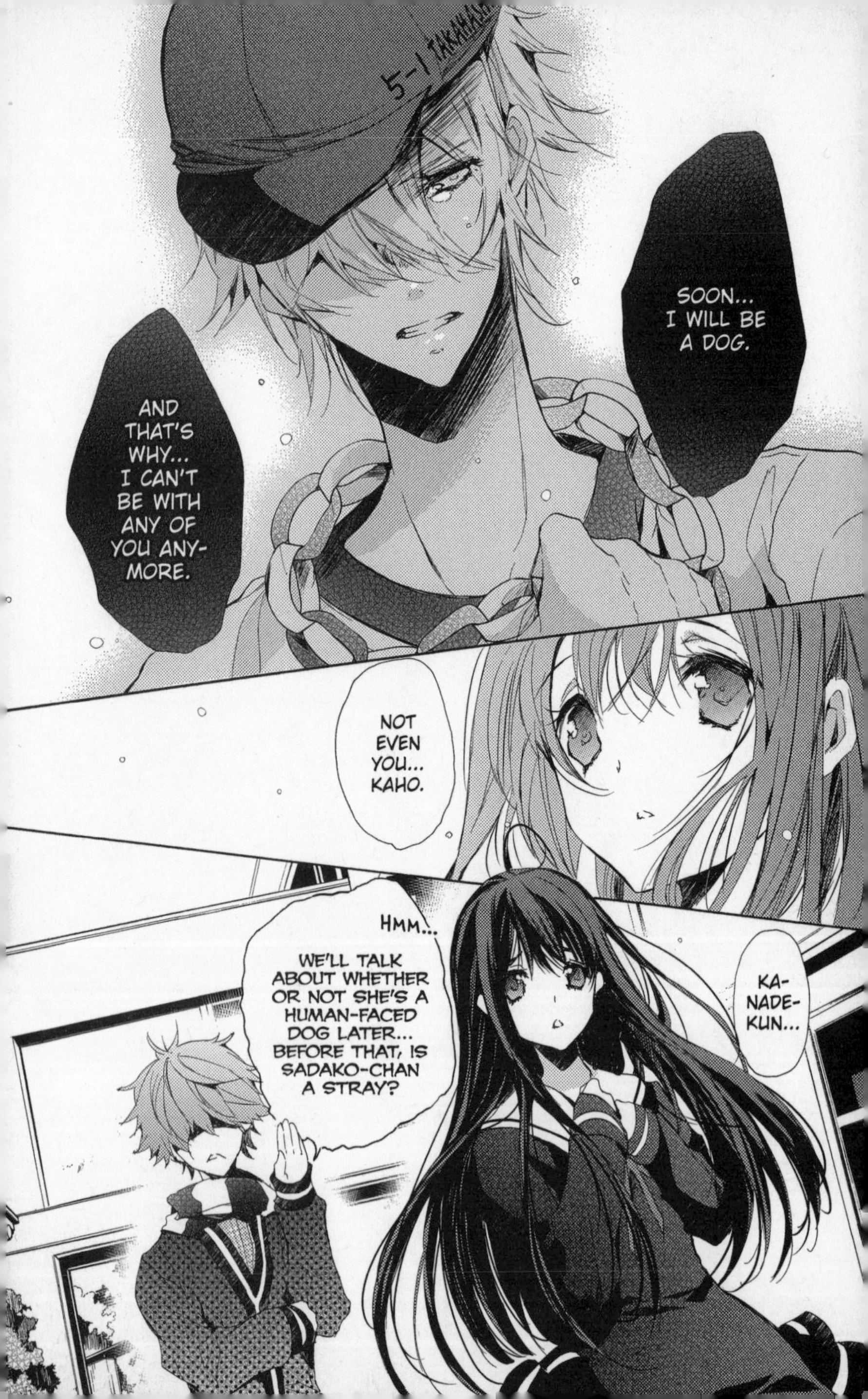
SOON... I WILL BE A DOG.
AND THAT'S WHY... I CAN'T BE WITH ANY OF YOU ANY-MORE.
NOT EVEN YOU... KAHO.
KA-NADE-KUN...
HMM...
WE'LL TALK ABOUT WHETHER OR NOT SHE'S A HUMAN-FACED DOG LATER... BEFORE THAT, IS SADAKO-CHAN A STRAY?

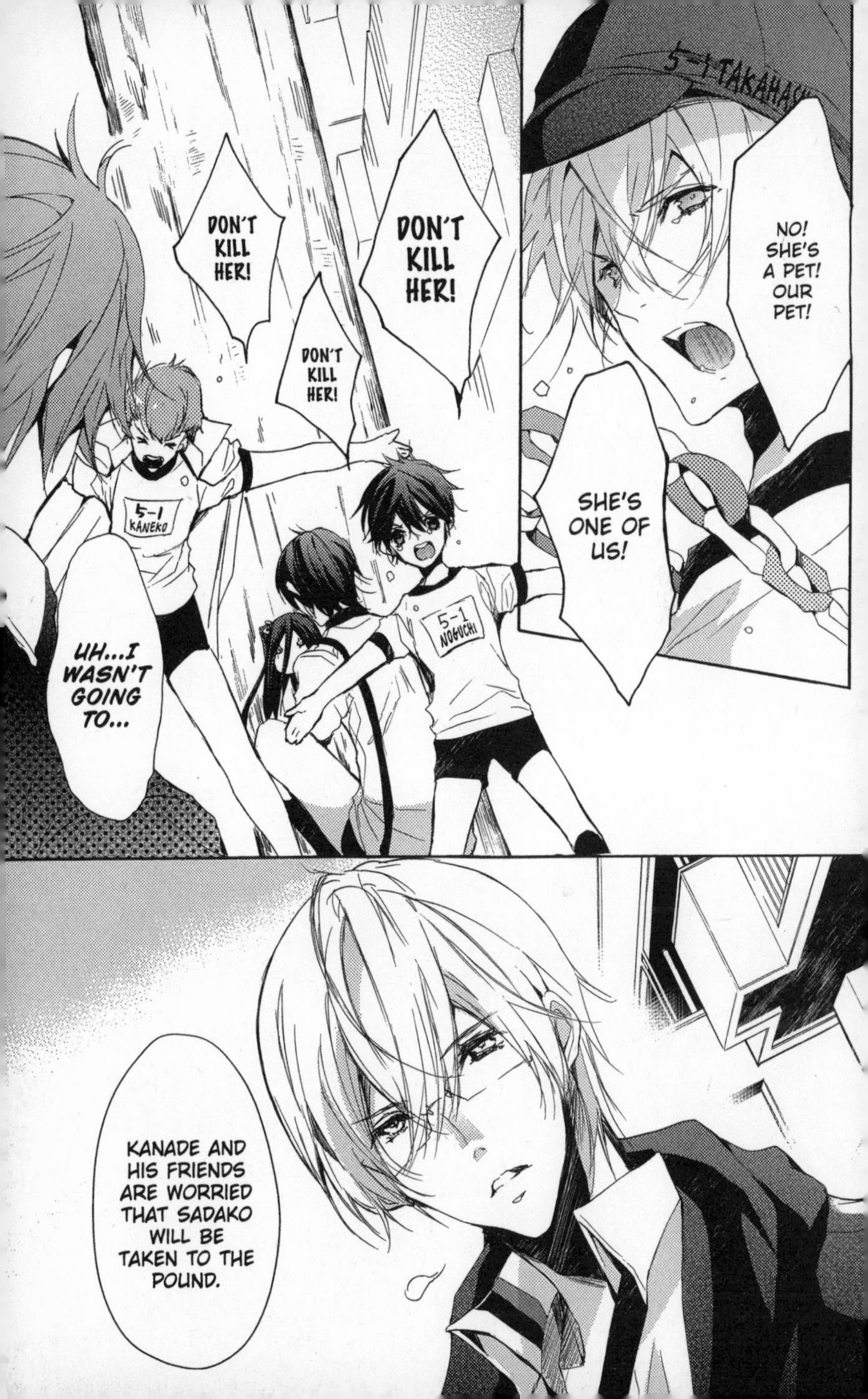
NO! SHE'S A PET! OUR PET!
SHE'S ONE OF US!
DON'T KILL HER!
DON'T KILL HER!
DON'T KILL HER!
5-1 KANEKO
5-1 NOGUCHI
UH...I WASN'T GOING TO...
KANADE AND HIS FRIENDS ARE WORRIED THAT SADAKO WILL BE TAKEN TO THE POUND.

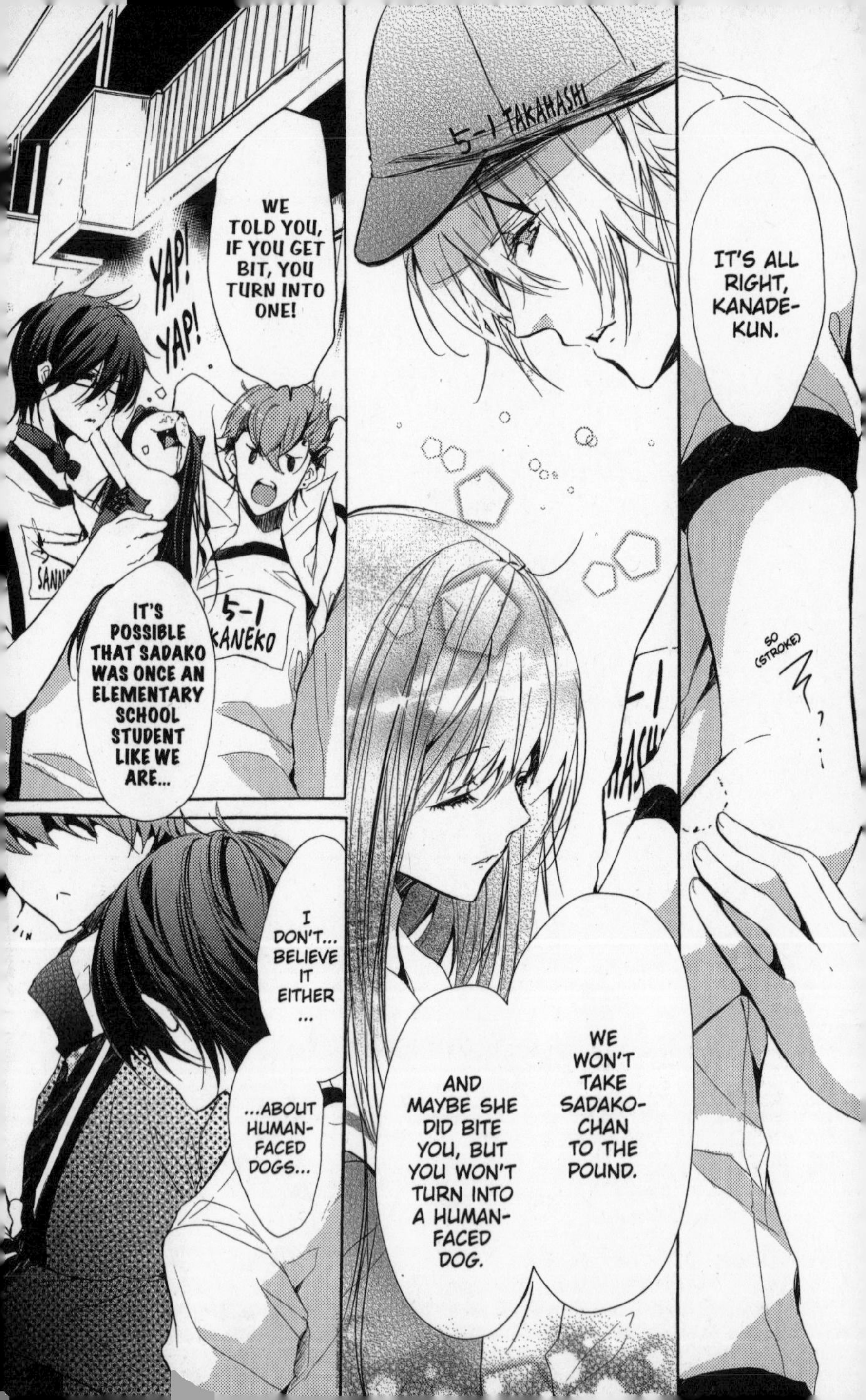
IT'S ALL RIGHT, KANADE-KUN.
SO (STROKE)
5-1 TAKAHASHI
WE WON'T TAKE SADAKO-CHAN TO THE POUND.
AND MAYBE SHE DID BITE YOU, BUT YOU WON'T TURN INTO A HUMAN-FACED DOG.
WE TOLD YOU, IF YOU GET BIT, YOU TURN INTO ONE!
YAP! YAP!
5-1 KANEKO
IT'S POSSIBLE THAT SADAKO WAS ONCE AN ELEMENTARY SCHOOL STUDENT LIKE WE ARE...
I DON'T... BELIEVE IT EITHER...
...ABOUT HUMAN-FACED DOGS...

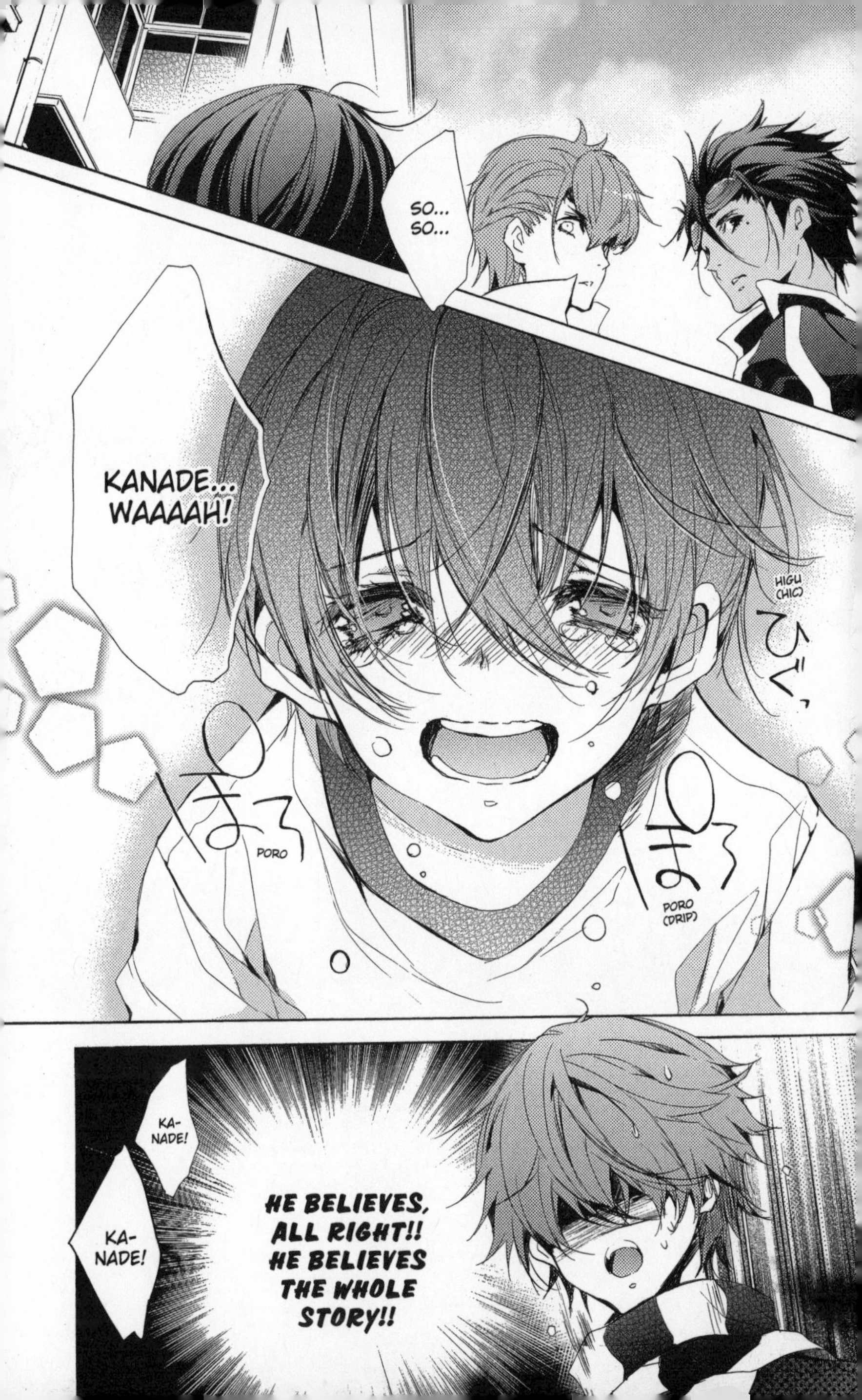
SO... SO...
KANADE... WAAAAH!
HIGU (HIC)
ひぐっ
ぽろ
PORO (DRIP)
ぽろ
PORO
HE BELIEVES, ALL RIGHT!! HE BELIEVES THE WHOLE STORY!!
KA-NADE!
KA-NADE!

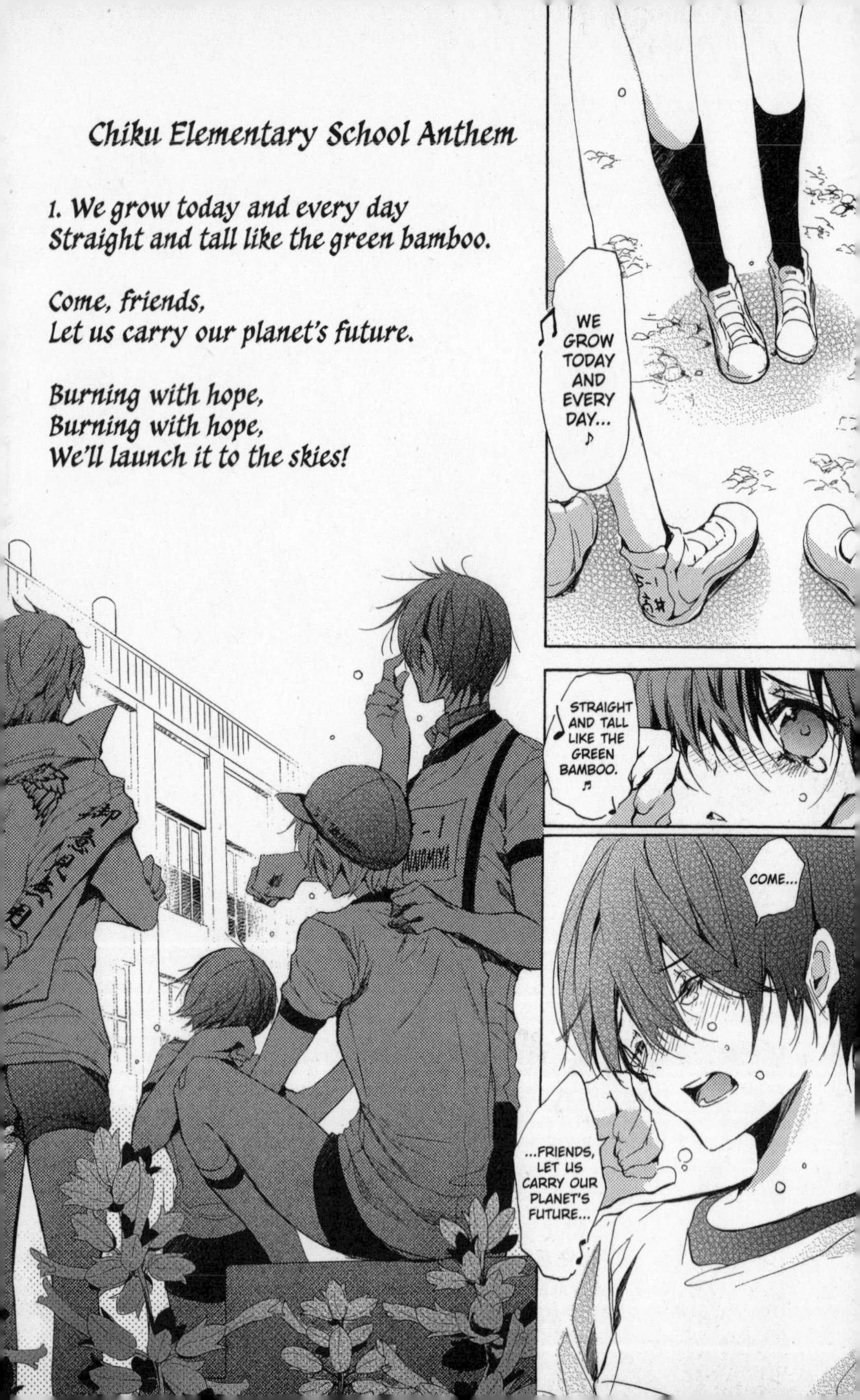
WE GROW TODAY AND EVERY DAY... ♪
STRAIGHT AND TALL LIKE THE GREEN BAMBOO. ♫
COME...
...FRIENDS, LET US CARRY OUR PLANET'S FUTURE...
Chiku Elementary School Anthem
1. We grow today and every day
Straight and tall like the green bamboo.
Come, friends,
Let us carry our planet's future.
Burning with hope,
Burning with hope,
We'll launch it to the skies!

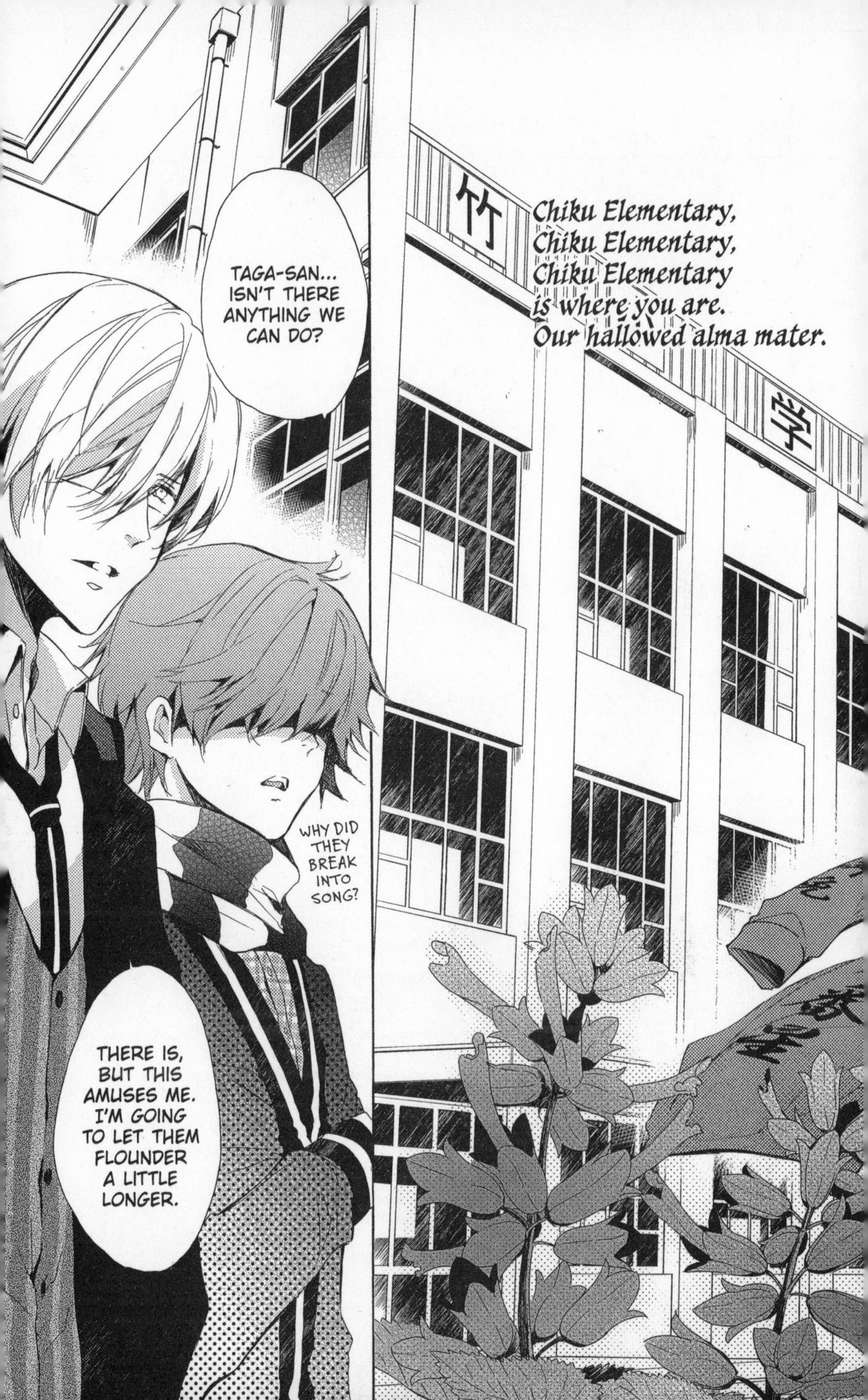
竹
学
Chiku Elementary,
Chiku Elementary,
Chiku Elementary
is where you are.
Our hallowed alma mater.
TAGA-SAN... ISN'T THERE ANYTHING WE CAN DO?
WHY DID THEY BREAK INTO SONG?
THERE IS, BUT THIS AMUSES ME. I'M GOING TO LET THEM FLOUNDER A LITTLE LONGER.

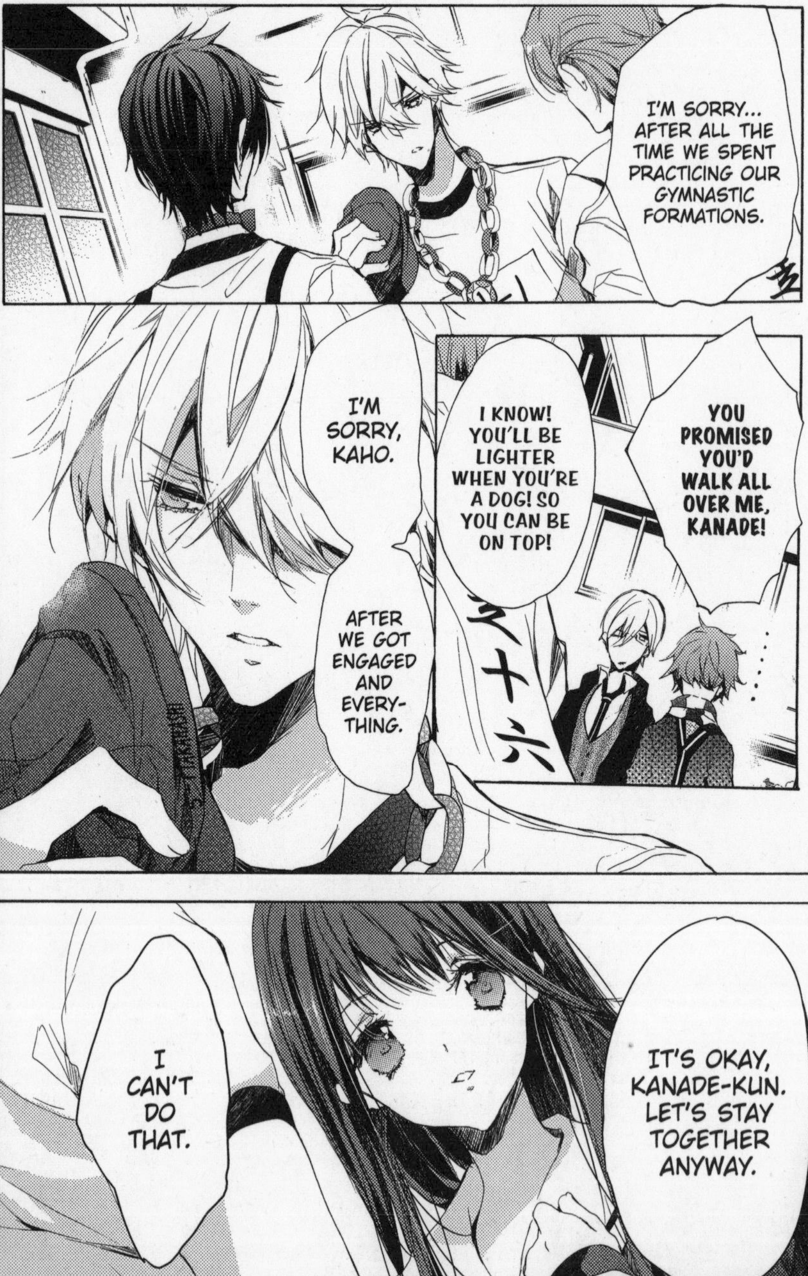
I'M SORRY... AFTER ALL THE TIME WE SPENT PRACTICING OUR GYMNASTIC FORMATIONS.
YOU PROMISED YOU'D WALK ALL OVER ME, KANADE!
I KNOW! YOU'LL BE LIGHTER WHEN YOU'RE A DOG! SO YOU CAN BE ON TOP!
I'M SORRY, KAHO.
AFTER WE GOT ENGAGED AND EVERY-THING.
IT'S OKAY, KANADE-KUN. LET'S STAY TOGETHER ANYWAY.
I CAN'T DO THAT.

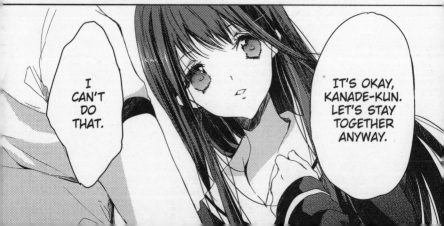

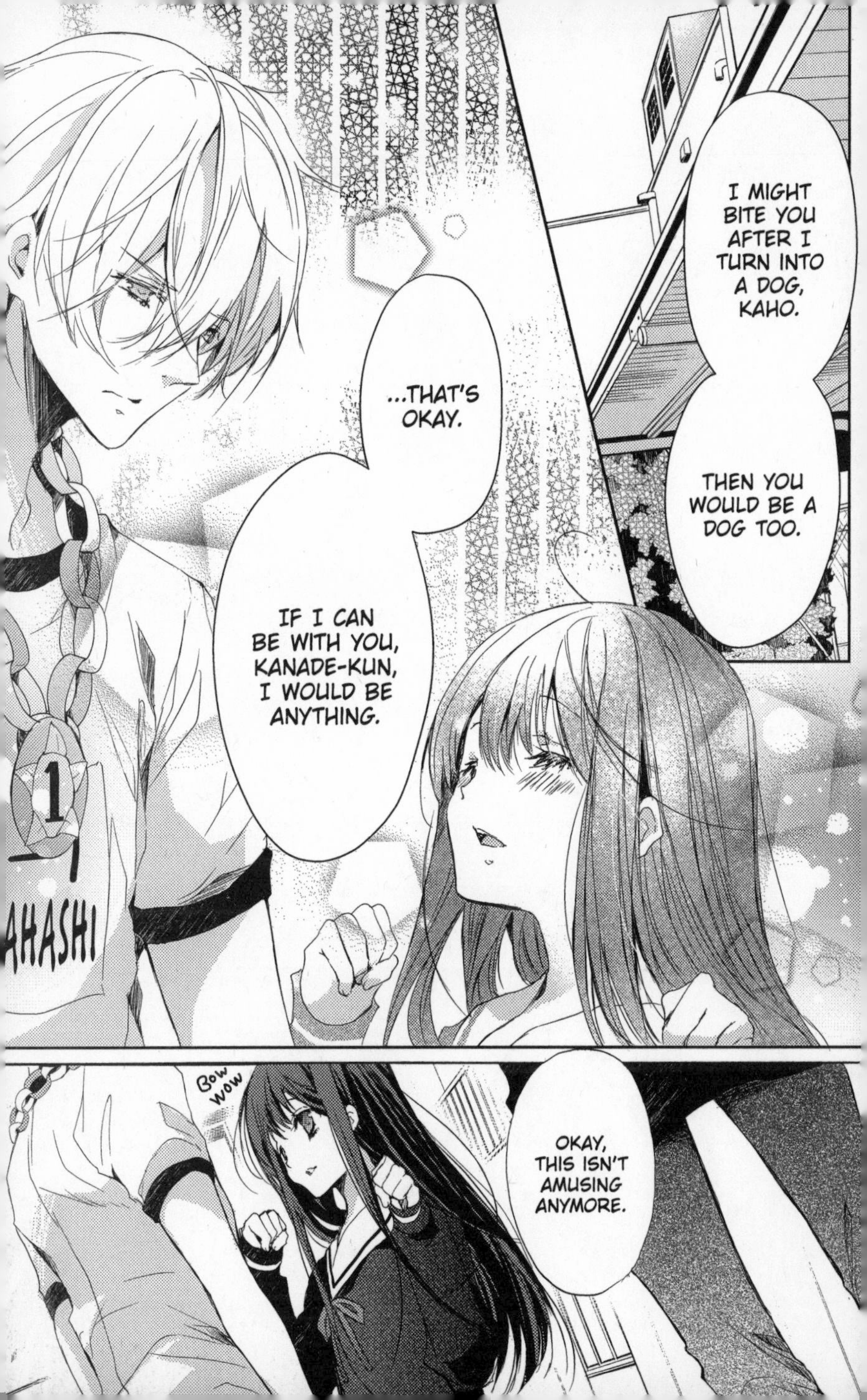
I MIGHT BITE YOU AFTER I TURN INTO A DOG, KAHO.
THEN YOU WOULD BE A DOG TOO.
...THAT'S OKAY.
IF I CAN BE WITH YOU, KANADE-KUN, I WOULD BE ANYTHING.
AHASHI
OKAY, THIS ISN'T AMUSING ANYMORE.
BOW WOW

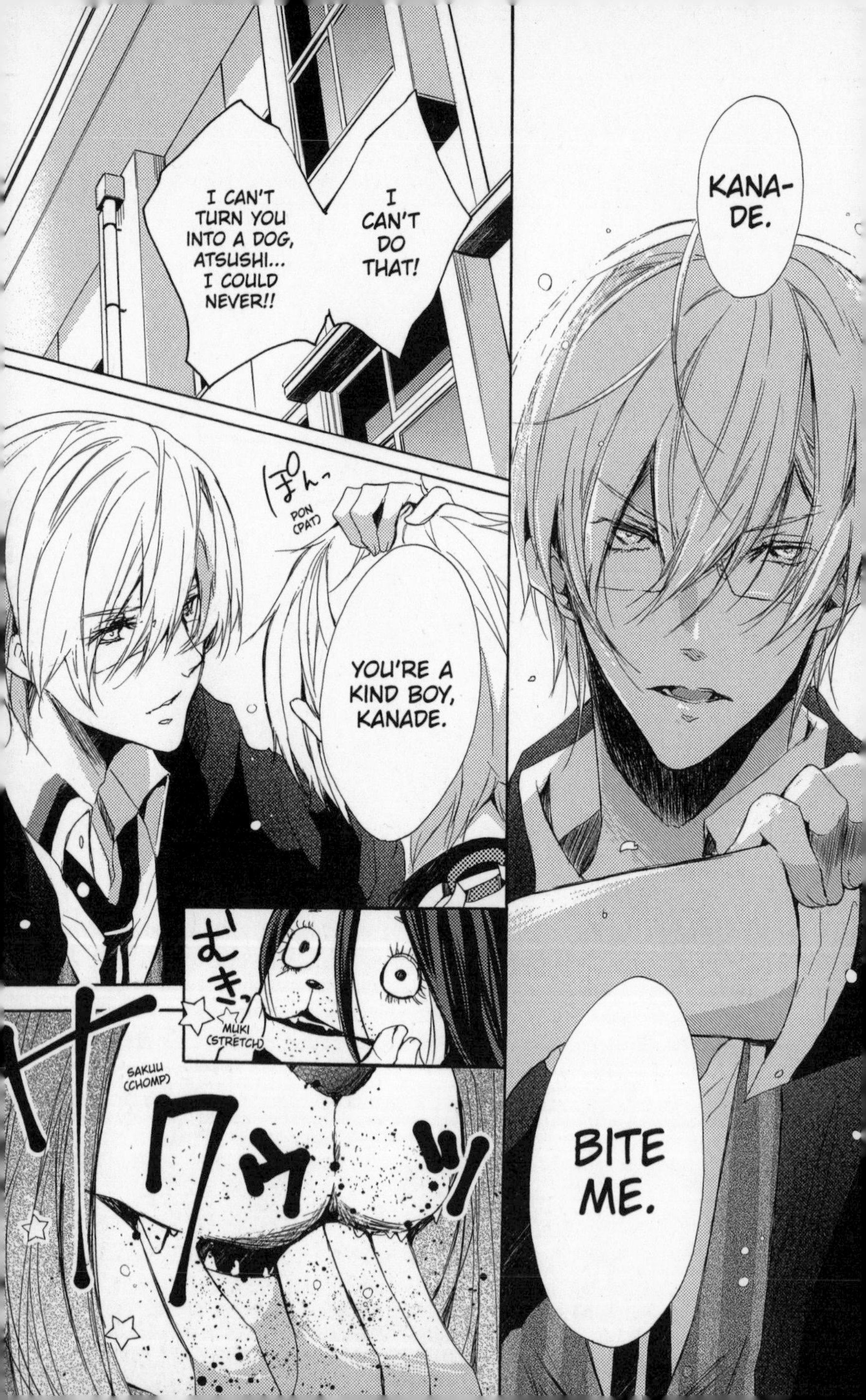
KANA-DE.
BITE ME.
I CAN'T DO THAT!
I CAN'T TURN YOU INTO A DOG, ATSUSHI... I COULD NEVER!!
ぽん
PON (PAT)
YOU'RE A KIND BOY, KANADE.
むき
MUKI (STRETCH)
サクゥ
SAKUU (CHOMP)

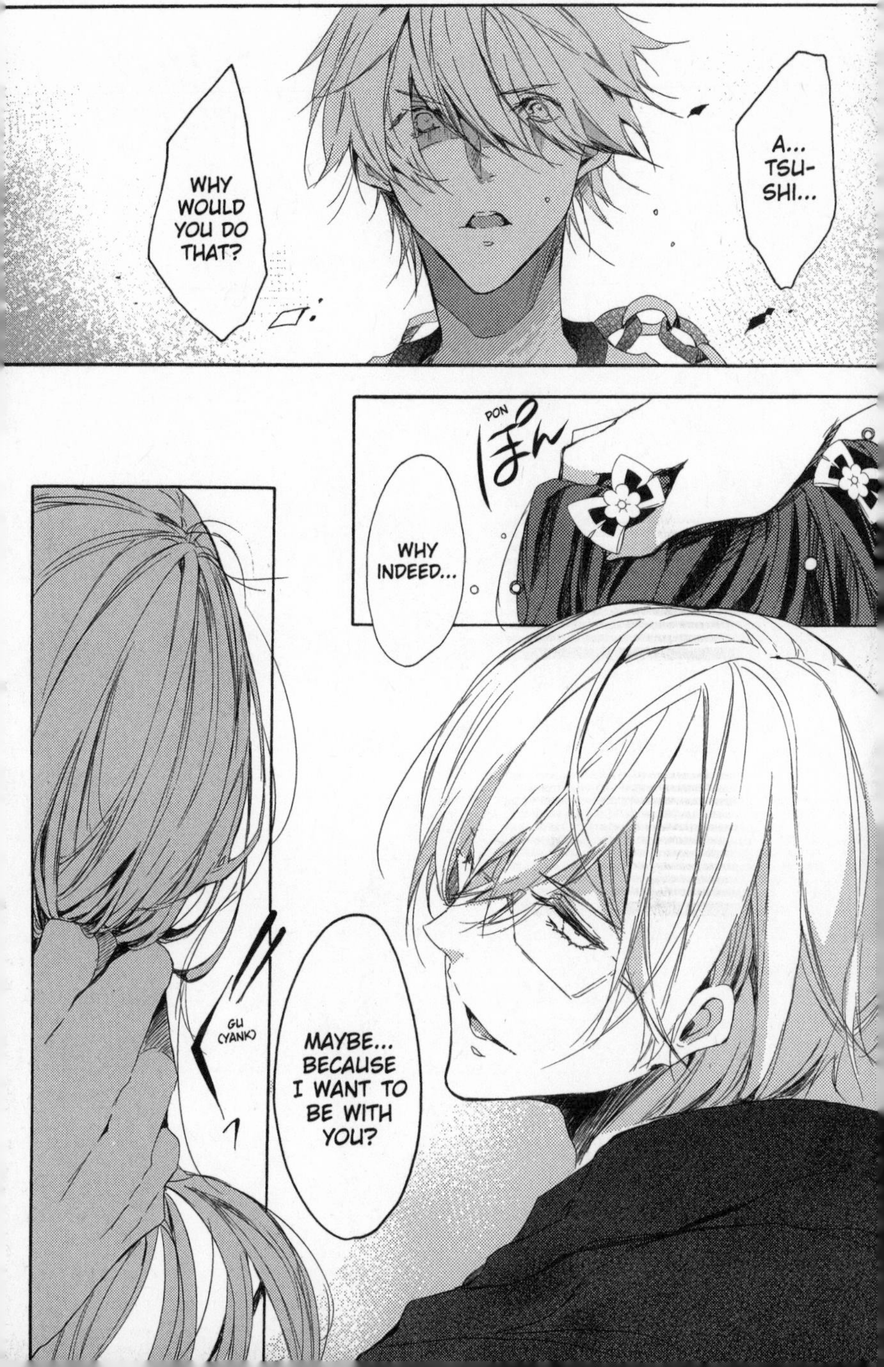
A... TSU-SHI...
WHY WOULD YOU DO THAT?
PON
ぽん
WHY INDEED...
MAYBE... BECAUSE I WANT TO BE WITH YOU?
GU (YANK)

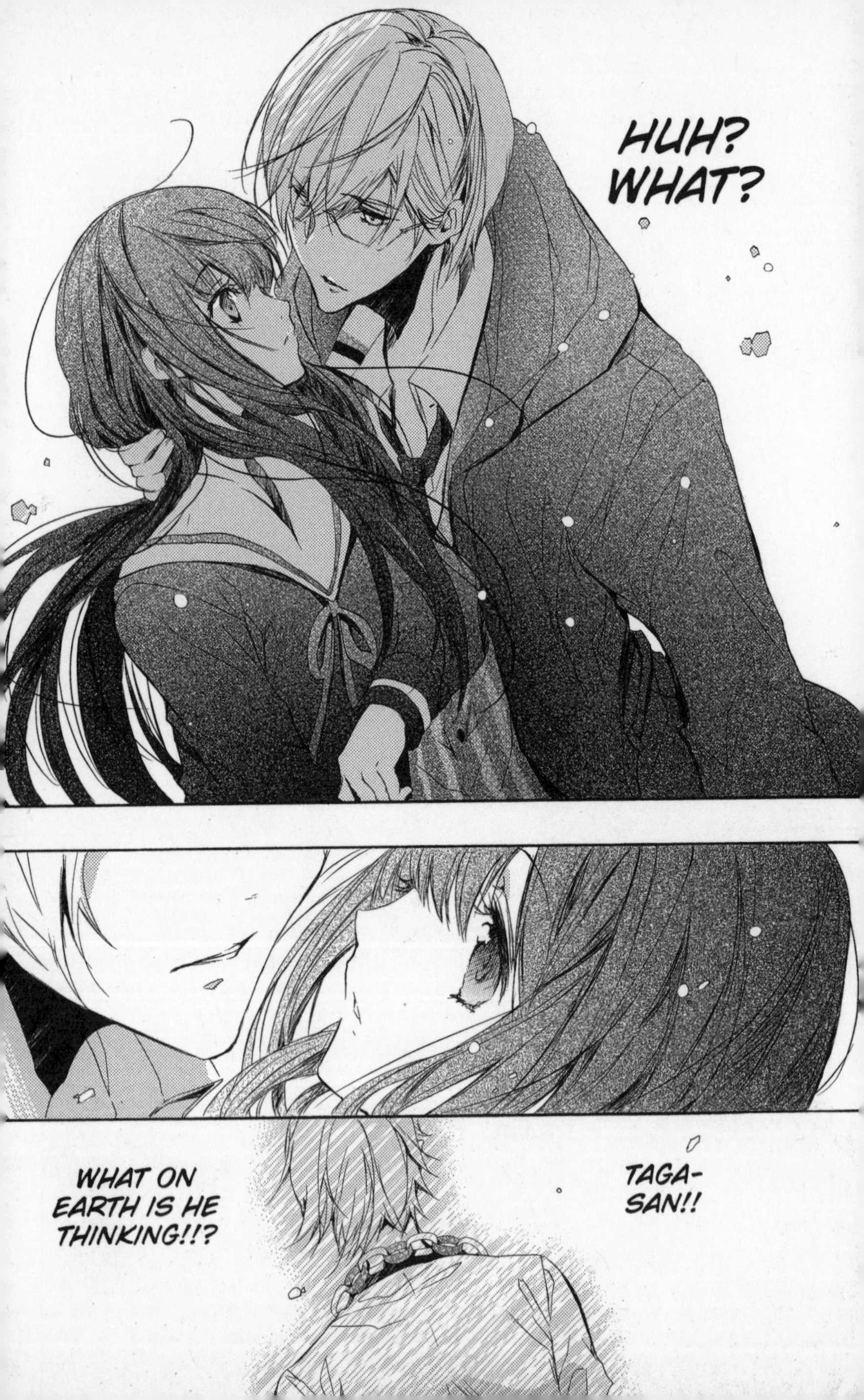
HUH? WHAT?
TAGA-SAN!!
WHAT ON EARTH IS HE THINKING!!?

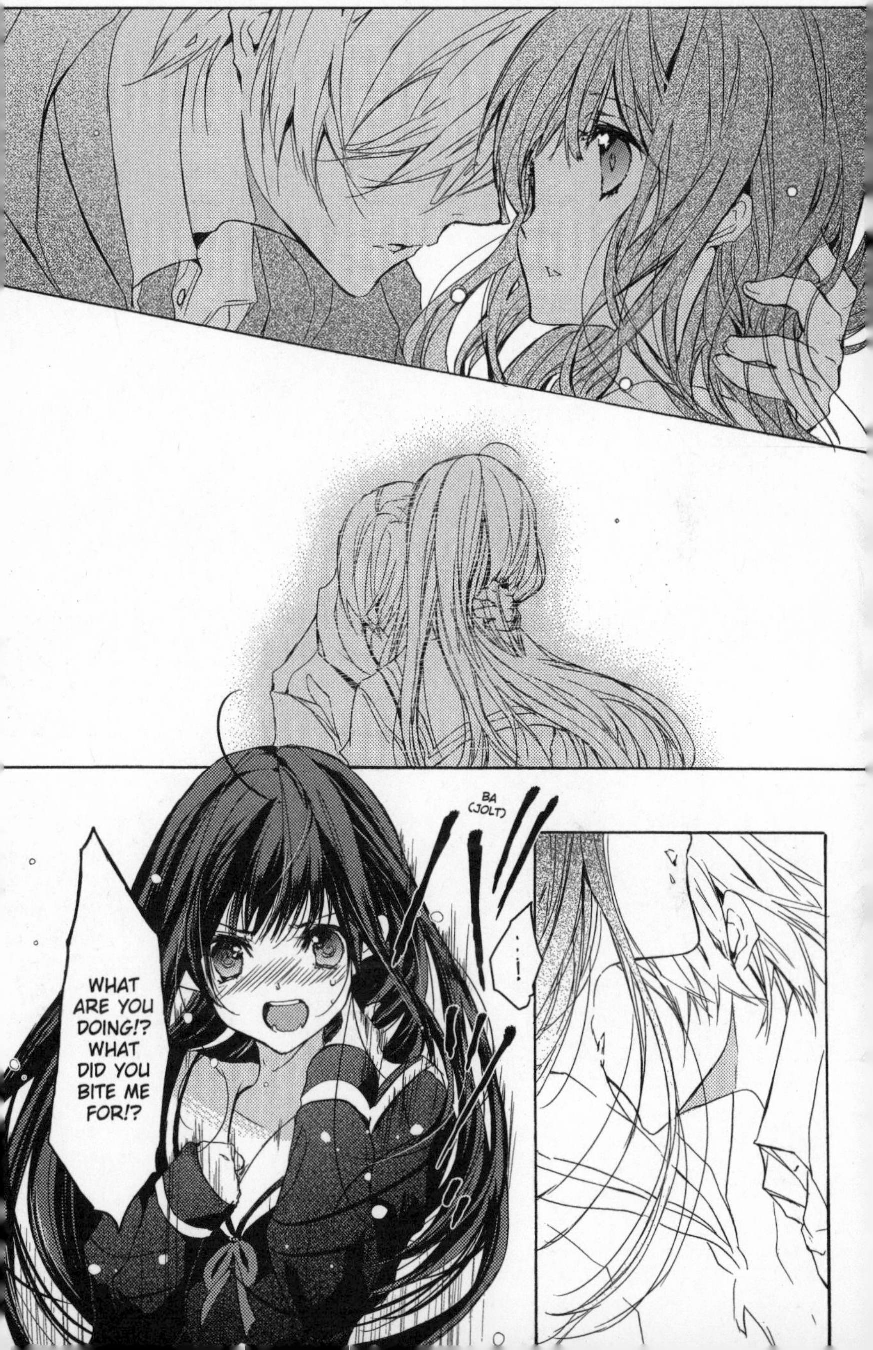
BA (JOLT)
...!
WHAT ARE YOU DOING!? WHAT DID YOU BITE ME FOR!?

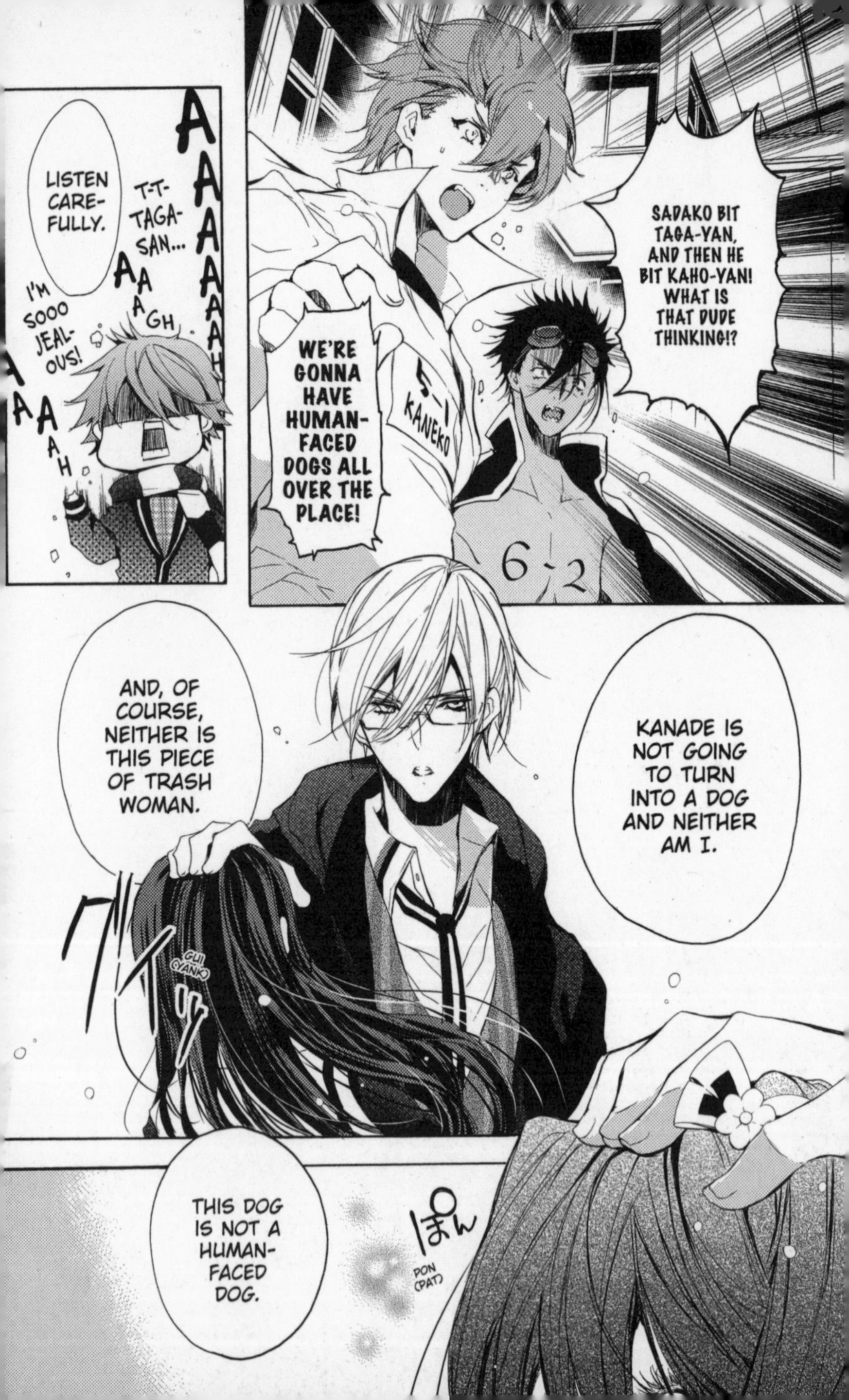
SADAKO BIT TAGA-YAN, AND THEN HE BIT KAHO-YAN! WHAT IS THAT DUDE THINKING!?
WE'RE GONNA HAVE HUMAN-FACED DOGS ALL OVER THE PLACE!
5-1 KANEKO
6-2
AAAAAAAAH
T-T-TAGA-SAN...
AAAGH
LISTEN CAREFULLY.
I'M SOOO JEALOUS!
AAAAH
KANADE IS NOT GOING TO TURN INTO A DOG AND NEITHER AM I.
AND, OF COURSE, NEITHER IS THIS PIECE OF TRASH WOMAN.
GUI (YANK)
PON (PAT)
THIS DOG IS NOT A HUMAN-FACED DOG.

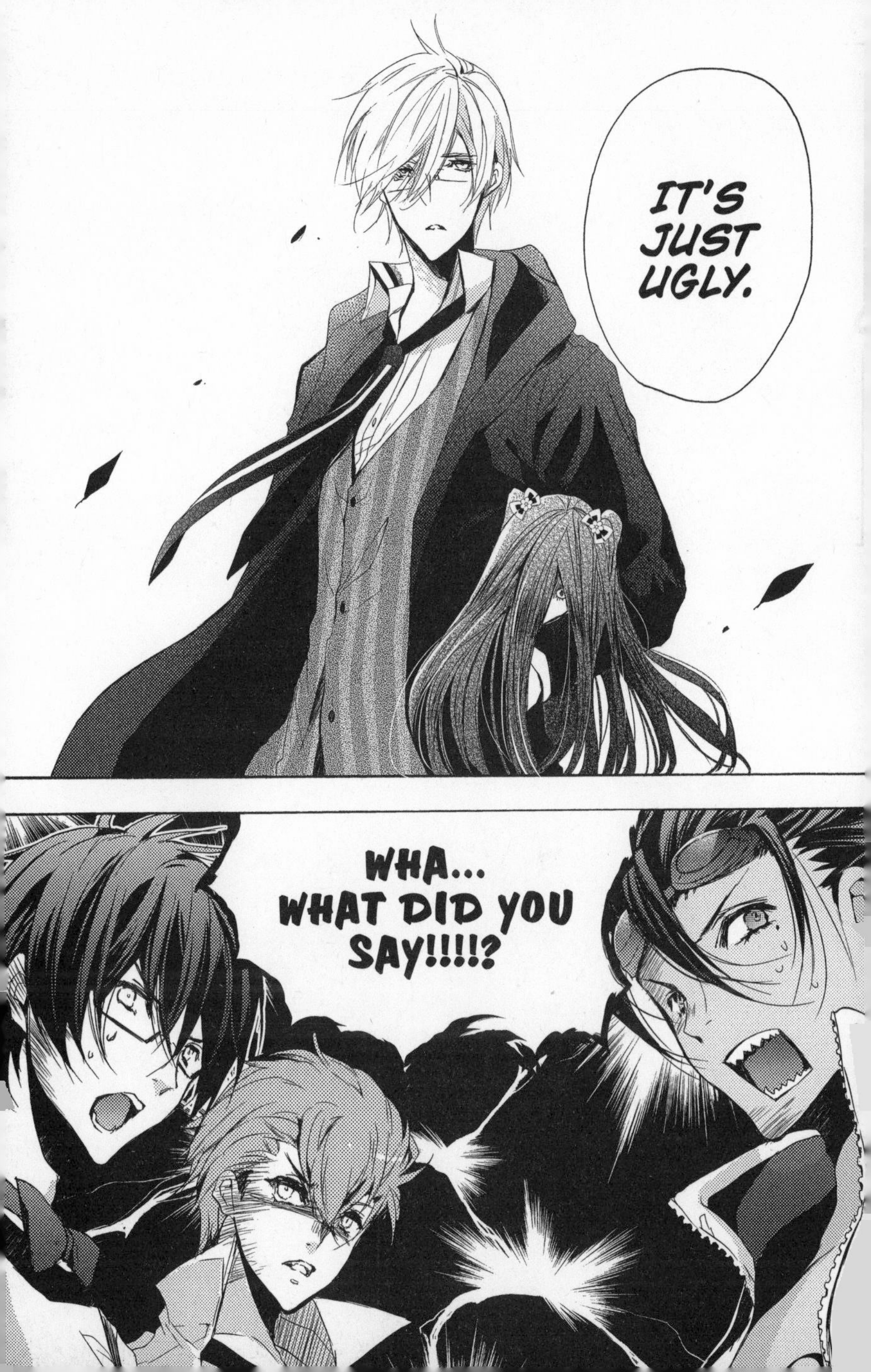
IT'S JUST UGLY.
WHA... WHAT DID YOU SAY!!!!?

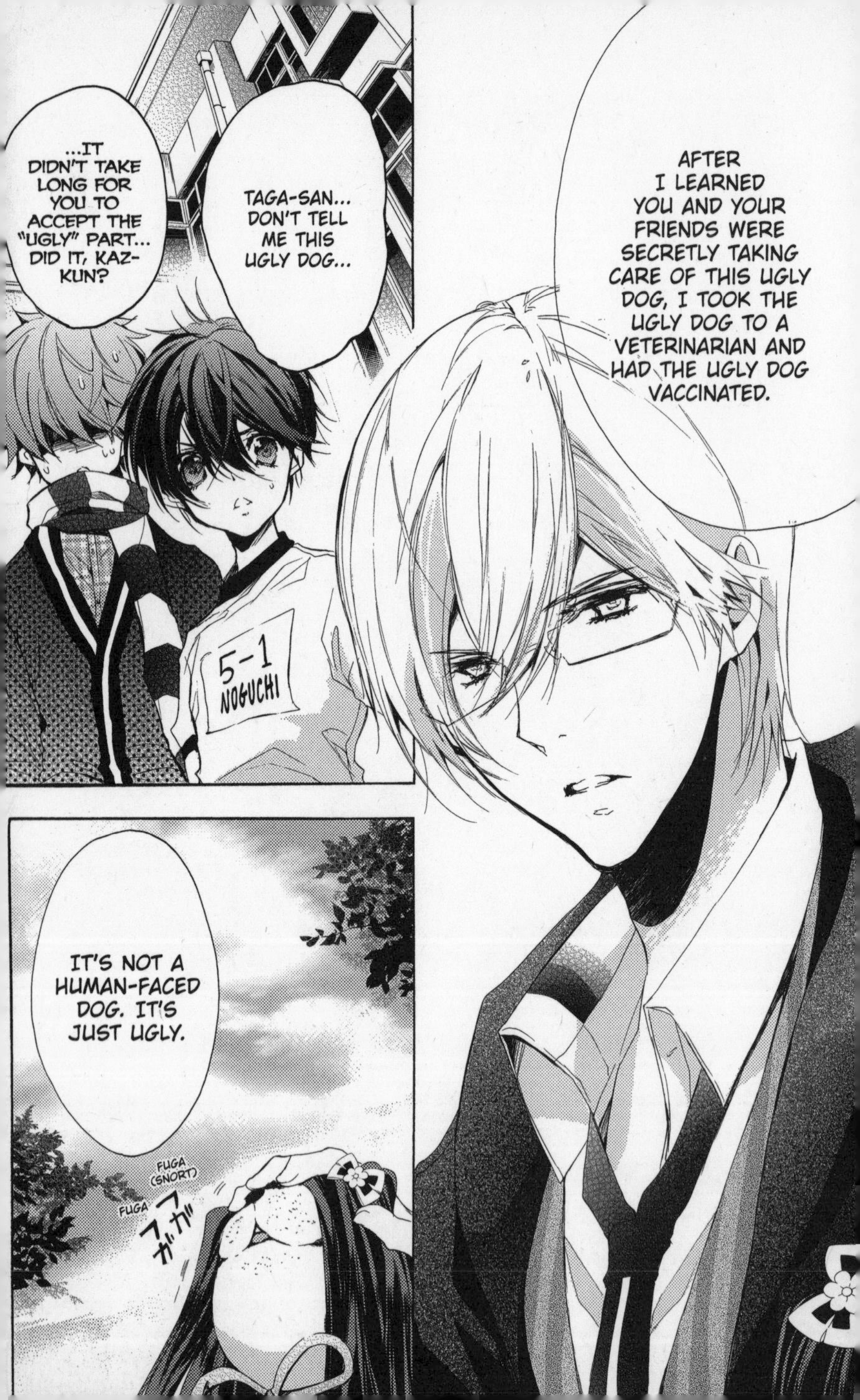
AFTER I LEARNED YOU AND YOUR FRIENDS WERE SECRETLY TAKING CARE OF THIS UGLY DOG, I TOOK THE UGLY DOG TO A VETERINARIAN AND HAD THE UGLY DOG VACCINATED.
TAGA-SAN... DON'T TELL ME THIS UGLY DOG...
...IT DIDN'T TAKE LONG FOR YOU TO ACCEPT THE "UGLY" PART... DID IT, KAZ-KUN?
5-1 NOGUCHI
IT'S NOT A HUMAN-FACED DOG. IT'S JUST UGLY.
FUGA (SNORT)
FUGA
フガフガ

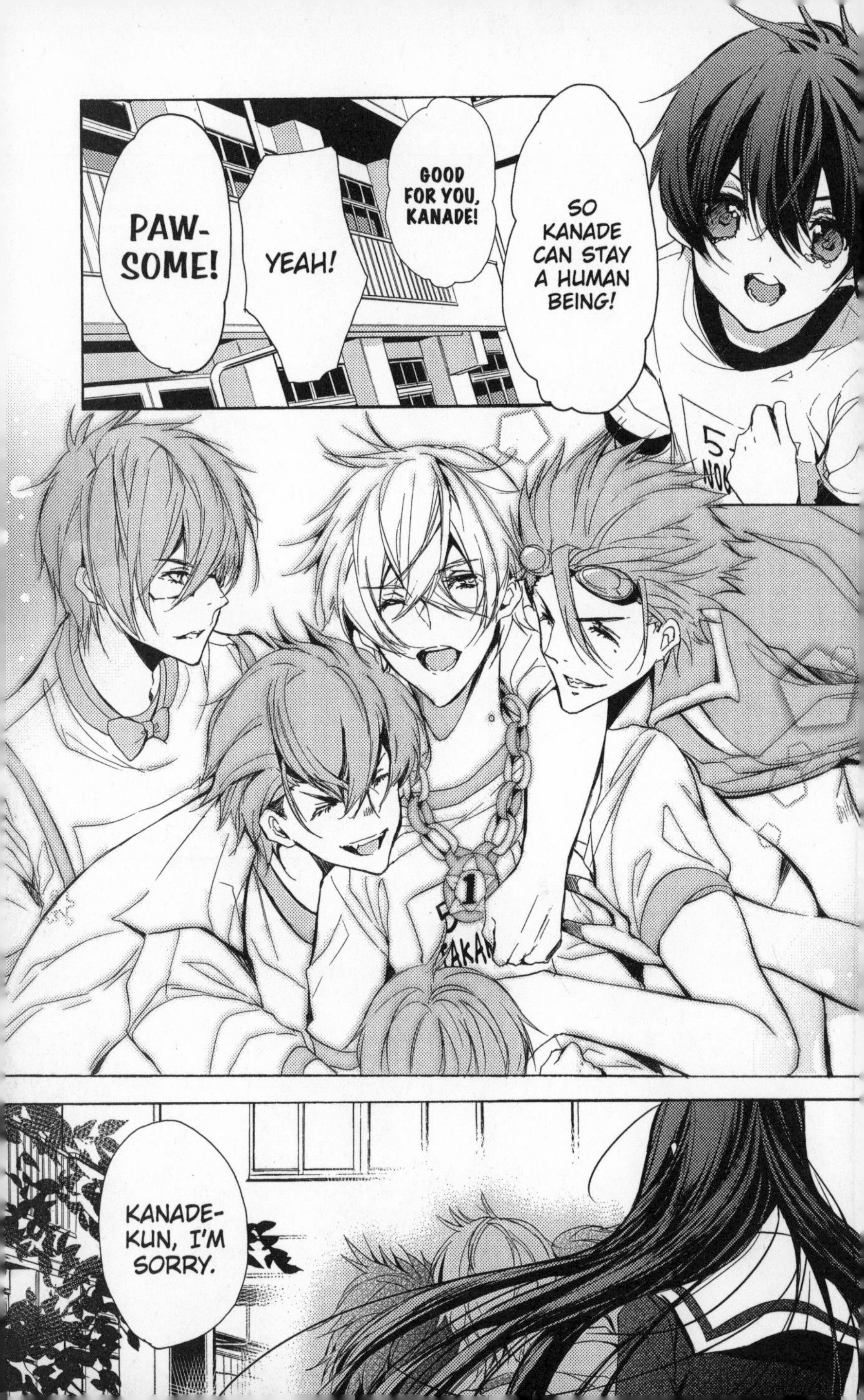
SO KANADE CAN STAY A HUMAN BEING!
GOOD FOR YOU, KANADE!
YEAH!
PAW-SOME!
KANADE-KUN, I'M SORRY.

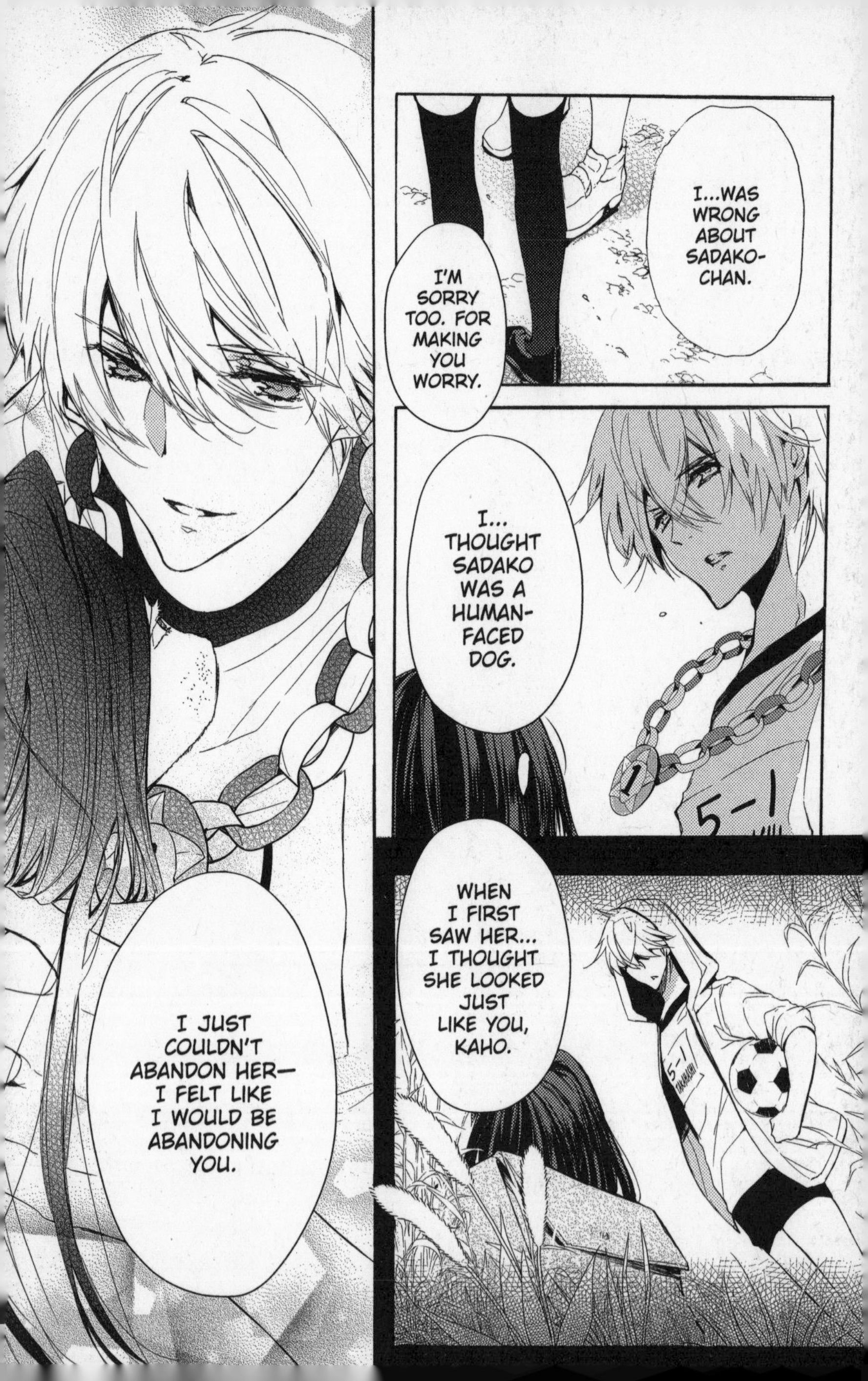
I...WAS WRONG ABOUT SADAKO-CHAN.
I'M SORRY TOO. FOR MAKING YOU WORRY.
I... THOUGHT SADAKO WAS A HUMAN-FACED DOG.
WHEN I FIRST SAW HER... I THOUGHT SHE LOOKED JUST LIKE YOU, KAHO.
I JUST COULDN'T ABANDON HER— I FELT LIKE I WOULD BE ABANDONING YOU.

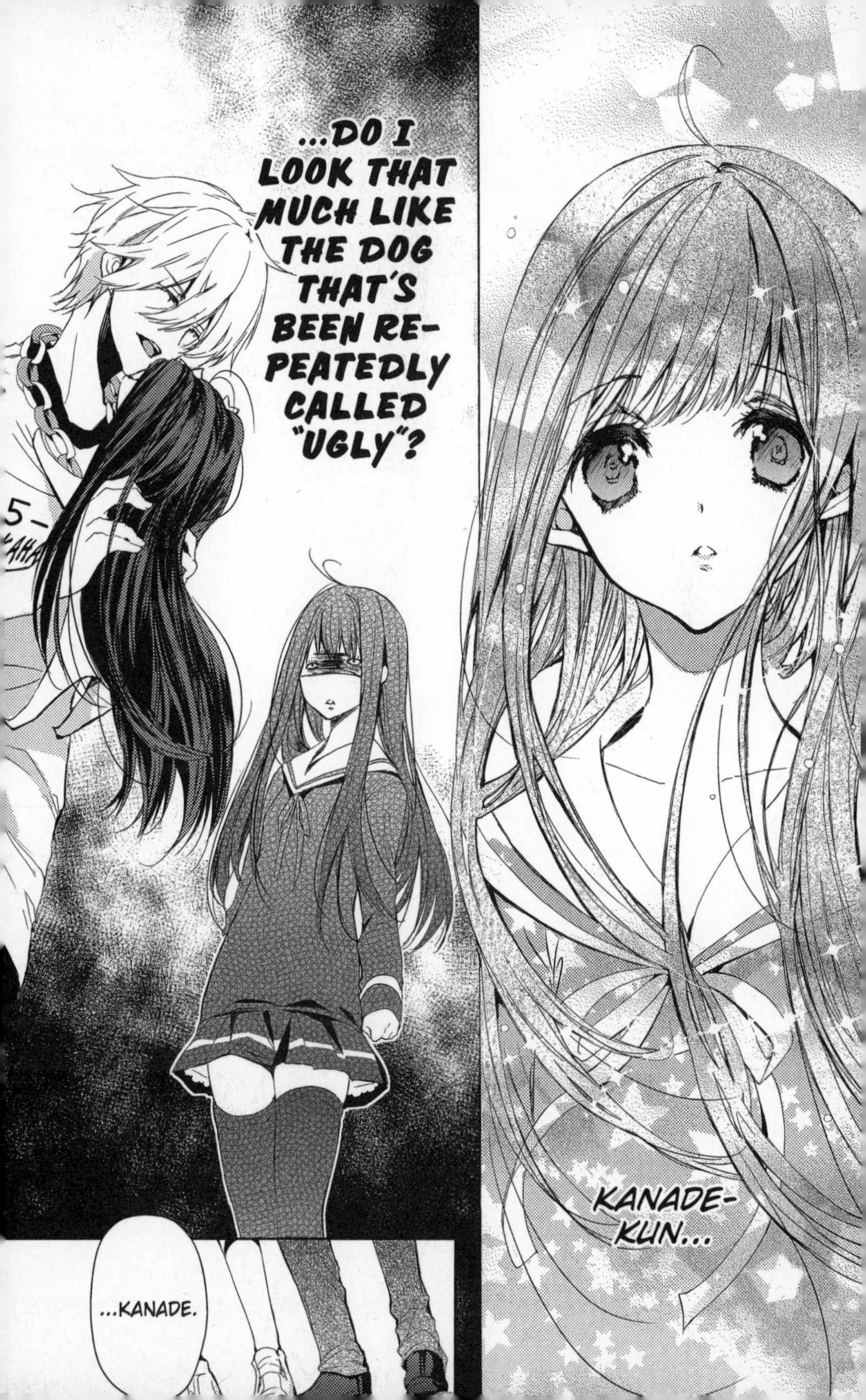
KANADE-KUN...
...DO I LOOK THAT MUCH LIKE THE DOG THAT'S BEEN RE-PEATEDLY CALLED "UGLY"?
...KANADE.

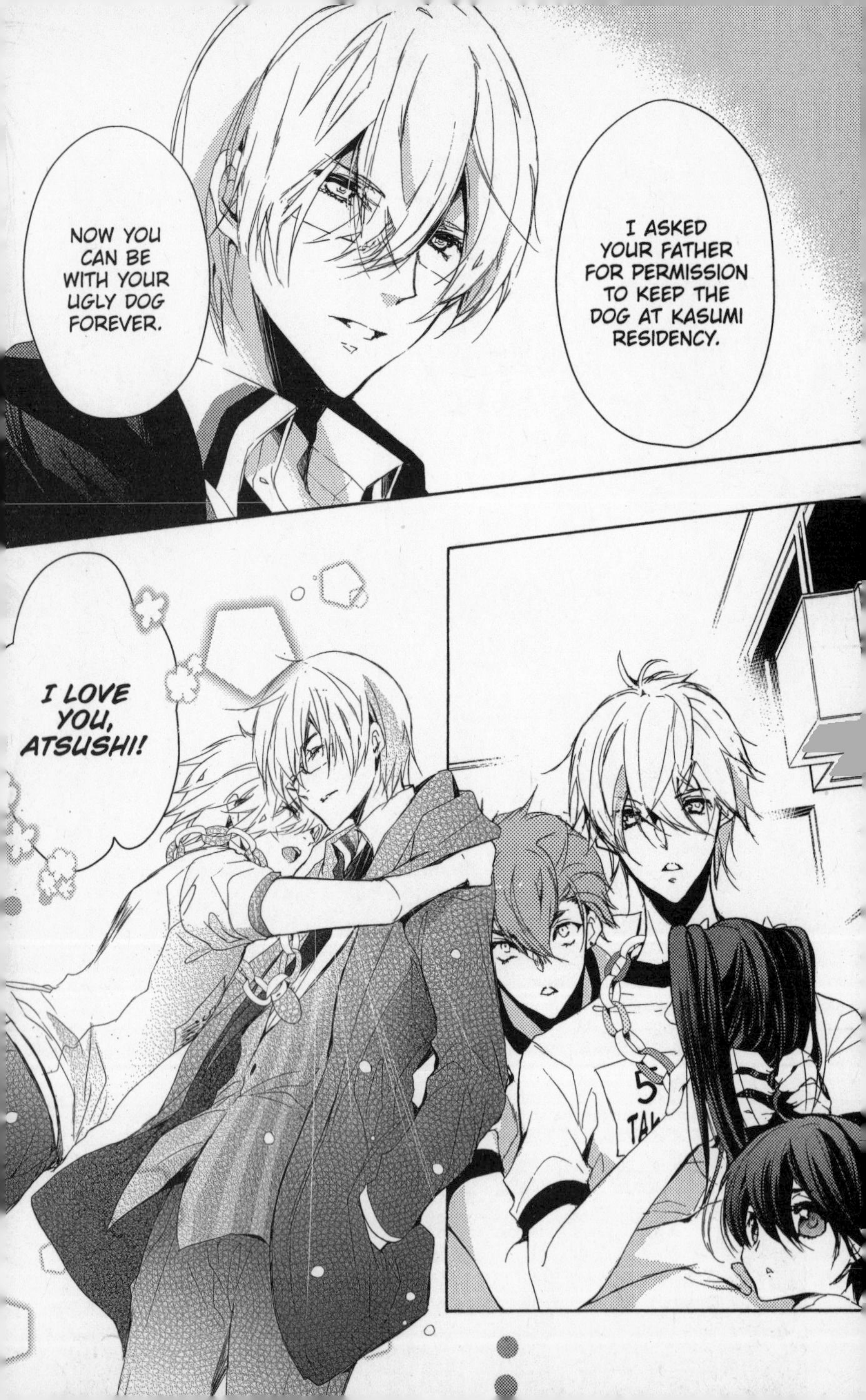
I ASKED YOUR FATHER FOR PERMISSION TO KEEP THE DOG AT KASUMI RESIDENCY.
NOW YOU CAN BE WITH YOUR UGLY DOG FOREVER.
I LOVE YOU, ATSUSHI!

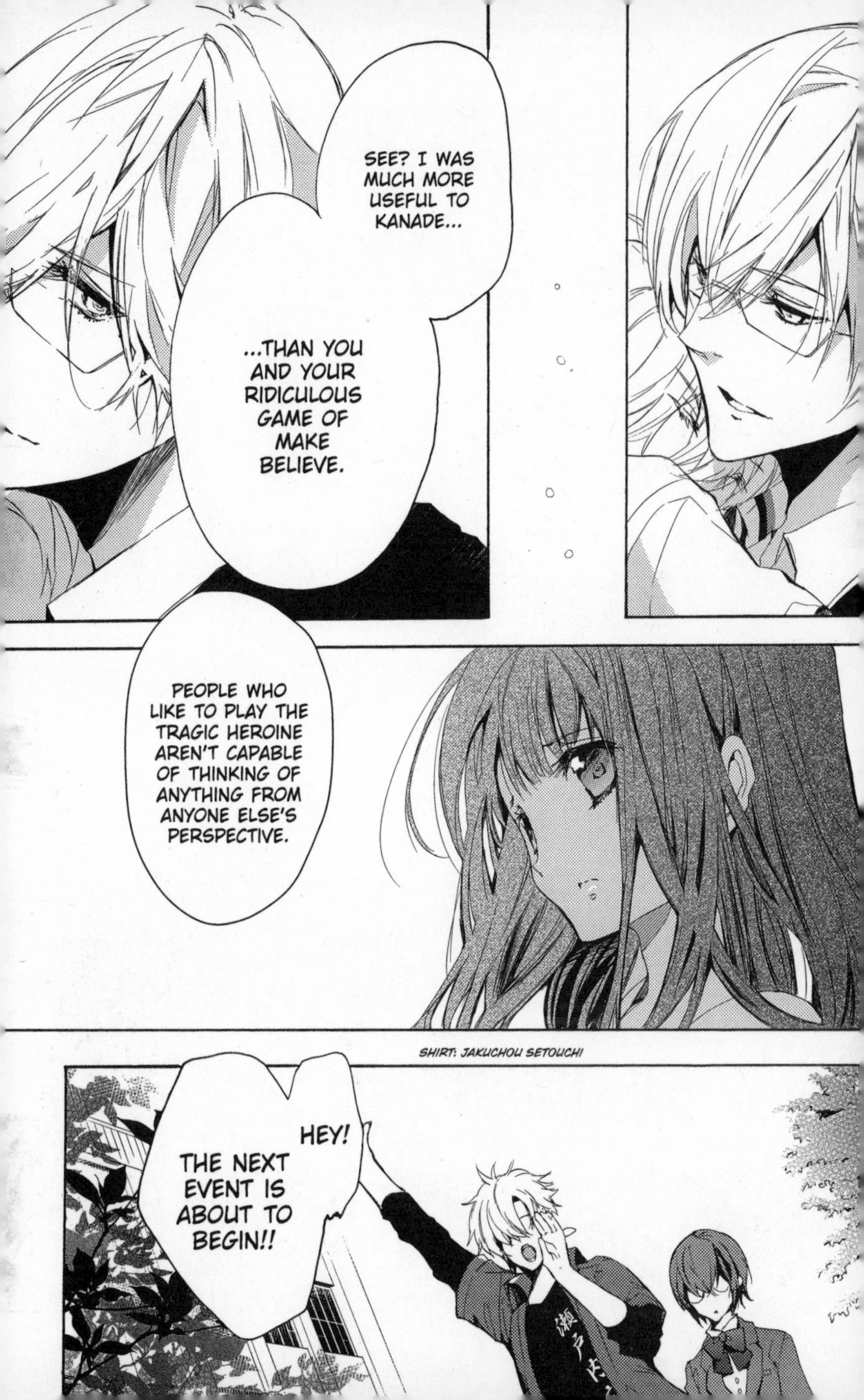
SEE? I WAS MUCH MORE USEFUL TO KANADE...
...THAN YOU AND YOUR RIDICULOUS GAME OF MAKE BELIEVE.
PEOPLE WHO LIKE TO PLAY THE TRAGIC HEROINE AREN'T CAPABLE OF THINKING OF ANYTHING FROM ANYONE ELSE'S PERSPECTIVE.
SHIRT: JAKUCHOU SETOUCHI
HEY!
THE NEXT EVENT IS ABOUT TO BEGIN!!

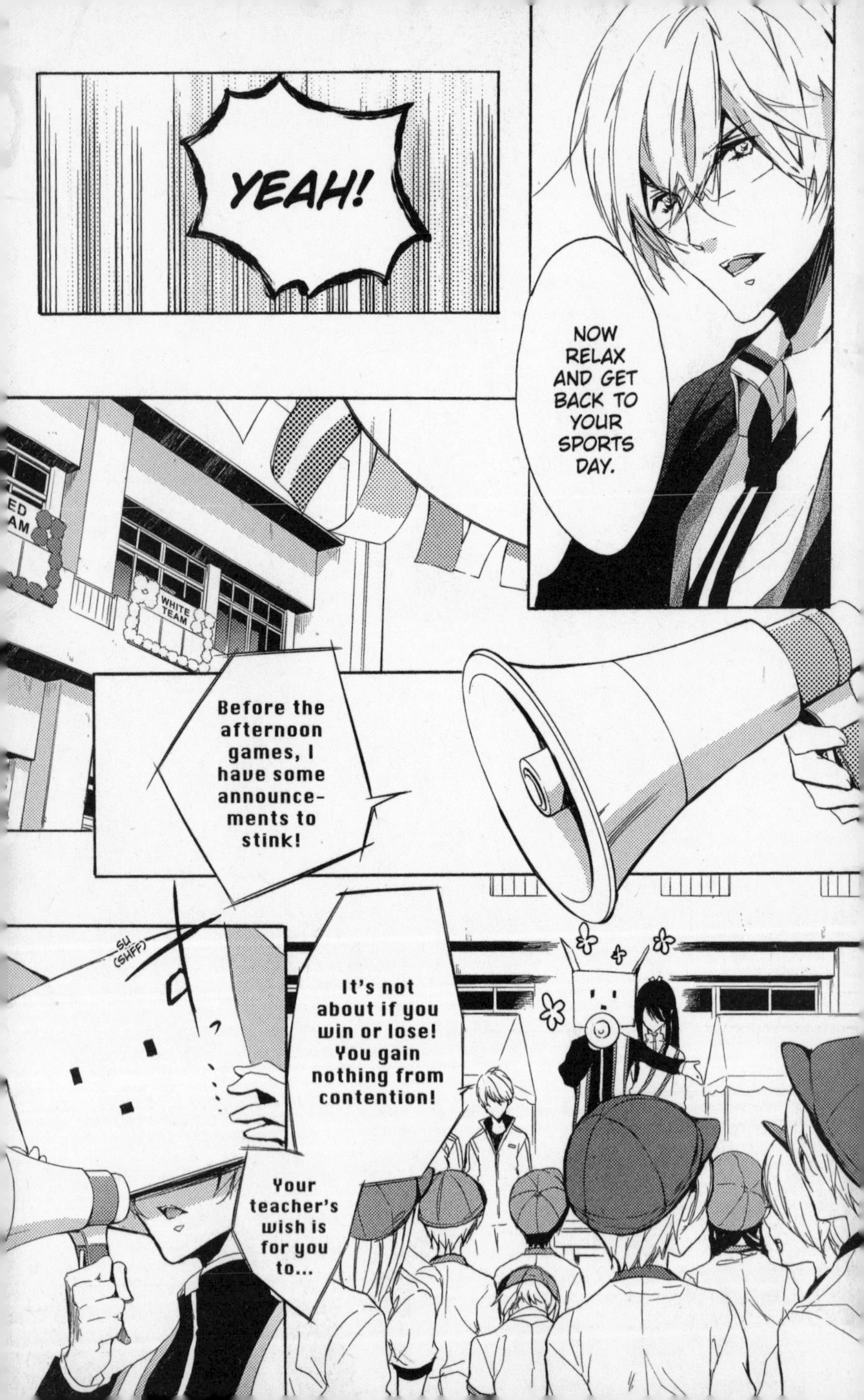
NOW RELAX AND GET BACK TO YOUR SPORTS DAY.
YEAH!
ED
AM
WHITE TEAM
Before the afternoon games, I have some announce-ments to stink!
It's not about if you win or lose! You gain nothing from contention!
SU (SHFF)
Your teacher's wish is for you to...

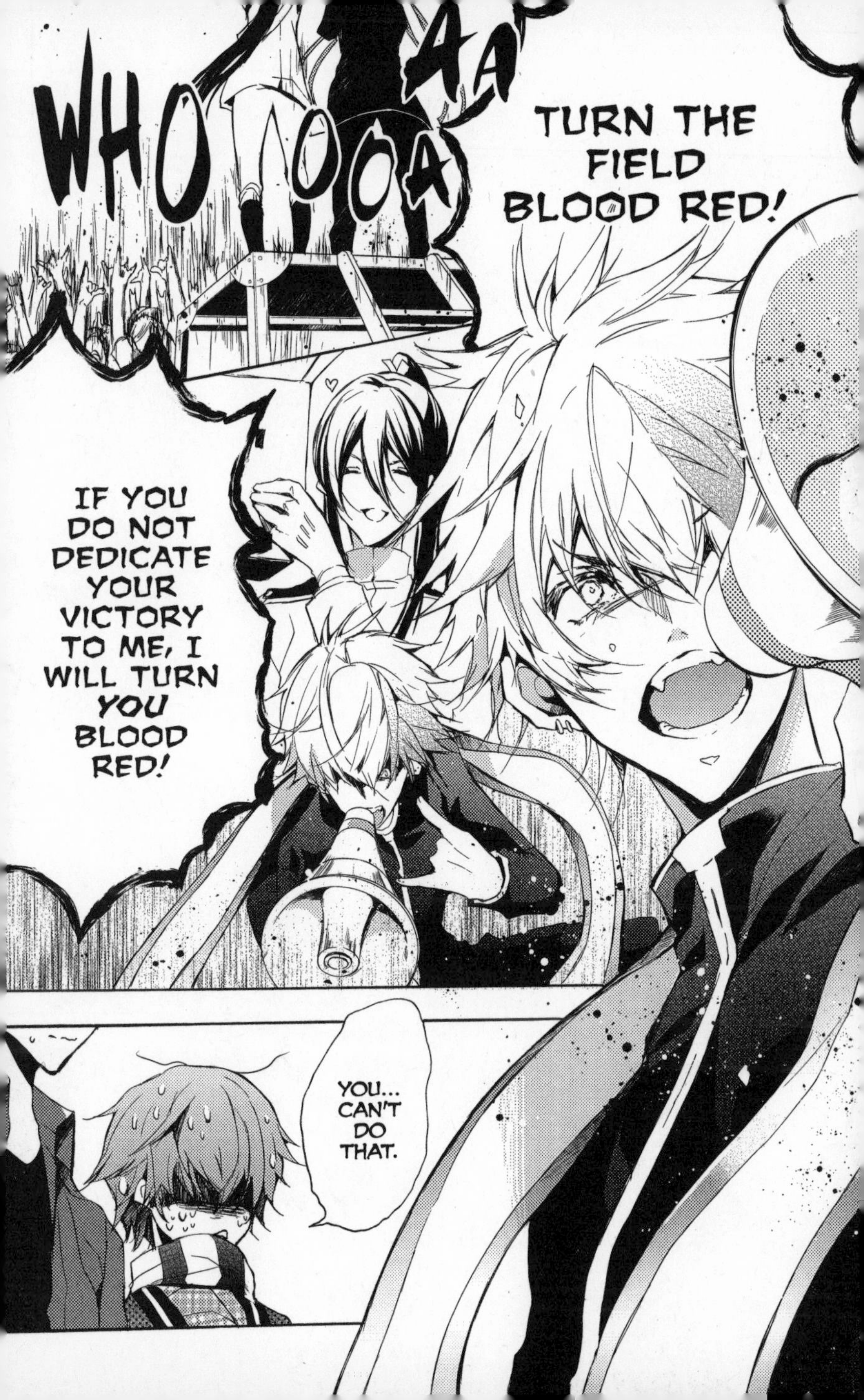
TURN THE FIELD BLOOD RED!
WHOOOAAAA
IF YOU DO NOT DEDICATE YOUR VICTORY TO ME, I WILL TURN *YOU* BLOOD RED!
YOU... CAN'T DO THAT.

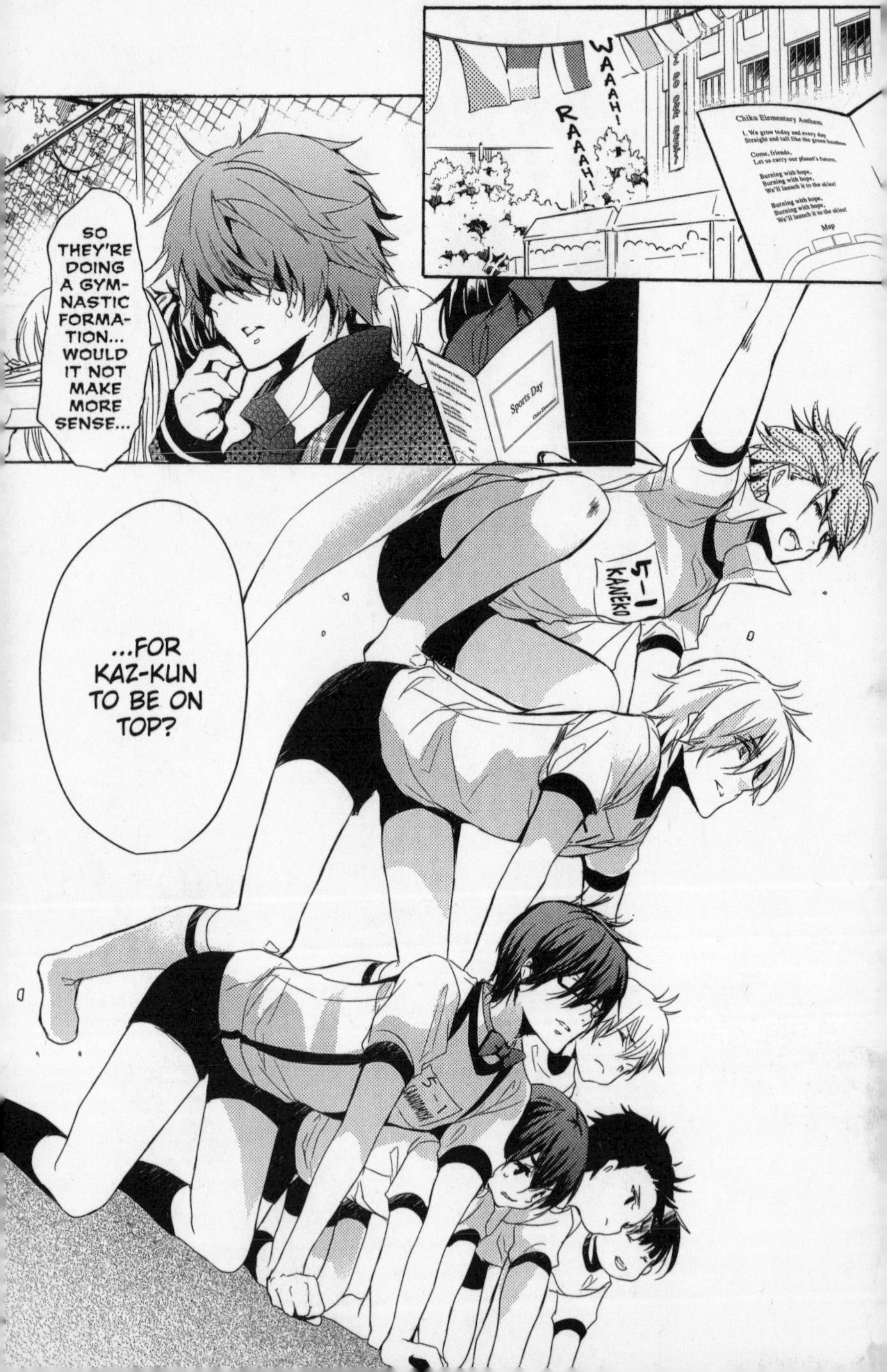
WAAAAH!
RAAAAH!
Chiku Elementary Anthem
1. We grow today and every day
Straight and tall like the green bamboo
Come, friends,
Let us carry our planet's future.
Burning with hope,
Burning with hope,
We'll launch it to the skies!
Burning with hope,
Burning with hope,
We'll launch it to the skies!
Map
SO THEY'RE DOING A GYM-NASTIC FORMA-TION... WOULD IT NOT MAKE MORE SENSE...
Sports Day
...FOR KAZ-KUN TO BE ON TOP?
5-1 KANEKO

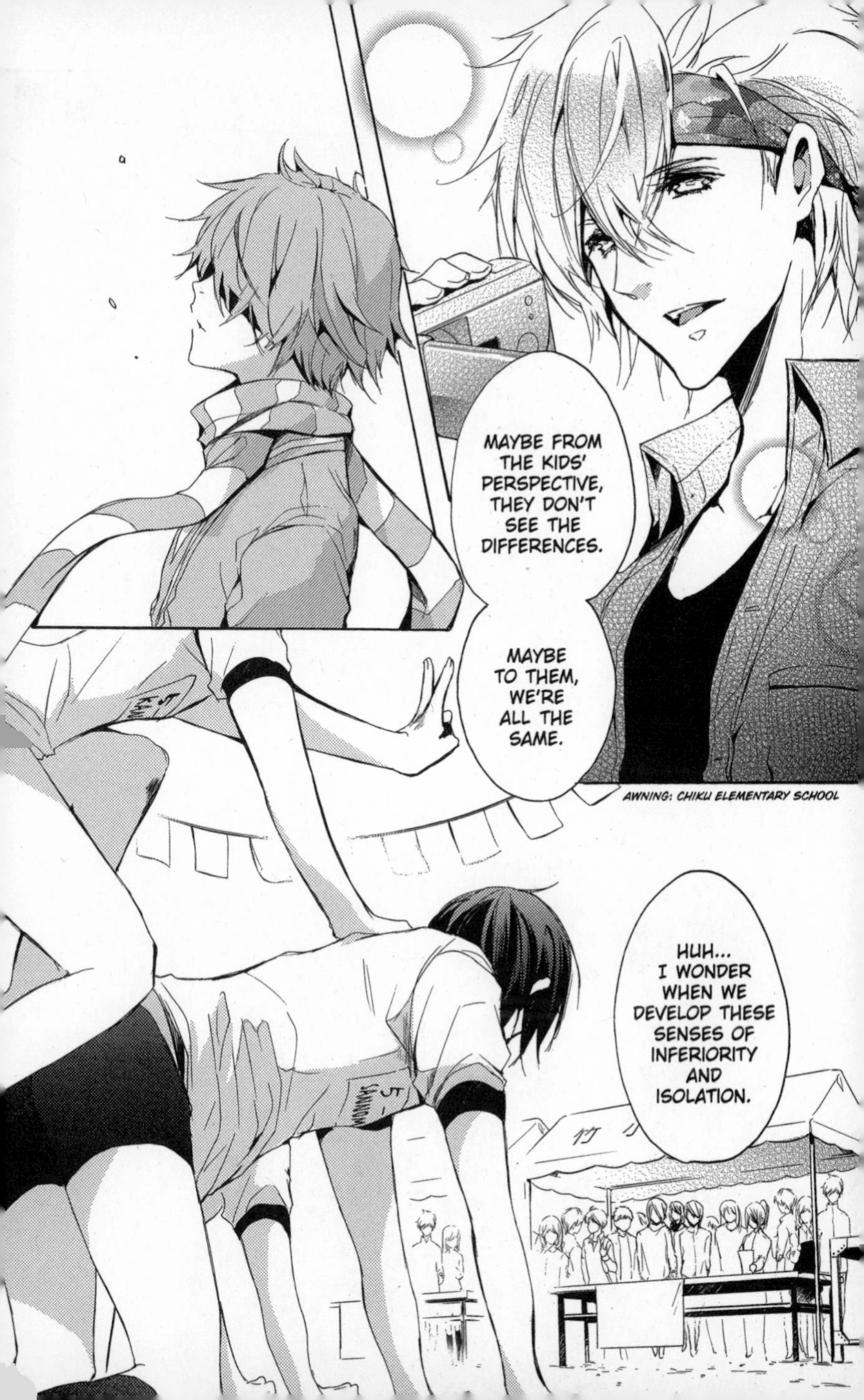
MAYBE FROM THE KIDS' PERSPECTIVE, THEY DON'T SEE THE DIFFERENCES.
MAYBE TO THEM, WE'RE ALL THE SAME.
AWNING: CHIKU ELEMENTARY SCHOOL
HUH... I WONDER WHEN WE DEVELOP THESE SENSES OF INFERIORITY AND ISOLATION.

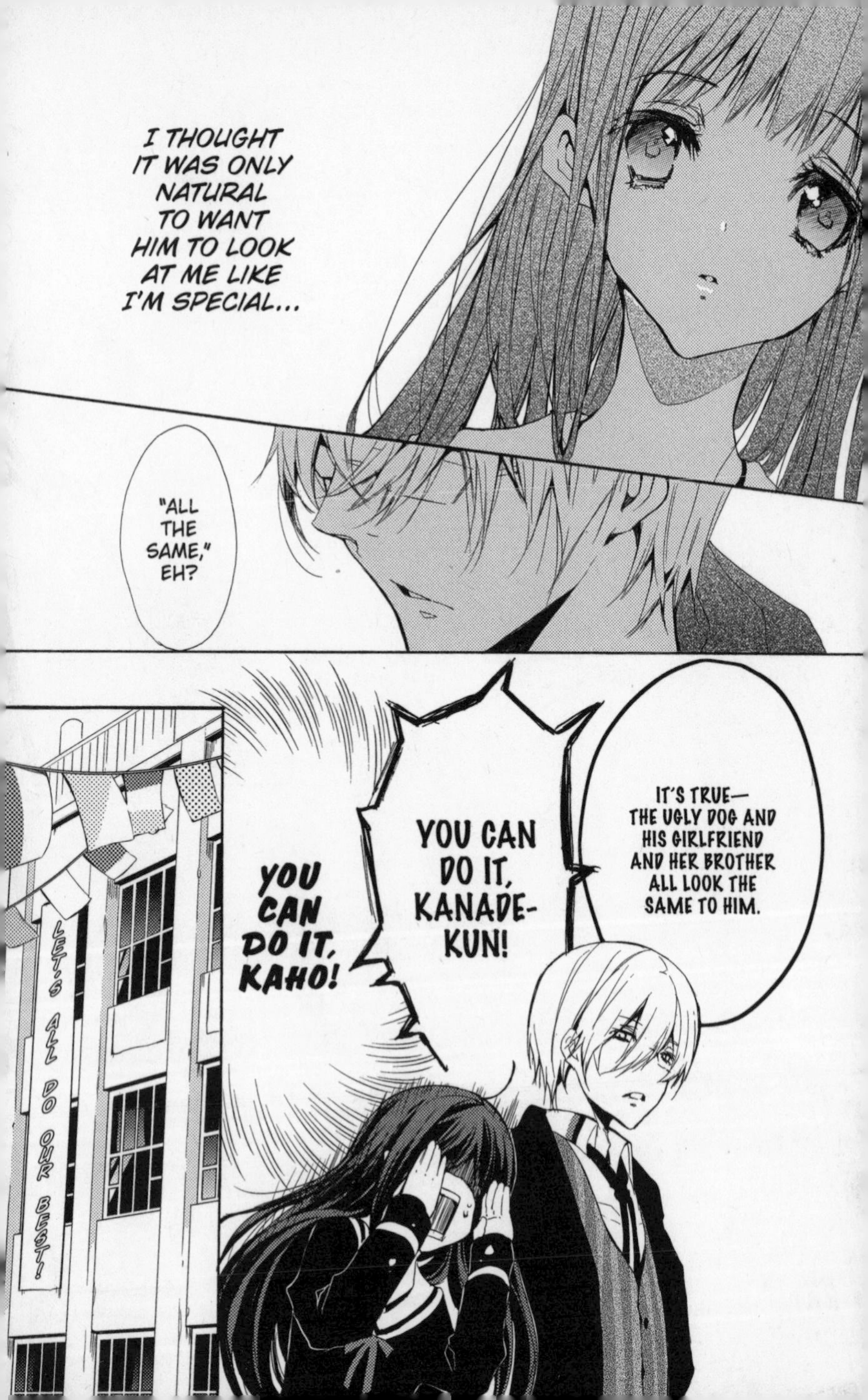
I THOUGHT IT WAS ONLY NATURAL TO WANT HIM TO LOOK AT ME LIKE I'M SPECIAL...
"ALL THE SAME," EH?
IT'S TRUE— THE UGLY DOG AND HIS GIRLFRIEND AND HER BROTHER ALL LOOK THE SAME TO HIM.
YOU CAN DO IT, KANADE-KUN!
YOU CAN DO IT, KAHO!
LET'S ALL DO OUR BEST!

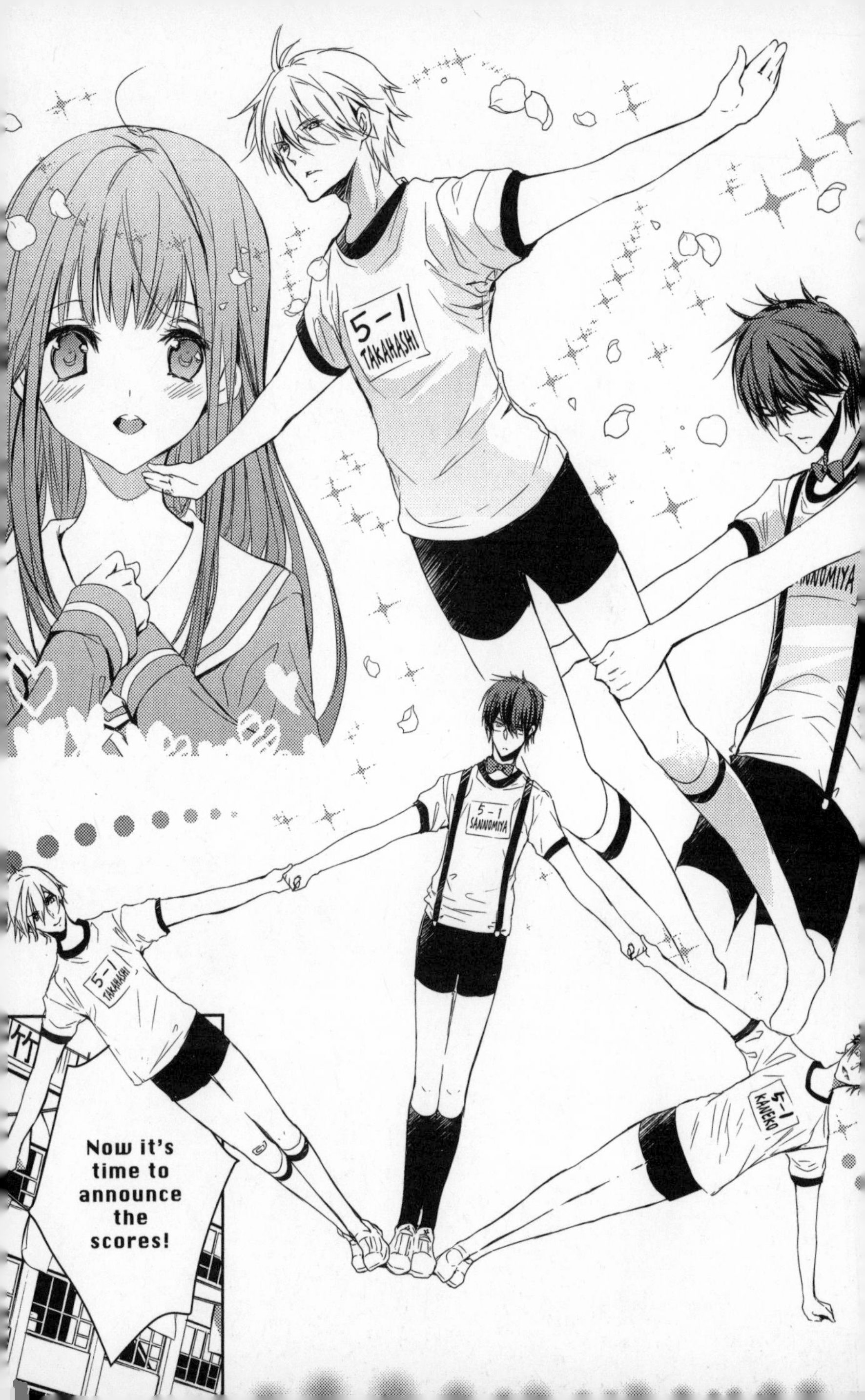
5-1
TAKAHASHI
SANNOMIYA
5-1
SANNOMIYA
5-1
TAKAHASHI
竹
5-1
KANEKO
Now it's time to announce the scores!

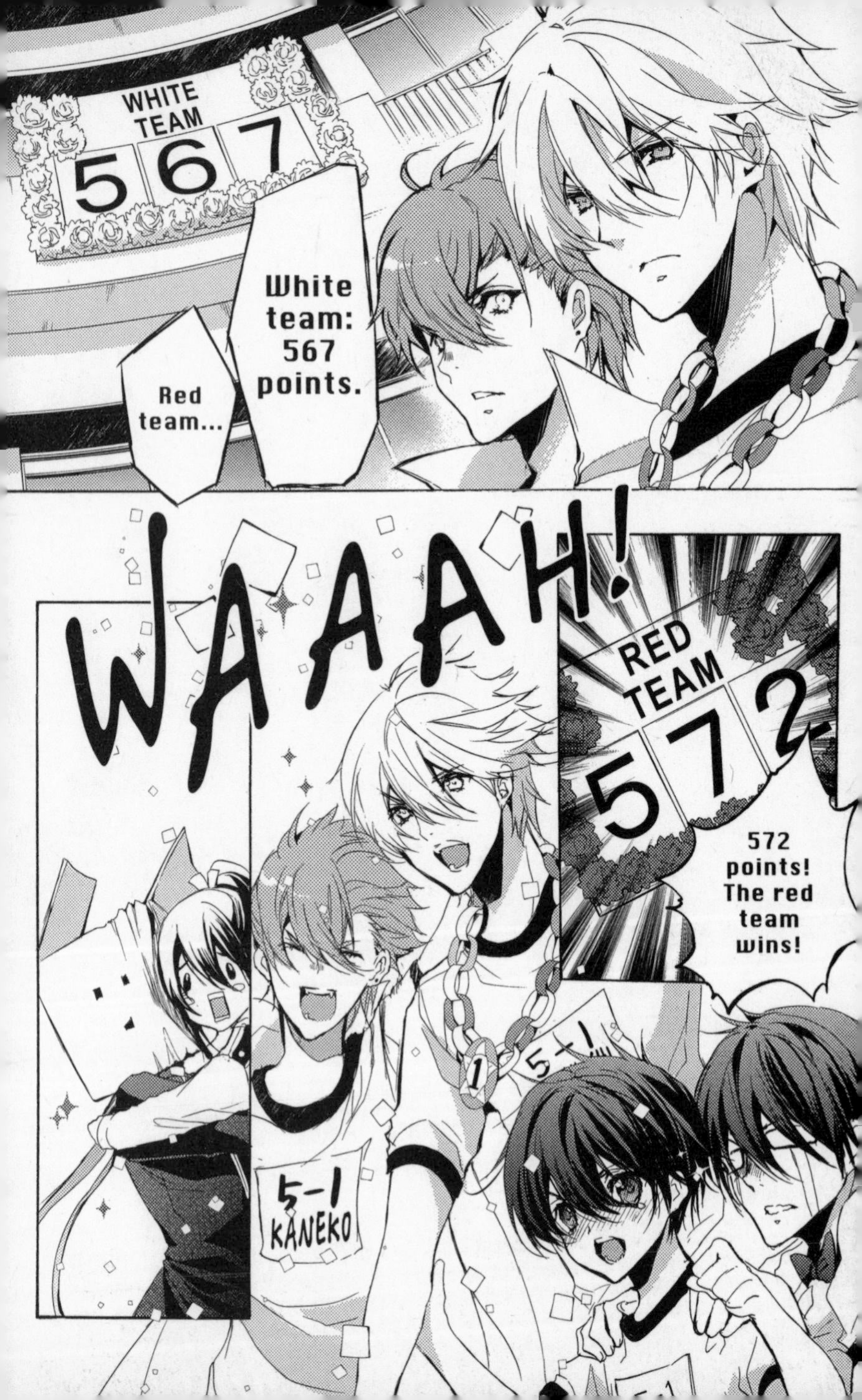
White team: 567 points.
WHITE TEAM 567
Red team...
572 points! The red team wins!
RED TEAM 572
WAAAH!
5-1
5-1 KANEKO

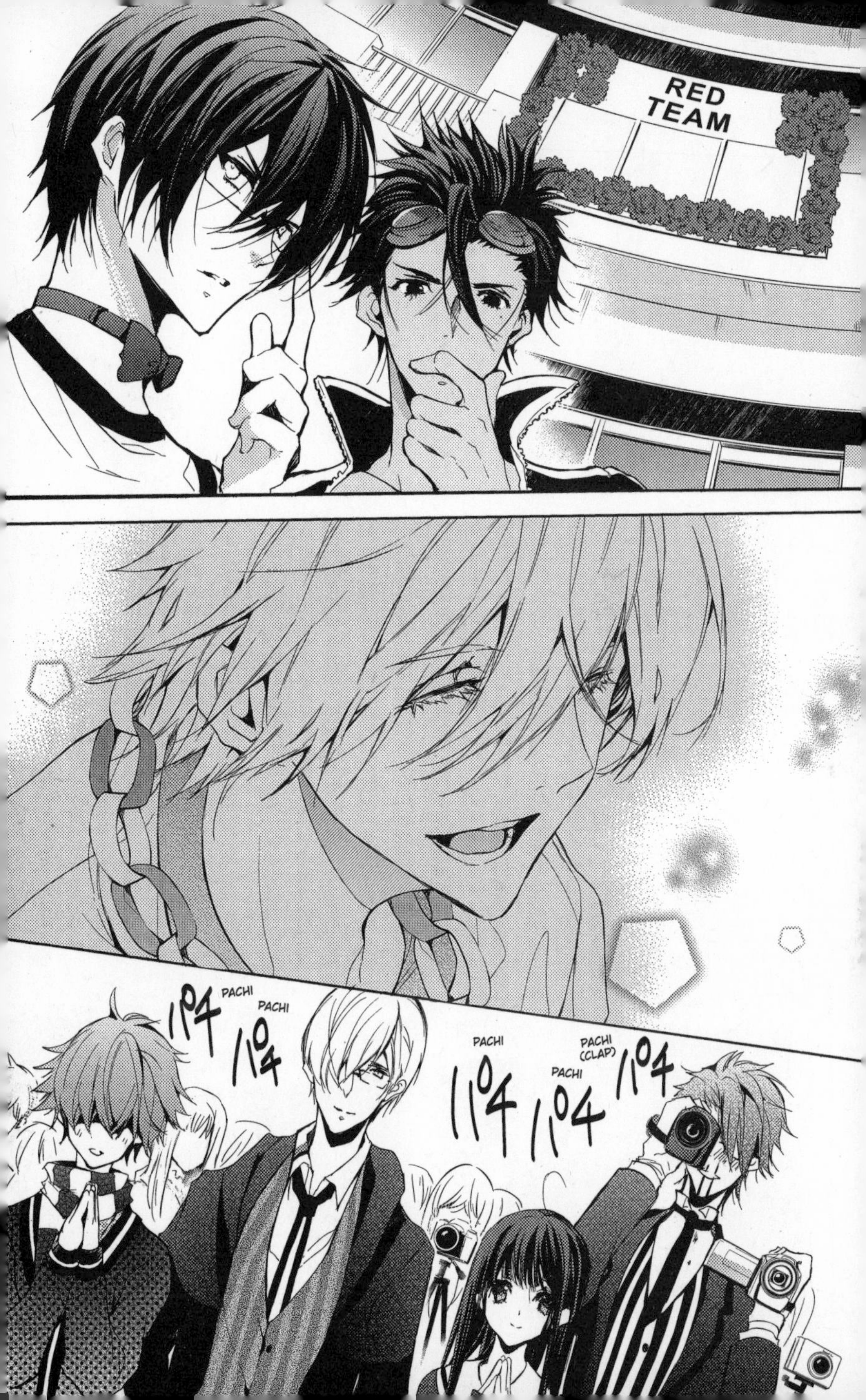
RED TEAM
PACHI (CLAP)
PACHI
PACHI
PACHI
PACHI

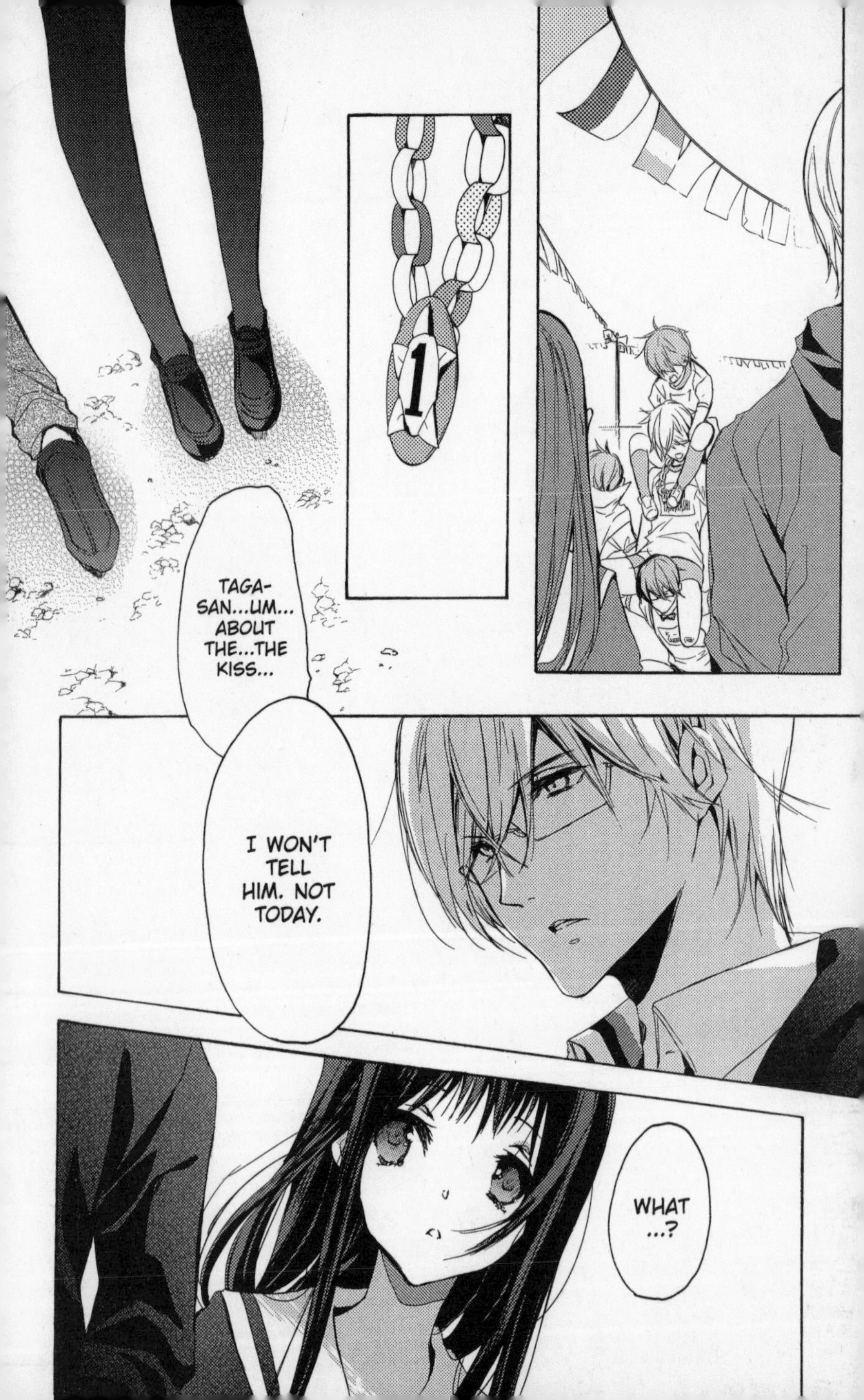
TAGA-SAN...UM... ABOUT THE...THE KISS...
I WON'T TELL HIM. NOT TODAY.
WHAT ...?

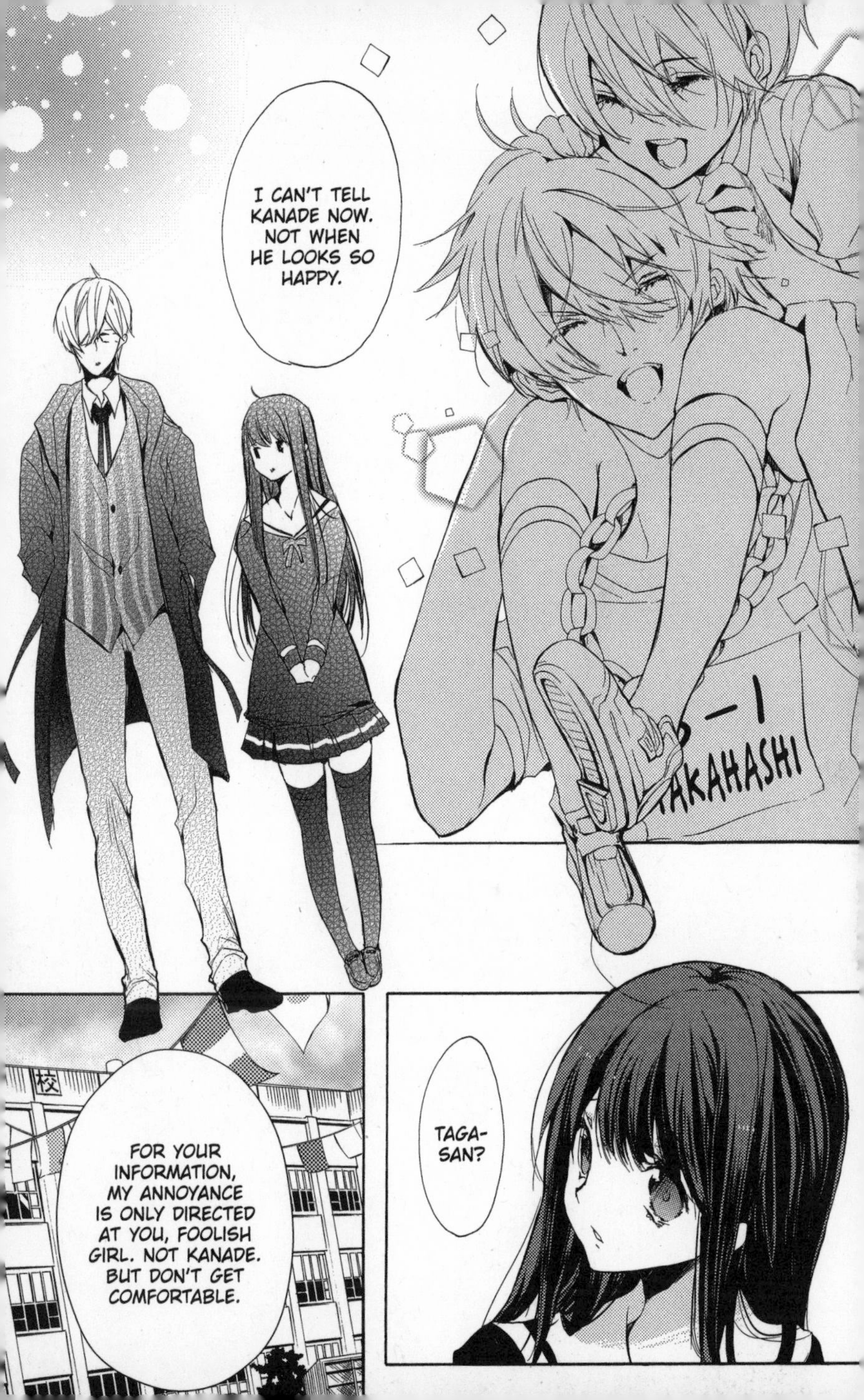
I CAN'T TELL KANADE NOW. NOT WHEN HE LOOKS SO HAPPY.
TAGA-SAN?
FOR YOUR INFORMATION, MY ANNOYANCE IS ONLY DIRECTED AT YOU, FOOLISH GIRL. NOT KANADE. BUT DON'T GET COMFORTABLE.

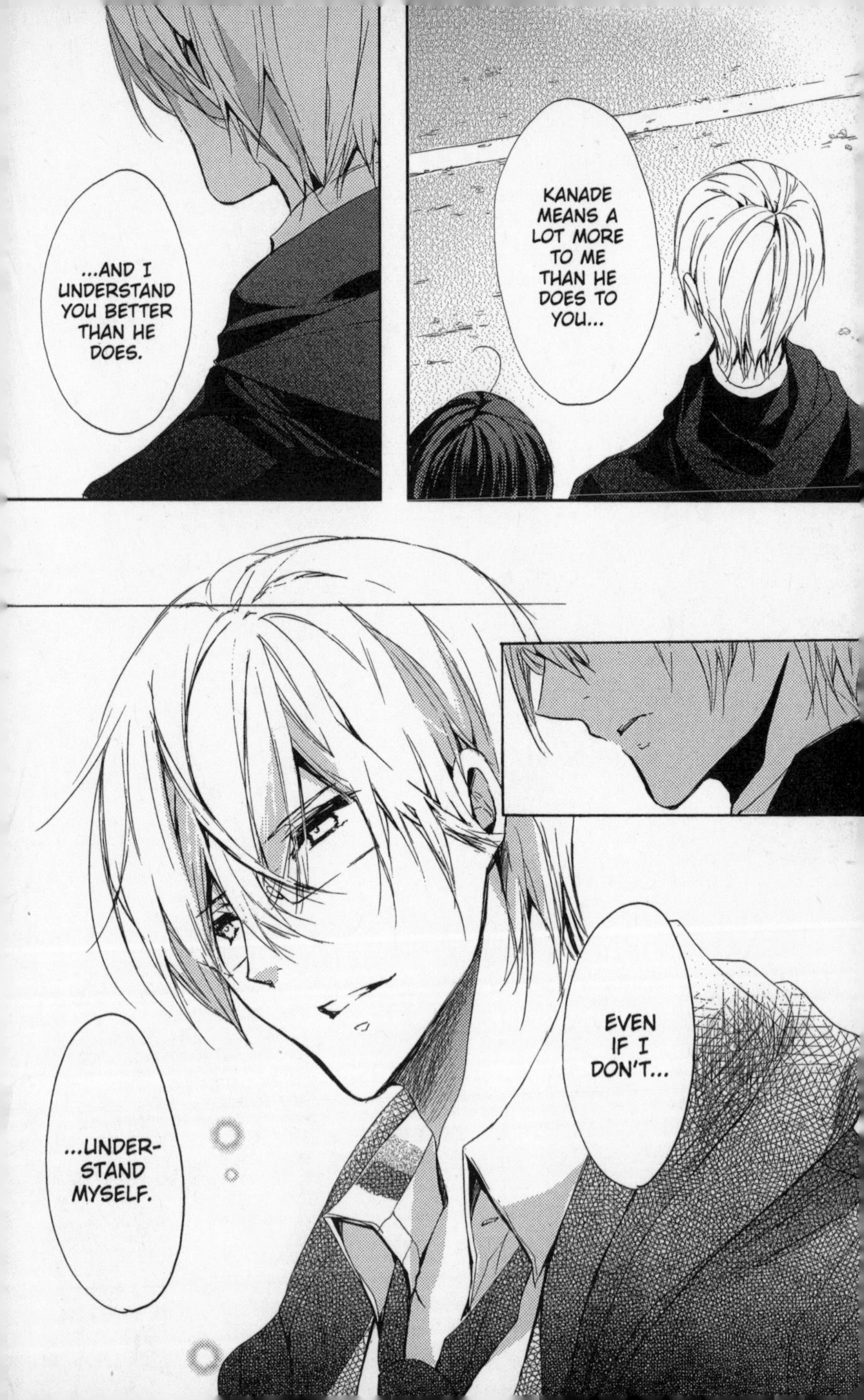
KANADE MEANS A LOT MORE TO ME THAN HE DOES TO YOU...
...AND I UNDERSTAND YOU BETTER THAN HE DOES.
EVEN IF I DON'T...
...UNDER-STAND MYSELF.

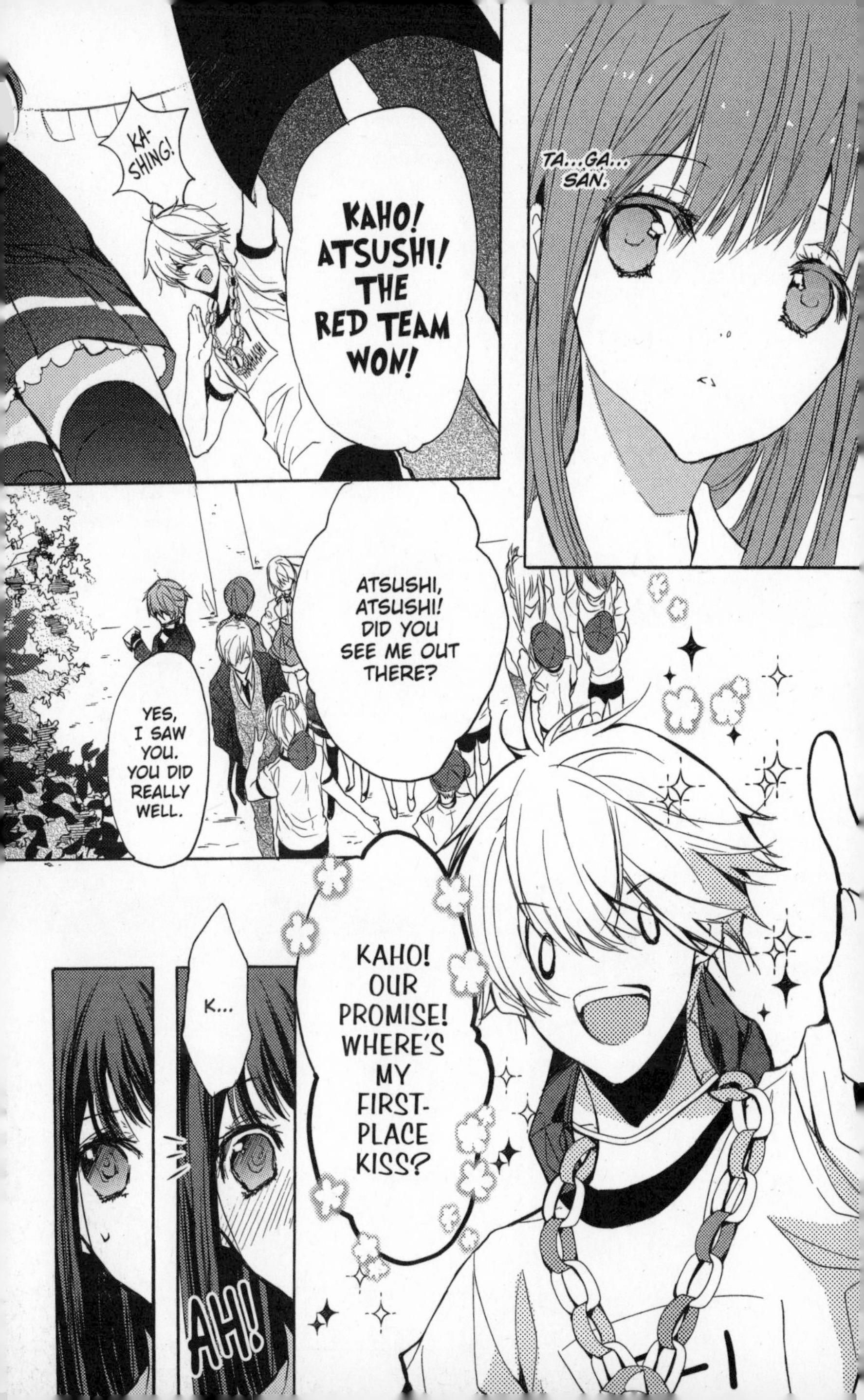
TA...GA... SAN.
KA-SHING!
KAHO! ATSUSHI! THE RED TEAM WON!
ATSUSHI, ATSUSHI! DID YOU SEE ME OUT THERE?
YES, I SAW YOU. YOU DID REALLY WELL.
KAHO! OUR PROMISE! WHERE'S MY FIRST-PLACE KISS?
K...
AH!

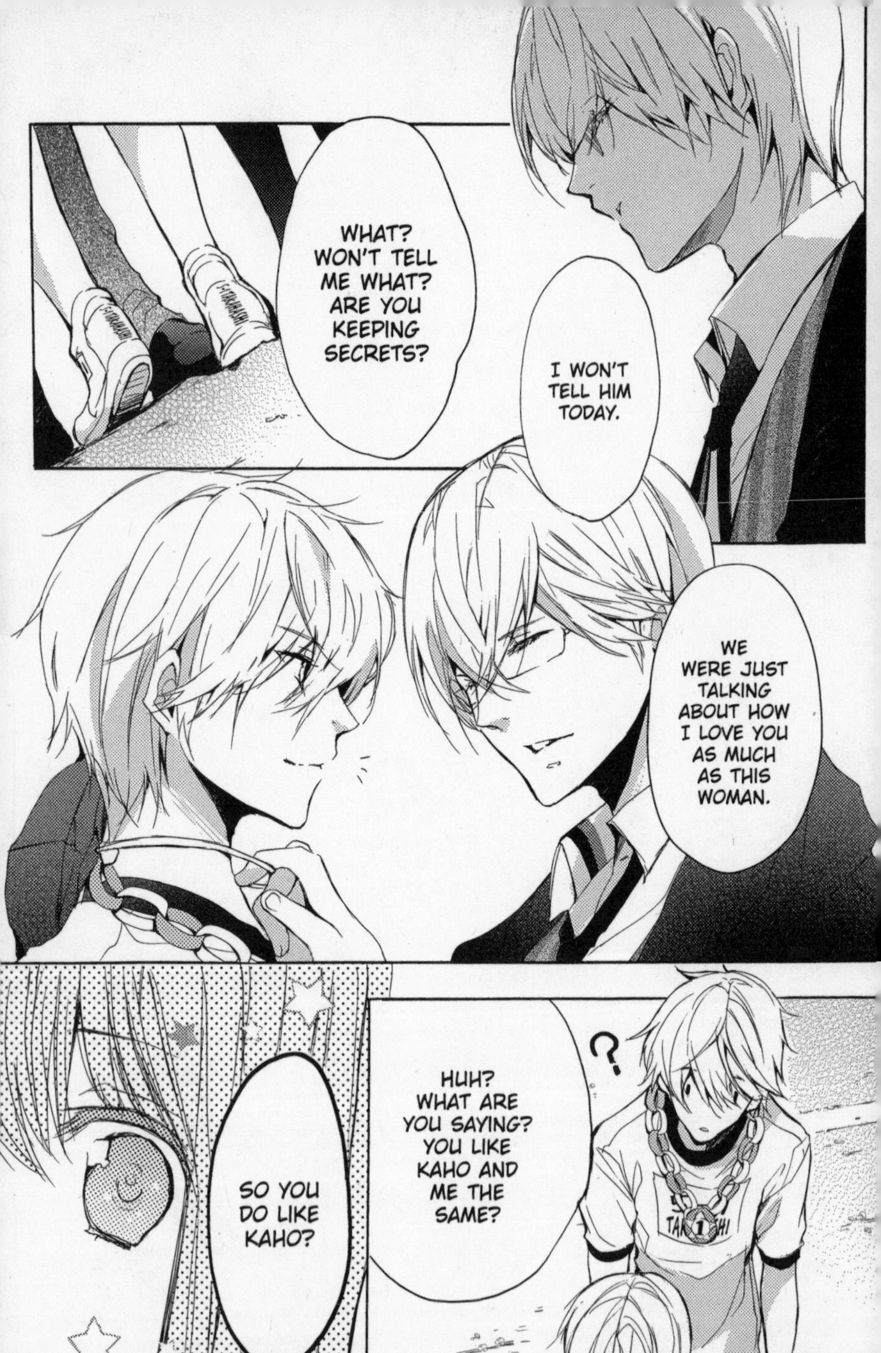
I WON'T TELL HIM TODAY.
WHAT? WON'T TELL ME WHAT? ARE YOU KEEPING SECRETS?
WE WERE JUST TALKING ABOUT HOW I LOVE YOU AS MUCH AS THIS WOMAN.
?
HUH? WHAT ARE YOU SAYING? YOU LIKE KAHO AND ME THE SAME?
SO YOU DO LIKE KAHO?

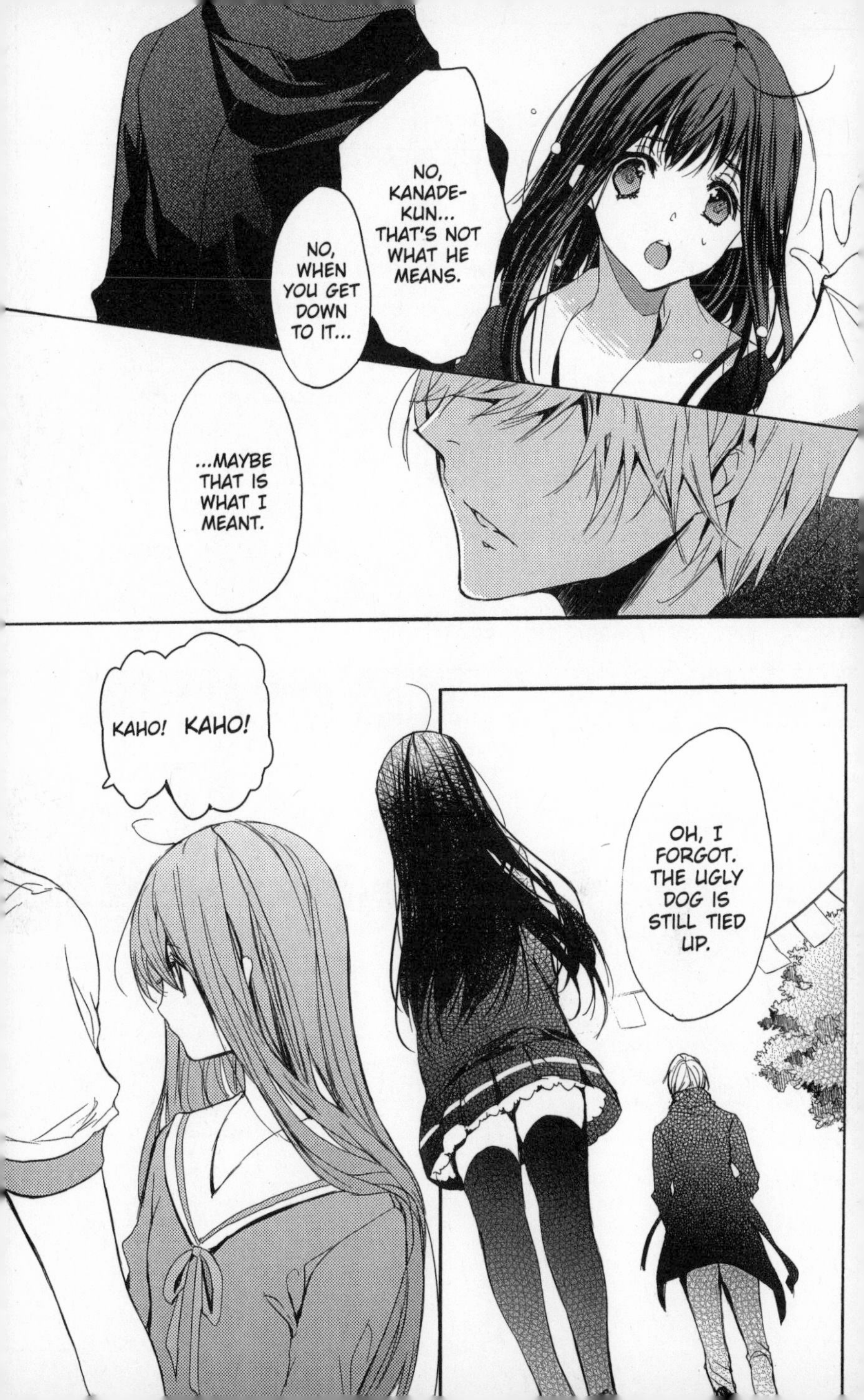
NO, KANADE-KUN... THAT'S NOT WHAT HE MEANS.
NO, WHEN YOU GET DOWN TO IT...
...MAYBE THAT IS WHAT I MEANT.
OH, I FORGOT. THE UGLY DOG IS STILL TIED UP.
KAHO! KAHO!

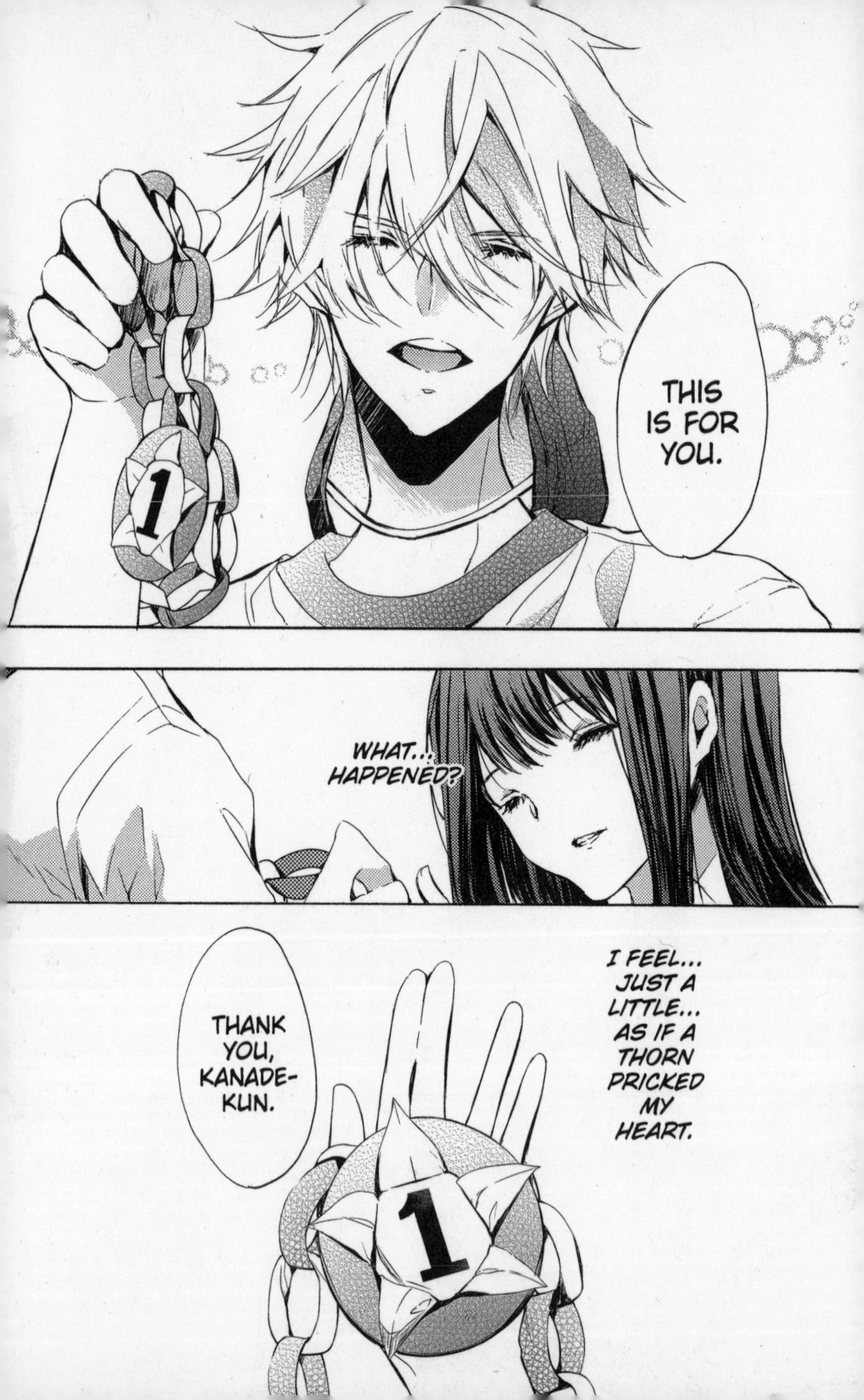
THIS IS FOR YOU.
WHAT... HAPPENED?
I FEEL... JUST A LITTLE... AS IF A THORN PRICKED MY HEART.
THANK YOU, KANADE-KUN.

Episode 22

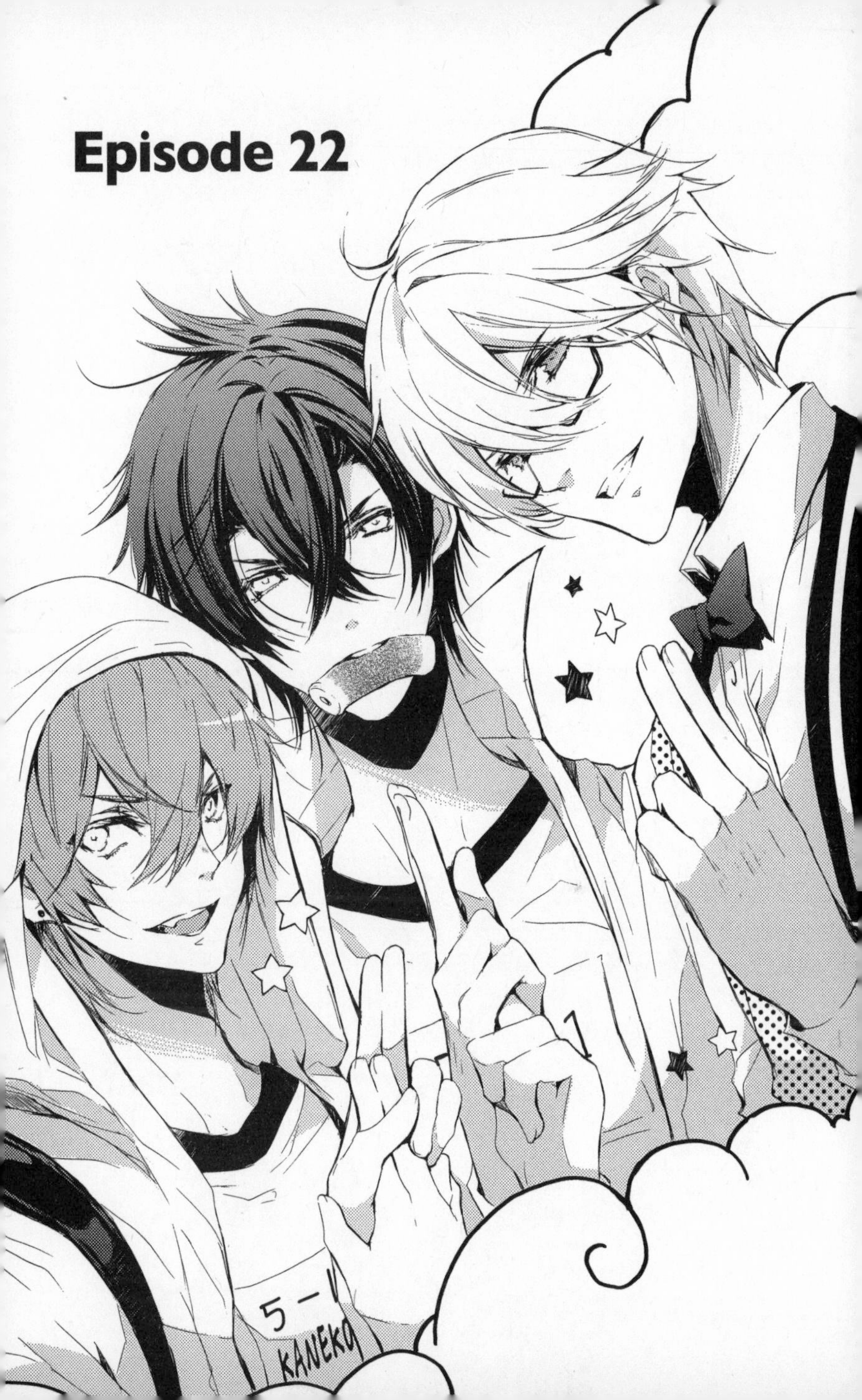
KANEKO

LABEL: FIRE HYDRANT

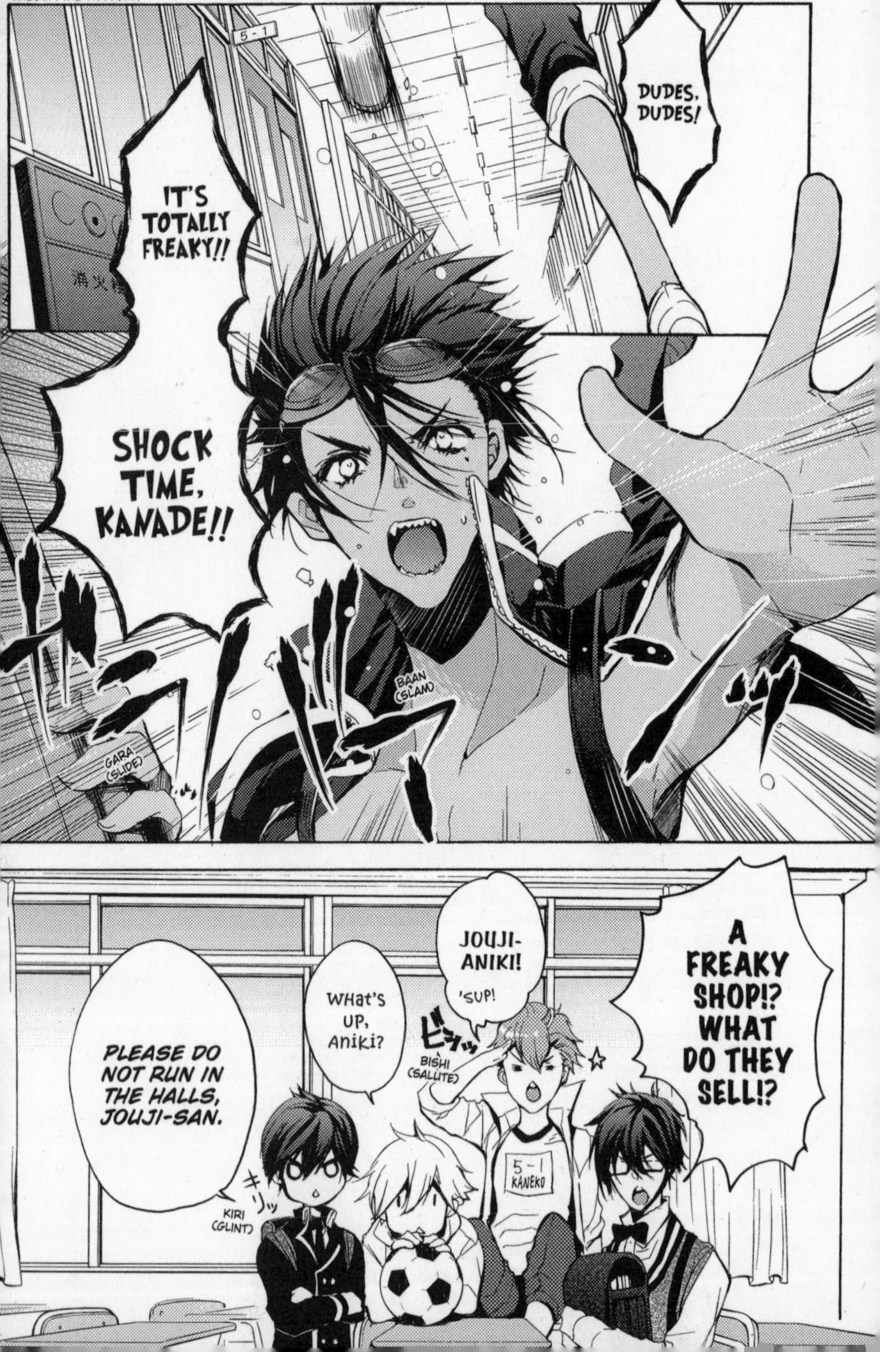
5-1
DUDES, DUDES!
IT'S TOTALLY FREAKY!!
GARA (SLIDE)
BAAN (SLAM)
SHOCK TIME, KANADE!!
A FREAKY SHOP!? WHAT DO THEY SELL!?
JOUJI-ANIKI!
'SUP!
BISHI (SALUTE)
WHAT'S UP, ANIKI?
5-1 KANEKO
PLEASE DO NOT RUN IN THE HALLS, JOUJI-SAN.
KIRI (GLINT)

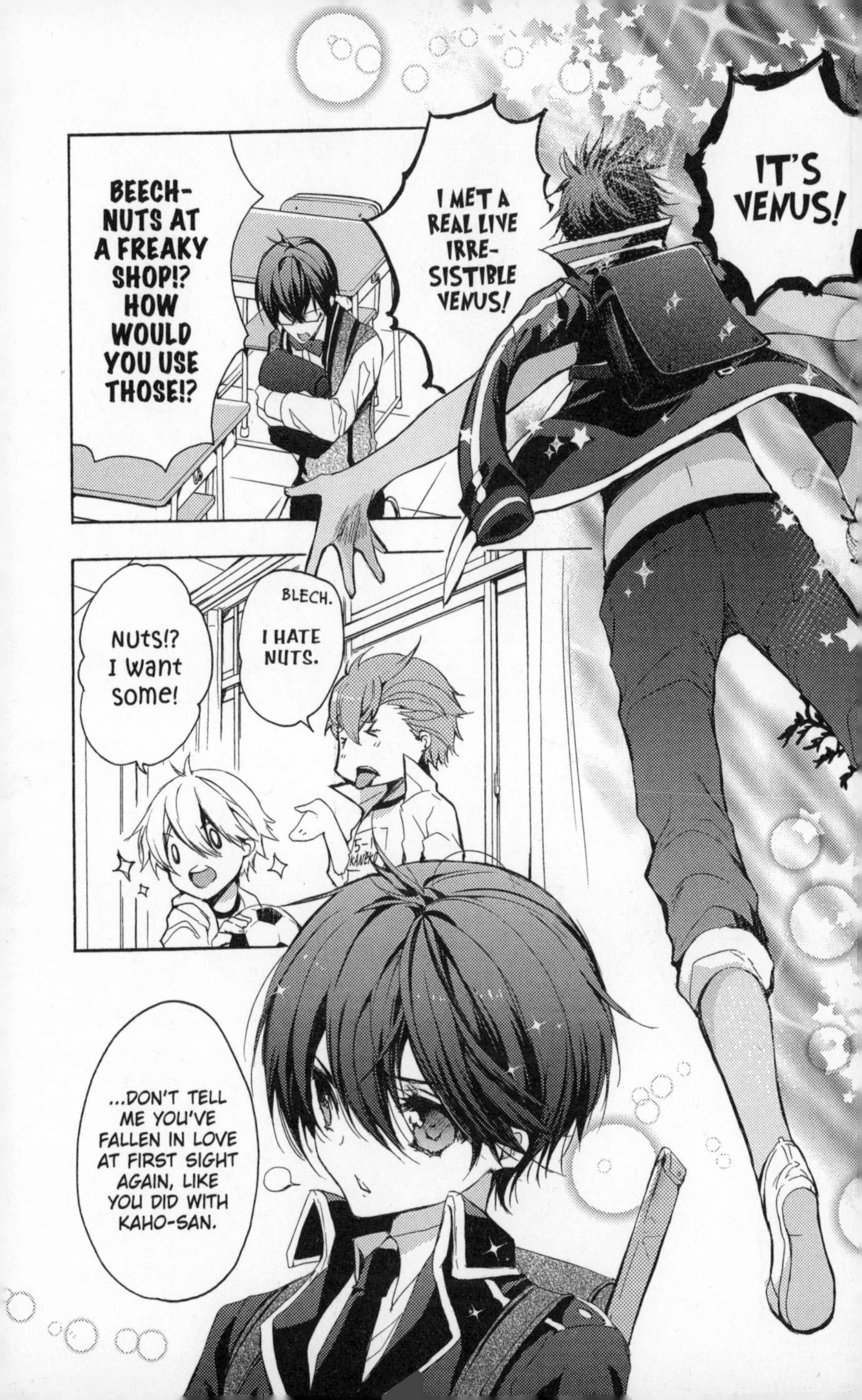
IT'S VENUS!
I MET A REAL LIVE IRRE-SISTIBLE VENUS!
BEECH-NUTS AT A FREAKY SHOP!? HOW WOULD YOU USE THOSE!?
BLECH.
I HATE NUTS.
NUts!? I want some!
5-1 KANEKO
...DON'T TELL ME YOU'VE FALLEN IN LOVE AT FIRST SIGHT AGAIN, LIKE YOU DID WITH KAHO-SAN.

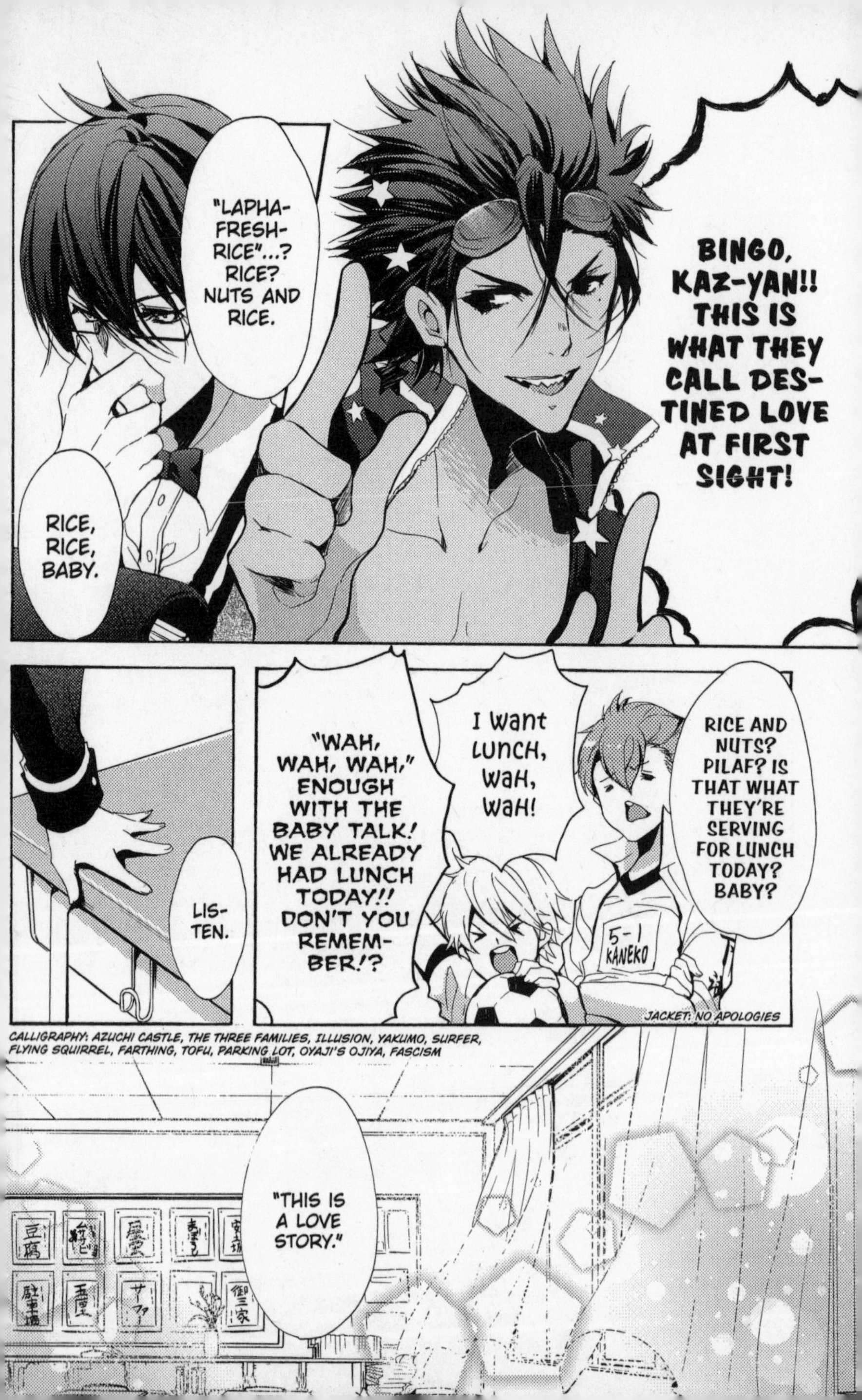
BINGO, KAZ-YAN!! THIS IS WHAT THEY CALL DES-TINED LOVE AT FIRST SIGHT!
"LAPHA-FRESH-RICE"...? RICE? NUTS AND RICE.
RICE, RICE, BABY.
RICE AND NUTS? PILAF? IS THAT WHAT THEY'RE SERVING FOR LUNCH TODAY? BABY?
I want lunch, wah, wah!
"WAH, WAH, WAH," ENOUGH WITH THE BABY TALK! WE ALREADY HAD LUNCH TODAY!! DON'T YOU REMEM-BER!?
5-1 KANEKO
JACKET: NO APOLOGIES
LIS-TEN.
CALLIGRAPHY: AZUCHI CASTLE, THE THREE FAMILIES, ILLUSION, YAKUMO, SURFER, FLYING SQUIRREL, FARTHING, TOFU, PARKING LOT, OYAJI'S OJIYA, FASCISM
"THIS IS A LOVE STORY."

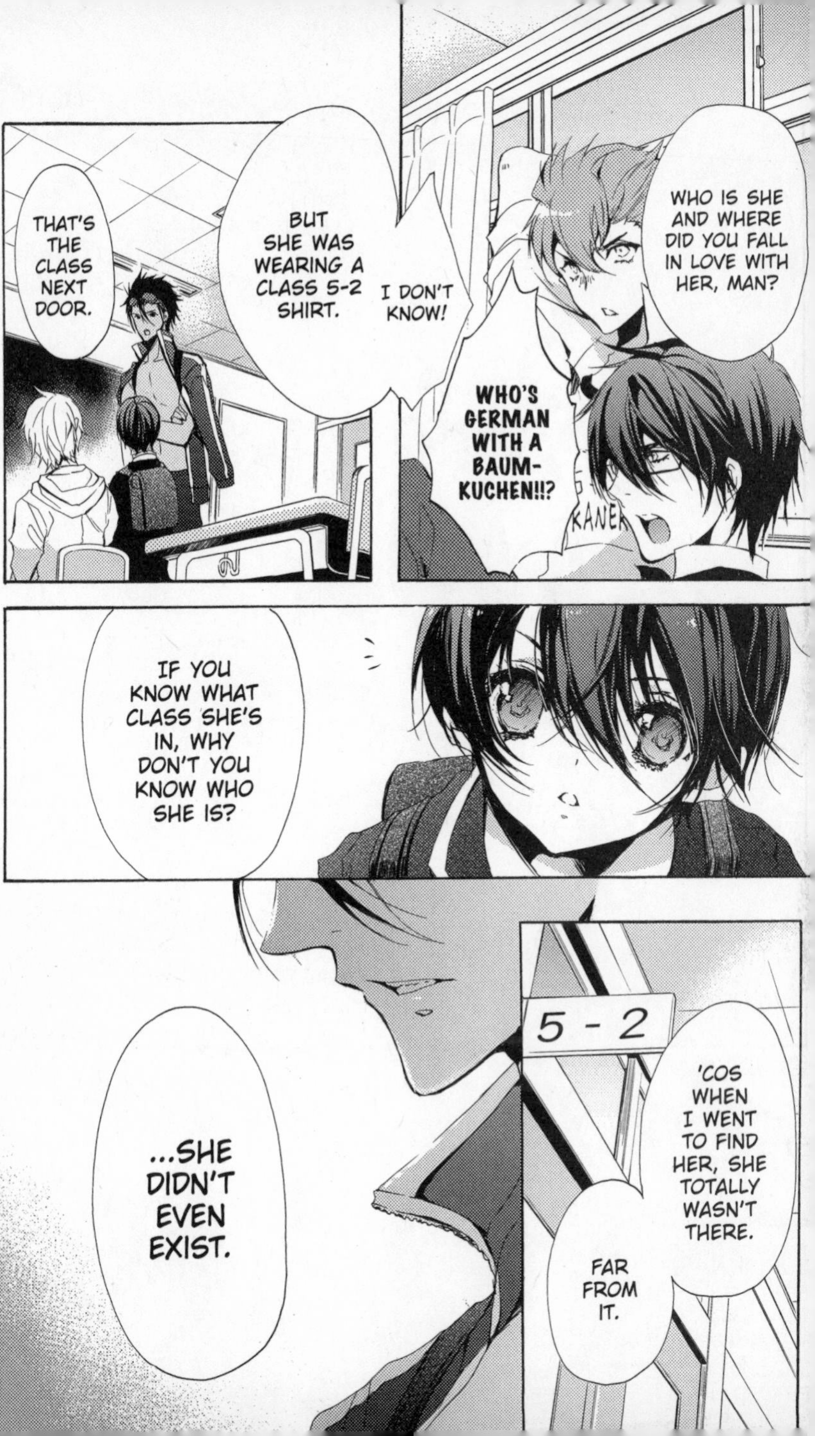
WHO IS SHE AND WHERE DID YOU FALL IN LOVE WITH HER, MAN?
WHO'S GERMAN WITH A BAUM-KUCHEN!!?
I DON'T KNOW!
BUT SHE WAS WEARING A CLASS 5-2 SHIRT.
THAT'S THE CLASS NEXT DOOR.
IF YOU KNOW WHAT CLASS SHE'S IN, WHY DON'T YOU KNOW WHO SHE IS?
5 - 2
'COS WHEN I WENT TO FIND HER, SHE TOTALLY WASN'T THERE.
FAR FROM IT.
...SHE DIDN'T EVEN EXIST.

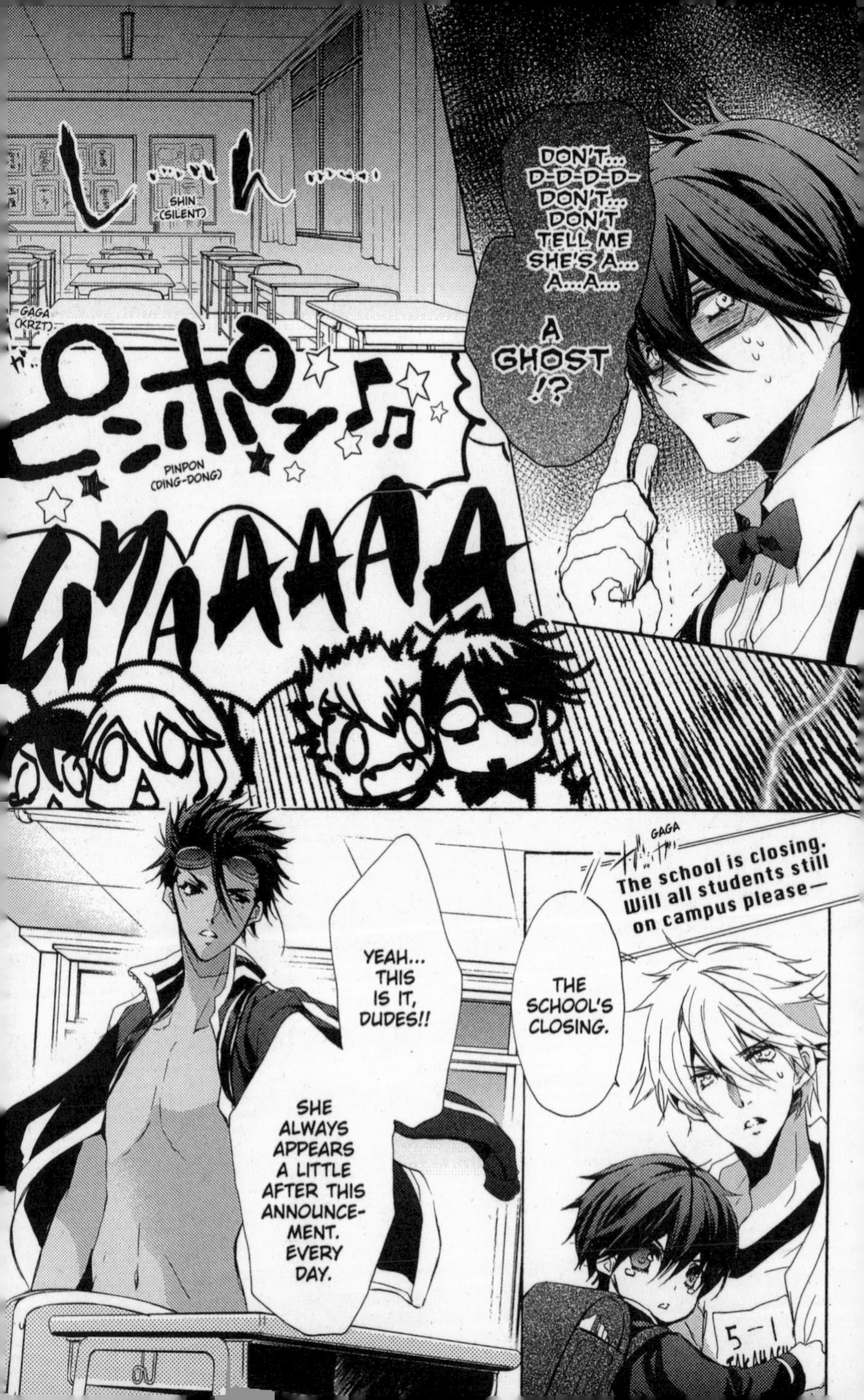
DON'T... D-D-D-D-DON'T... DON'T TELL ME SHE'S A... A...A...
A GHOST!?
SHIN (SILENT)
GAGA (KRZT)
PINPON (DING-DONG)
GYAAAA
GAGA
The school is closing. Will all students still on campus please—
THE SCHOOL'S CLOSING.
YEAH... THIS IS IT, DUDES!!
SHE ALWAYS APPEARS A LITTLE AFTER THIS ANNOUNCEMENT. EVERY DAY.
5-1

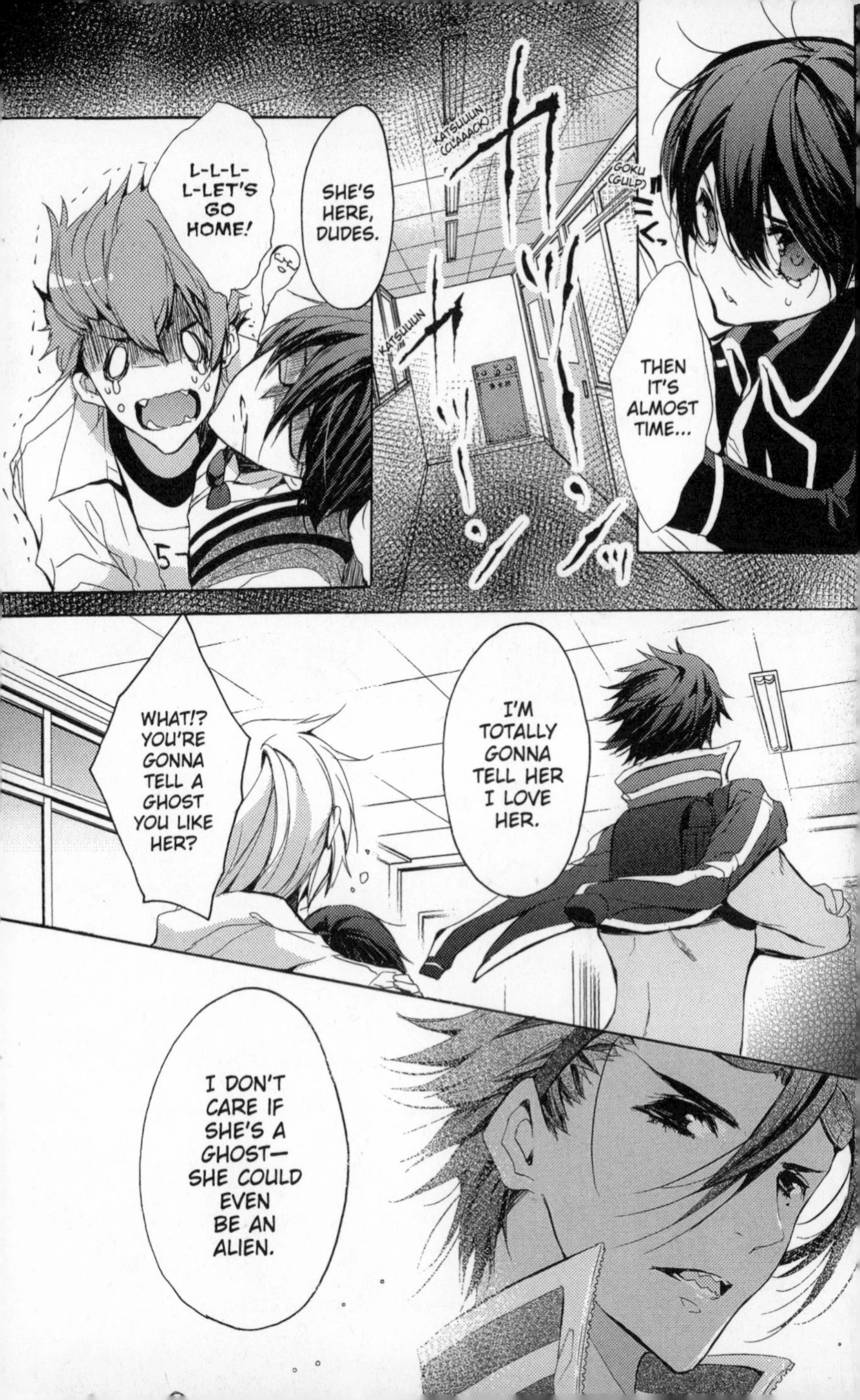
GOKU (GULP)
THEN IT'S ALMOST TIME...
KATSUUUN (CLAAACK)
KATSUUUN
SHE'S HERE, DUDES.
L-L-L-L-LET'S GO HOME!
I'M TOTALLY GONNA TELL HER I LOVE HER.
WHAT!? YOU'RE GONNA TELL A GHOST YOU LIKE HER?
I DON'T CARE IF SHE'S A GHOST—SHE COULD EVEN BE AN ALIEN.

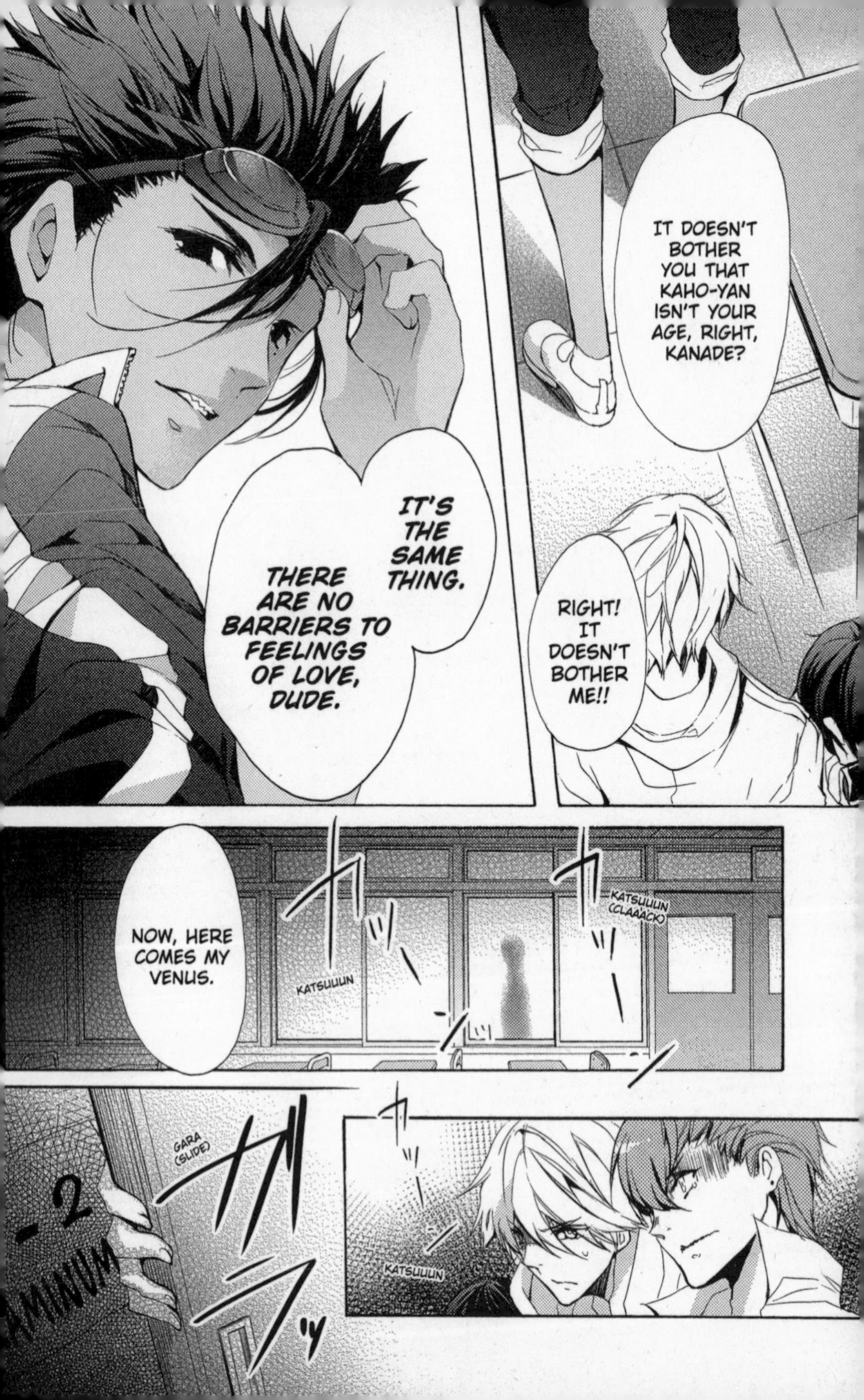
IT DOESN'T BOTHER YOU THAT KAHO-YAN ISN'T YOUR AGE, RIGHT, KANADE?
RIGHT! IT DOESN'T BOTHER ME!!
IT'S THE SAME THING.
THERE ARE NO BARRIERS TO FEELINGS OF LOVE, DUDE.
KATSUUUN (CLAAACK)
KATSUUUN
NOW, HERE COMES MY VENUS.
KATSUUUN
GARA (SLIDE)

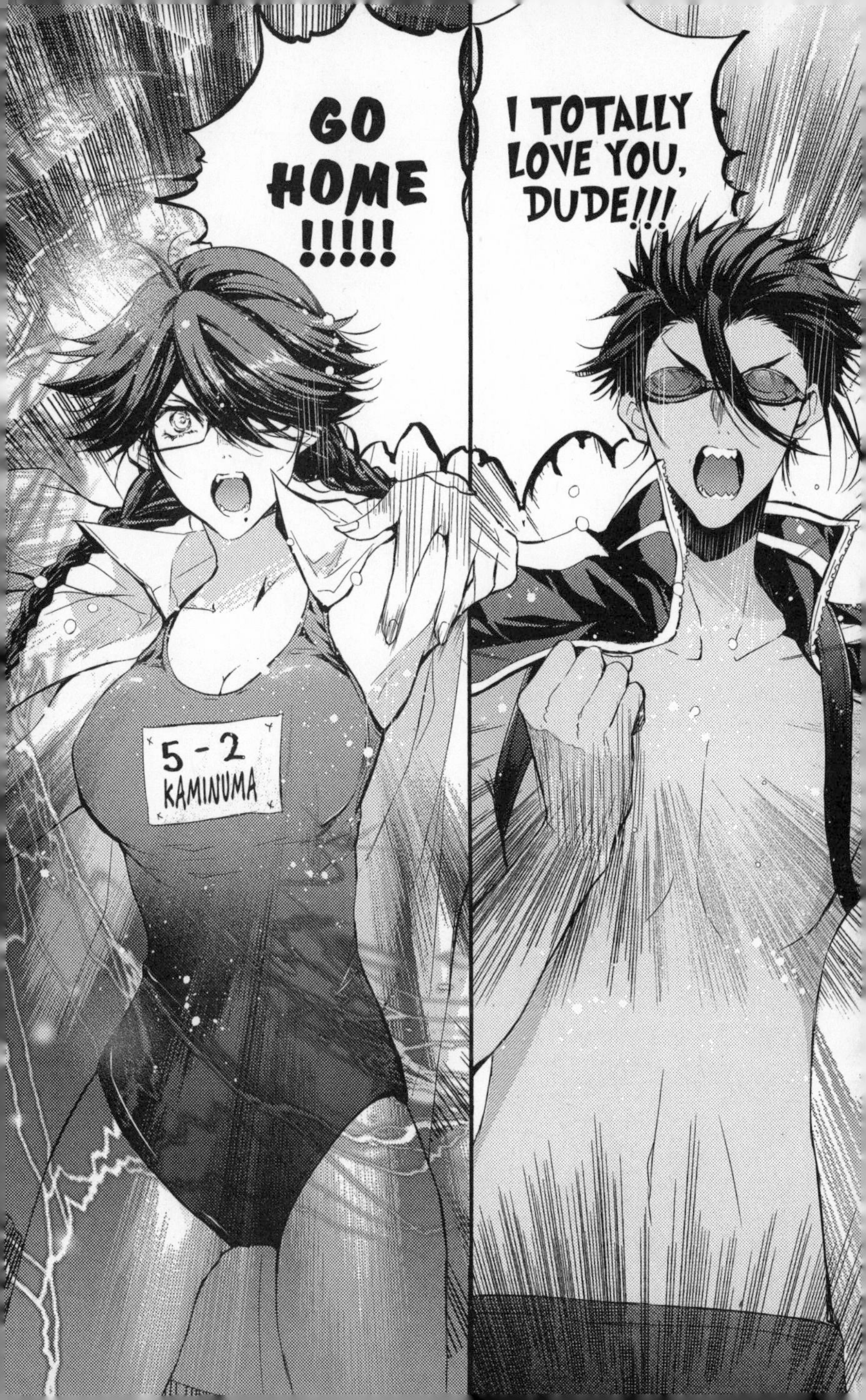
I TOTALLY LOVE YOU, DUDE!!!
GO HOME!!!!!
5-2
KAMINUMA

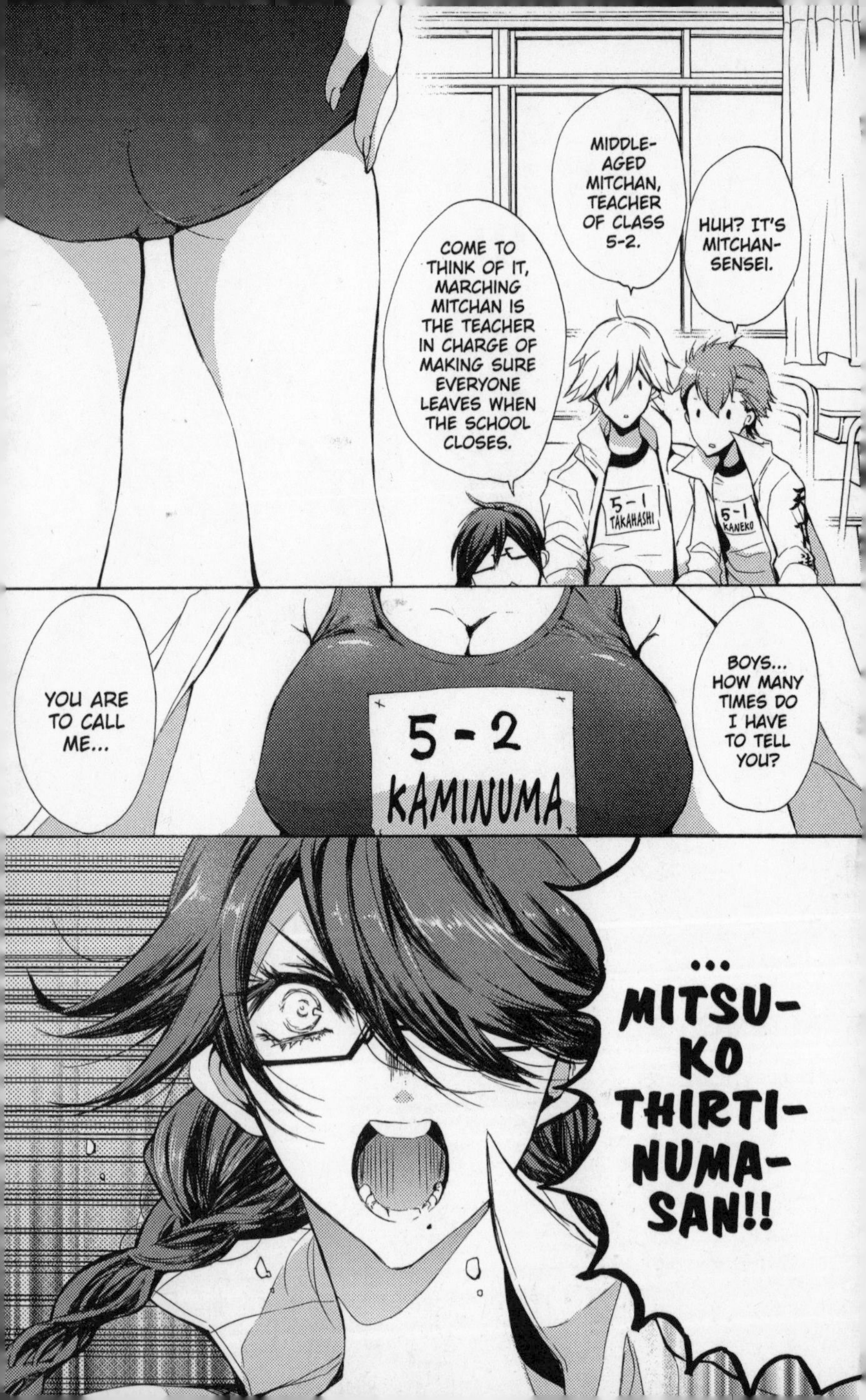
HUH? IT'S MITCHAN-SENSEI.
MIDDLE-AGED MITCHAN, TEACHER OF CLASS 5-2.
COME TO THINK OF IT, MARCHING MITCHAN IS THE TEACHER IN CHARGE OF MAKING SURE EVERYONE LEAVES WHEN THE SCHOOL CLOSES.
5-1 KANEKO
5-1 TAKAHASHI
BOYS... HOW MANY TIMES DO I HAVE TO TELL YOU?
5-2 KAMINUMA
YOU ARE TO CALL ME...
...MITSU-KO THIRTI-NUMA-SAN!!

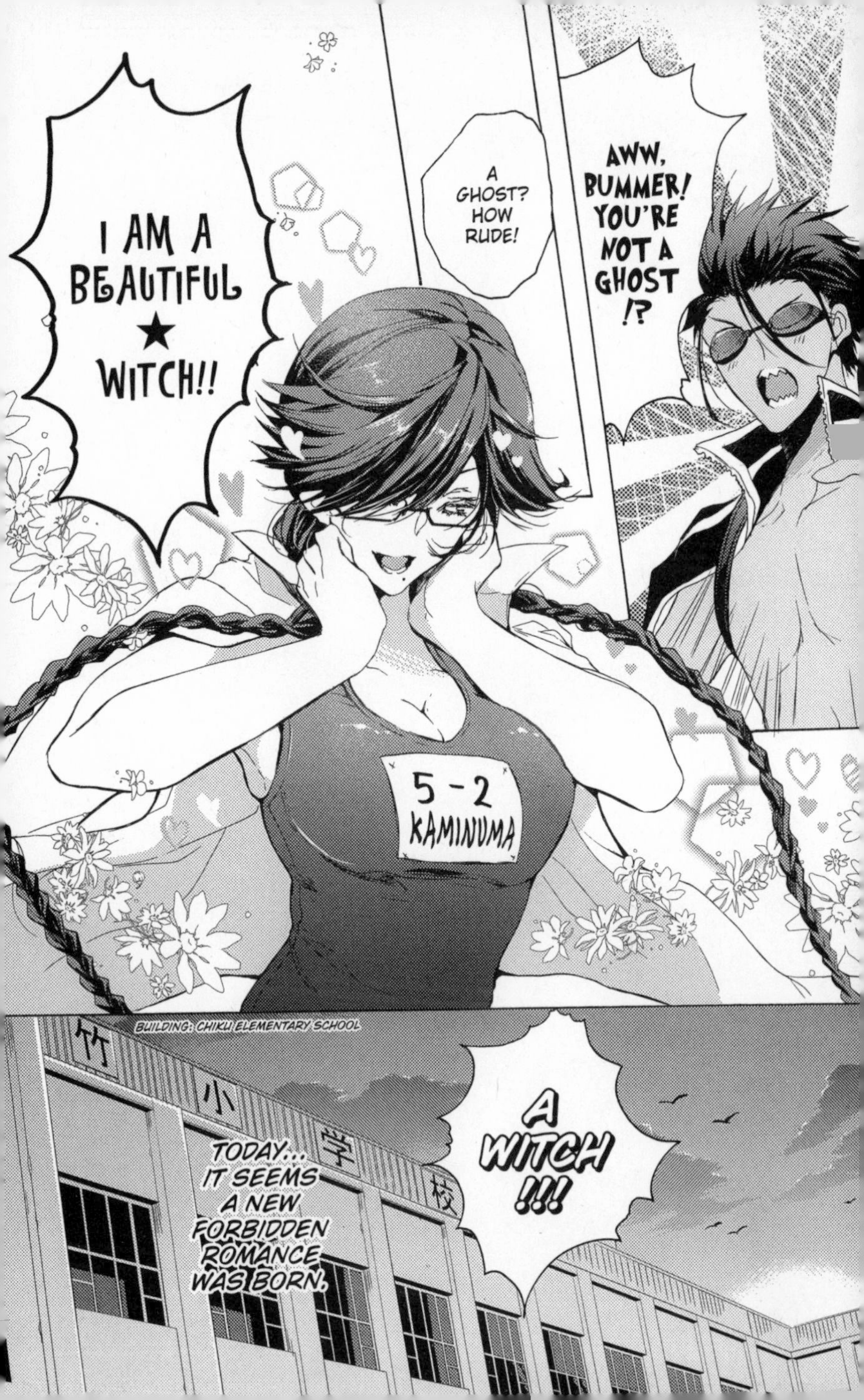
AWW, BUMMER! YOU'RE NOT A GHOST!?
A GHOST? HOW RUDE!
I AM A BEAUTIFUL ★ WITCH!!
5-2 KAMINUMA
A WITCH!!!
BUILDING: CHIKU ELEMENTARY SCHOOL
竹小学校
TODAY... IT SEEMS A NEW FORBIDDEN ROMANCE WAS BORN.

first love monster

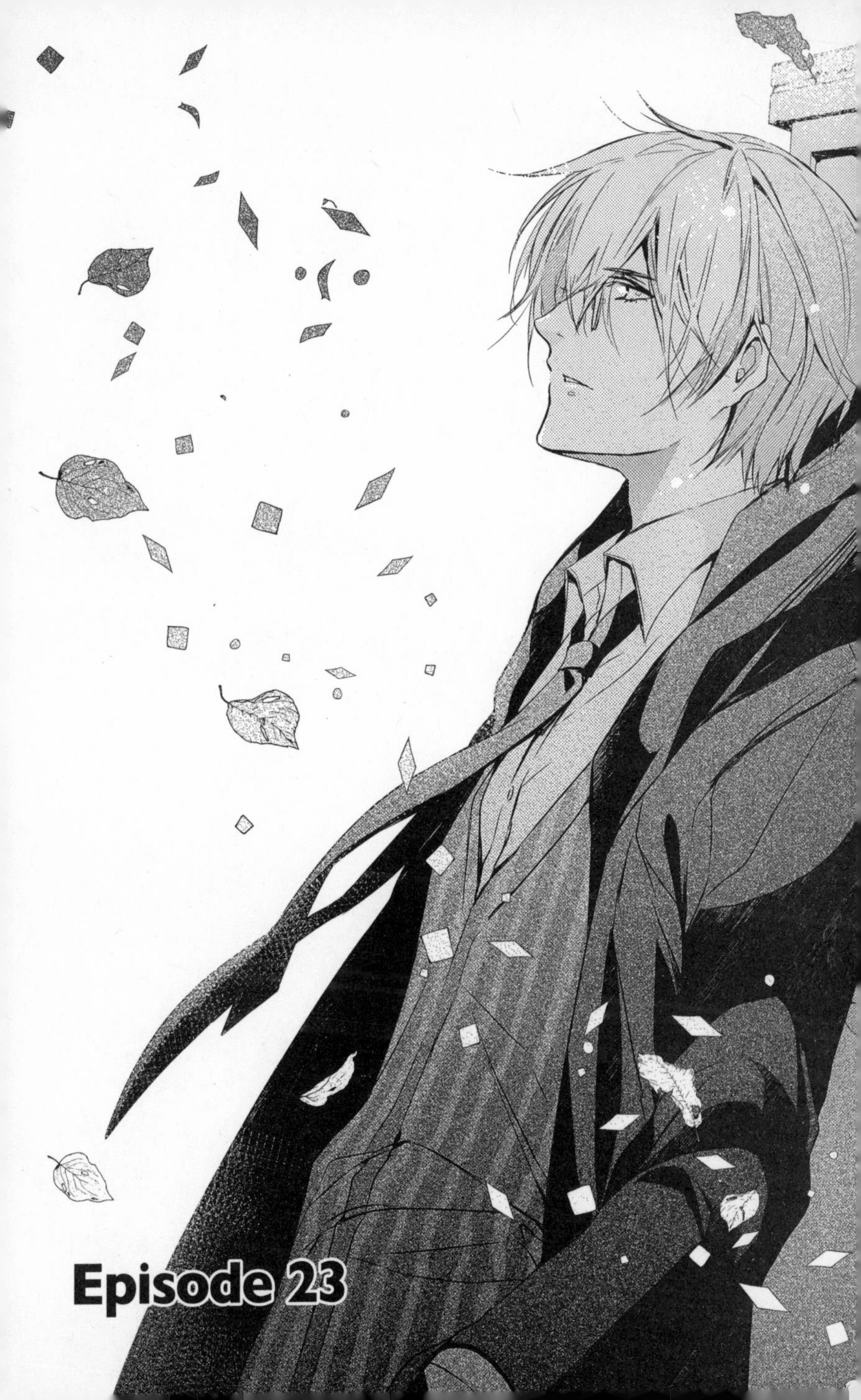
Episode 23

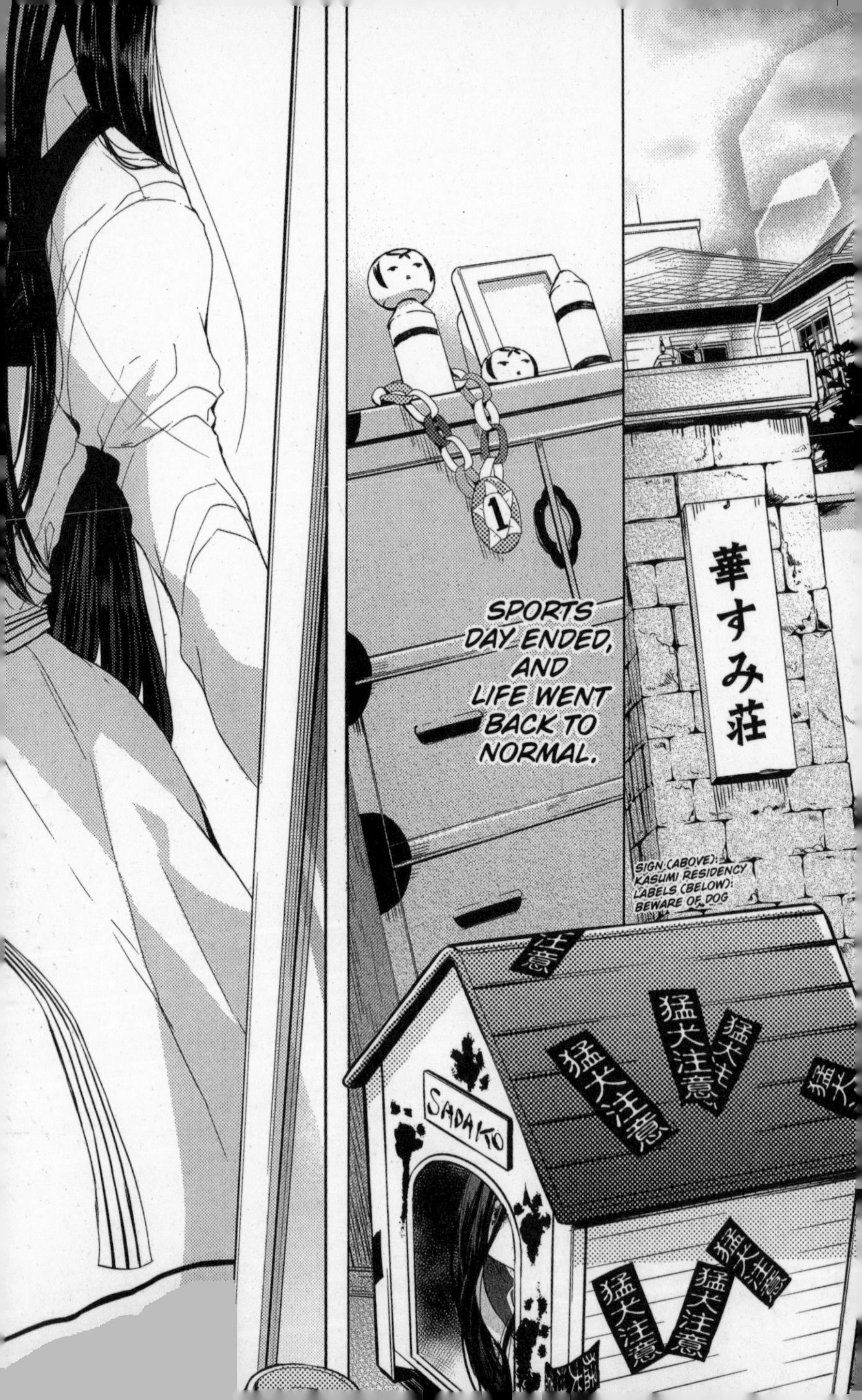
華すみ荘
SIGN (ABOVE): KASUMI RESIDENCY
LABELS (BELOW): BEWARE OF DOG
猛犬注意
SADAKO
SPORTS DAY ENDED, AND LIFE WENT BACK TO NORMAL.

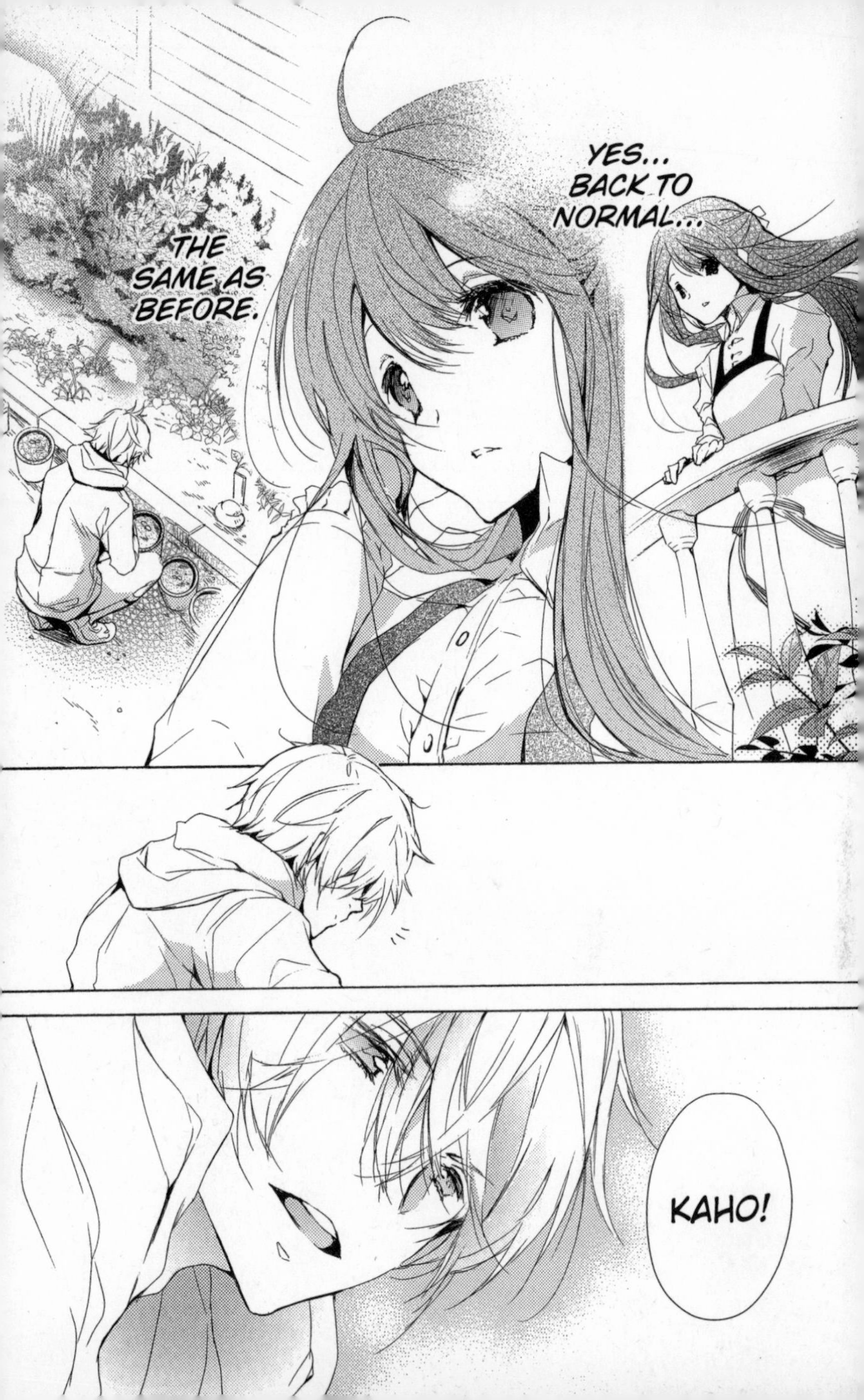
YES... BACK TO NORMAL...
THE SAME AS BEFORE.
KAHO!

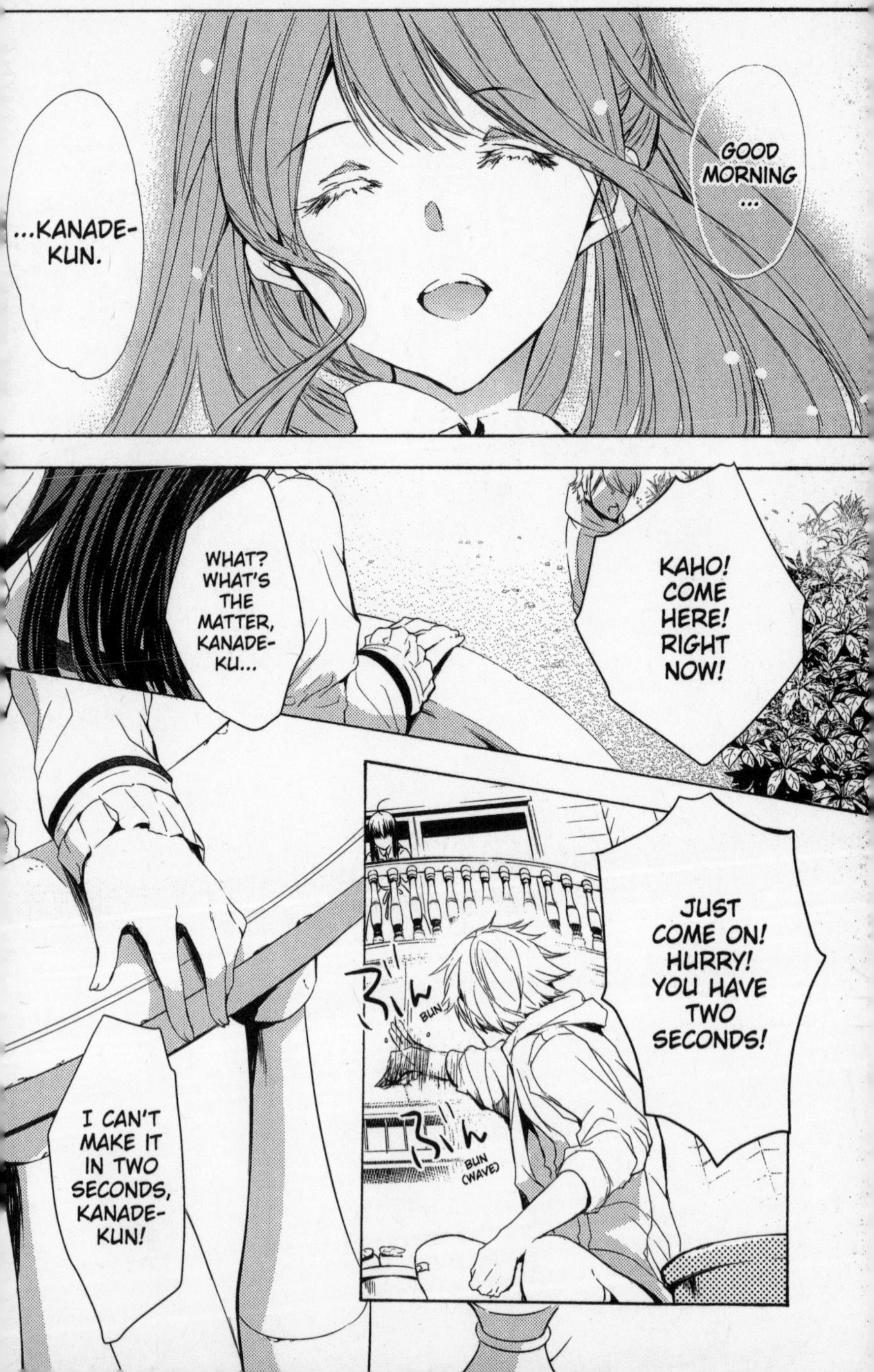
GOOD MORNING ...
...KANADE-KUN.
KAHO! COME HERE! RIGHT NOW!
WHAT? WHAT'S THE MATTER, KANADE-KU...
JUST COME ON! HURRY! YOU HAVE TWO SECONDS!
ぶん
BUN
ぶん
BUN (WAVE)
I CAN'T MAKE IT IN TWO SECONDS, KANADE-KUN!

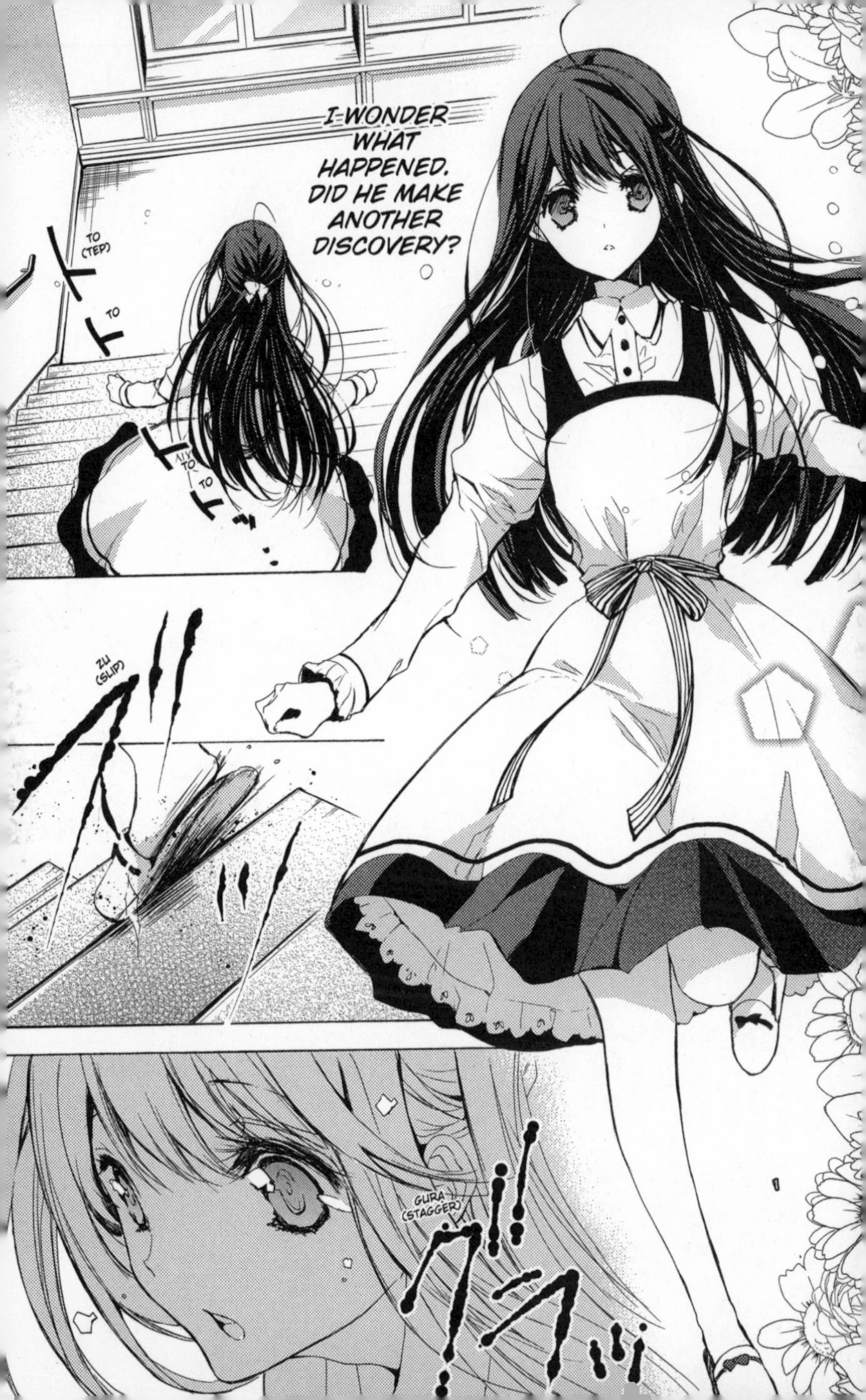
I-WONDER WHAT HAPPENED. DID HE MAKE ANOTHER DISCOVERY?
TO (TEP)
TO
TO
TO
ZU (SLIP)
GURA (STAGGER)

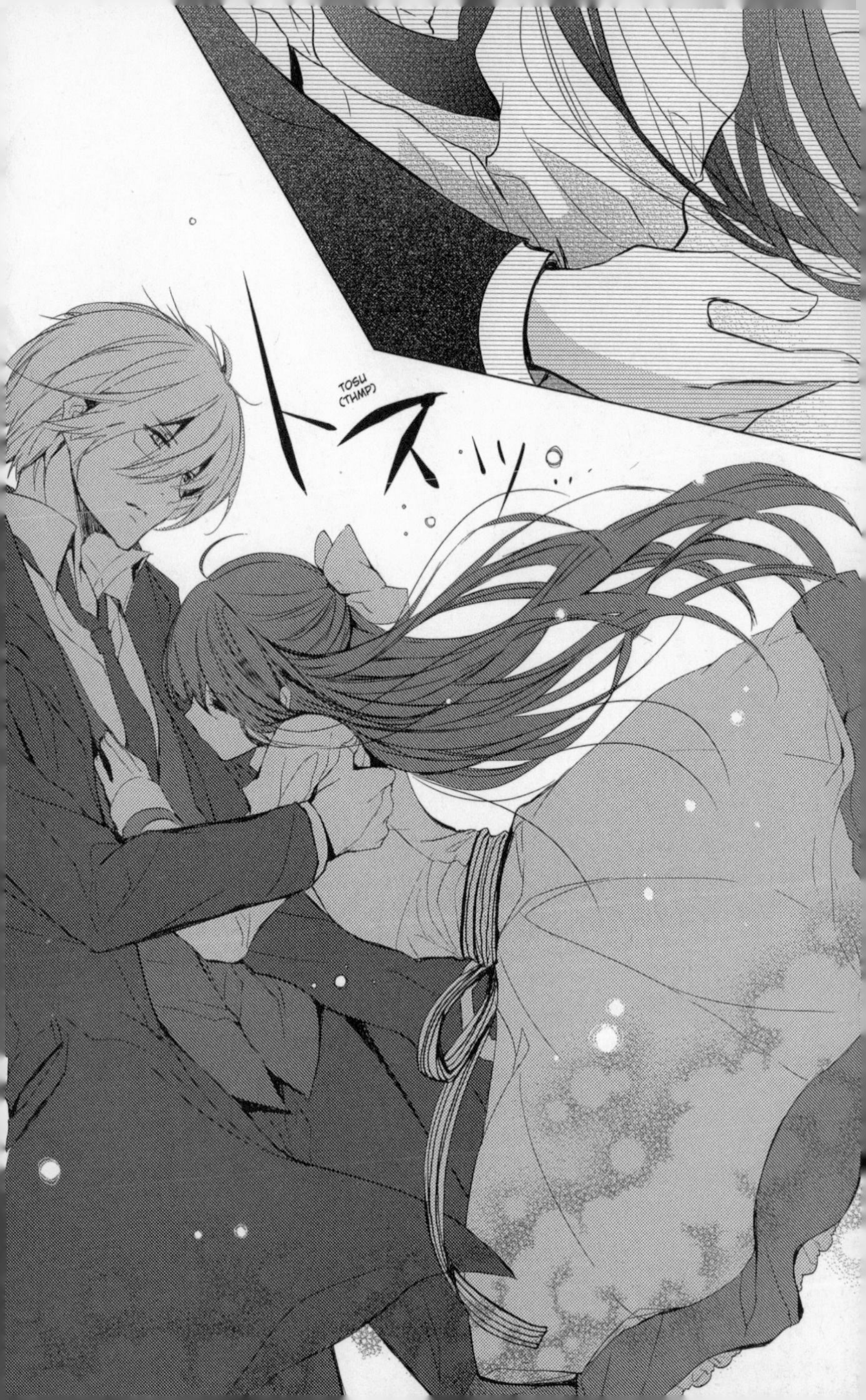
TOSU
(THMP)

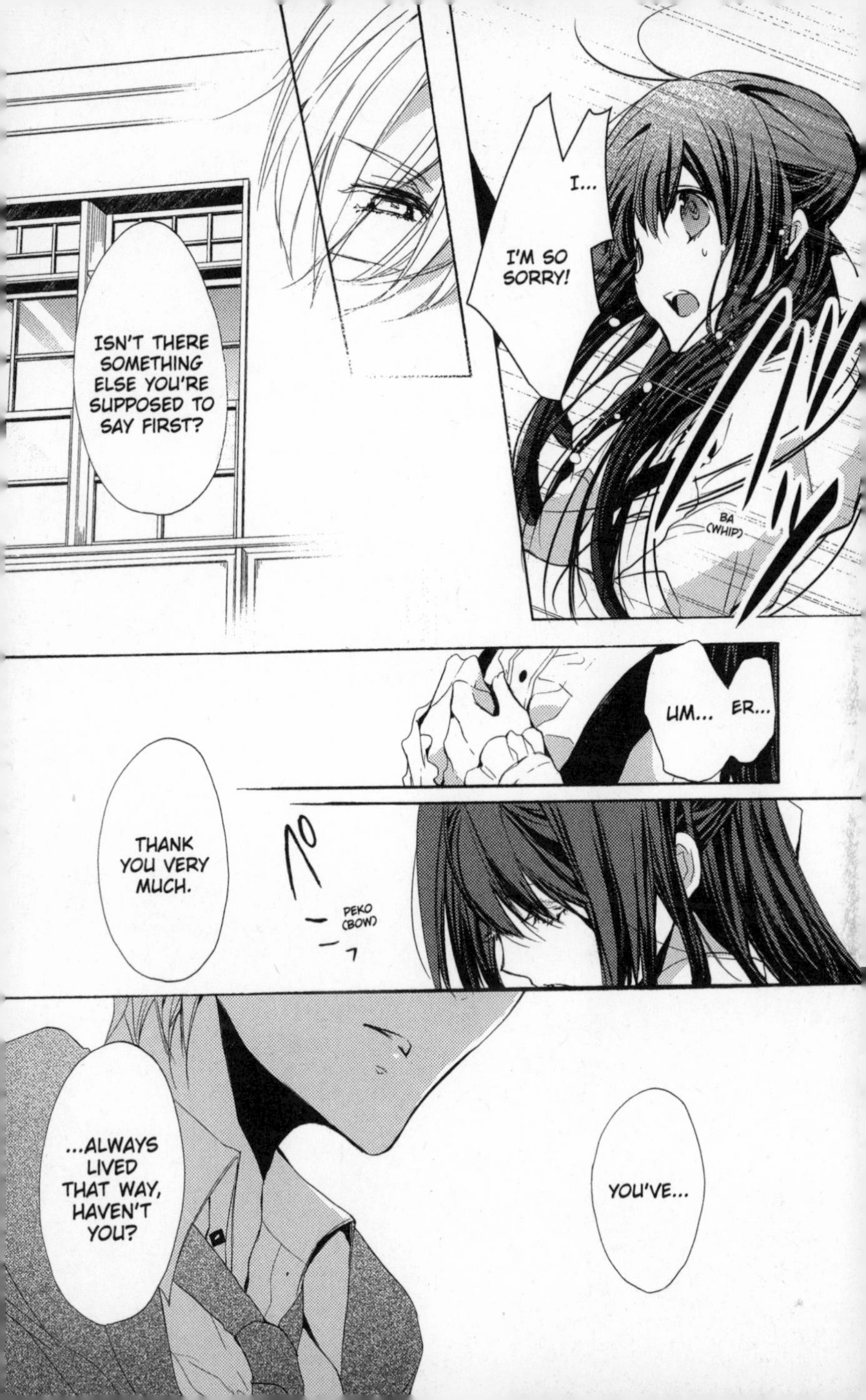
I...
I'M SO SORRY!
BA (WHIP)
ISN'T THERE SOMETHING ELSE YOU'RE SUPPOSED TO SAY FIRST?
UM... ER...
PEKO (BOW)
THANK YOU VERY MUCH.
YOU'VE...
...ALWAYS LIVED THAT WAY, HAVEN'T YOU?

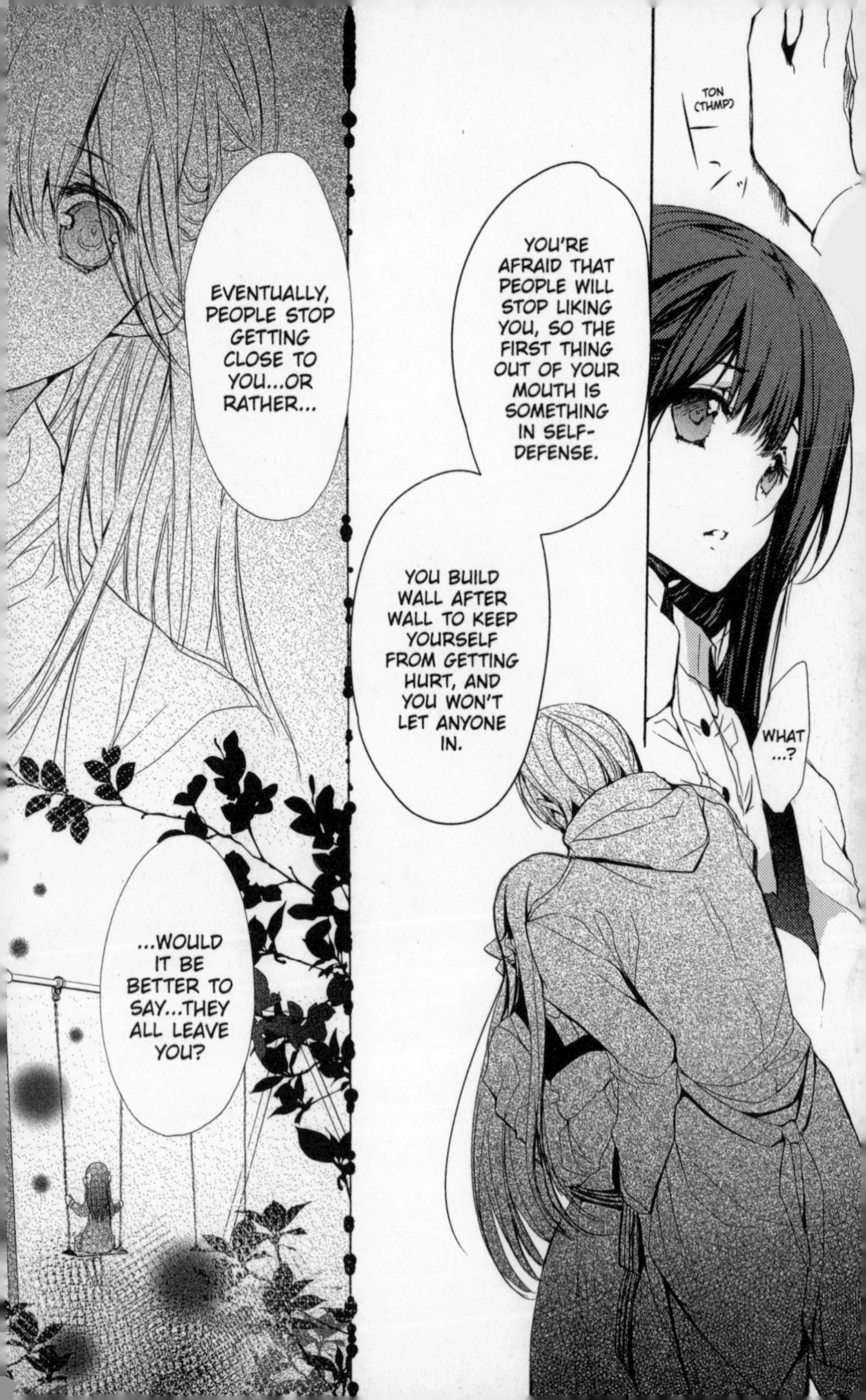
TON (THMP)
YOU'RE AFRAID THAT PEOPLE WILL STOP LIKING YOU, SO THE FIRST THING OUT OF YOUR MOUTH IS SOMETHING IN SELF-DEFENSE.
YOU BUILD WALL AFTER WALL TO KEEP YOURSELF FROM GETTING HURT, AND YOU WON'T LET ANYONE IN.
WHAT ...?
EVENTUALLY, PEOPLE STOP GETTING CLOSE TO YOU...OR RATHER...
...WOULD IT BE BETTER TO SAY...THEY ALL LEAVE YOU?

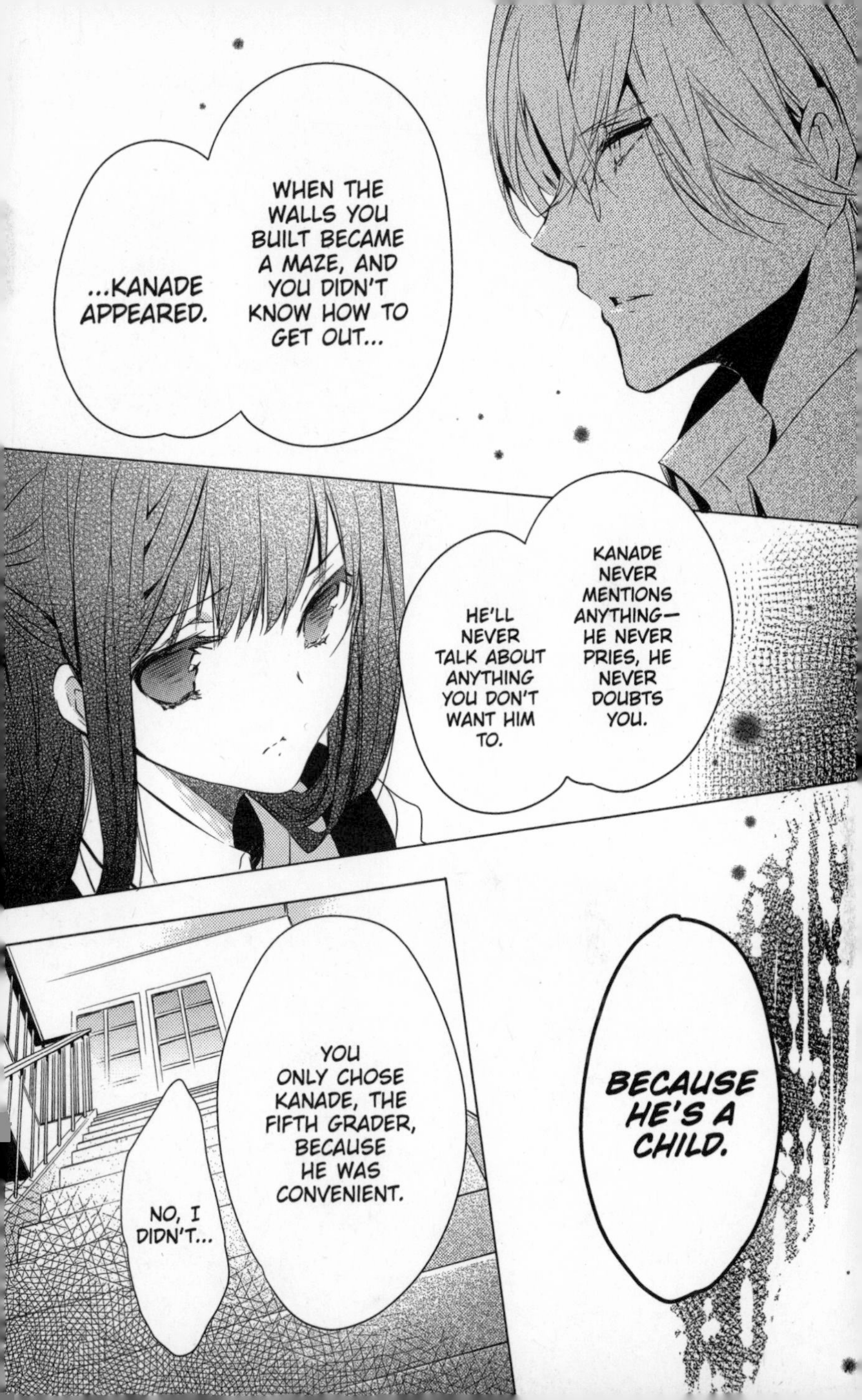
WHEN THE WALLS YOU BUILT BECAME A MAZE, AND YOU DIDN'T KNOW HOW TO GET OUT...
...KANADE APPEARED.
KANADE NEVER MENTIONS ANYTHING—HE NEVER PRIES, HE NEVER DOUBTS YOU.
HE'LL NEVER TALK ABOUT ANYTHING YOU DON'T WANT HIM TO.
BECAUSE HE'S A CHILD.
YOU ONLY CHOSE KANADE, THE FIFTH GRADER, BECAUSE HE WAS CONVENIENT.
NO, I DIDN'T...

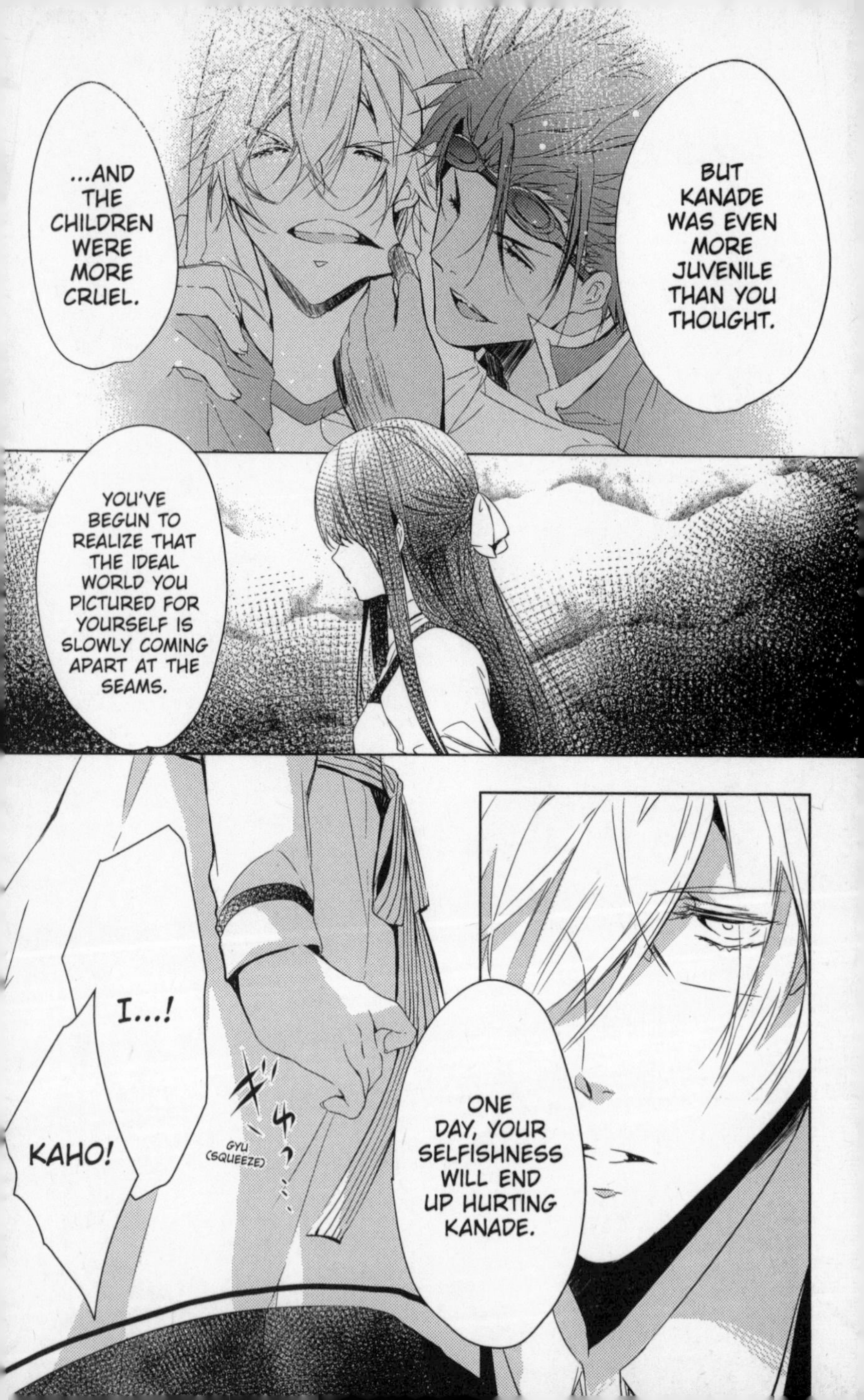
BUT KANADE WAS EVEN MORE JUVENILE THAN YOU THOUGHT.
...AND THE CHILDREN WERE MORE CRUEL.
YOU'VE BEGUN TO REALIZE THAT THE IDEAL WORLD YOU PICTURED FOR YOURSELF IS SLOWLY COMING APART AT THE SEAMS.
ONE DAY, YOUR SELFISHNESS WILL END UP HURTING KANADE.
I...!
GYU (SQUEEZE)
KAHO!

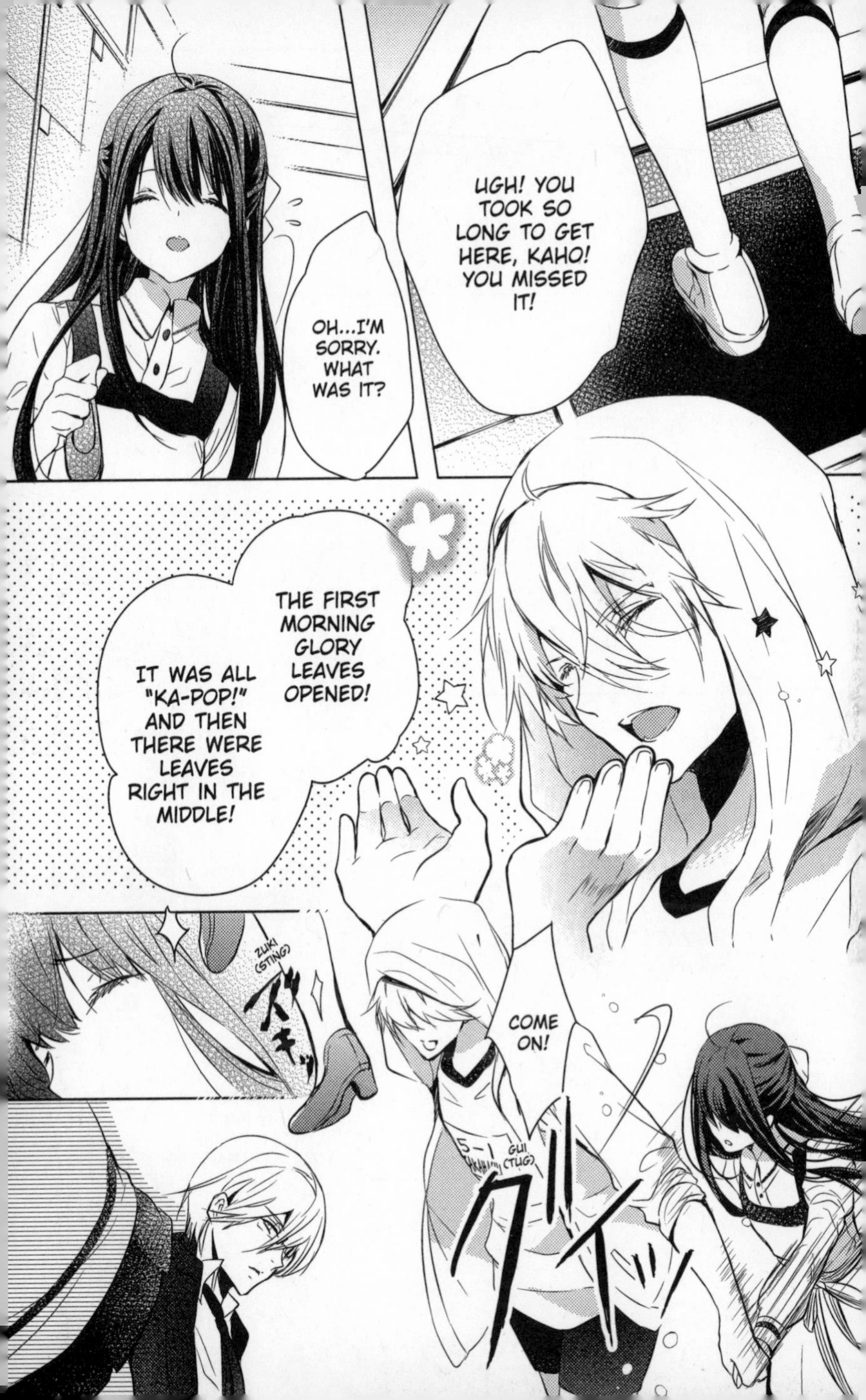
UGH! YOU TOOK SO LONG TO GET HERE, KAHO! YOU MISSED IT!
OH...I'M SORRY. WHAT WAS IT?
THE FIRST MORNING GLORY LEAVES OPENED!
IT WAS ALL "KA-POP!" AND THEN THERE WERE LEAVES RIGHT IN THE MIDDLE!
COME ON!
GUI (TUG)
ZUKI (STING)

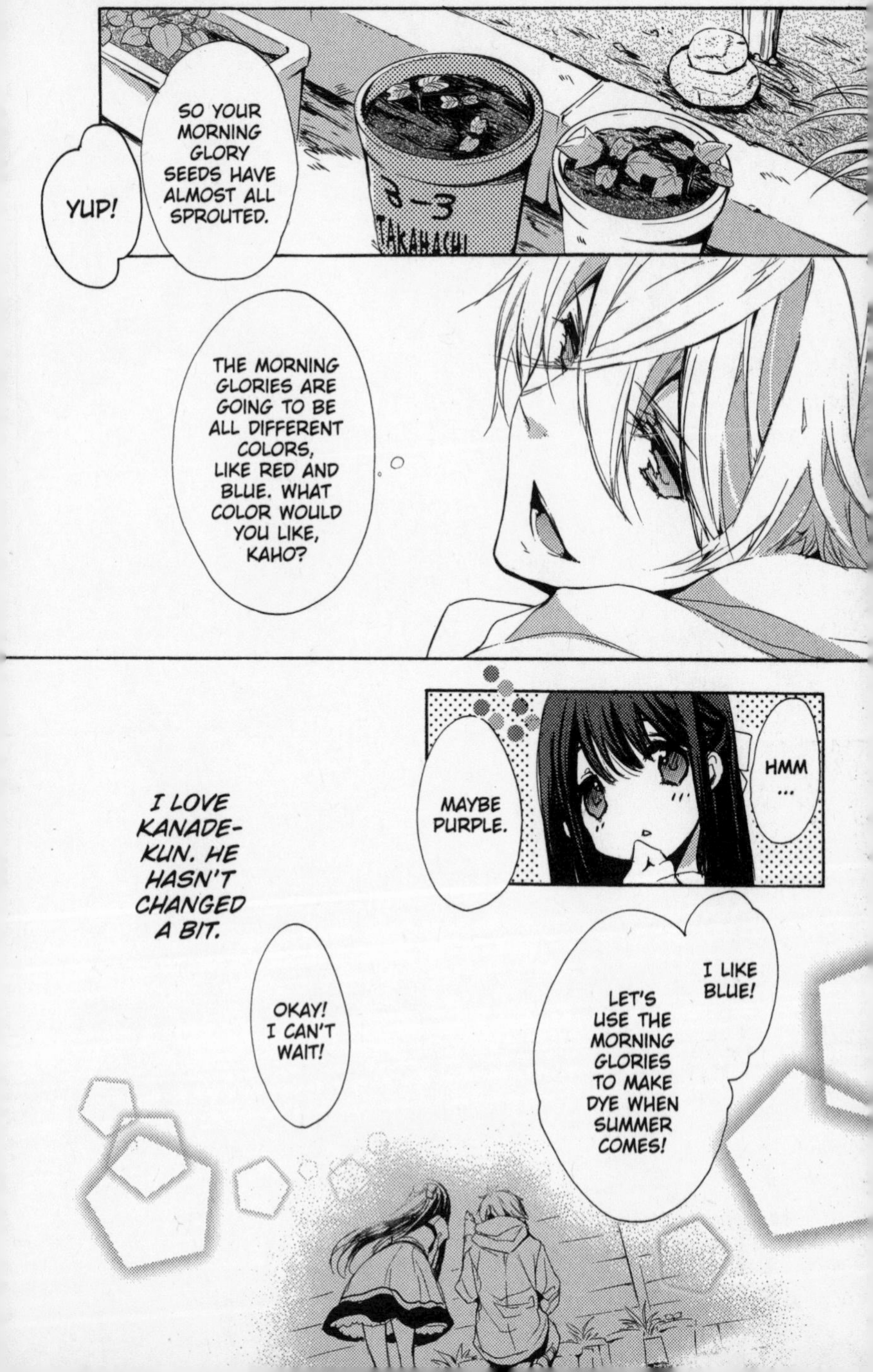
SO YOUR MORNING GLORY SEEDS HAVE ALMOST ALL SPROUTED.
YUP!
TAKAHASHI
THE MORNING GLORIES ARE GOING TO BE ALL DIFFERENT COLORS, LIKE RED AND BLUE. WHAT COLOR WOULD YOU LIKE, KAHO?
HMM ...
MAYBE PURPLE.
I LOVE KANADE-KUN. HE HASN'T CHANGED A BIT.
I LIKE BLUE!
LET'S USE THE MORNING GLORIES TO MAKE DYE WHEN SUMMER COMES!
OKAY! I CAN'T WAIT!

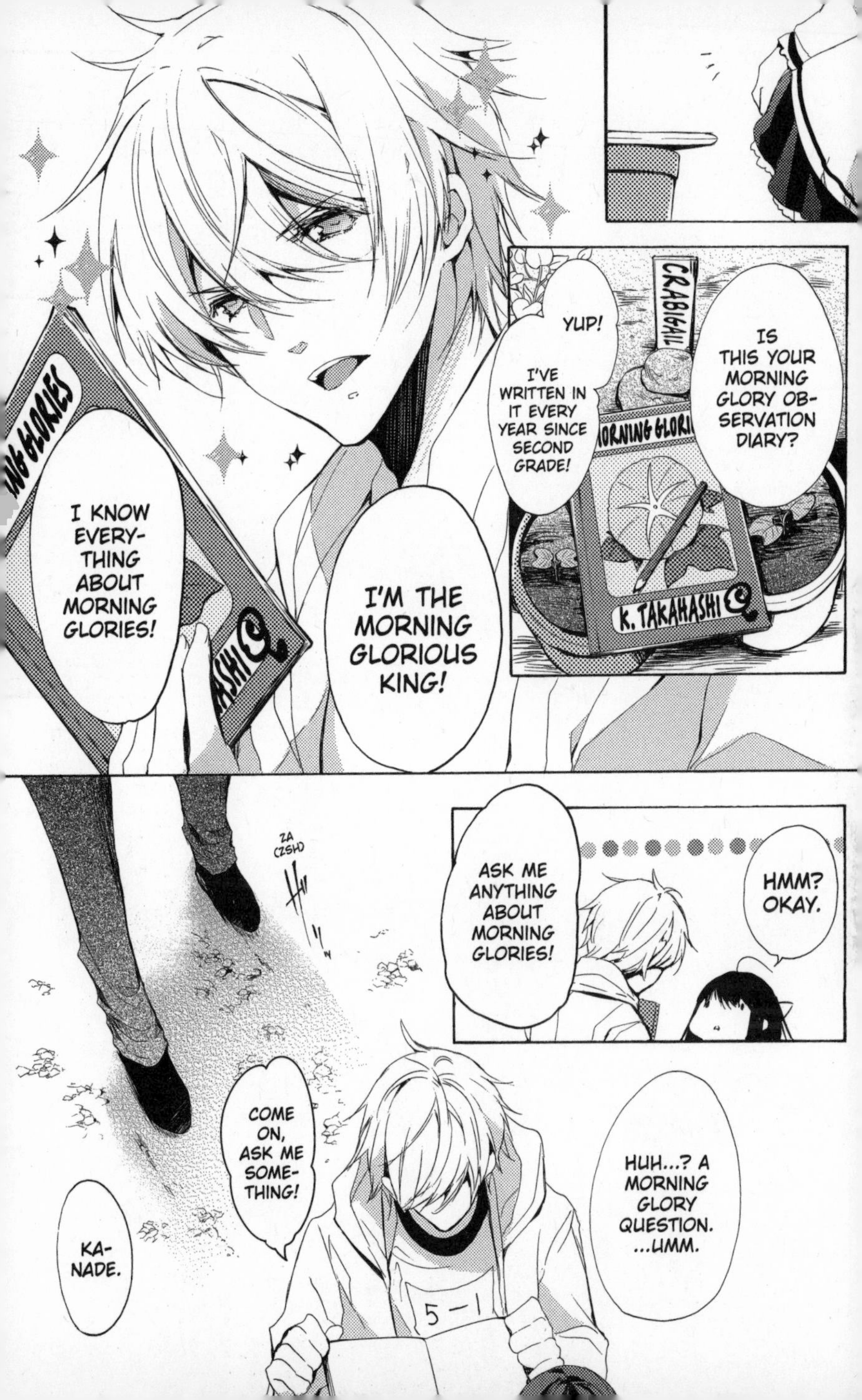
IS THIS YOUR MORNING GLORY OB-SERVATION DIARY?
CRABIGAIL
MORNING GLORIE
K. TAKAHASHI
YUP! I'VE WRITTEN IN IT EVERY YEAR SINCE SECOND GRADE!
I'M THE MORNING GLORIOUS KING!
I KNOW EVERY-THING ABOUT MORNING GLORIES!
HMM? OKAY.
ASK ME ANYTHING ABOUT MORNING GLORIES!
HUH...? A MORNING GLORY QUESTION. ...UMM.
5-1
COME ON, ASK ME SOME-THING!
ZA (ZSH)
KA-NADE.

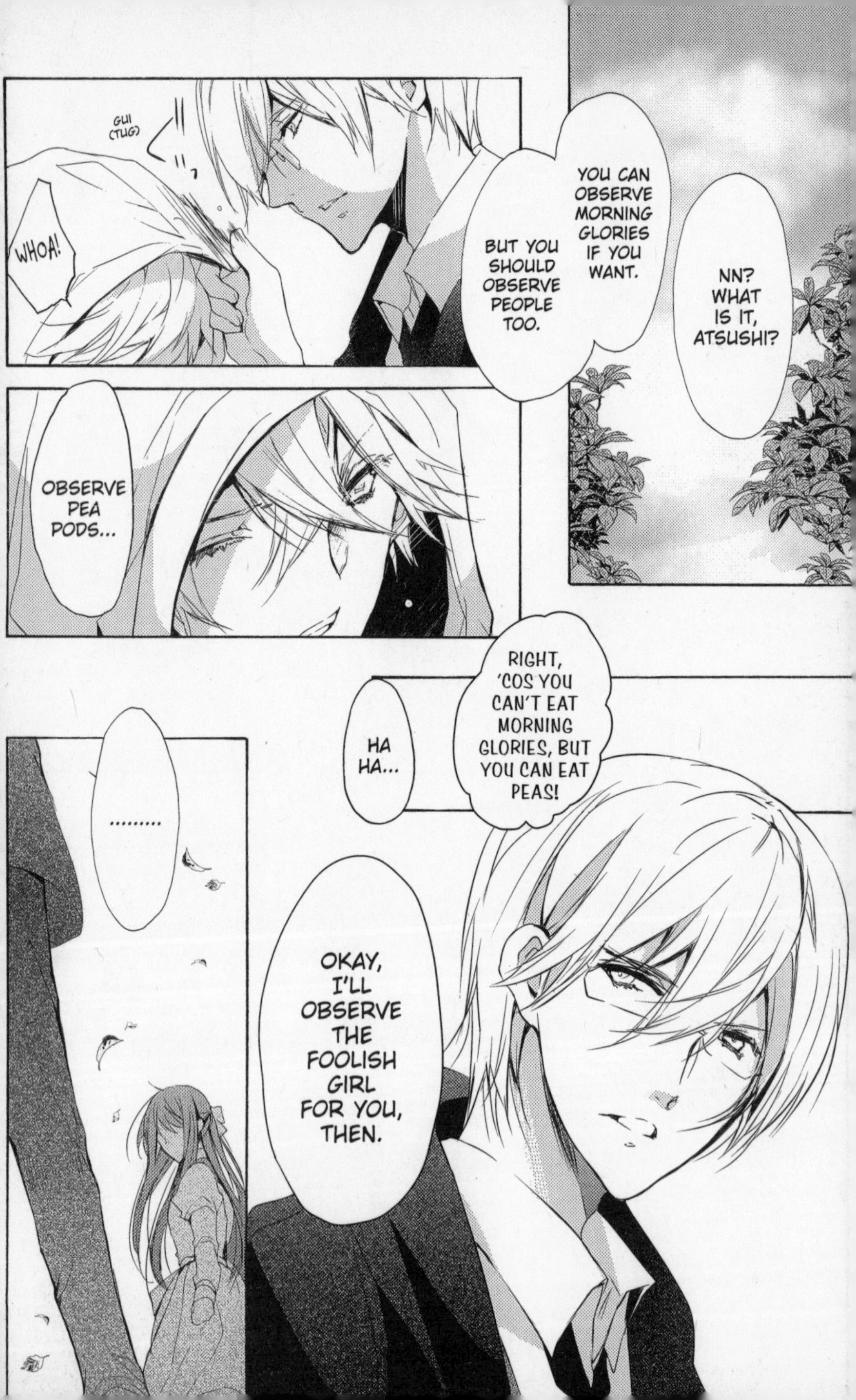

NN? WHAT IS IT, ATSUSHI?
YOU CAN OBSERVE MORNING GLORIES IF YOU WANT.
BUT YOU SHOULD OBSERVE PEOPLE TOO.
GUI (TUG)
WHOA!
OBSERVE PEA PODS...
RIGHT, 'COS YOU CAN'T EAT MORNING GLORIES, BUT YOU CAN EAT PEAS!
HA HA...
OKAY, I'LL OBSERVE THE FOOLISH GIRL FOR YOU, THEN.
....

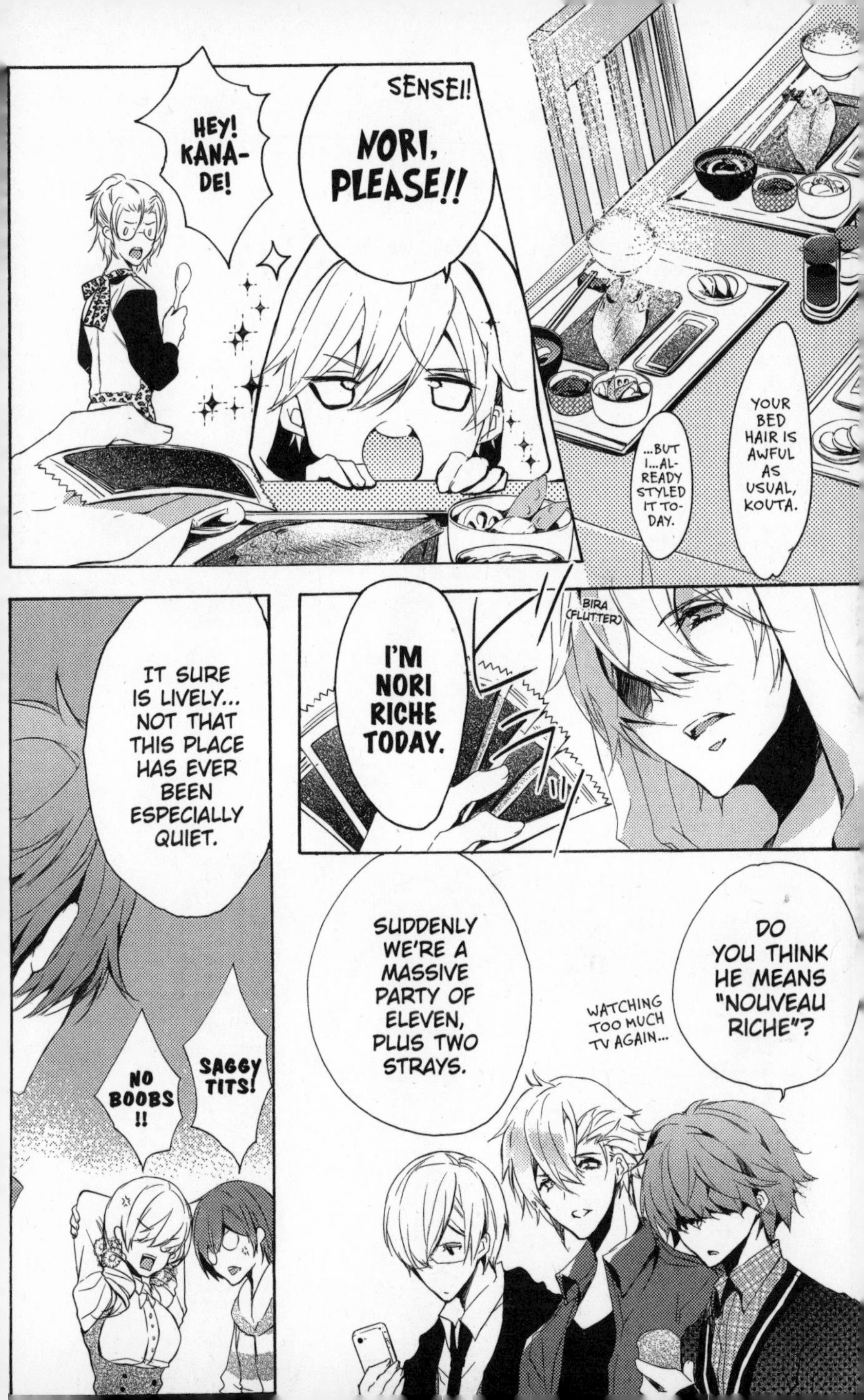
YOUR BED HAIR IS AWFUL AS USUAL, KOUTA.
...BUT I...AL-READY STYLED IT TO-DAY.
SENSEI!
NORI, PLEASE!!
HEY! KANA-DE!
BIRA (FLUTTER)
I'M NORI RICHE TODAY.
DO YOU THINK HE MEANS "NOUVEAU RICHE"?
WATCHING TOO MUCH TV AGAIN...
SUDDENLY WE'RE A MASSIVE PARTY OF ELEVEN, PLUS TWO STRAYS.
IT SURE IS LIVELY... NOT THAT THIS PLACE HAS EVER BEEN ESPECIALLY QUIET.
SAGGY TITS!
NO BOOBS !!

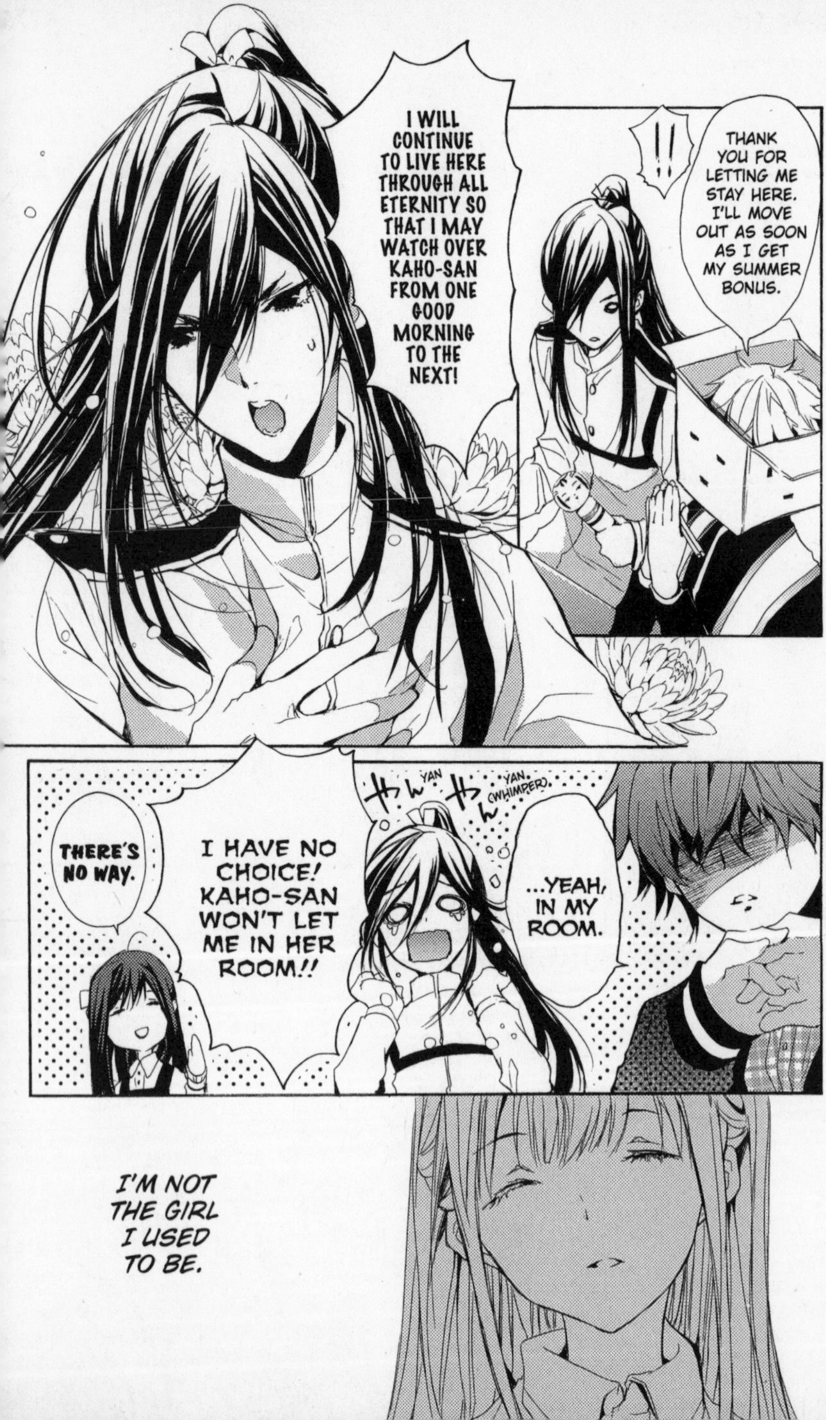
!!
THANK YOU FOR LETTING ME STAY HERE. I'LL MOVE OUT AS SOON AS I GET MY SUMMER BONUS.
I WILL CONTINUE TO LIVE HERE THROUGH ALL ETERNITY SO THAT I MAY WATCH OVER KAHO-SAN FROM ONE GOOD MORNING TO THE NEXT!
...YEAH, IN MY ROOM.
やん YAN やん YAN. (WHIMPER)
I HAVE NO CHOICE! KAHO-SAN WON'T LET ME IN HER ROOM!!
THERE'S NO WAY.
I'M NOT THE GIRL I USED TO BE.

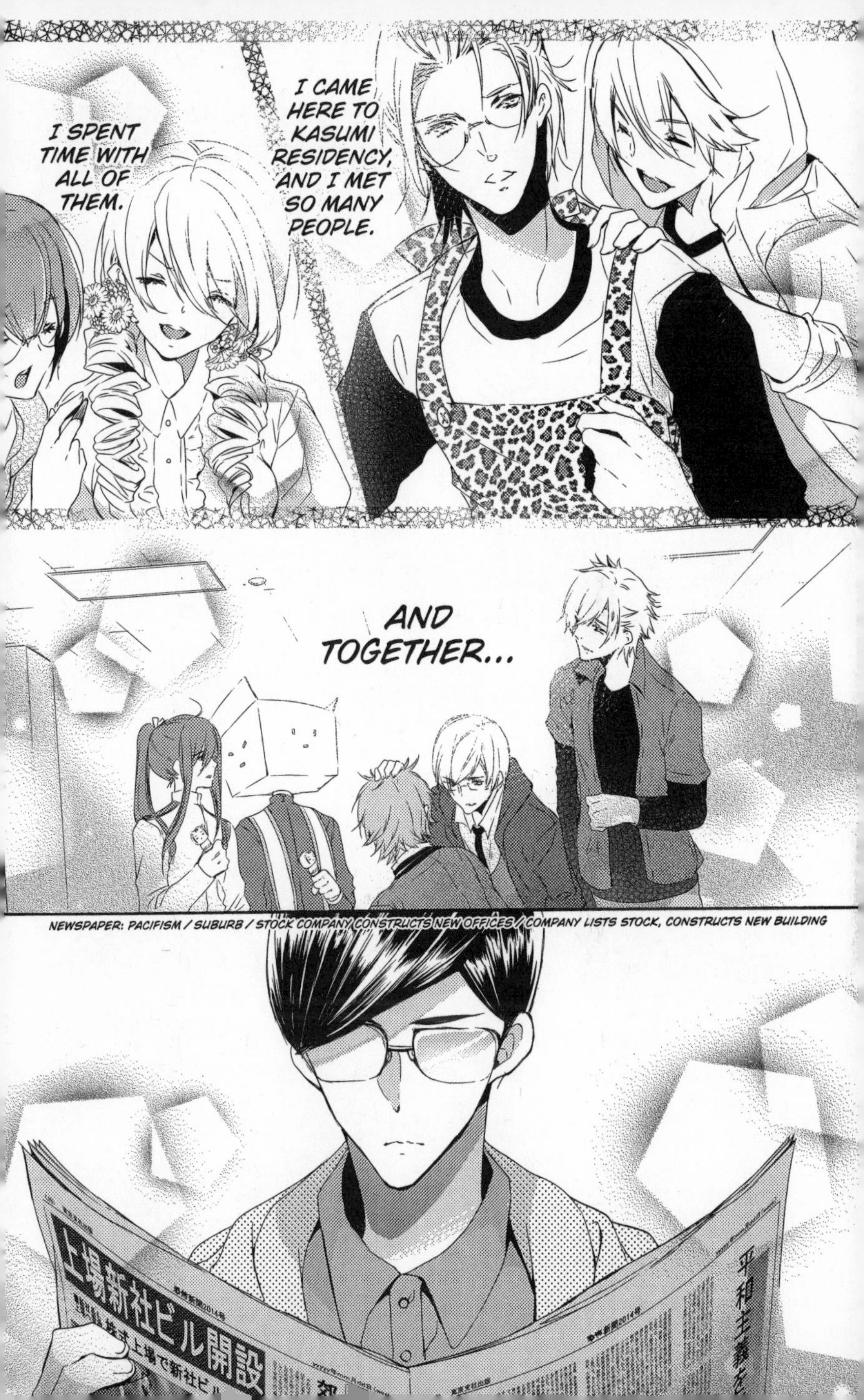
I CAME HERE TO KASUMI RESIDENCY, AND I MET SO MANY PEOPLE.
I SPENT TIME WITH ALL OF THEM.
AND TOGETHER...
NEWSPAPER: PACIFISM / SUBURB / STOCK COMPANY CONSTRUCTS NEW OFFICES / COMPANY LISTS STOCK, CONSTRUCTS NEW BUILDING
平和主義
上場新社ビル開設

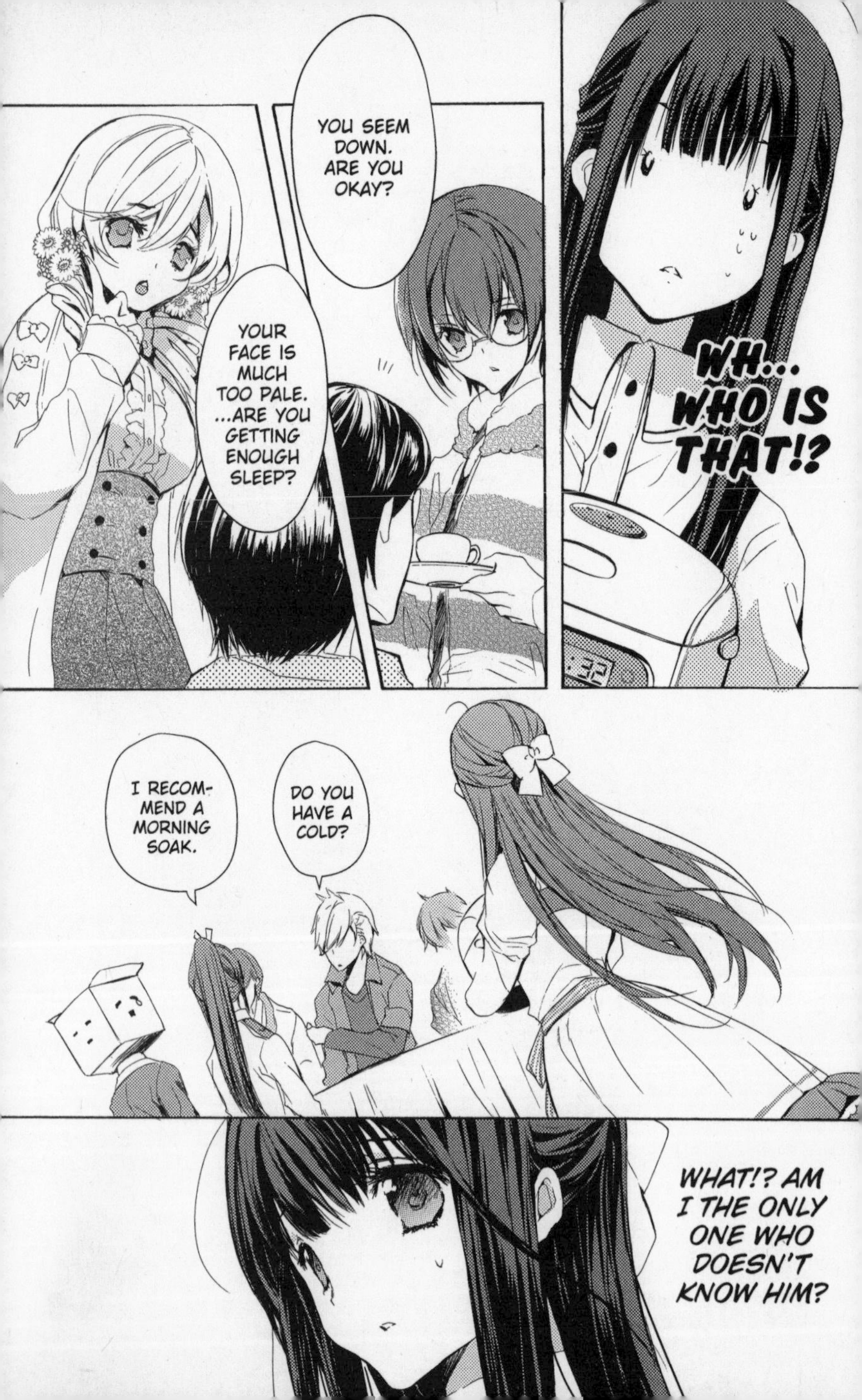
WH... WHO IS THAT!?
YOU SEEM DOWN. ARE YOU OKAY?
YOUR FACE IS MUCH TOO PALE. ...ARE YOU GETTING ENOUGH SLEEP?
DO YOU HAVE A COLD?
I RECOM-MEND A MORNING SOAK.
WHAT!? AM I THE ONLY ONE WHO DOESN'T KNOW HIM?

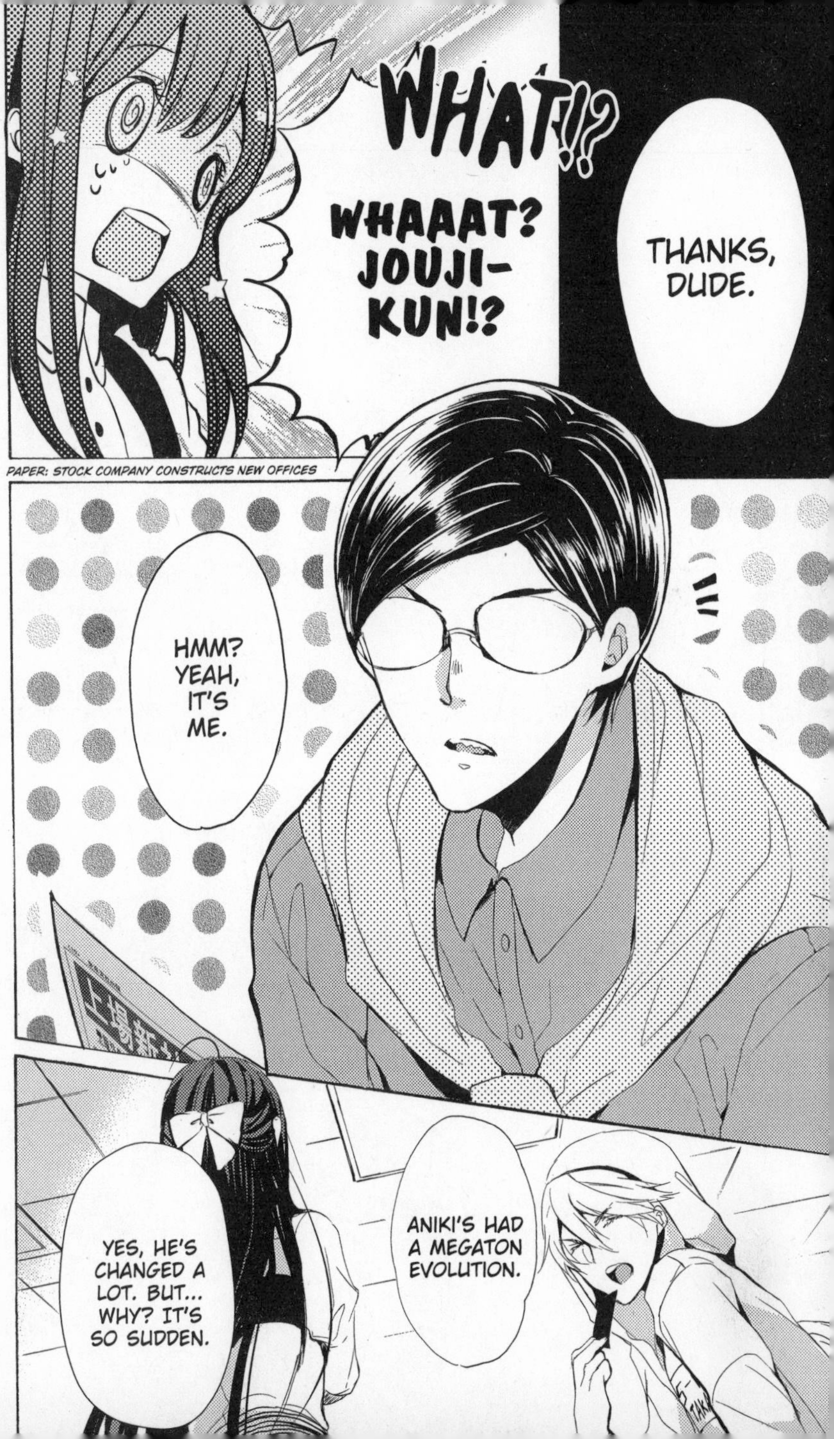
THANKS, DUDE.
WHAT!?
WHAAAT? JOUJI-KUN!?
PAPER: STOCK COMPANY CONSTRUCTS NEW OFFICES
HMM? YEAH, IT'S ME.
ANIKI'S HAD A MEGATON EVOLUTION.
YES, HE'S CHANGED A LOT. BUT... WHY? IT'S SO SUDDEN.

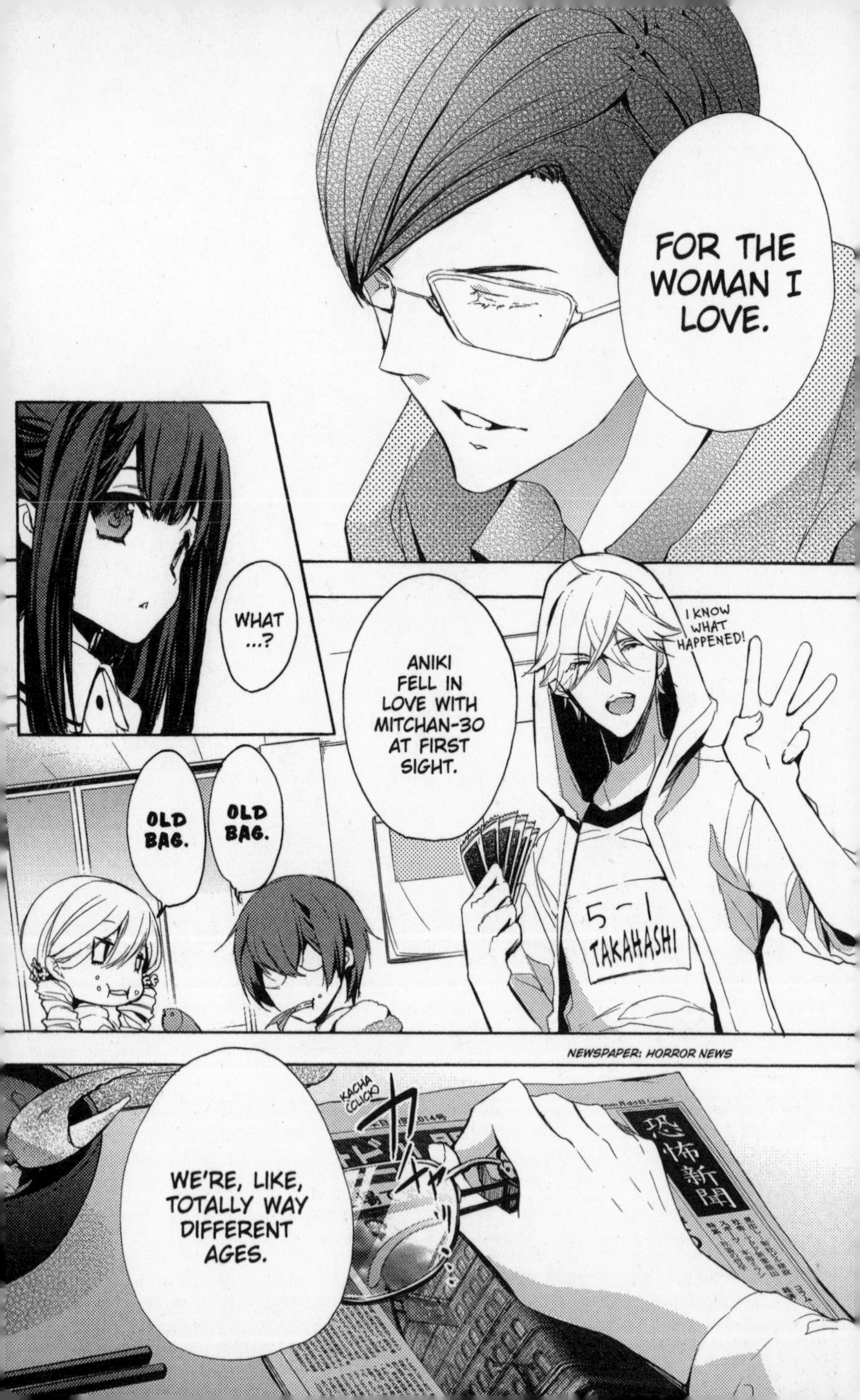
FOR THE WOMAN I LOVE.
I KNOW WHAT HAPPENED!
ANIKI FELL IN LOVE WITH MITCHAN-30 AT FIRST SIGHT.
WHAT ...?
OLD BAG.
OLD BAG.
5-1 TAKAHASHI
NEWSPAPER: HORROR NEWS
KACHA (CLICK)
恐怖新聞
WE'RE, LIKE, TOTALLY WAY DIFFERENT AGES.

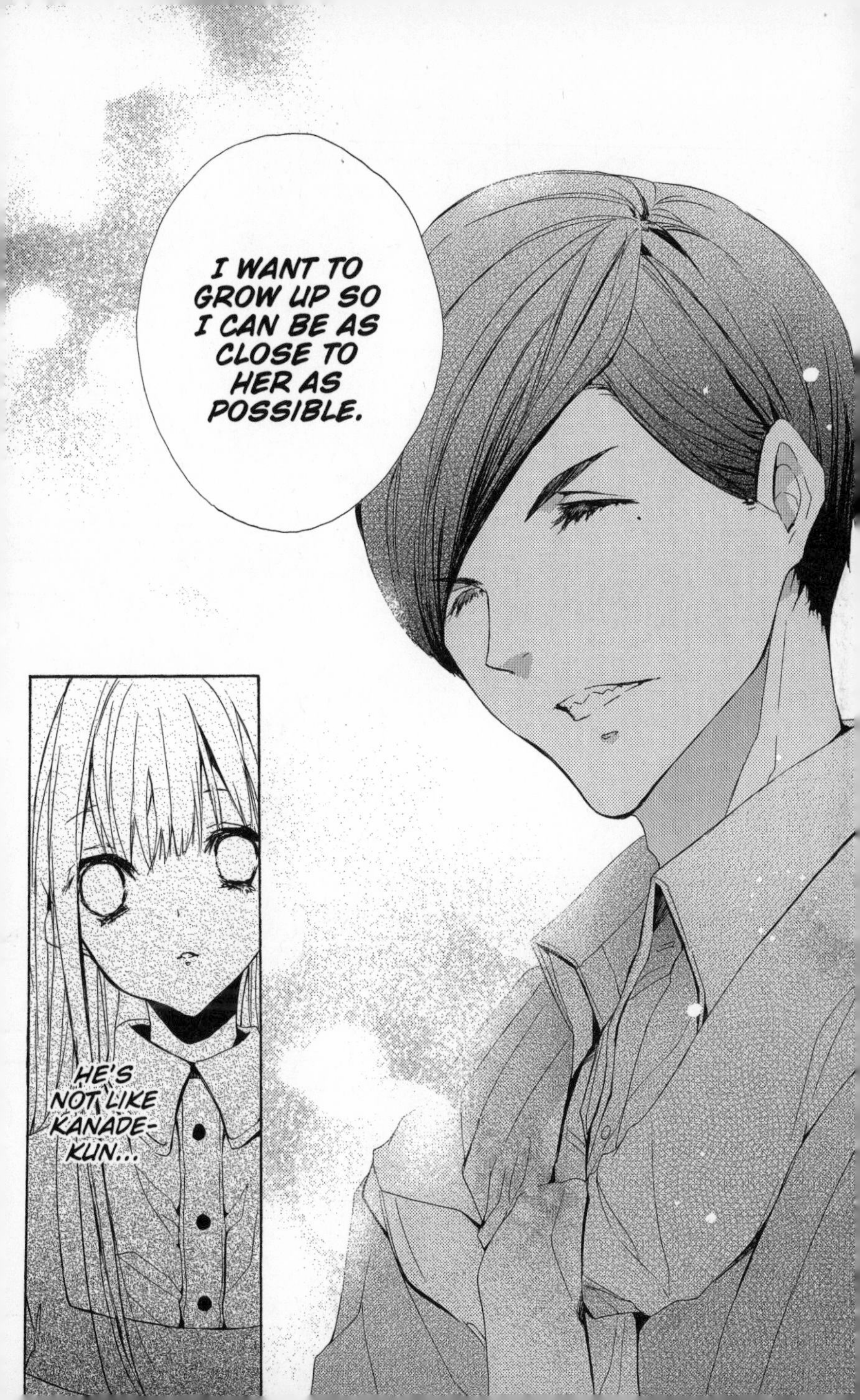
I WANT TO GROW UP SO I CAN BE AS CLOSE TO HER AS POSSIBLE.
HE'S NOT LIKE KANADE-KUN...

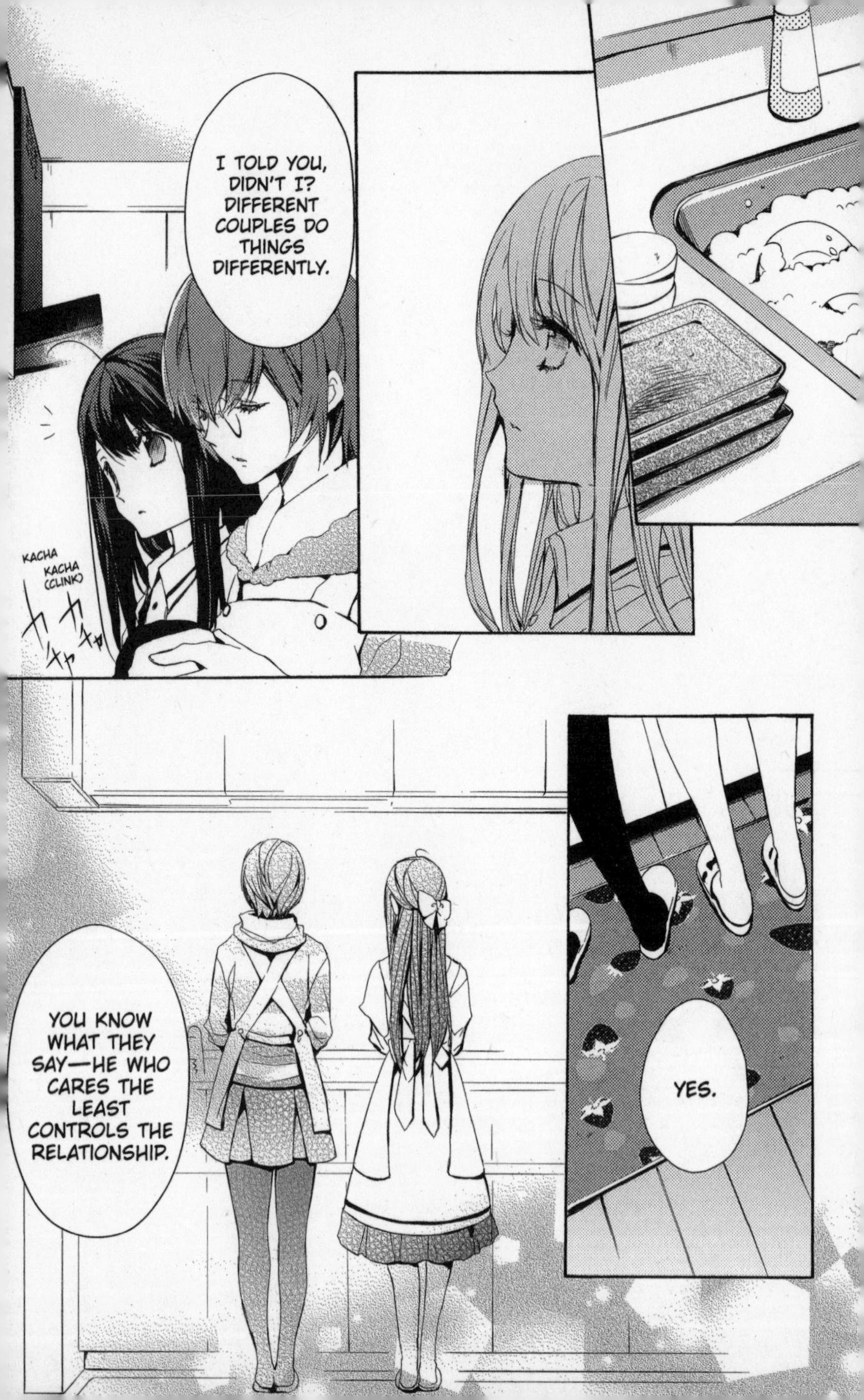
I TOLD YOU, DIDN'T I? DIFFERENT COUPLES DO THINGS DIFFERENTLY.
KACHA KACHA (CLINK)
YES.
YOU KNOW WHAT THEY SAY—HE WHO CARES THE LEAST CONTROLS THE RELATIONSHIP.

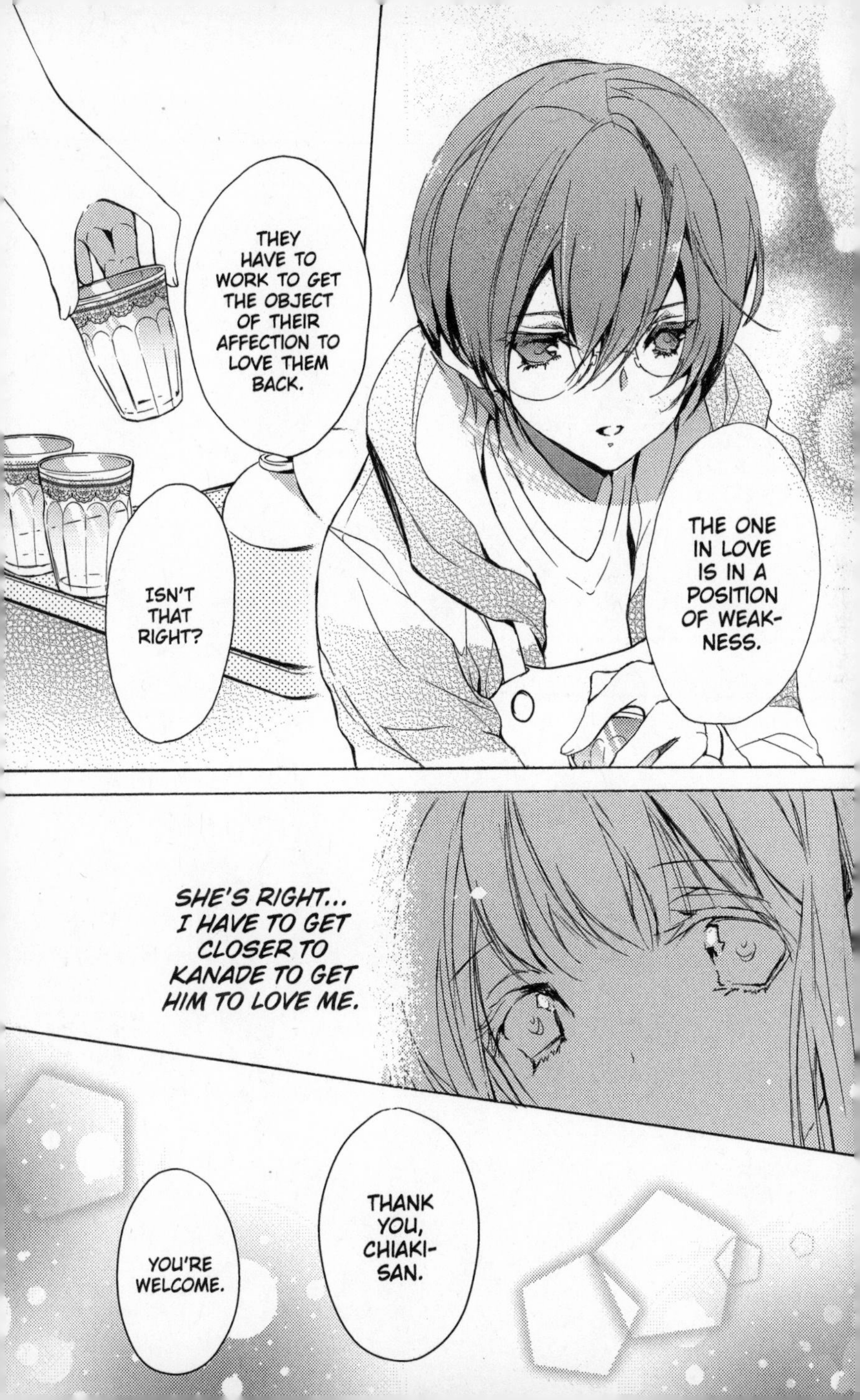
THE ONE IN LOVE IS IN A POSITION OF WEAK-NESS.
THEY HAVE TO WORK TO GET THE OBJECT OF THEIR AFFECTION TO LOVE THEM BACK.
ISN'T THAT RIGHT?
SHE'S RIGHT... I HAVE TO GET CLOSER TO KANADE TO GET HIM TO LOVE ME.
THANK YOU, CHIAKI-SAN.
YOU'RE WELCOME.

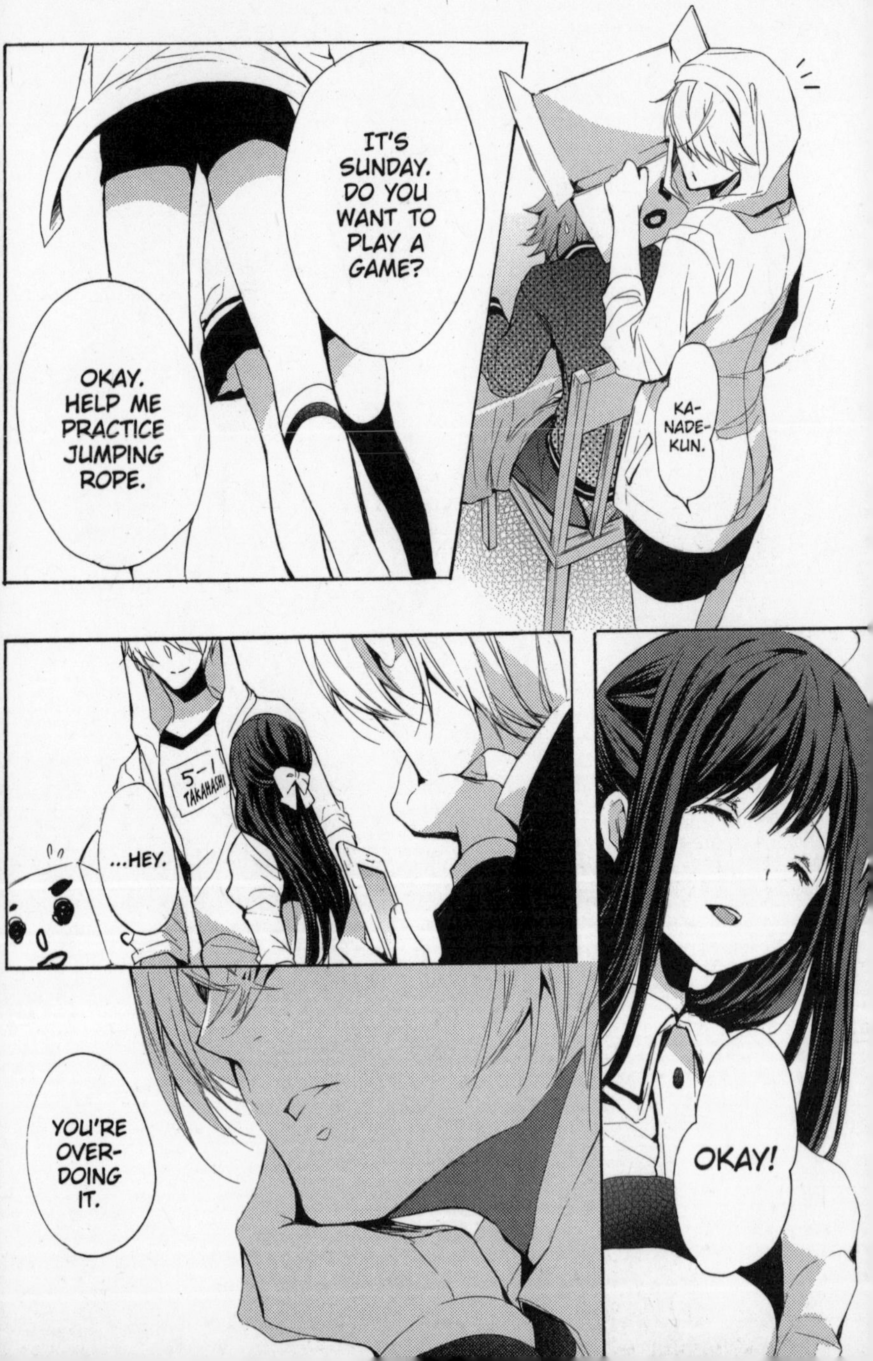
KA-NADE-KUN.
IT'S SUNDAY. DO YOU WANT TO PLAY A GAME?
OKAY. HELP ME PRACTICE JUMPING ROPE.
OKAY!
...HEY.
YOU'RE OVER-DOING IT.

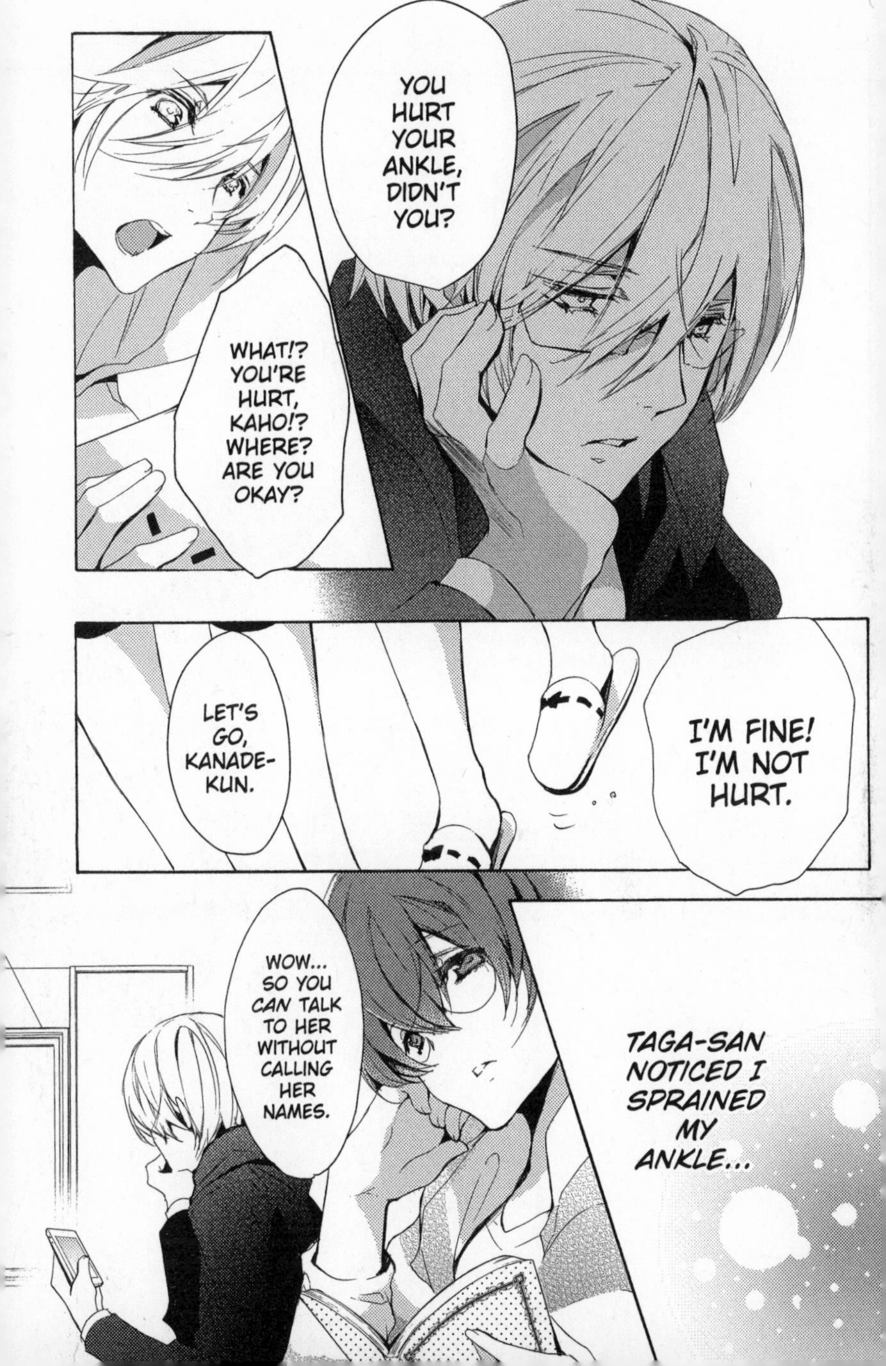
YOU HURT YOUR ANKLE, DIDN'T YOU?
WHAT!? YOU'RE HURT, KAHO!? WHERE? ARE YOU OKAY?
I'M FINE! I'M NOT HURT.
LET'S GO, KANADE-KUN.
TAGA-SAN NOTICED I SPRAINED MY ANKLE...
WOW... SO YOU CAN TALK TO HER WITHOUT CALLING HER NAMES.

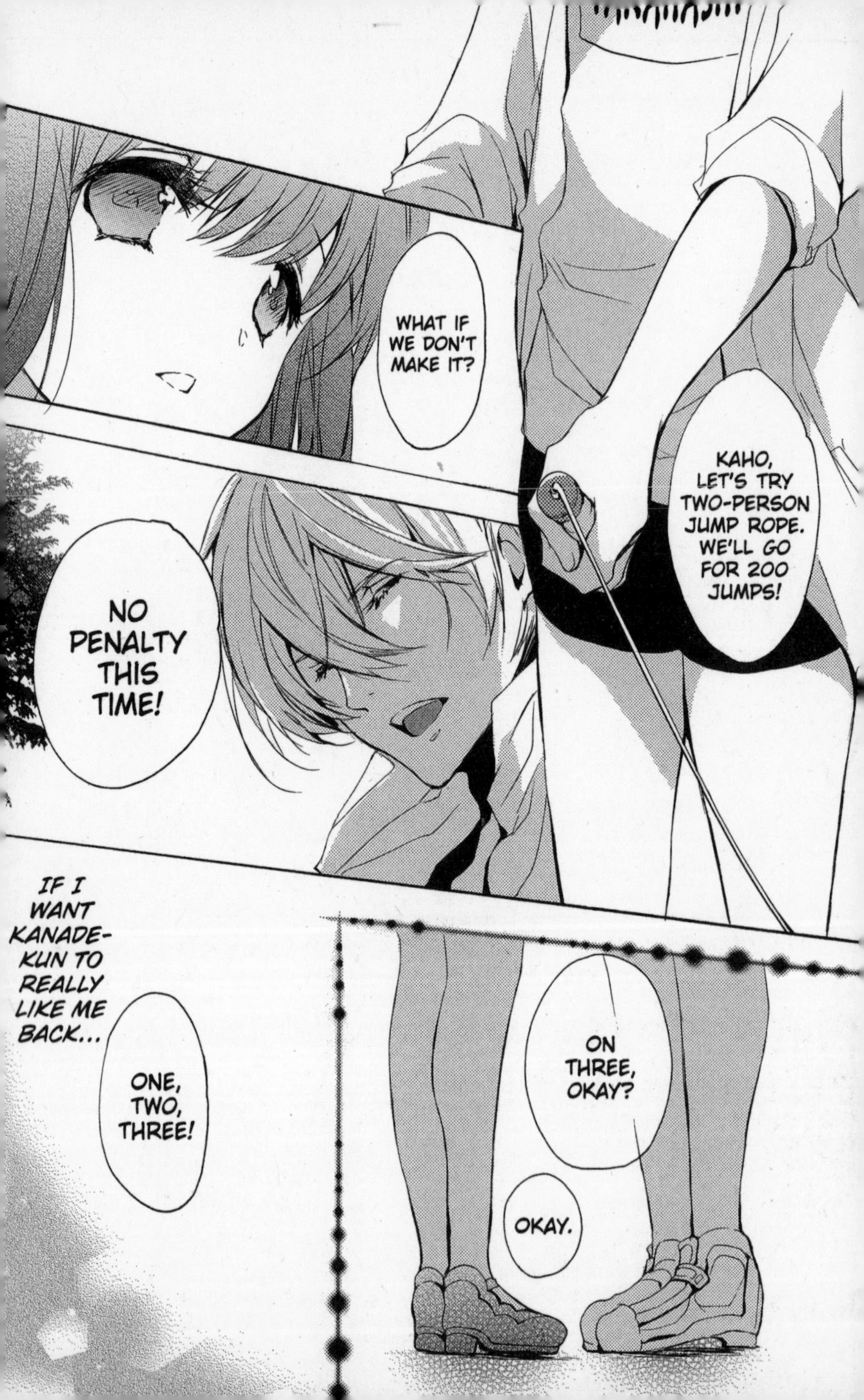
KAHO, LET'S TRY TWO-PERSON JUMP ROPE. WE'LL GO FOR 200 JUMPS!
WHAT IF WE DON'T MAKE IT?
NO PENALTY THIS TIME!
ON THREE, OKAY?
OKAY.
IF I WANT KANADE-KUN TO REALLY LIKE ME BACK...
ONE, TWO, THREE!

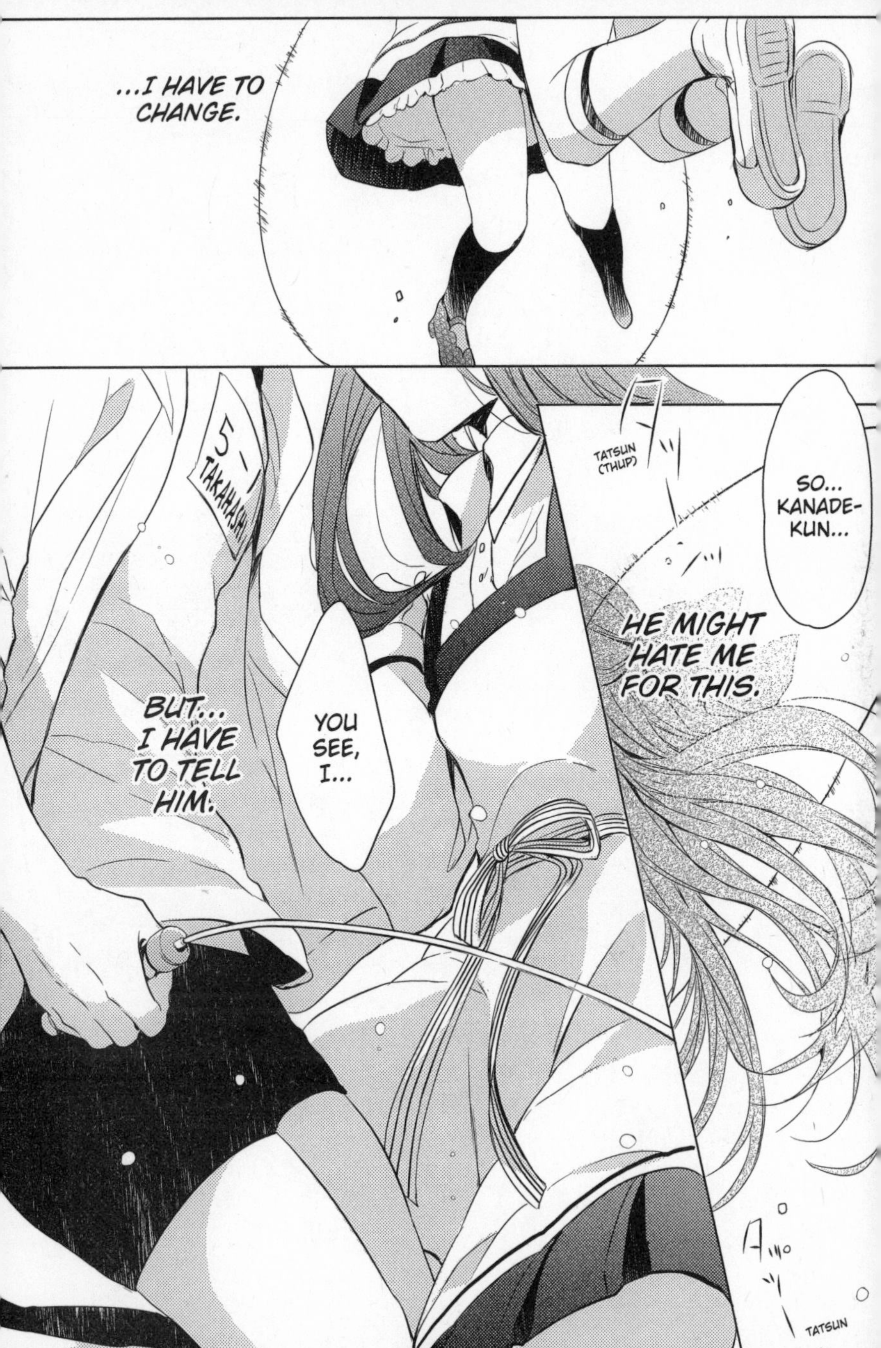
...I HAVE TO CHANGE.
TATSUN (THUP)
SO... KANADE-KUN...
HE MIGHT HATE ME FOR THIS.
TATSUN
5-1 TAKAHASHI
YOU SEE, I...
BUT... I HAVE TO TELL HIM.

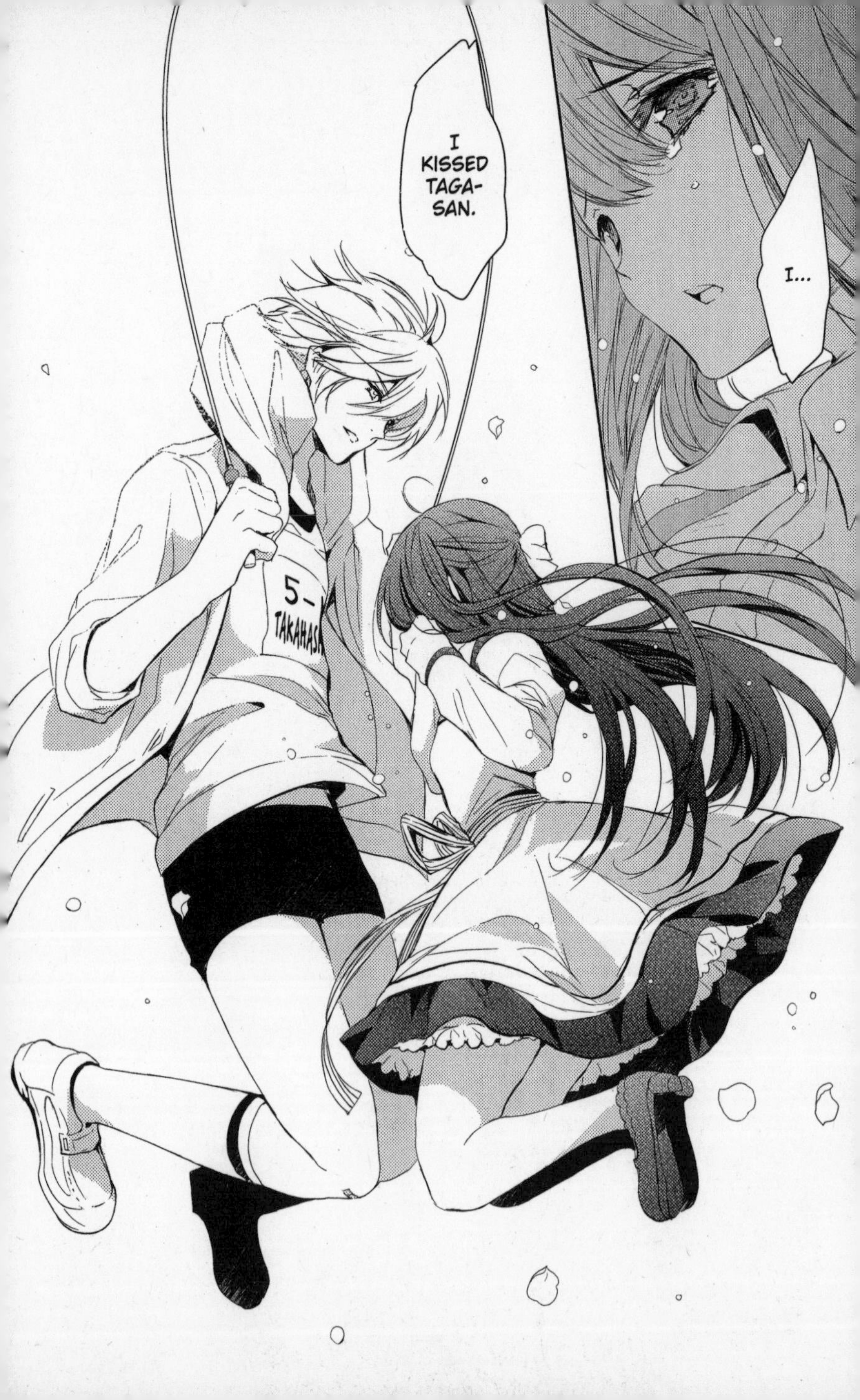
I...
I KISSED TAGA-SAN.

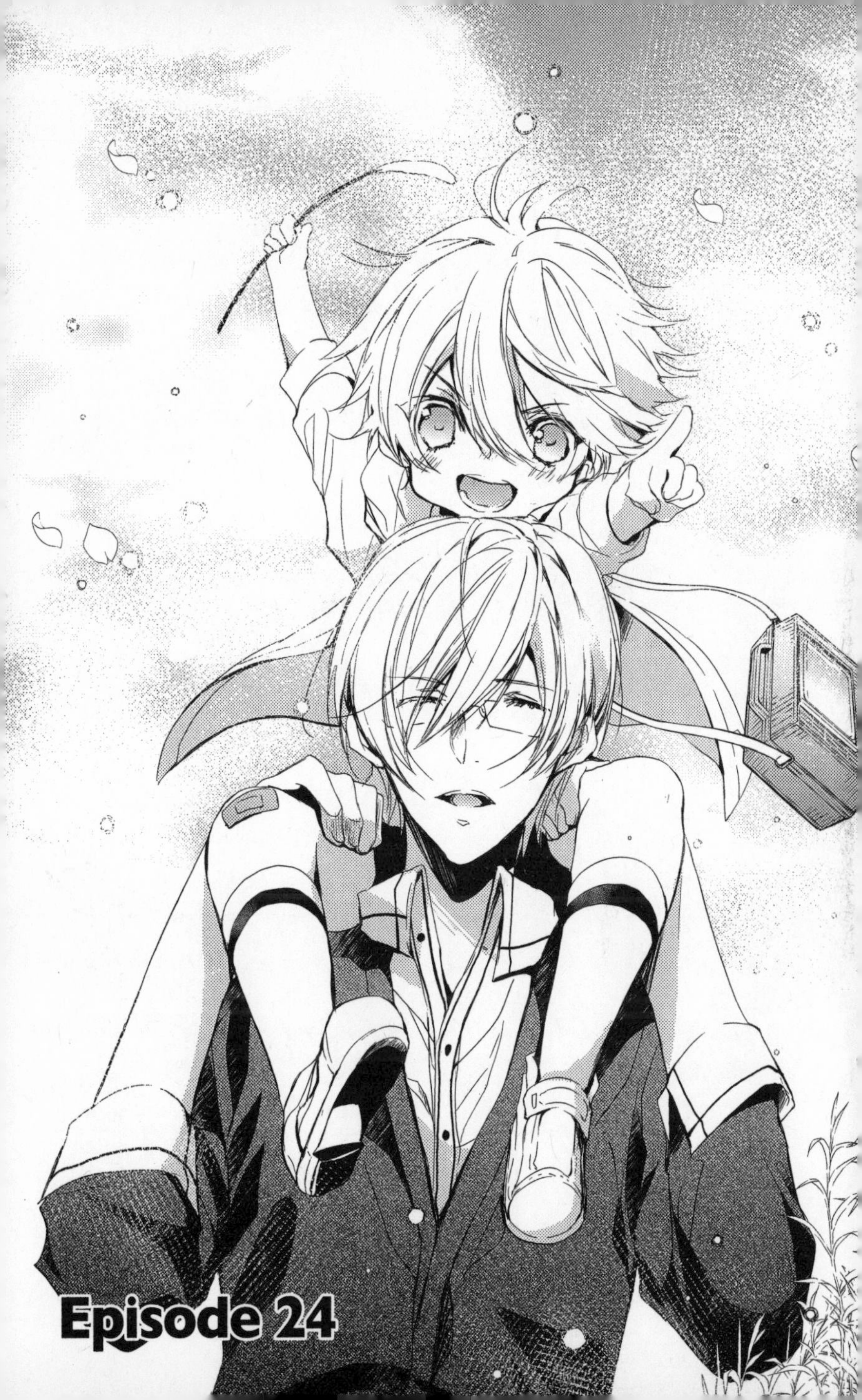

Episode 24

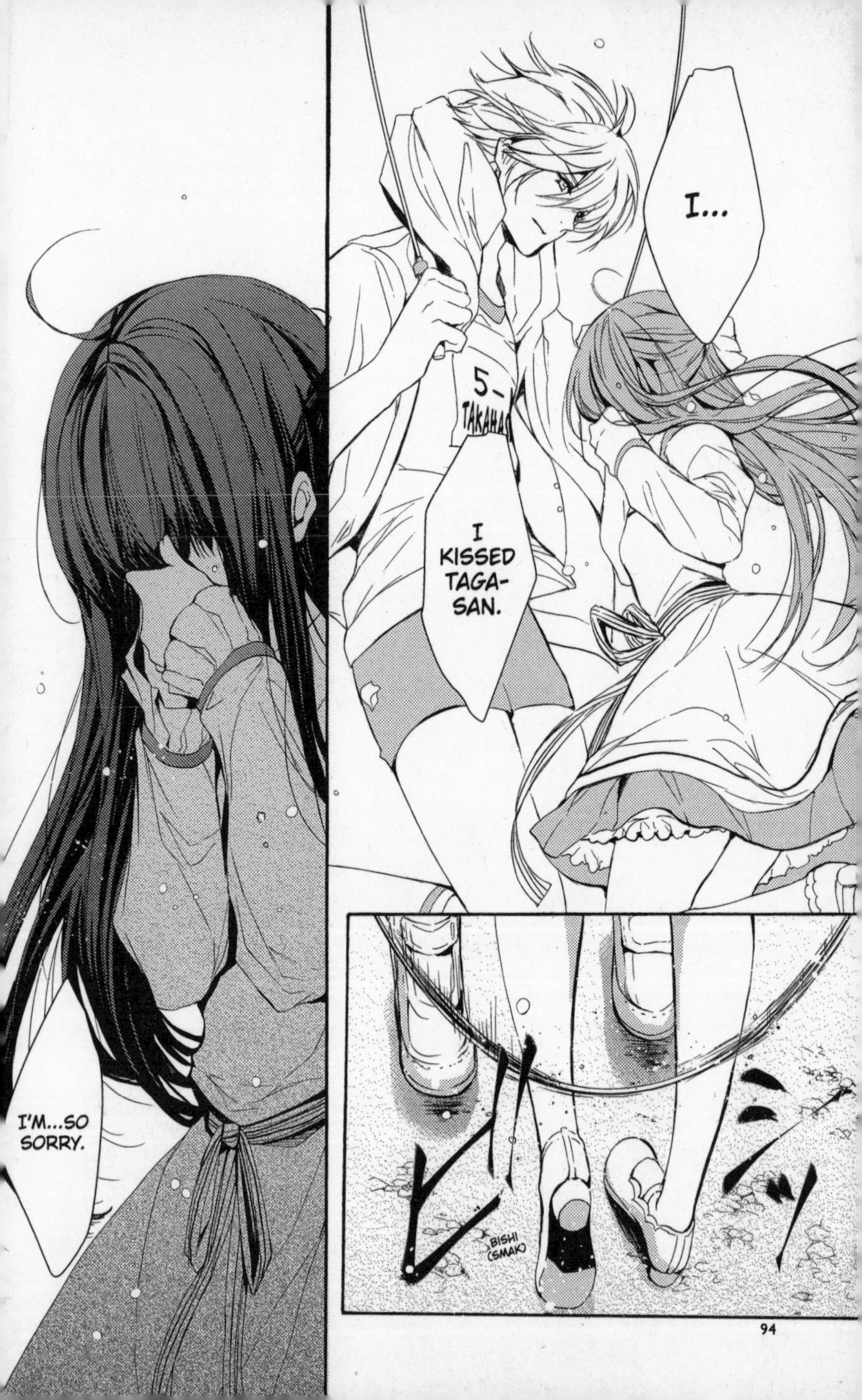
I...
I KISSED TAGA-SAN.
BISHI (SMAK)
I'M...SO SORRY.

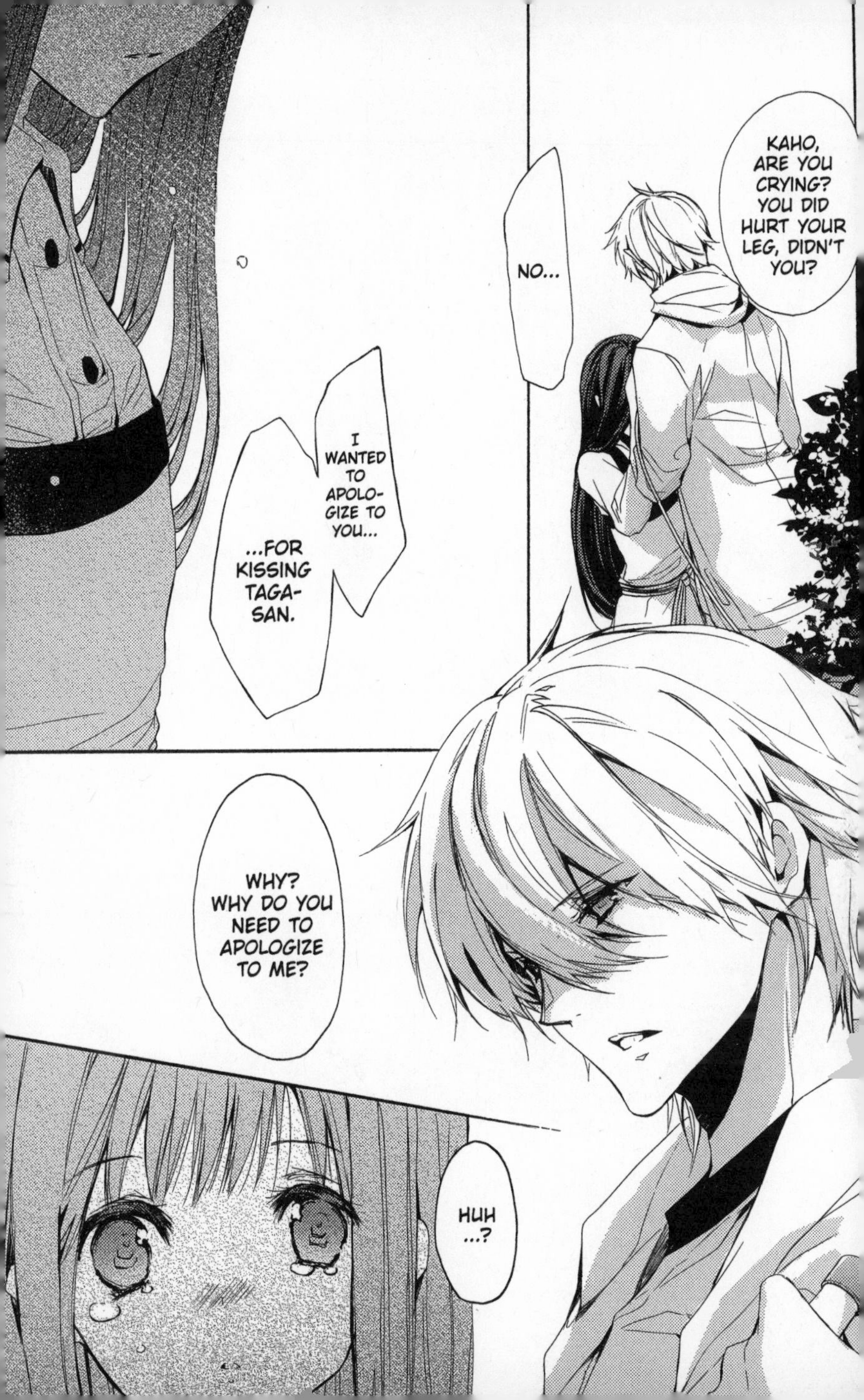
KAHO, ARE YOU CRYING? YOU DID HURT YOUR LEG, DIDN'T YOU?
NO...
I WANTED TO APOLO-GIZE TO YOU...
...FOR KISSING TAGA-SAN.
WHY? WHY DO YOU NEED TO APOLOGIZE TO ME?
HUH ...?

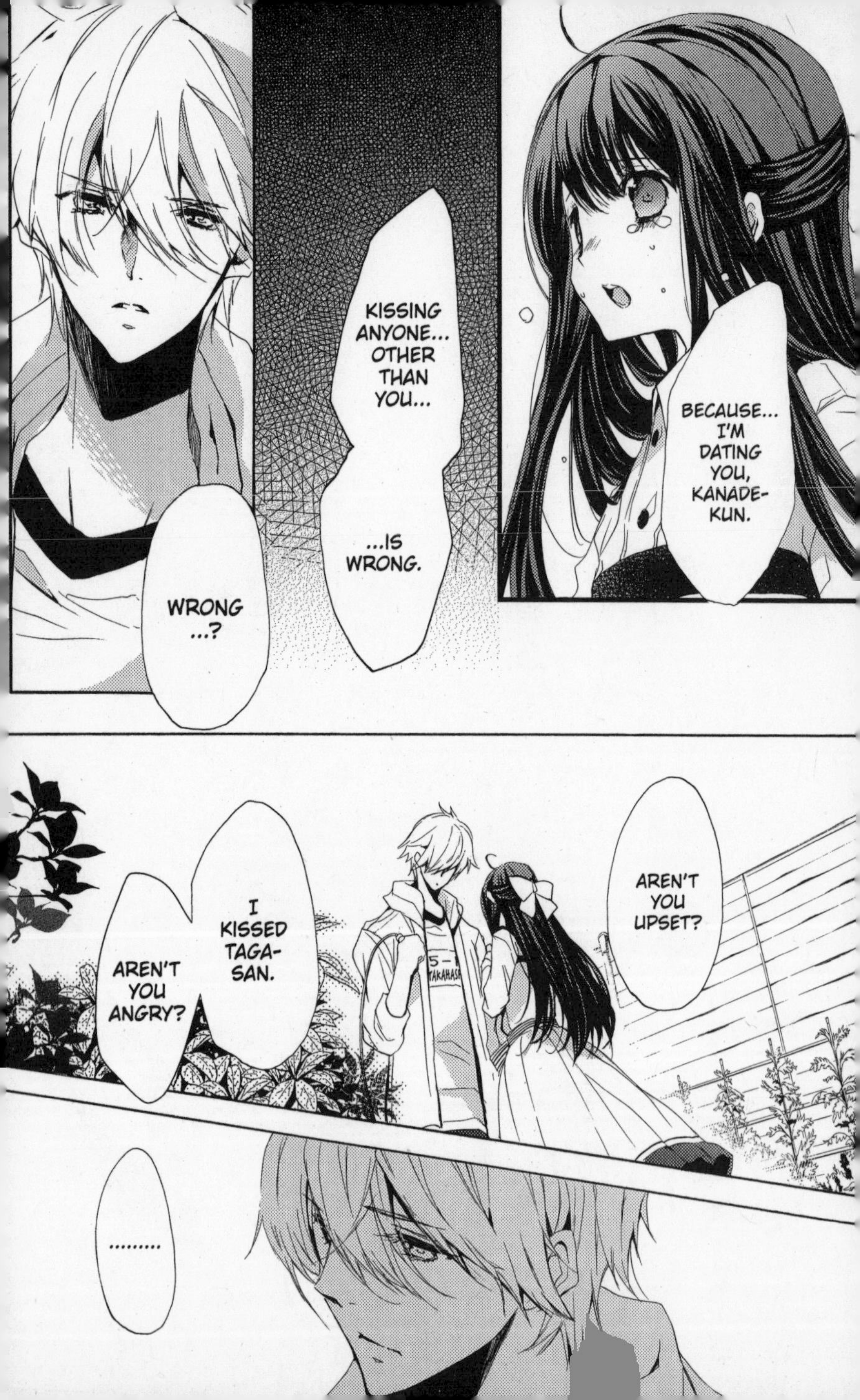
BECAUSE... I'M DATING YOU, KANADE-KUN.
KISSING ANYONE... OTHER THAN YOU...
...IS WRONG.
WRONG ...?
AREN'T YOU UPSET?
I KISSED TAGA-SAN.
AREN'T YOU ANGRY?
....

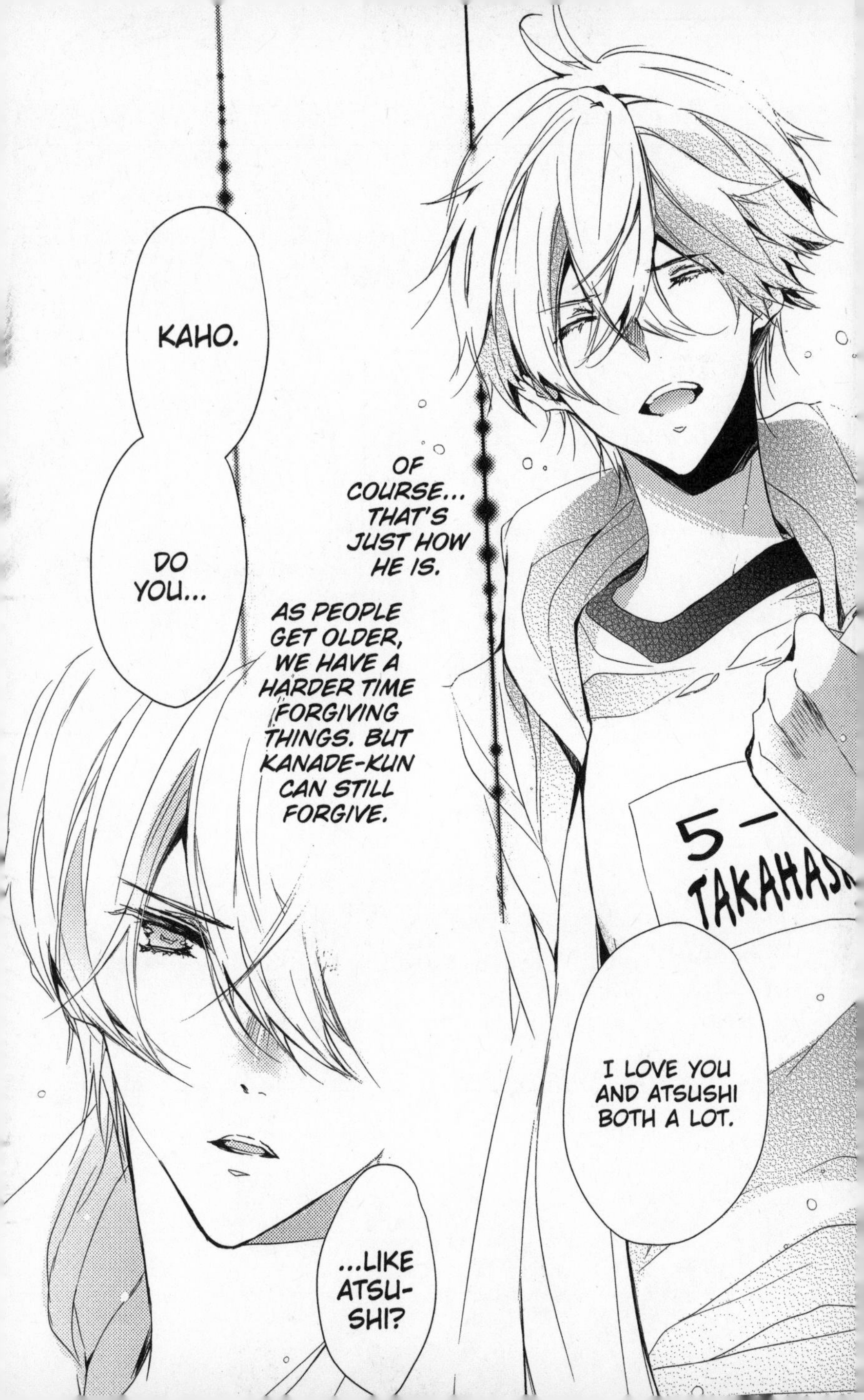
OF COURSE... THAT'S JUST HOW HE IS.
AS PEOPLE GET OLDER, WE HAVE A HARDER TIME FORGIVING THINGS. BUT KANADE-KUN CAN STILL FORGIVE.
5-
TAKAHAS
KAHO.
DO YOU...
...LIKE ATSU-SHI?
I LOVE YOU AND ATSUSHI BOTH A LOT.

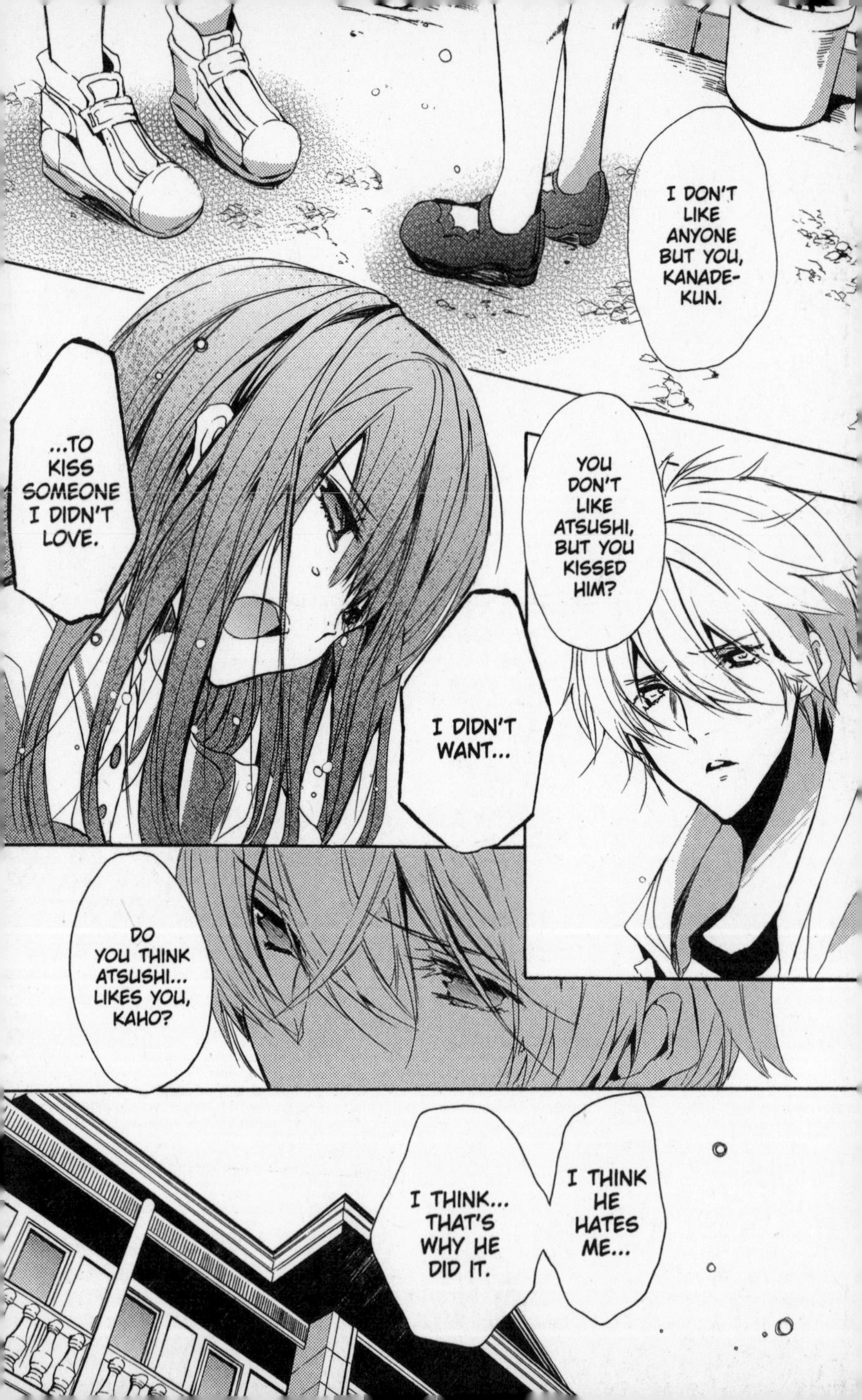
I DON'T LIKE ANYONE BUT YOU, KANADE-KUN.
YOU DON'T LIKE ATSUSHI, BUT YOU KISSED HIM?
I DIDN'T WANT...
...TO KISS SOMEONE I DIDN'T LOVE.
DO YOU THINK ATSUSHI... LIKES YOU, KAHO?
I THINK HE HATES ME...
I THINK... THAT'S WHY HE DID IT.

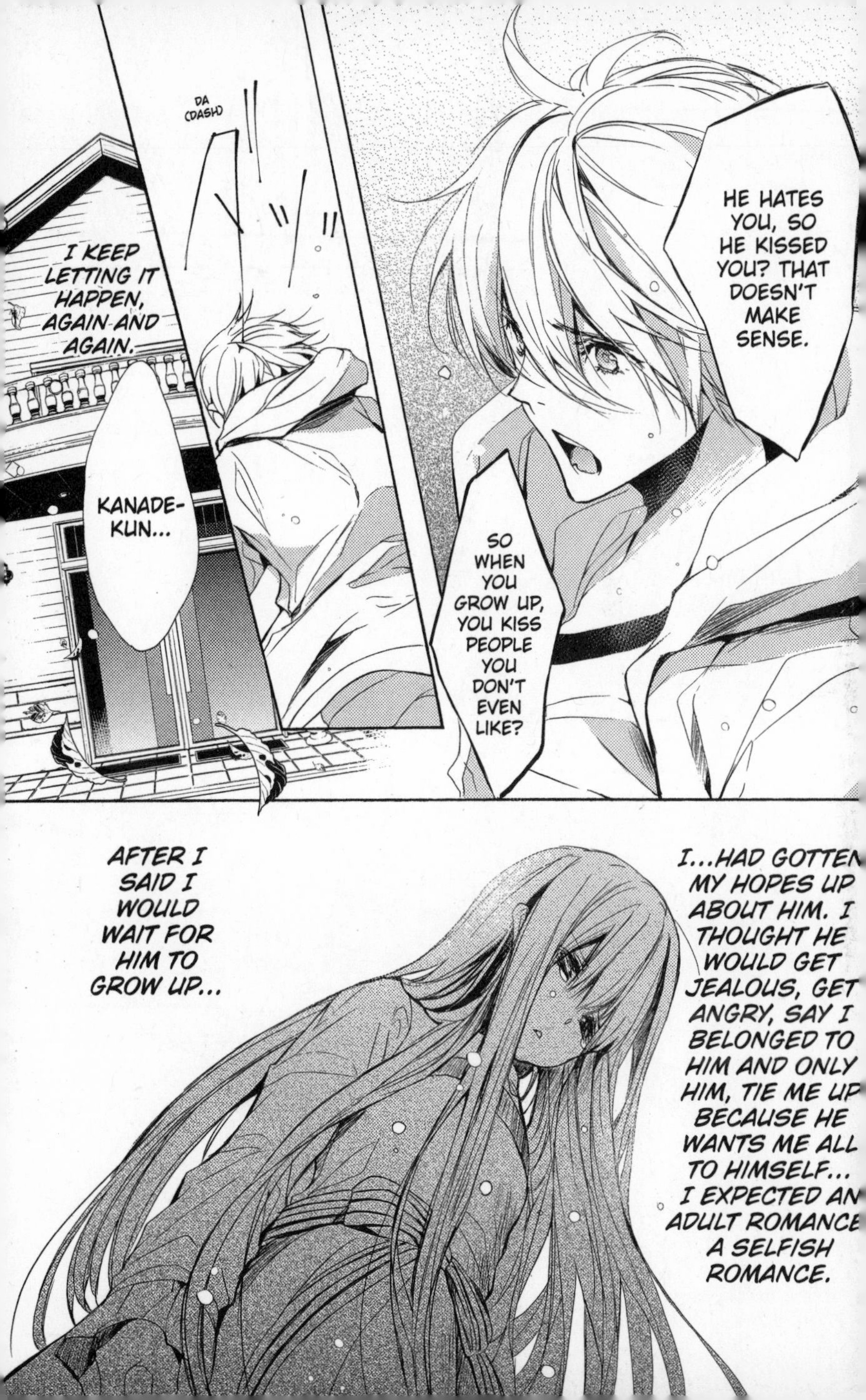
HE HATES YOU, SO HE KISSED YOU? THAT DOESN'T MAKE SENSE.
SO WHEN YOU GROW UP, YOU KISS PEOPLE YOU DON'T EVEN LIKE?
DA (DASH)
I KEEP LETTING IT HAPPEN, AGAIN AND AGAIN.
KANADE-KUN...
I...HAD GOTTEN MY HOPES UP ABOUT HIM. I THOUGHT HE WOULD GET JEALOUS, GET ANGRY, SAY I BELONGED TO HIM AND ONLY HIM, TIE ME UP BECAUSE HE WANTS ME ALL TO HIMSELF... I EXPECTED AN ADULT ROMANCE A SELFISH ROMANCE.
AFTER I SAID I WOULD WAIT FOR HIM TO GROW UP...

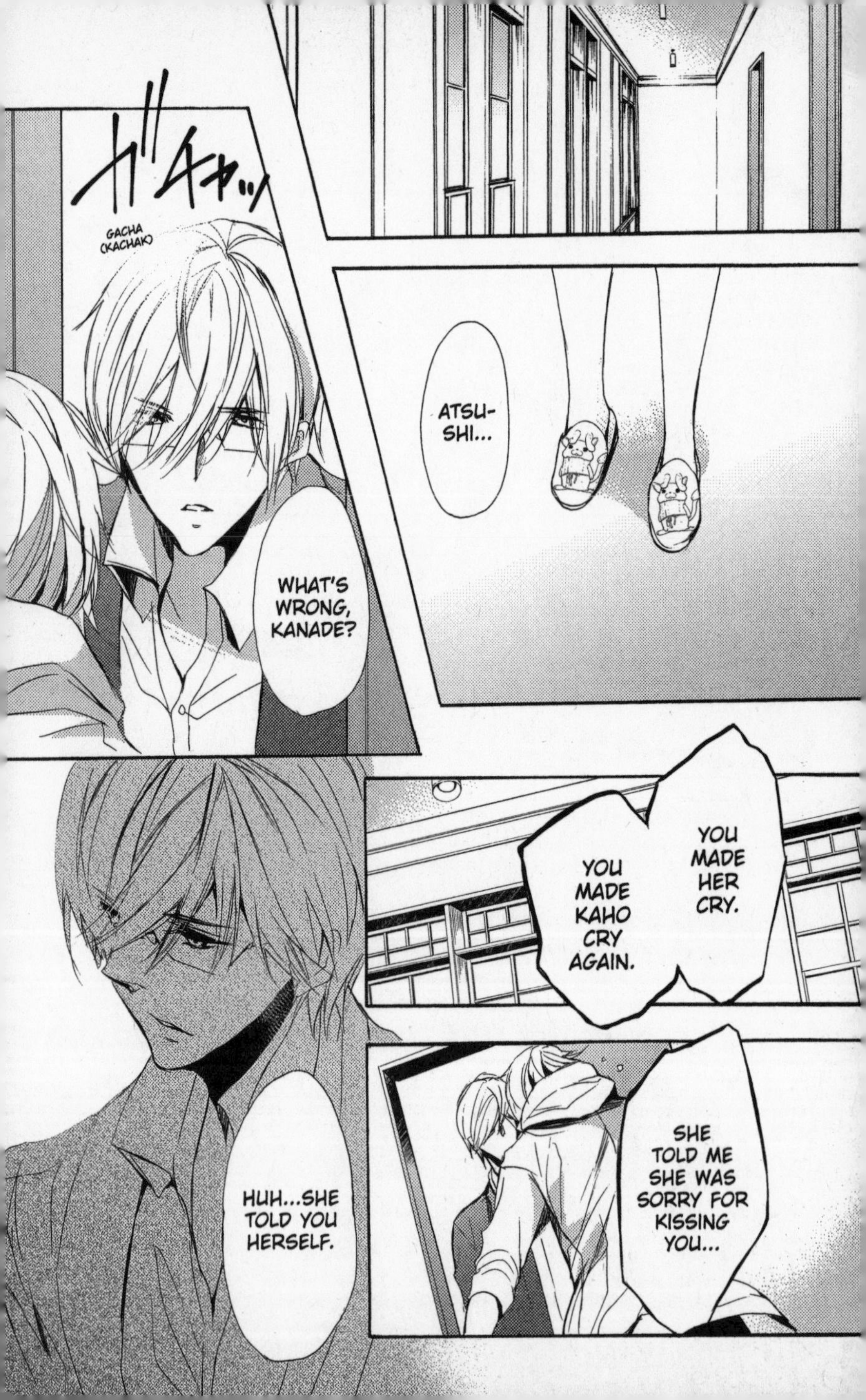
ATSU-SHI...
GACHA (KACHAK)
WHAT'S WRONG, KANADE?
YOU MADE HER CRY.
YOU MADE KAHO CRY AGAIN.
SHE TOLD ME SHE WAS SORRY FOR KISSING YOU...
HUH...SHE TOLD YOU HERSELF.

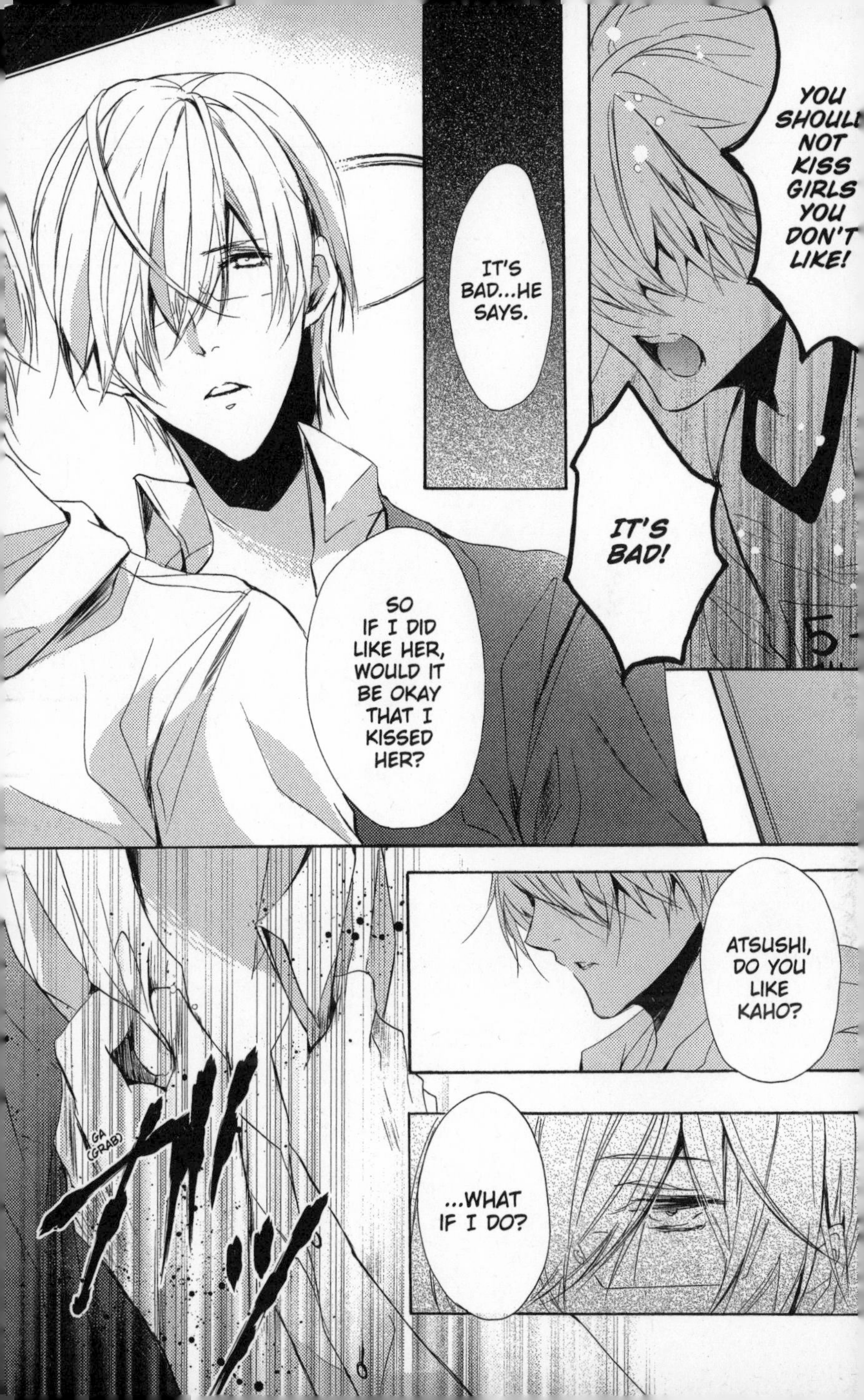
YOU SHOUL NOT KISS GIRLS YOU DON'T LIKE!
IT'S BAD!
IT'S BAD...HE SAYS.
SO IF I DID LIKE HER, WOULD IT BE OKAY THAT I KISSED HER?
ATSUSHI, DO YOU LIKE KAHO?
...WHAT IF I DO?
GA (GRAB)

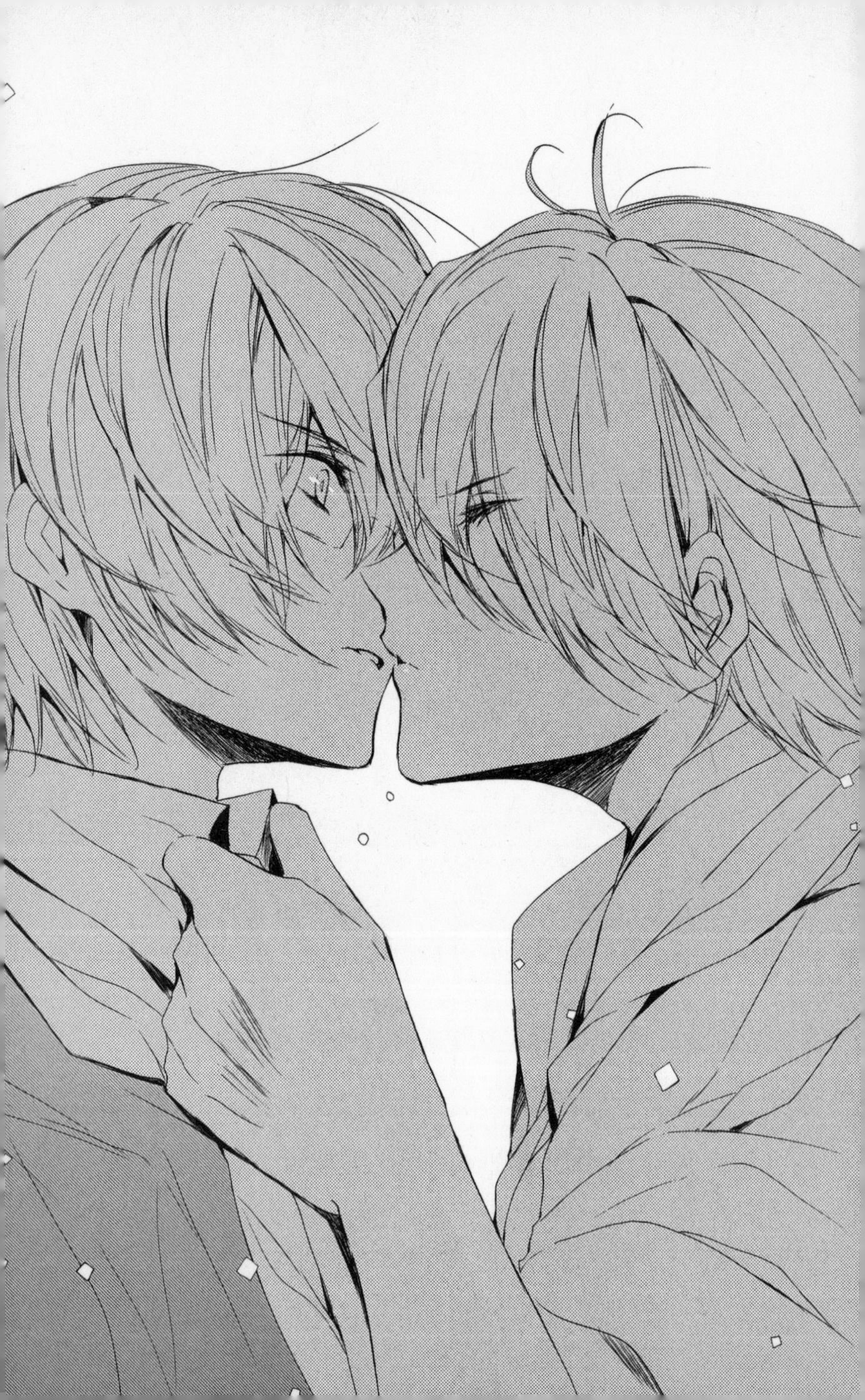

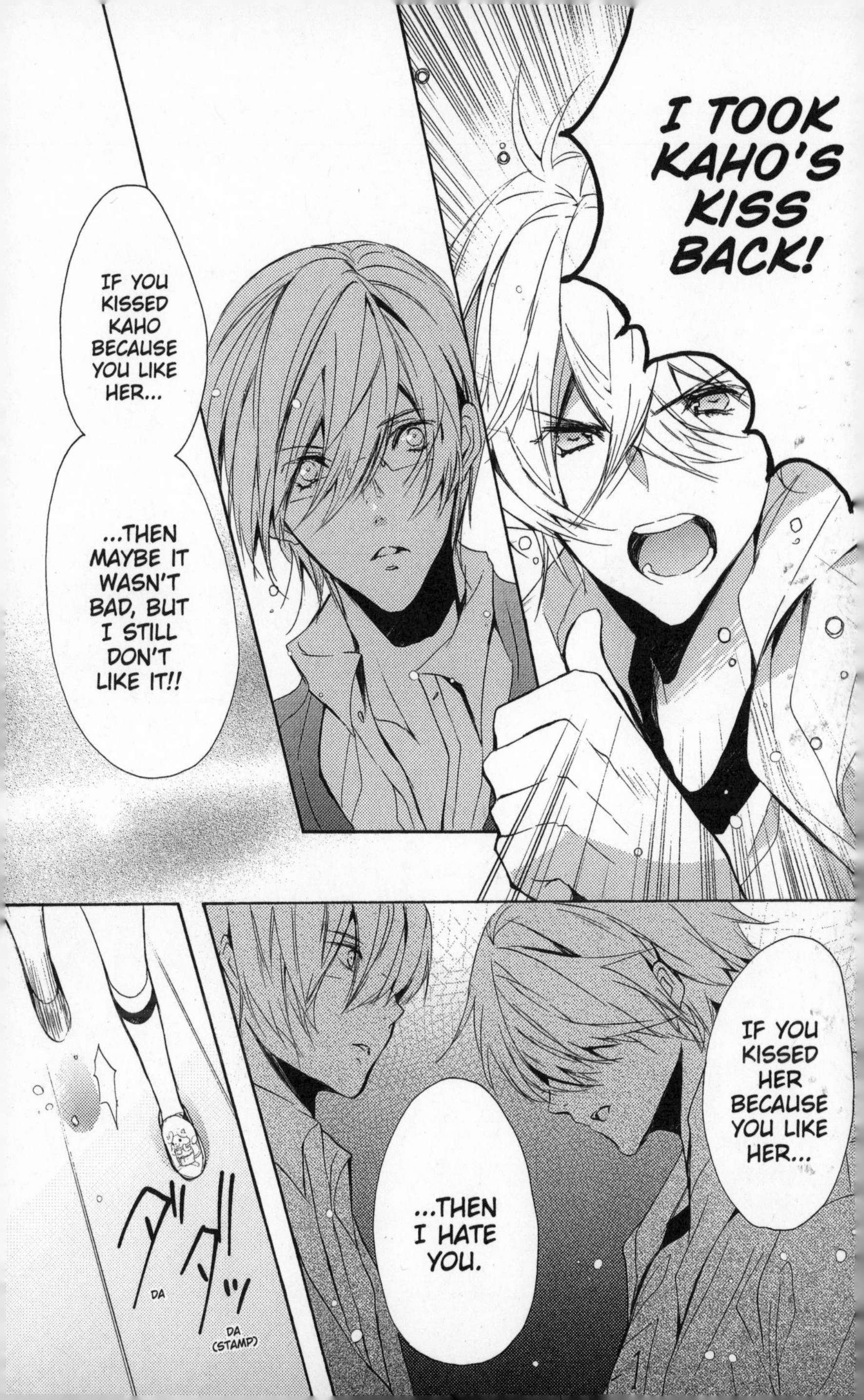
I TOOK KAHO'S KISS BACK!
IF YOU KISSED KAHO BECAUSE YOU LIKE HER...
...THEN MAYBE IT WASN'T BAD, BUT I STILL DON'T LIKE IT!!
IF YOU KISSED HER BECAUSE YOU LIKE HER...
...THEN I HATE YOU.
DA
DA (STAMP)

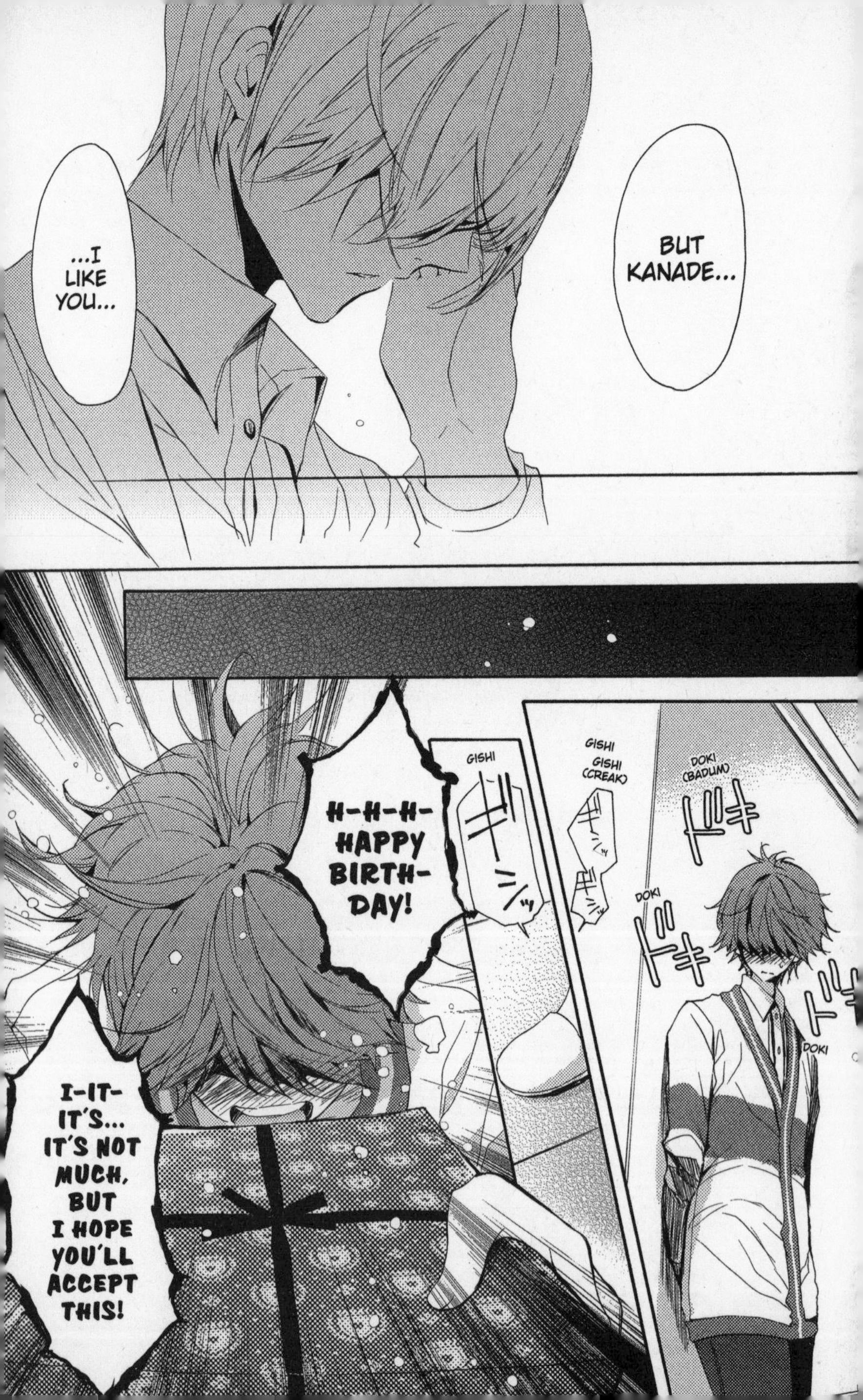
BUT KANADE...
...I LIKE YOU...
DOKI (BADUM)
DOKI
DOKI
GISHI GISHI (CREAK)
GISHI
H-H-H-HAPPY BIRTHDAY!
I-IT-IT'S... IT'S NOT MUCH, BUT I HOPE YOU'LL ACCEPT THIS!

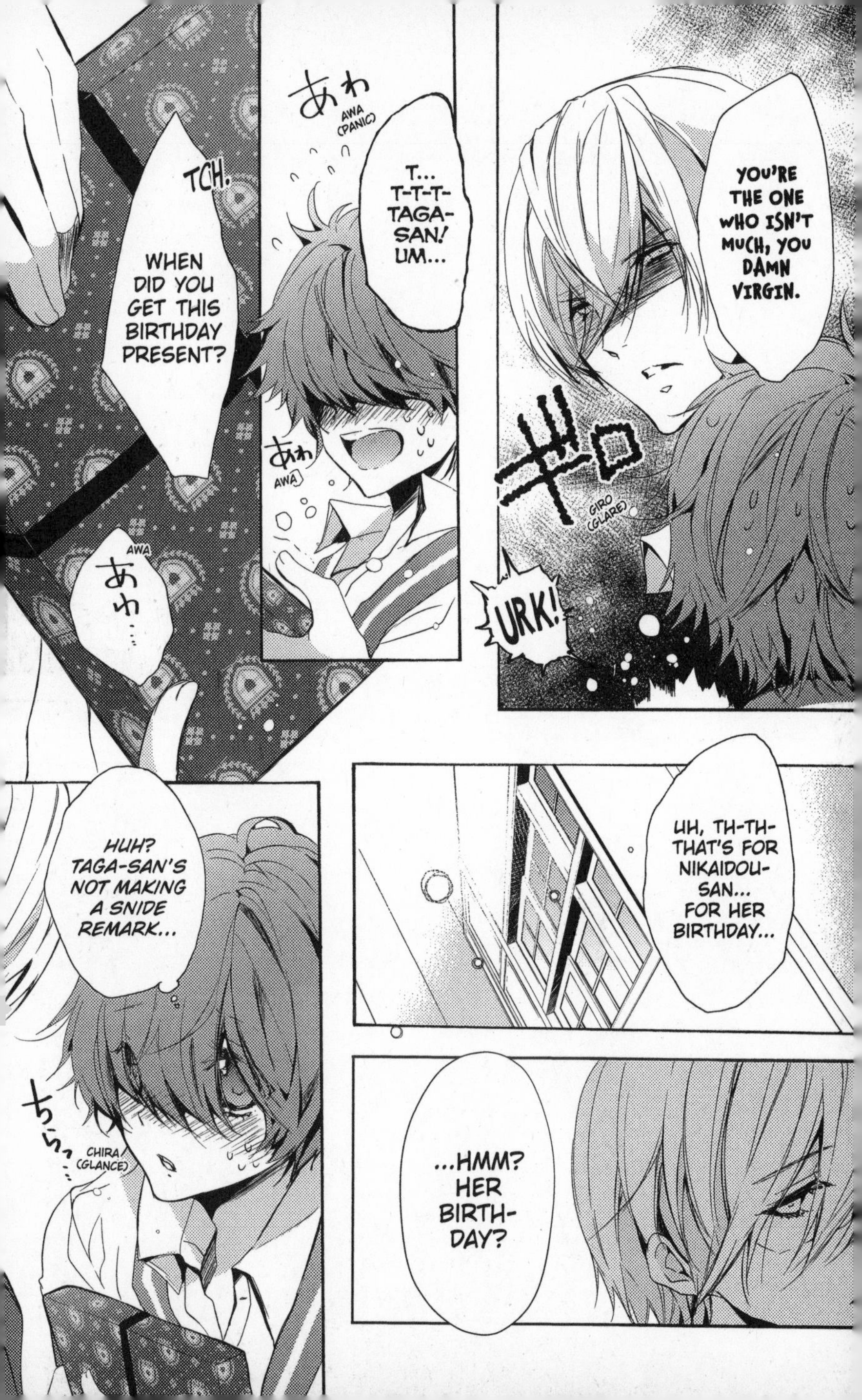

YOU'RE THE ONE WHO ISN'T MUCH, YOU DAMN VIRGIN.
ギロ
GIRO (GLARE)
URK!
あわ
AWA (PANIC)
T... T-T-T-TAGA-SAN! UM...
あわ
AWA
TCH.
WHEN DID YOU GET THIS BIRTHDAY PRESENT?
AWA
あわ...
UH, TH-TH-THAT'S FOR NIKAIDOU-SAN... FOR HER BIRTHDAY...
...HMM? HER BIRTH-DAY?
HUH? TAGA-SAN'S NOT MAKING A SNIDE REMARK...
ちらっ
CHIRA (GLANCE)

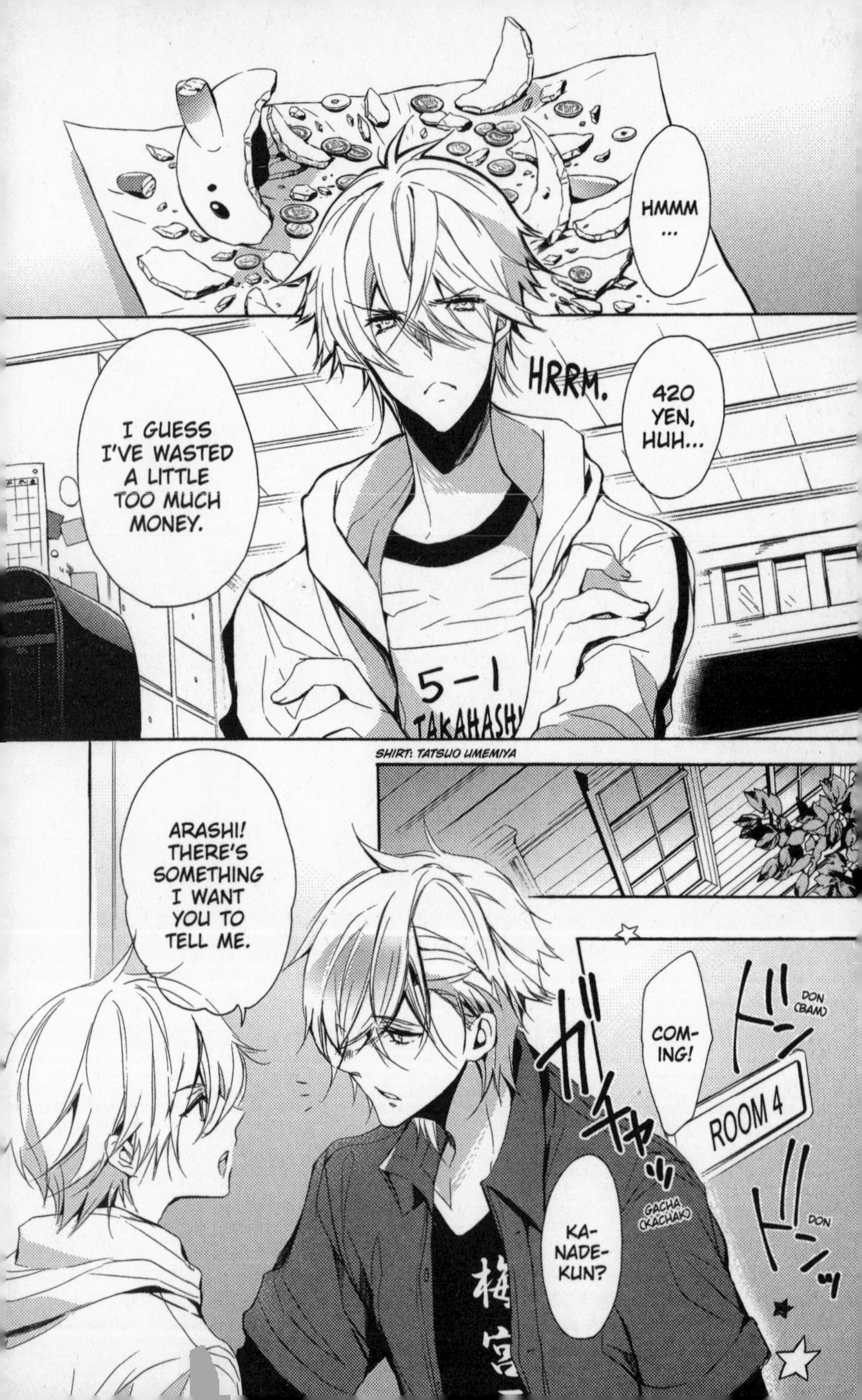
HMMM ...
420 YEN, HUH...
HRRM.
I GUESS I'VE WASTED A LITTLE TOO MUCH MONEY.
5-1 TAKAHASHI
SHIRT: TATSUO UMEMIYA
DON (BAM)
DON
ROOM 4
COM-ING!
GACHA (KACHAK)
KA-NADE-KUN?
ARASHI! THERE'S SOMETHING I WANT YOU TO TELL ME.

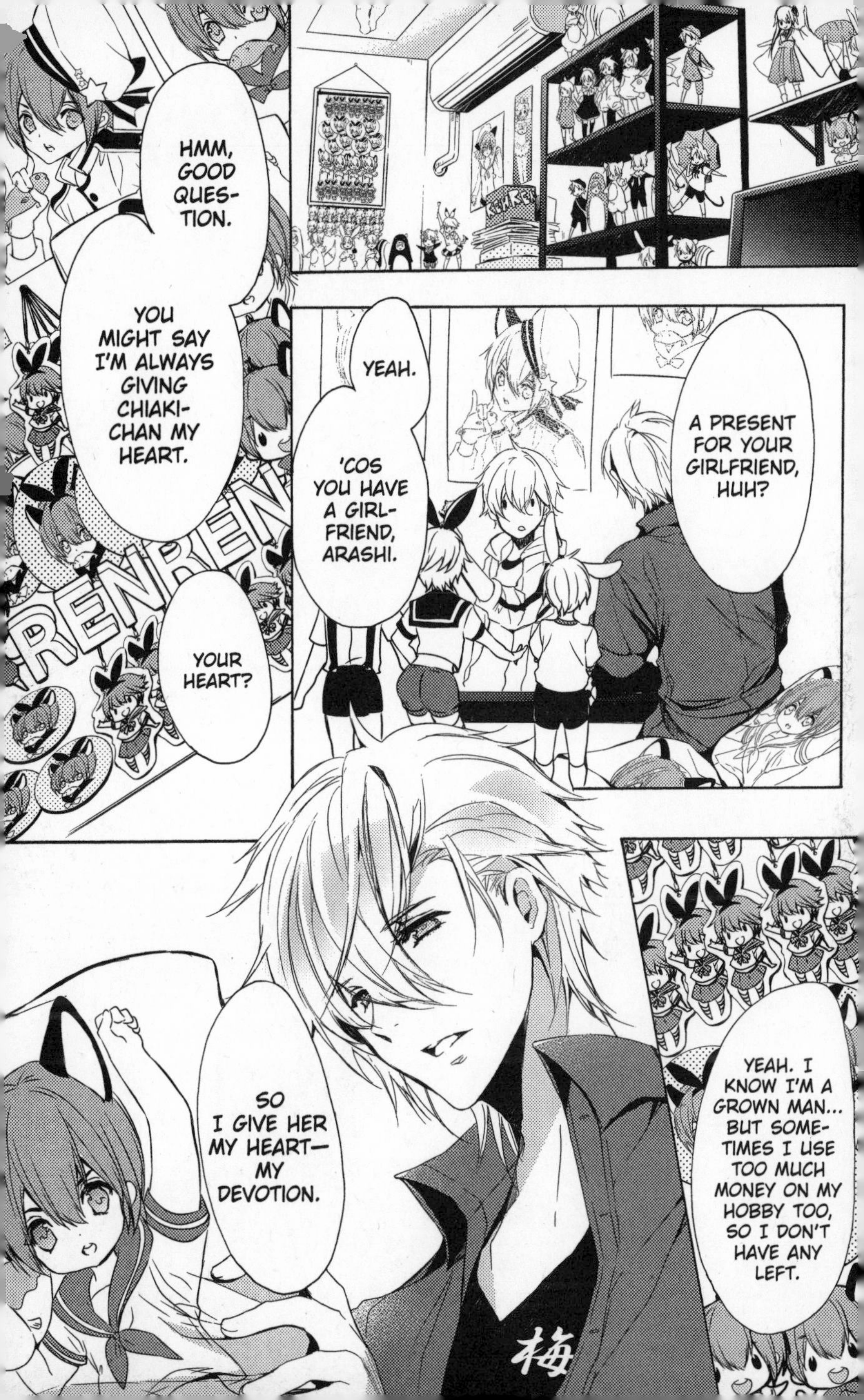
A PRESENT FOR YOUR GIRLFRIEND, HUH?
YEAH.
'COS YOU HAVE A GIRL-FRIEND, ARASHI.
HMM, GOOD QUES-TION.
YOU MIGHT SAY I'M ALWAYS GIVING CHIAKI-CHAN MY HEART.
YOUR HEART?
RENREN
YEAH. I KNOW I'M A GROWN MAN... BUT SOME-TIMES I USE TOO MUCH MONEY ON MY HOBBY TOO, SO I DON'T HAVE ANY LEFT.
SO I GIVE HER MY HEART—MY DEVOTION.
梅

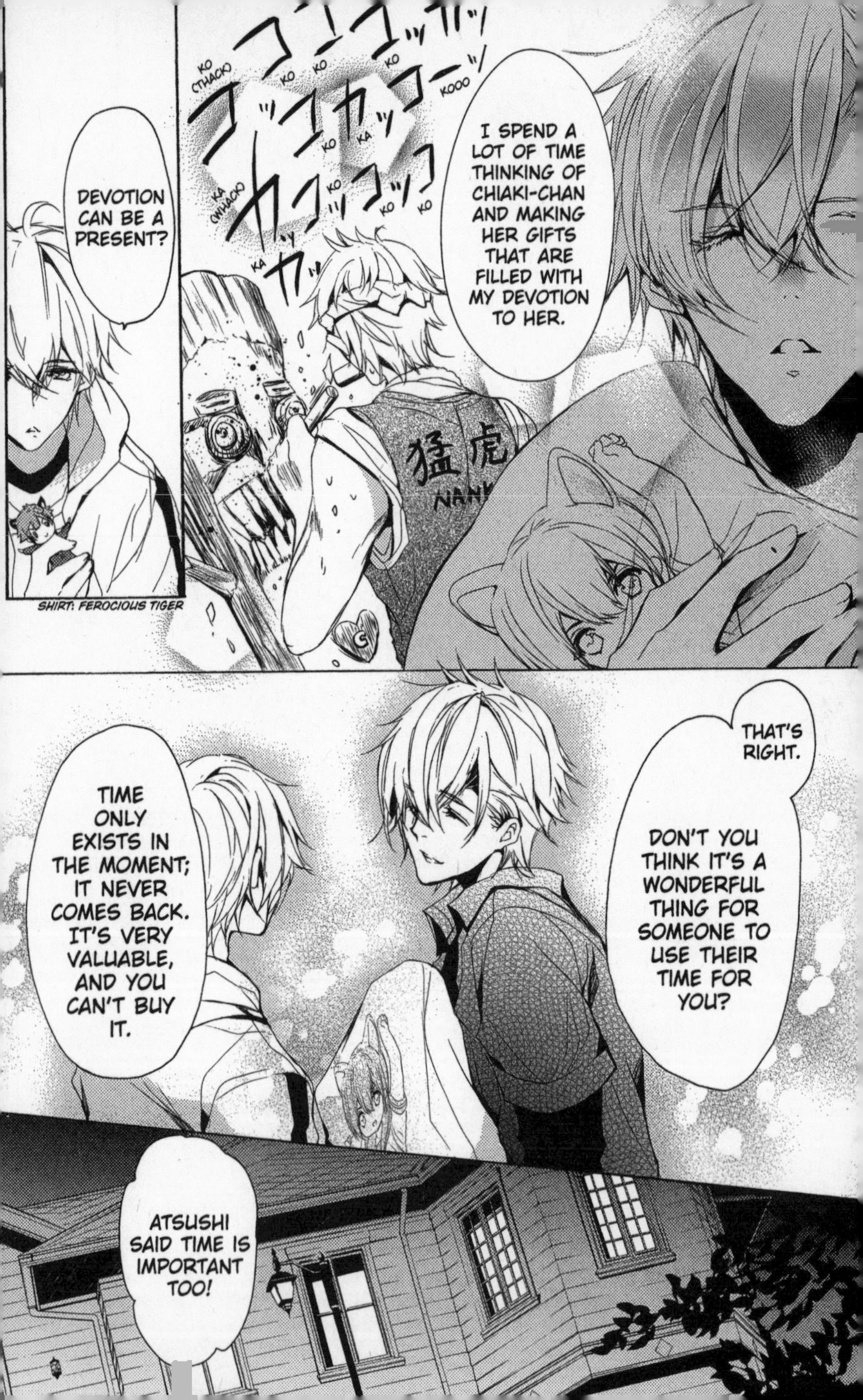
I SPEND A LOT OF TIME THINKING OF CHIAKI-CHAN AND MAKING HER GIFTS THAT ARE FILLED WITH MY DEVOTION TO HER.
KO (THACK) KO KO KO KOOO
KO KA KA (WHACK) KO KO KO KA
猛虎
DEVOTION CAN BE A PRESENT?
SHIRT: FEROCIOUS TIGER
THAT'S RIGHT.
DON'T YOU THINK IT'S A WONDERFUL THING FOR SOMEONE TO USE THEIR TIME FOR YOU?
TIME ONLY EXISTS IN THE MOMENT; IT NEVER COMES BACK. IT'S VERY VALUABLE, AND YOU CAN'T BUY IT.
ATSUSHI SAID TIME IS IMPORTANT TOO!

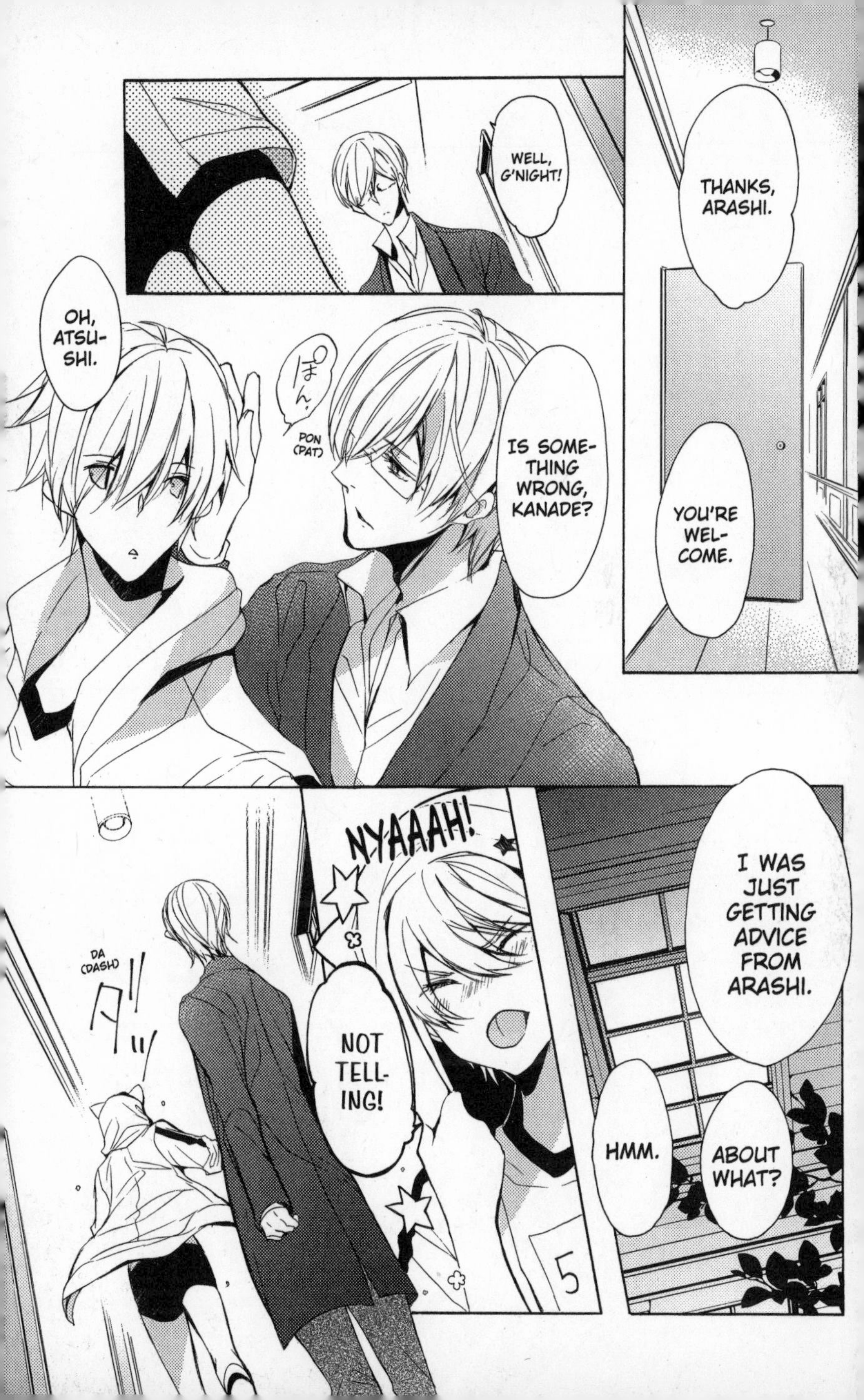
THANKS, ARASHI.
YOU'RE WELCOME.
WELL, G'NIGHT!
IS SOME-THING WRONG, KANADE?
ぽん
PON (PAT)
OH, ATSU-SHI.
I WAS JUST GETTING ADVICE FROM ARASHI.
HMM.
ABOUT WHAT?
NYAAAH!
NOT TELL-ING!
DA (DASH)
5

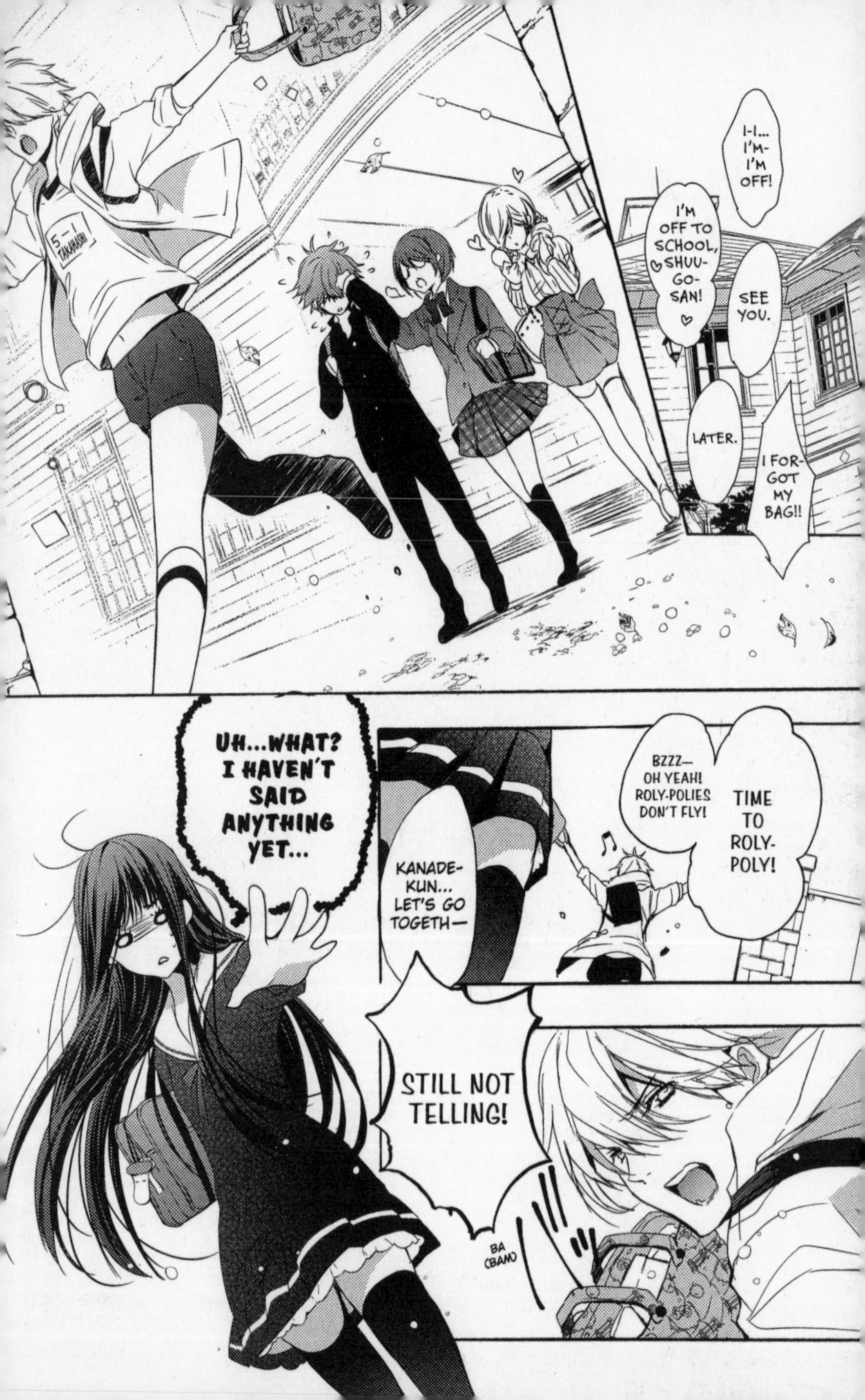

I-I... I'M- I'M OFF!
I'M OFF TO SCHOOL, SHUU-GO-SAN!
SEE YOU.
LATER.
I FOR-GOT MY BAG!!
5-1 TAKAHASHI
TIME TO ROLY-POLY!
BZZZ— OH YEAH! ROLY-POLIES DON'T FLY!
KANADE-KUN... LET'S GO TOGETH—
STILL NOT TELLING!
BA (BAM)
UH...WHAT? I HAVEN'T SAID ANYTHING YET...

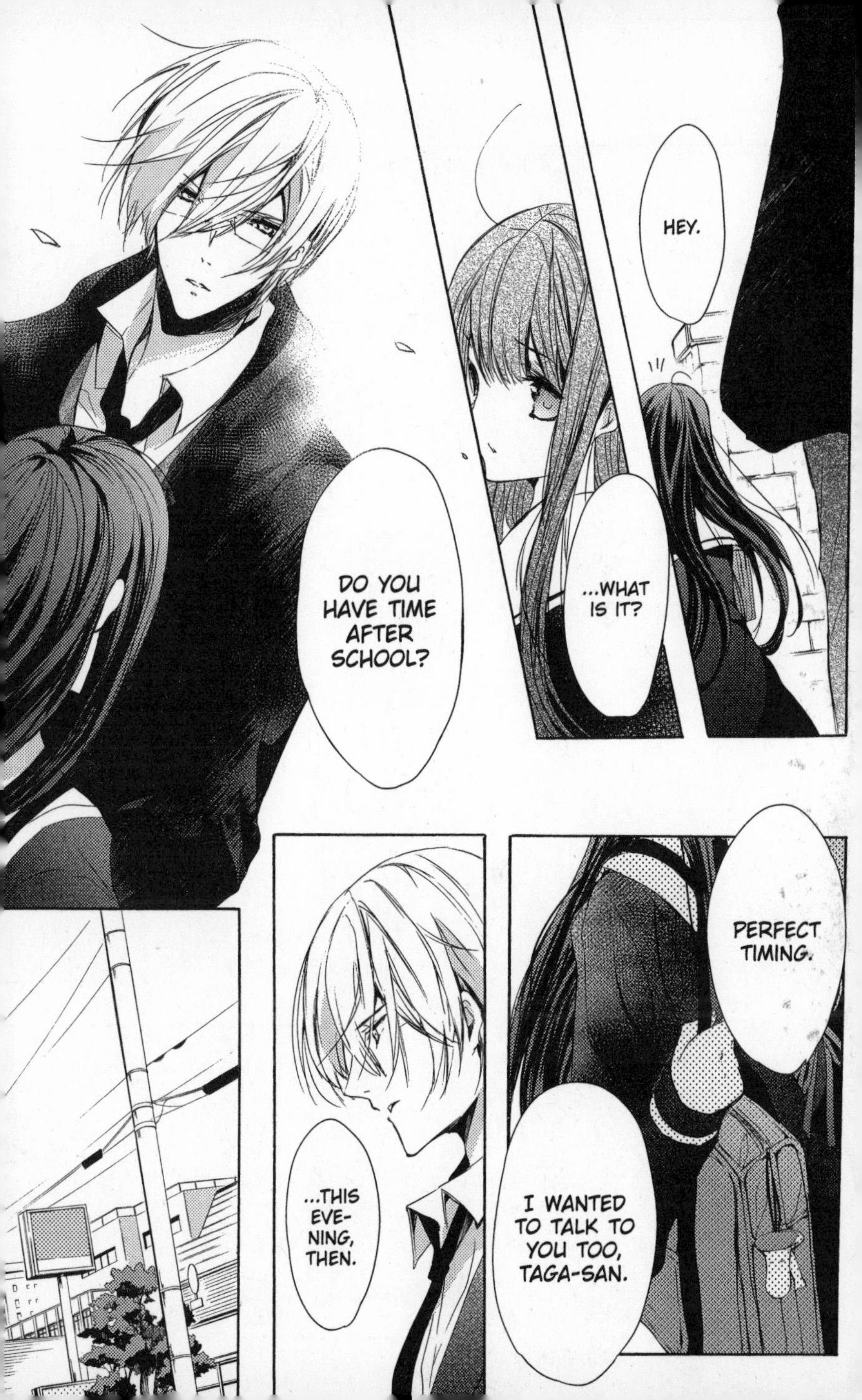
HEY.
...WHAT IS IT?
DO YOU HAVE TIME AFTER SCHOOL?
PERFECT TIMING.
I WANTED TO TALK TO YOU TOO, TAGA-SAN.
...THIS EVE-NING, THEN.

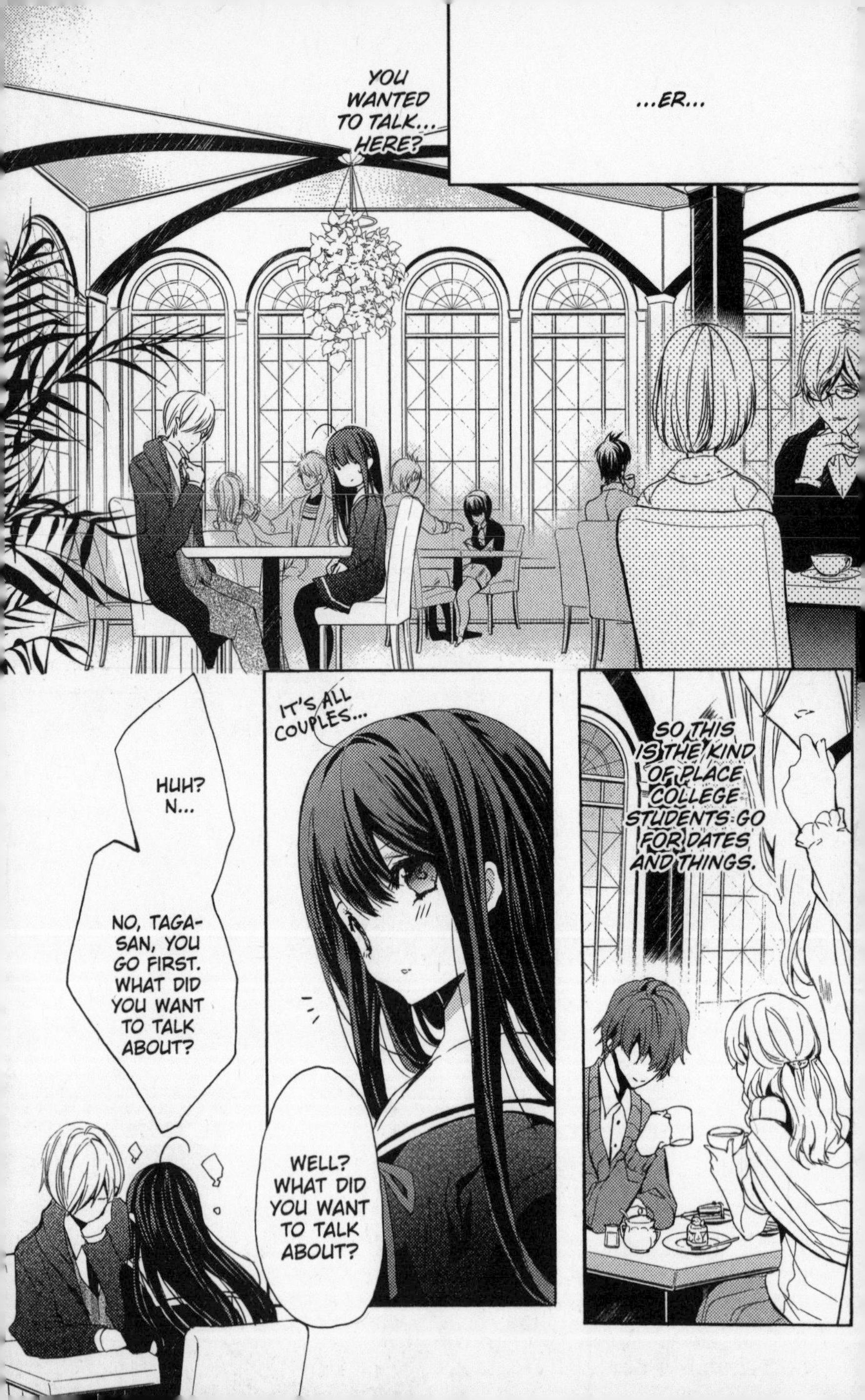
...ER...
YOU WANTED TO TALK... HERE?
SO THIS IS THE KIND OF PLACE COLLEGE STUDENTS GO FOR DATES AND THINGS.
IT'S ALL COUPLES...
WELL? WHAT DID YOU WANT TO TALK ABOUT?
HUH? N...
NO, TAGA-SAN, YOU GO FIRST. WHAT DID YOU WANT TO TALK ABOUT?

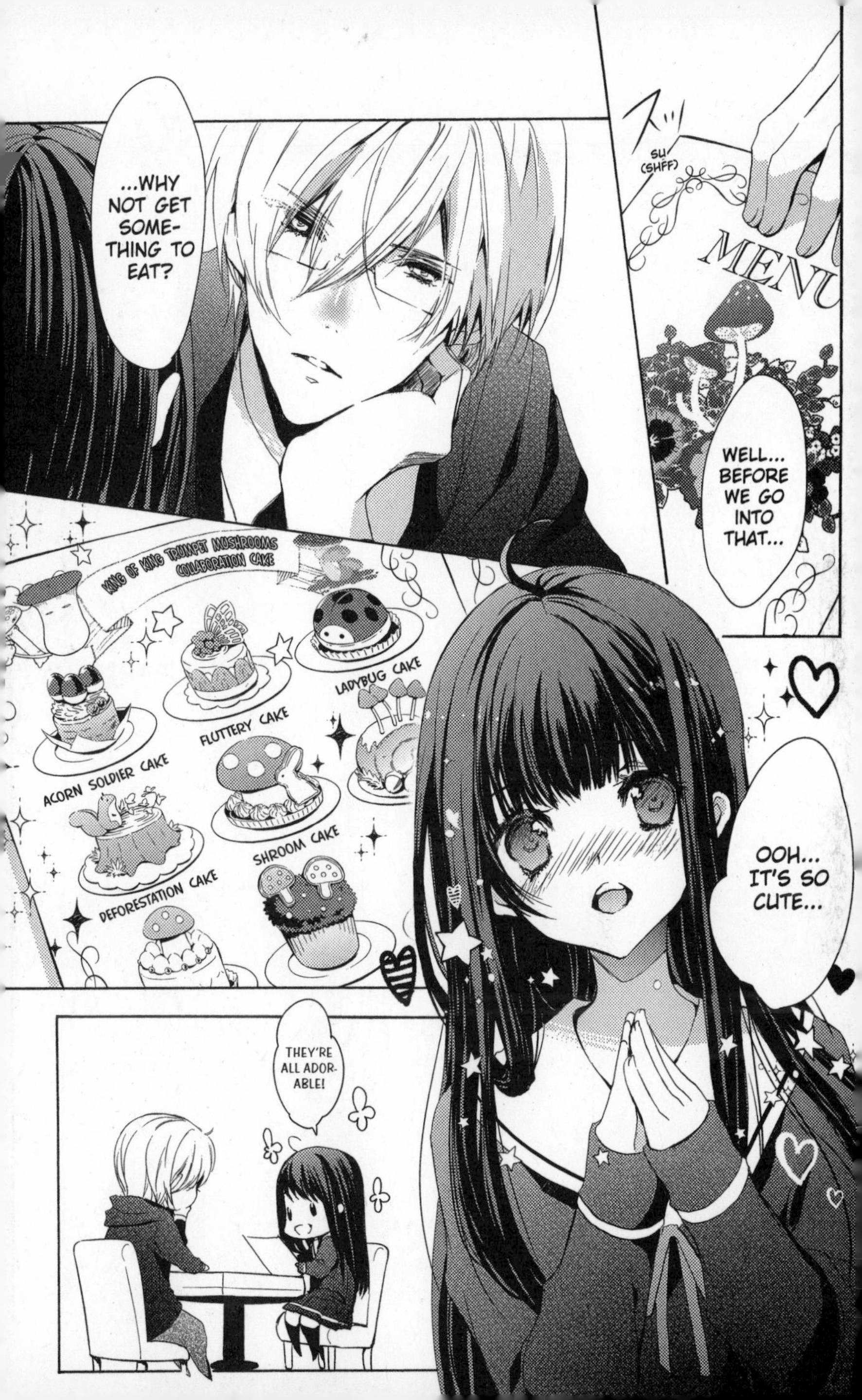
ズッ
SU (SHFF)
MENU
WELL... BEFORE WE GO INTO THAT...
...WHY NOT GET SOME-THING TO EAT?
OOH... IT'S SO CUTE...
KING OF KING TRUMPET MUSHROOMS COLLABORATION CAKE
LADYBUG CAKE
FLUTTERY CAKE
ACORN SOLDIER CAKE
SHROOM CAKE
DEFORESTATION CAKE
THEY'RE ALL ADOR-ABLE!

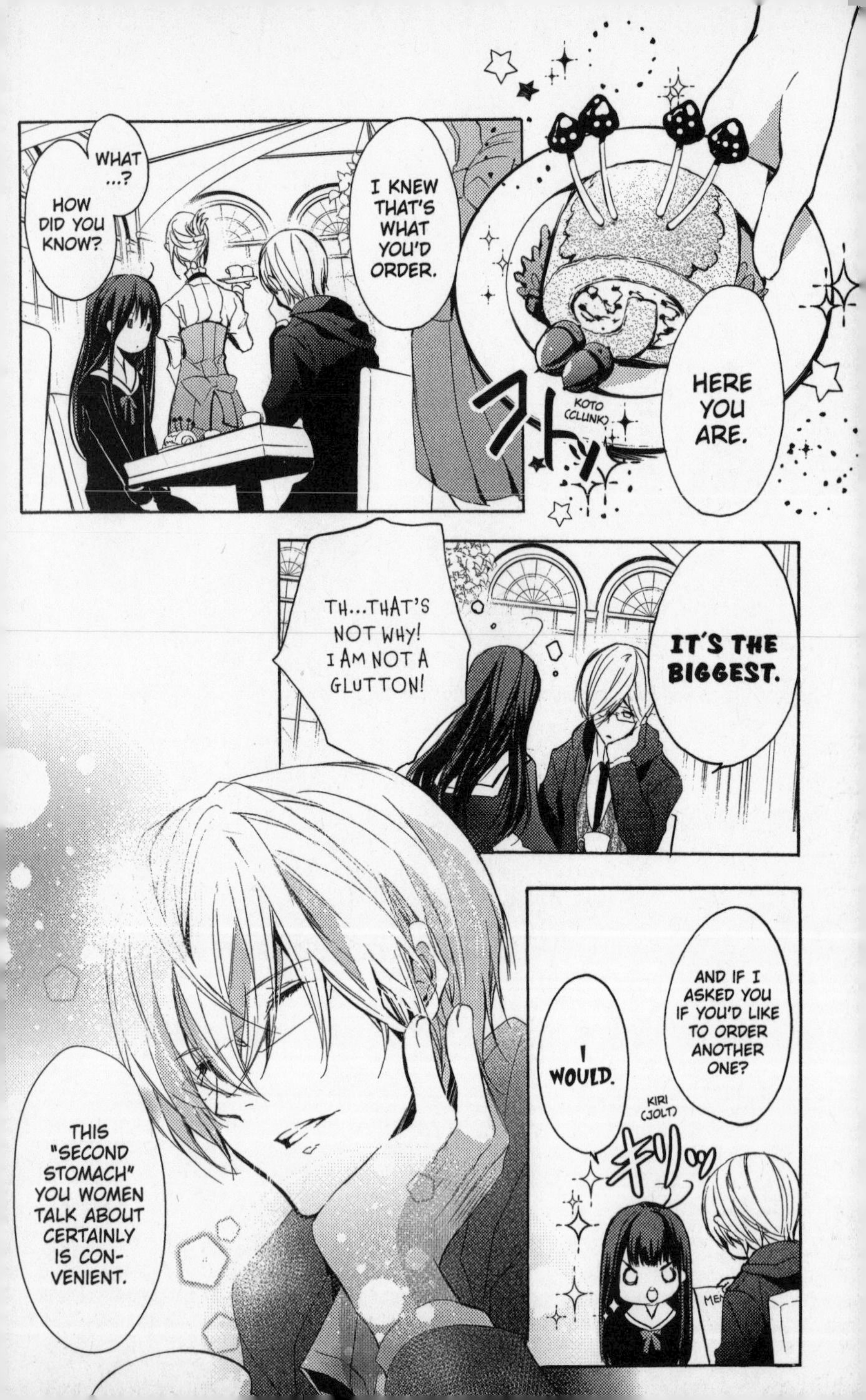
HERE YOU ARE.
KOTO (CLUNK)
I KNEW THAT'S WHAT YOU'D ORDER.
WHAT ...? HOW DID YOU KNOW?
IT'S THE BIGGEST.
TH...THAT'S NOT WHY! I AM NOT A GLUTTON!
AND IF I ASKED YOU IF YOU'D LIKE TO ORDER ANOTHER ONE?
I WOULD.
KIRI (JOLT)
THIS "SECOND STOMACH" YOU WOMEN TALK ABOUT CERTAINLY IS CON-VENIENT.

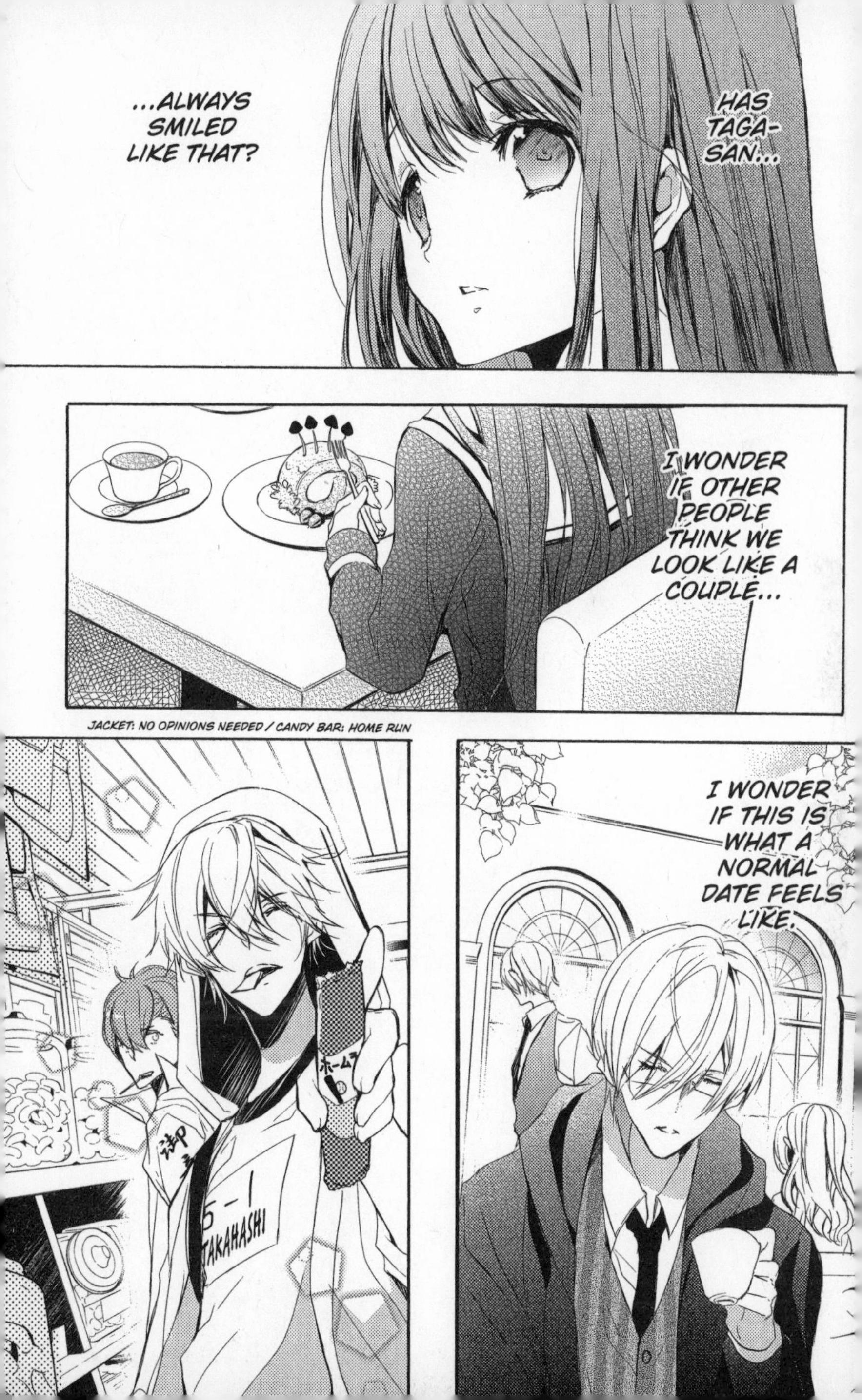
HAS TAGA-SAN...
...ALWAYS SMILED LIKE THAT?
I WONDER IF OTHER PEOPLE THINK WE LOOK LIKE A COUPLE...
JACKET: NO OPINIONS NEEDED / CANDY BAR: HOME RUN
I WONDER IF THIS IS WHAT A NORMAL DATE FEELS LIKE.
5-1
TAKAHASHI

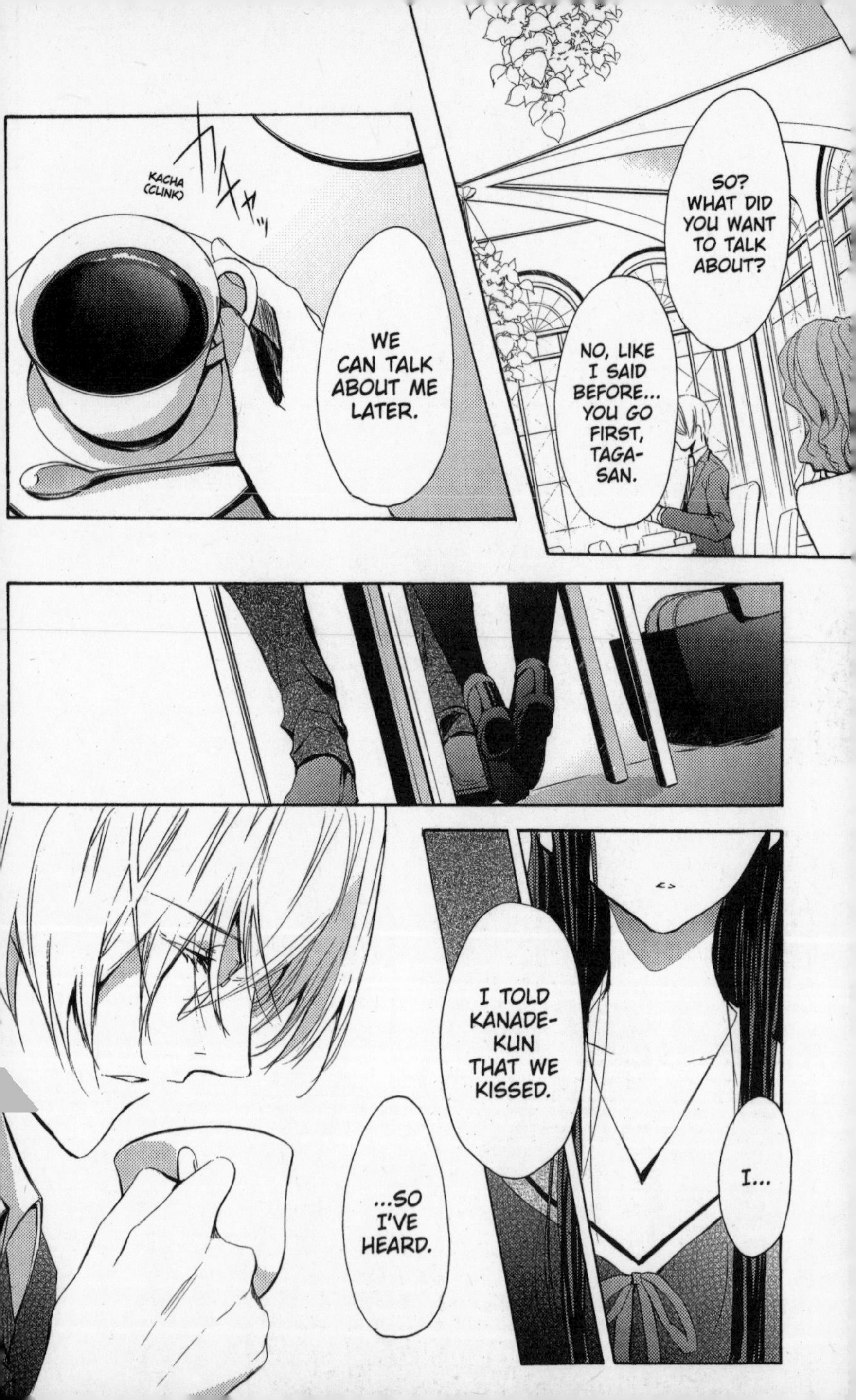
SO? WHAT DID YOU WANT TO TALK ABOUT?
NO, LIKE I SAID BEFORE... YOU GO FIRST, TAGA-SAN.
KACHA (CLINK)
WE CAN TALK ABOUT ME LATER.
I...
I TOLD KANADE-KUN THAT WE KISSED.
...SO I'VE HEARD.

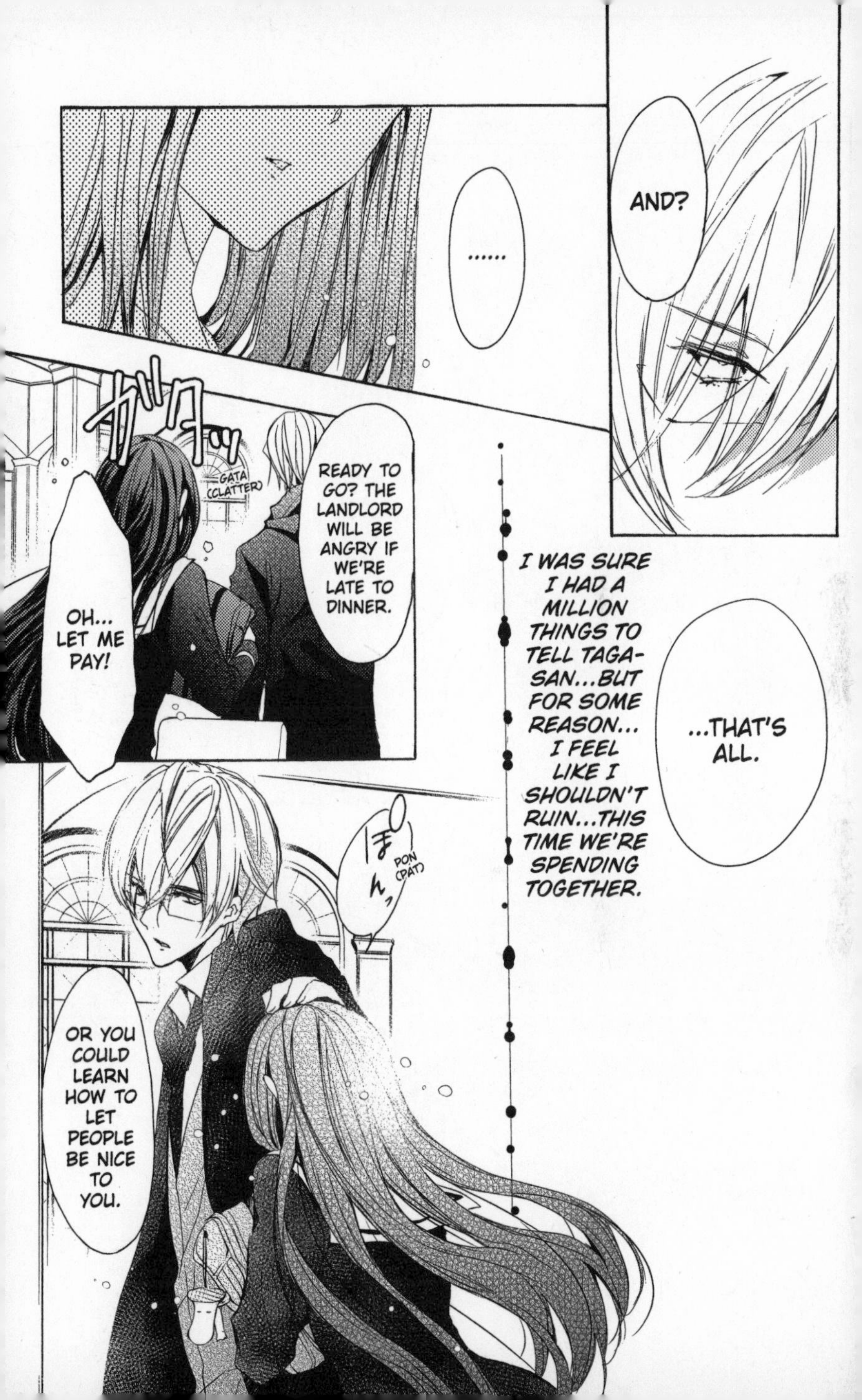
AND?
......
...THAT'S ALL.
I WAS SURE I HAD A MILLION THINGS TO TELL TAGA-SAN...BUT FOR SOME REASON... I FEEL LIKE I SHOULDN'T RUIN...THIS TIME WE'RE SPENDING TOGETHER.
READY TO GO? THE LANDLORD WILL BE ANGRY IF WE'RE LATE TO DINNER.
GATA (CLATTER)
OH... LET ME PAY!
PON (PAT)
OR YOU COULD LEARN HOW TO LET PEOPLE BE NICE TO YOU.

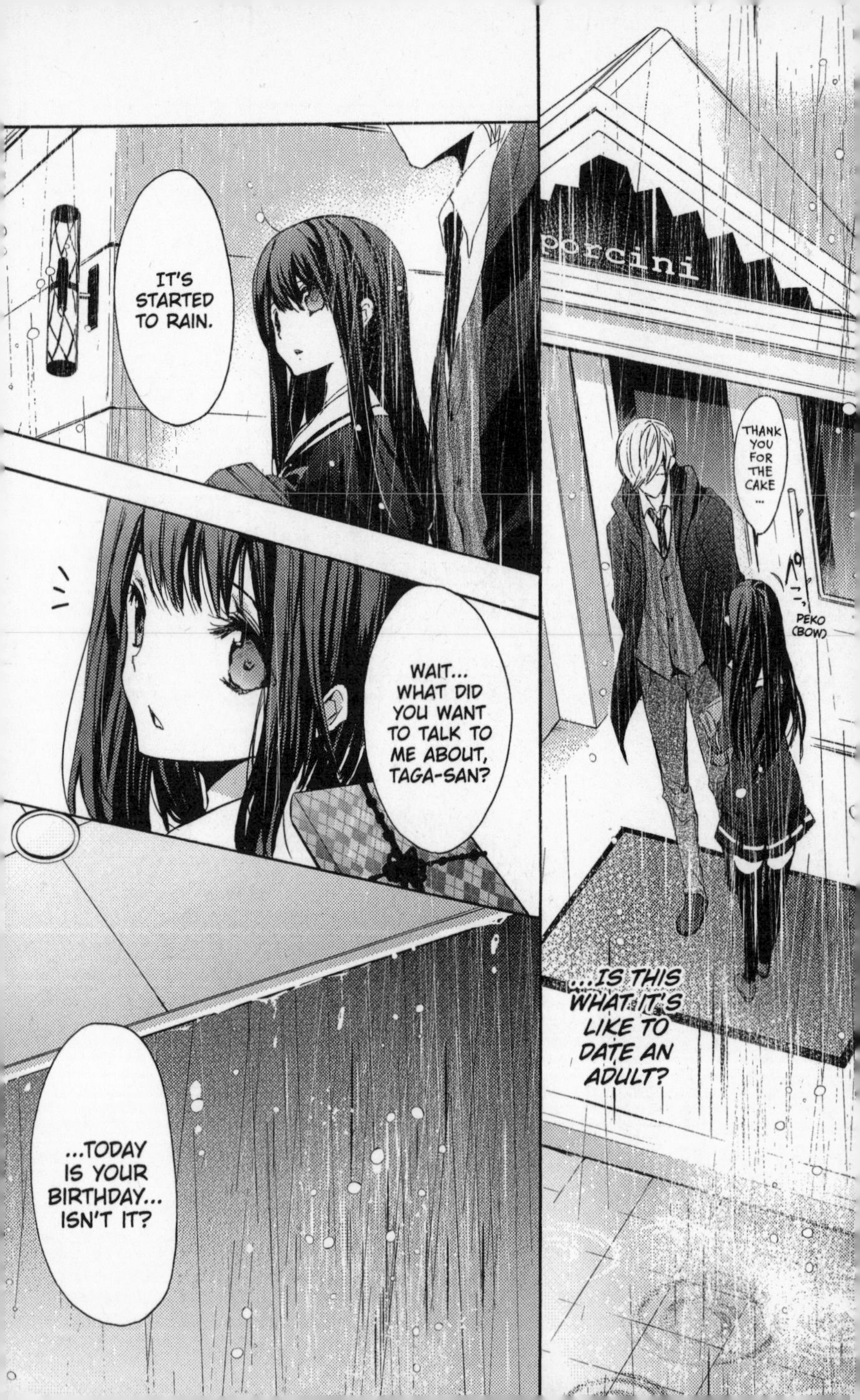
porcini
THANK YOU FOR THE CAKE ...
PEKO (BOW)
...IS THIS WHAT IT'S LIKE TO DATE AN ADULT?
IT'S STARTED TO RAIN.
WAIT... WHAT DID YOU WANT TO TALK TO ME ABOUT, TAGA-SAN?
...TODAY IS YOUR BIRTHDAY... ISN'T IT?

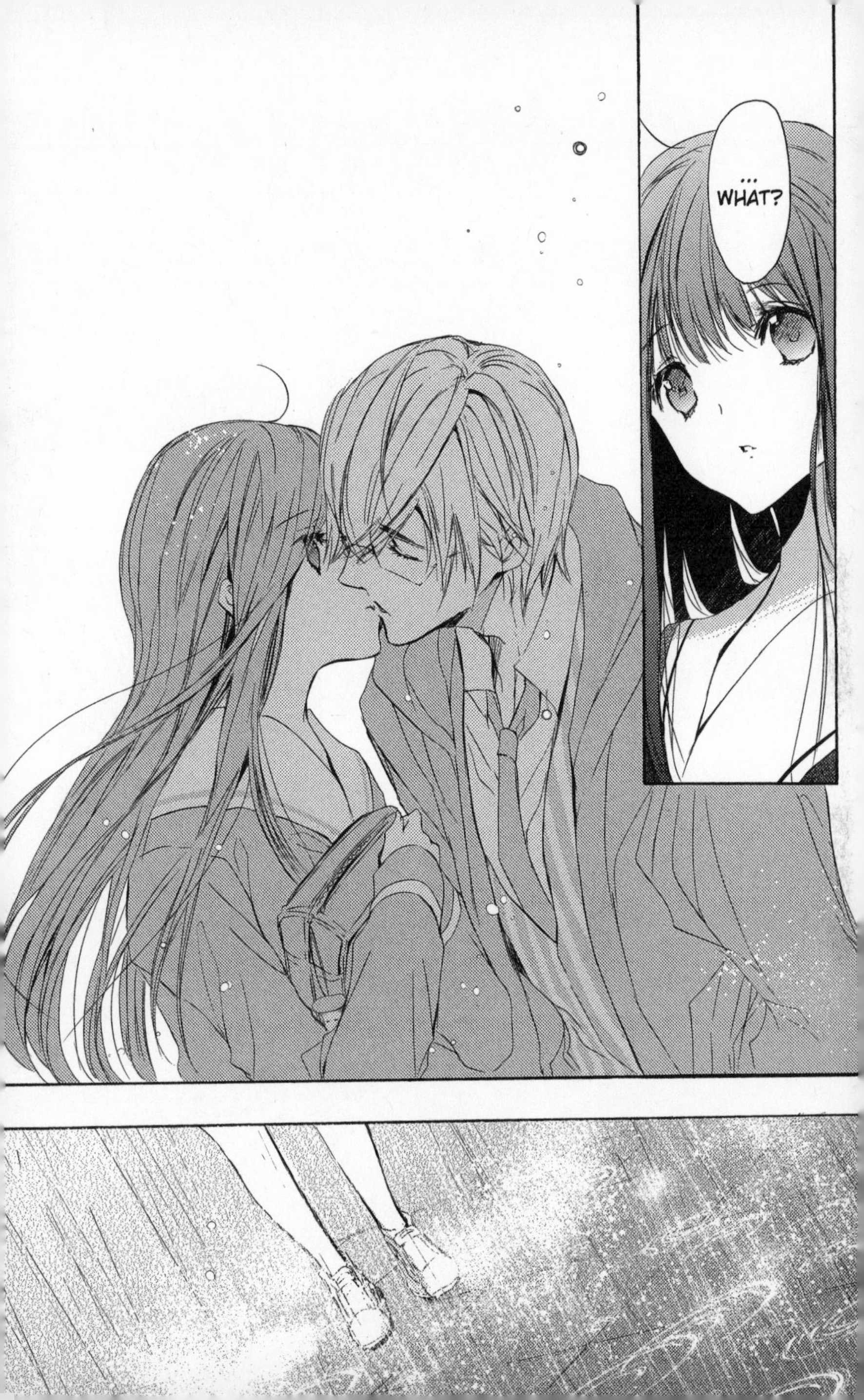
... WHAT?

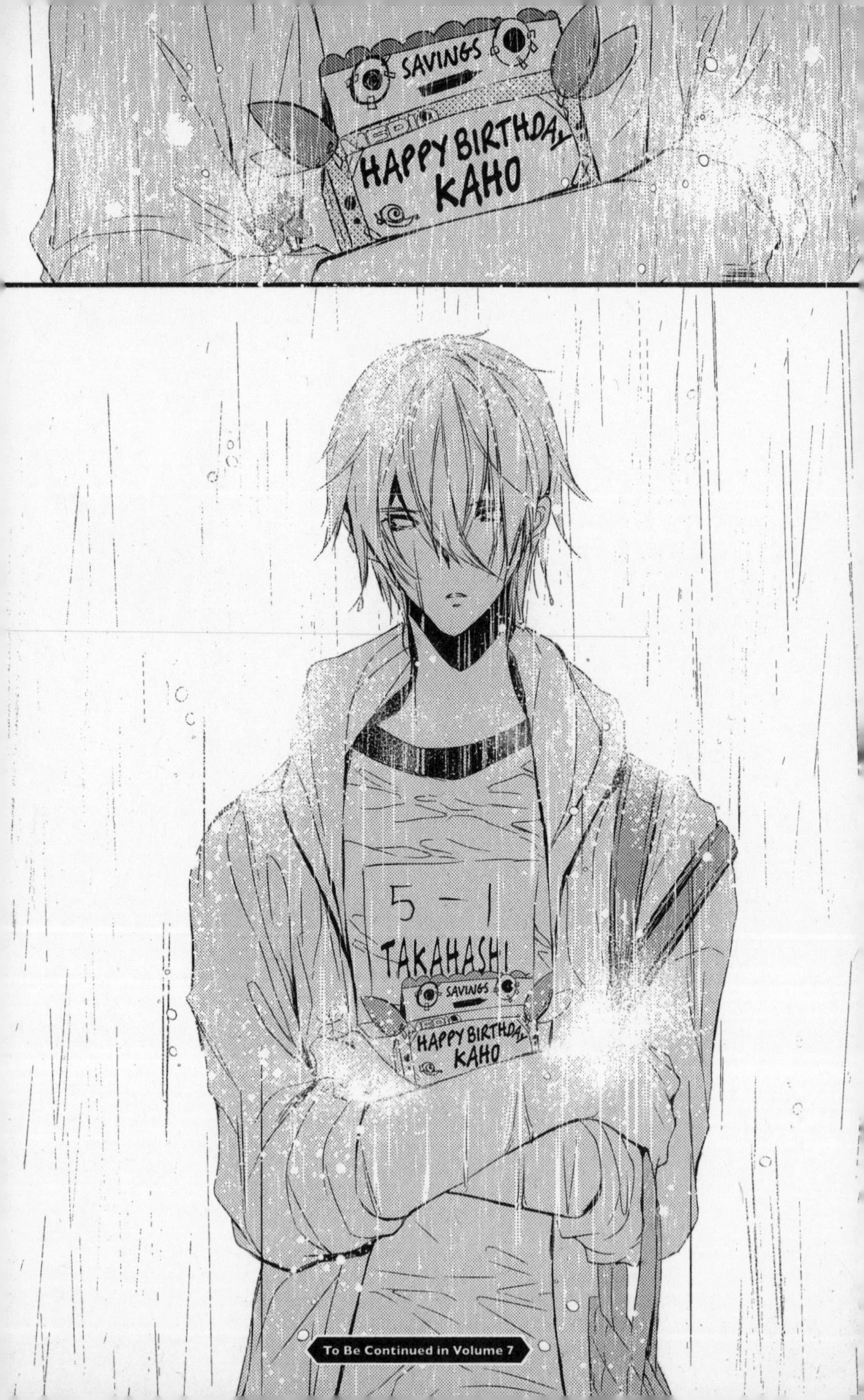
SAVINGS
HAPPY BIRTHDAY KAHO
5-1
TAKAHASHI
SAVINGS
HAPPY BIRTHDAY KAHO
To Be Continued in Volume 7

first love monster

first love monster

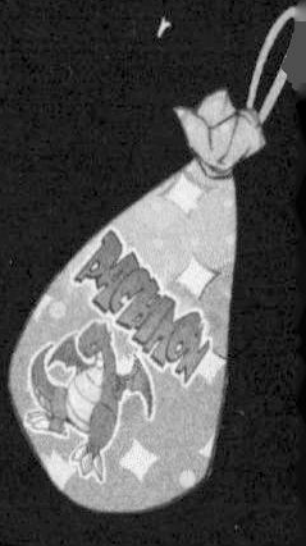

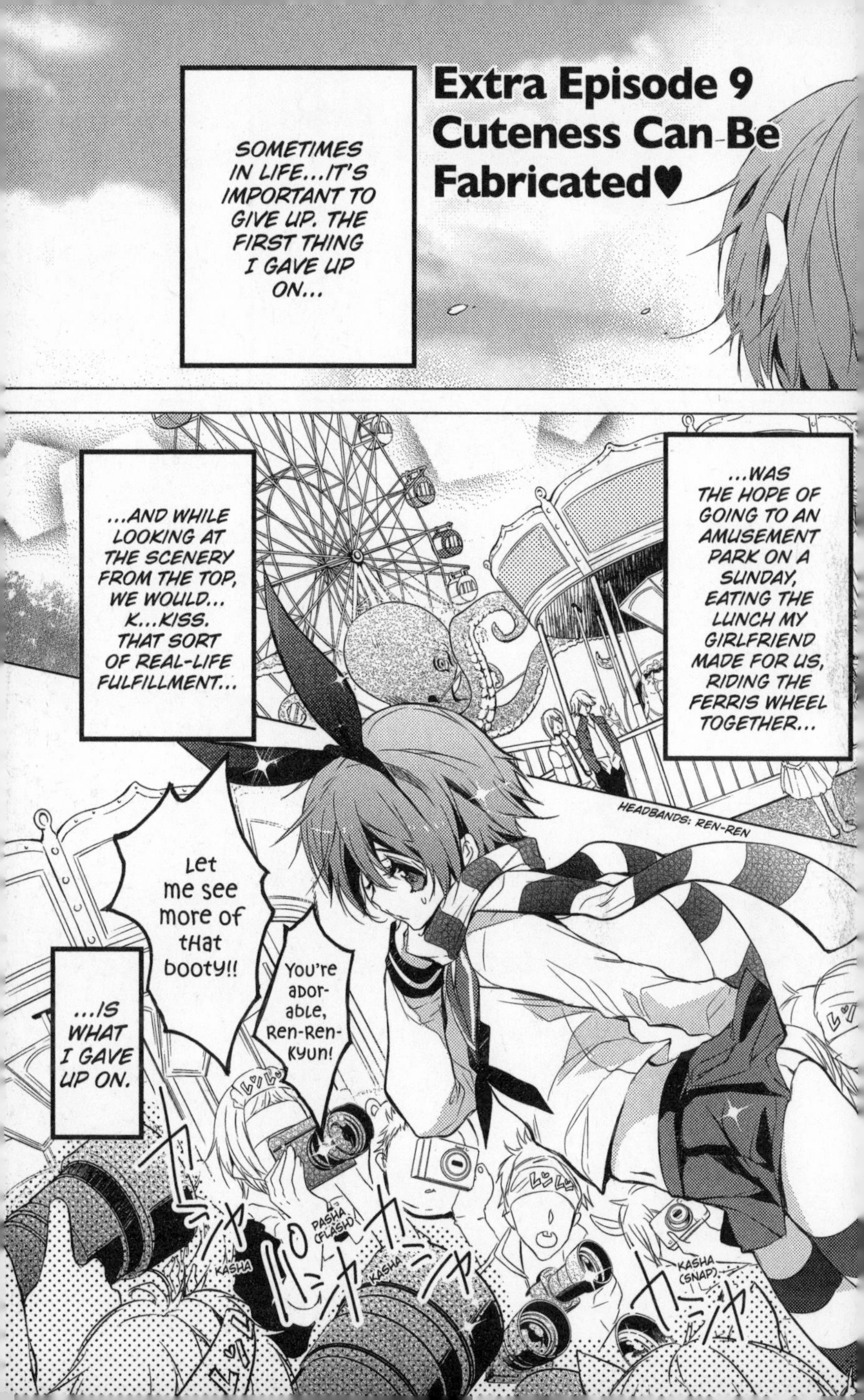
Extra Episode 9
Cuteness Can Be Fabricated♥
SOMETIMES IN LIFE...IT'S IMPORTANT TO GIVE UP. THE FIRST THING I GAVE UP ON...
...WAS THE HOPE OF GOING TO AN AMUSEMENT PARK ON A SUNDAY, EATING THE LUNCH MY GIRLFRIEND MADE FOR US, RIDING THE FERRIS WHEEL TOGETHER...
...AND WHILE LOOKING AT THE SCENERY FROM THE TOP, WE WOULD... K...KISS. THAT SORT OF REAL-LIFE FULFILLMENT...
HEADBANDS: REN-REN
Let me see more of that booty!!
You're adorable, Ren-Ren-kyun!
...IS WHAT I GAVE UP ON.
PASHA (FLASH)
KASHA (SNAP)
KASHA
KASHA

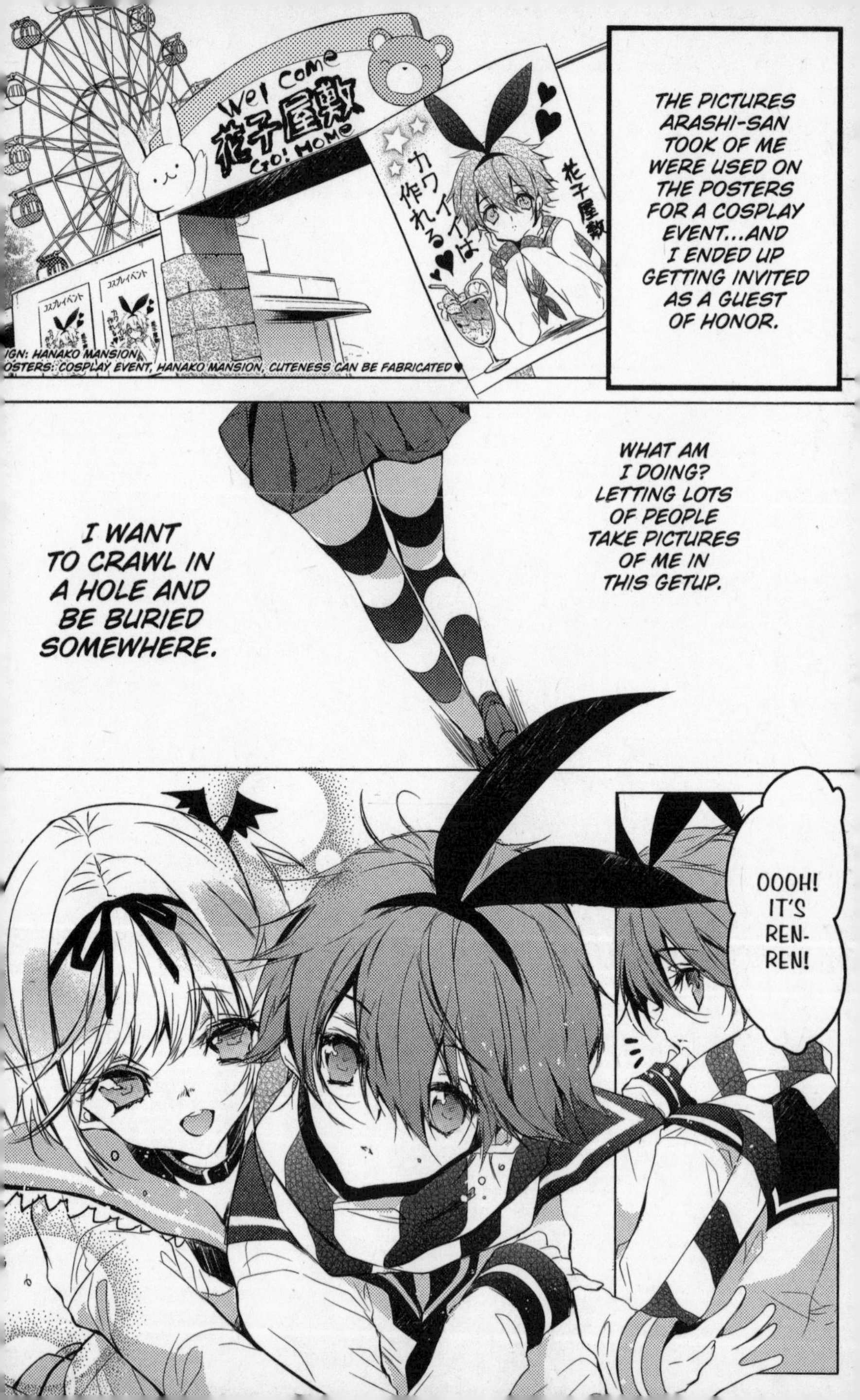
THE PICTURES ARASHI-SAN TOOK OF ME WERE USED ON THE POSTERS FOR A COSPLAY EVENT...AND I ENDED UP GETTING INVITED AS A GUEST OF HONOR.
花子屋敷
カワイイは作れる♥
Wel come
花子屋敷
GO! HOME
コスプレイベント
コスプレイベント
IGN: HANAKO MANSION
OSTERS: COSPLAY EVENT, HANAKO MANSION, CUTENESS CAN BE FABRICATED♥
WHAT AM I DOING? LETTING LOTS OF PEOPLE TAKE PICTURES OF ME IN THIS GETUP.
I WANT TO CRAWL IN A HOLE AND BE BURIED SOMEWHERE.
OOOH! IT'S REN-REN!

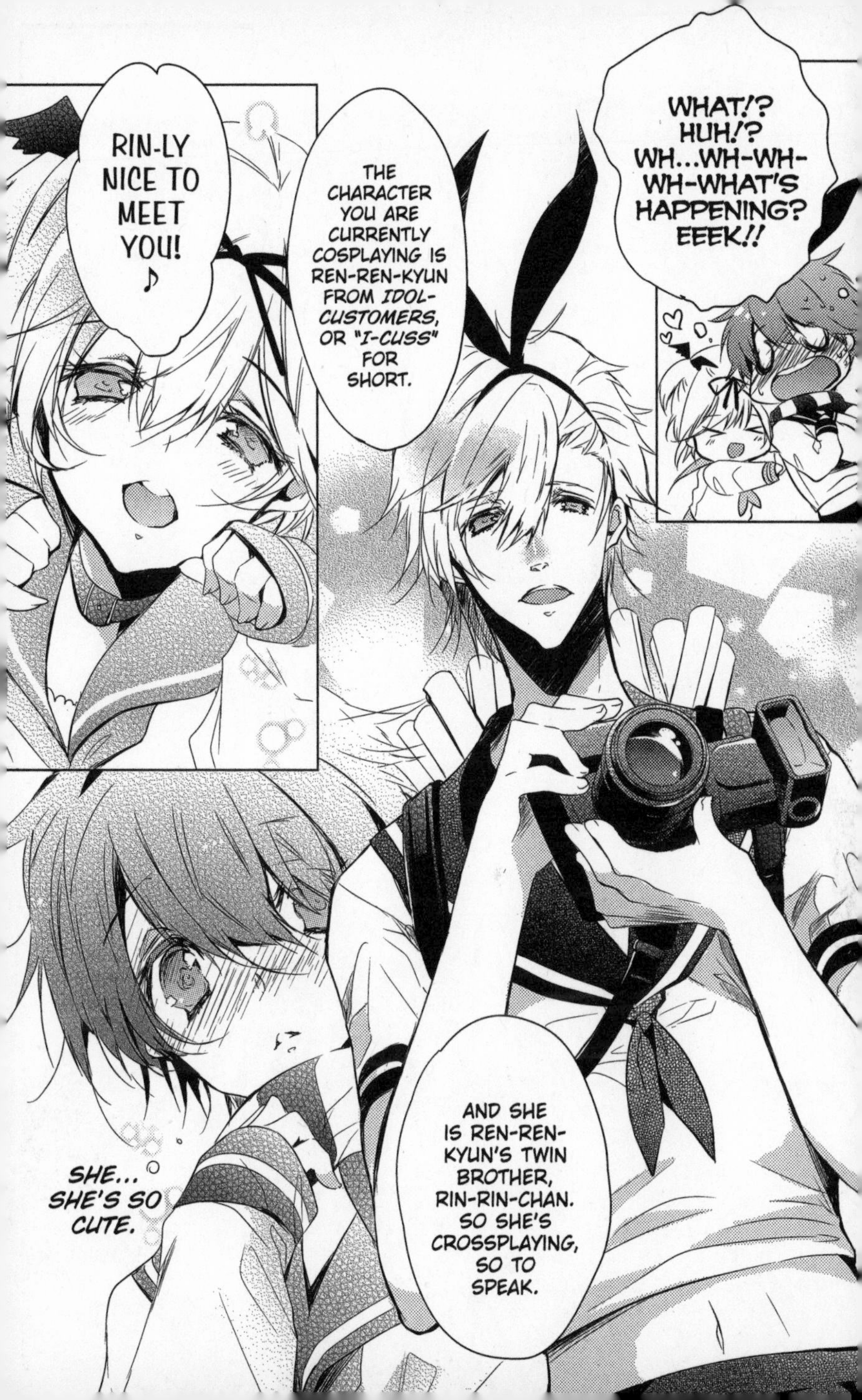
WHAT!? HUH!? WH...WH-WH-WH-WHAT'S HAPPENING? EEEK!!
THE CHARACTER YOU ARE CURRENTLY COSPLAYING IS REN-REN-KYUN FROM *IDOL-CUSTOMERS*, OR "*I-CUSS*" FOR SHORT.
RIN-LY NICE TO MEET YOU! ♪
AND SHE IS REN-REN-KYUN'S TWIN BROTHER, RIN-RIN-CHAN. SO SHE'S CROSSPLAYING, SO TO SPEAK.
SHE... SHE'S SO CUTE.

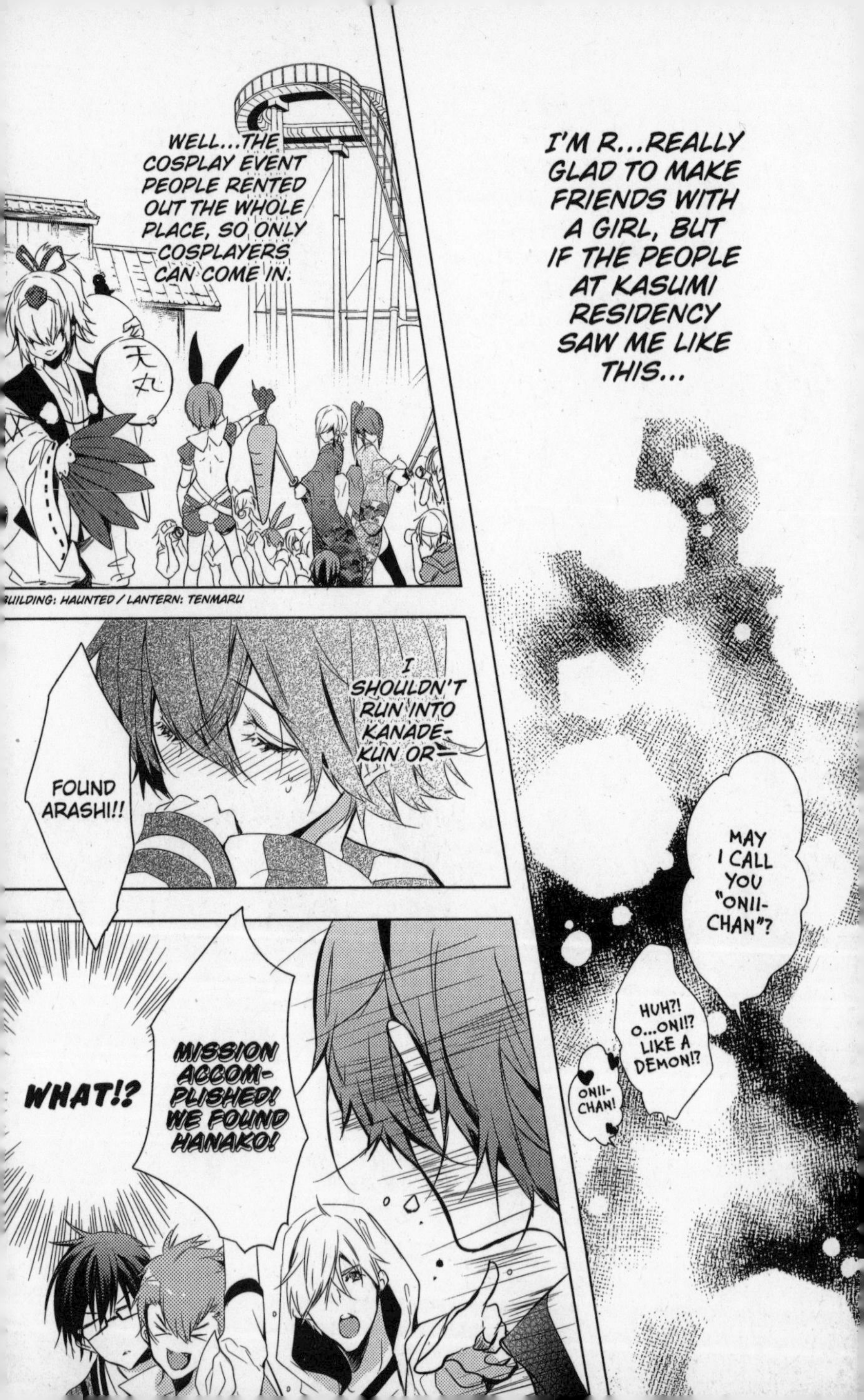
I'M R...REALLY GLAD TO MAKE FRIENDS WITH A GIRL, BUT IF THE PEOPLE AT KASUMI RESIDENCY SAW ME LIKE THIS...
MAY I CALL YOU "ONII-CHAN"?
HUH?! O...ONI!? LIKE A DEMON!?
ONII-CHAN!
WELL...THE COSPLAY EVENT PEOPLE RENTED OUT THE WHOLE PLACE, SO ONLY COSPLAYERS CAN COME IN.
天丸
BUILDING: HAUNTED / LANTERN: TENMARU
I SHOULDN'T RUN INTO KANADE-KUN OR—
FOUND ARASHI!!
MISSION ACCOMPLISHED! WE FOUND HANAKO!
WHAT!?

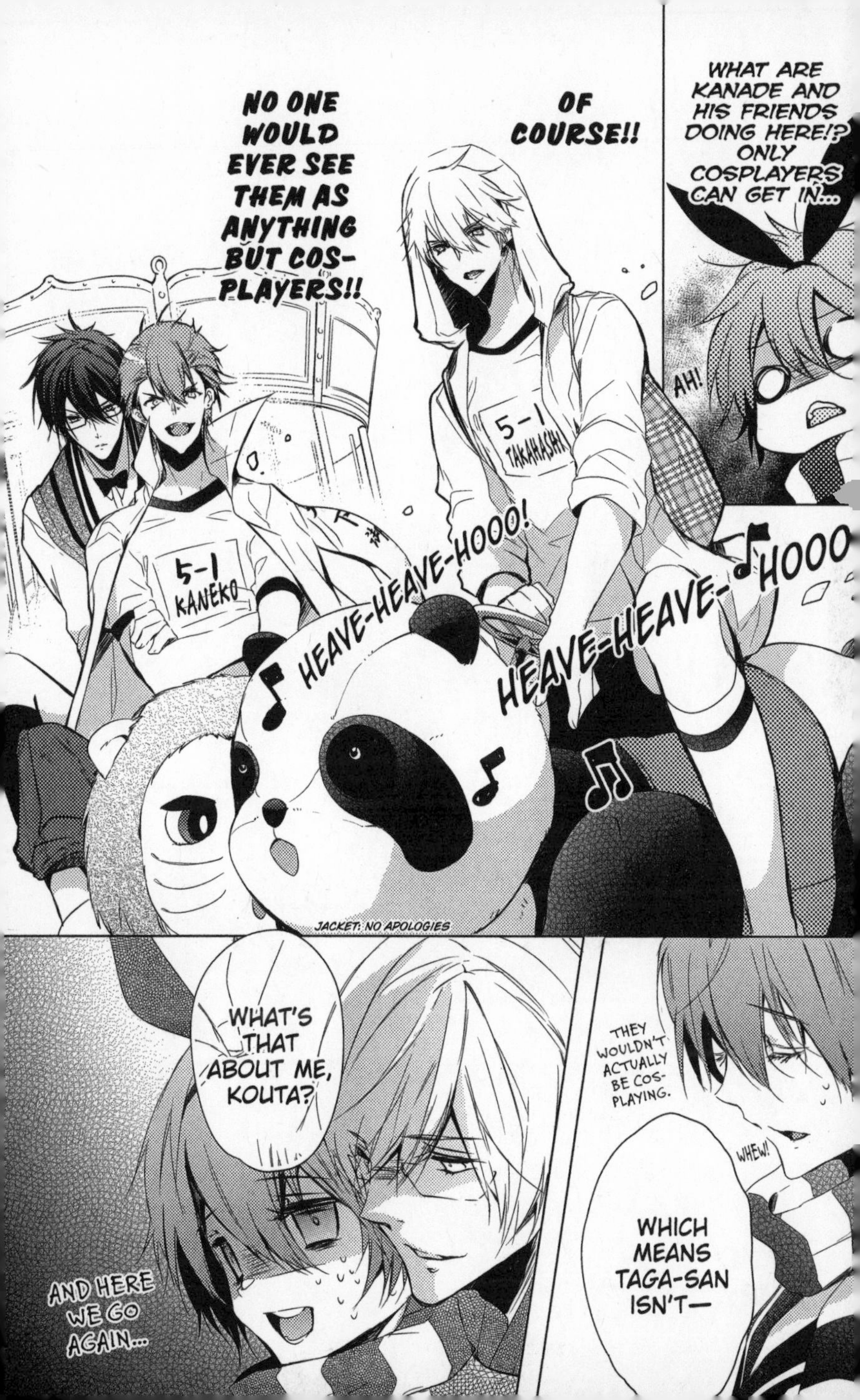
WHAT ARE KANADE AND HIS FRIENDS DOING HERE!? ONLY COSPLAYERS CAN GET IN...
AH!
OF COURSE!!
NO ONE WOULD EVER SEE THEM AS ANYTHING BUT COS-PLAYERS!!
5-1 TAKAHASHI
5-1 KANEKO
HEAVE-HEAVE-♪HOOO
♪HEAVE-HEAVE-HEAVE-HOOO!
JACKET: NO APOLOGIES
THEY WOULDN'T ACTUALLY BE COS-PLAYING.
WHEW!
WHICH MEANS TAGA-SAN ISN'T—
WHAT'S THAT ABOUT ME, KOUTA?
AND HERE WE GO AGAIN...

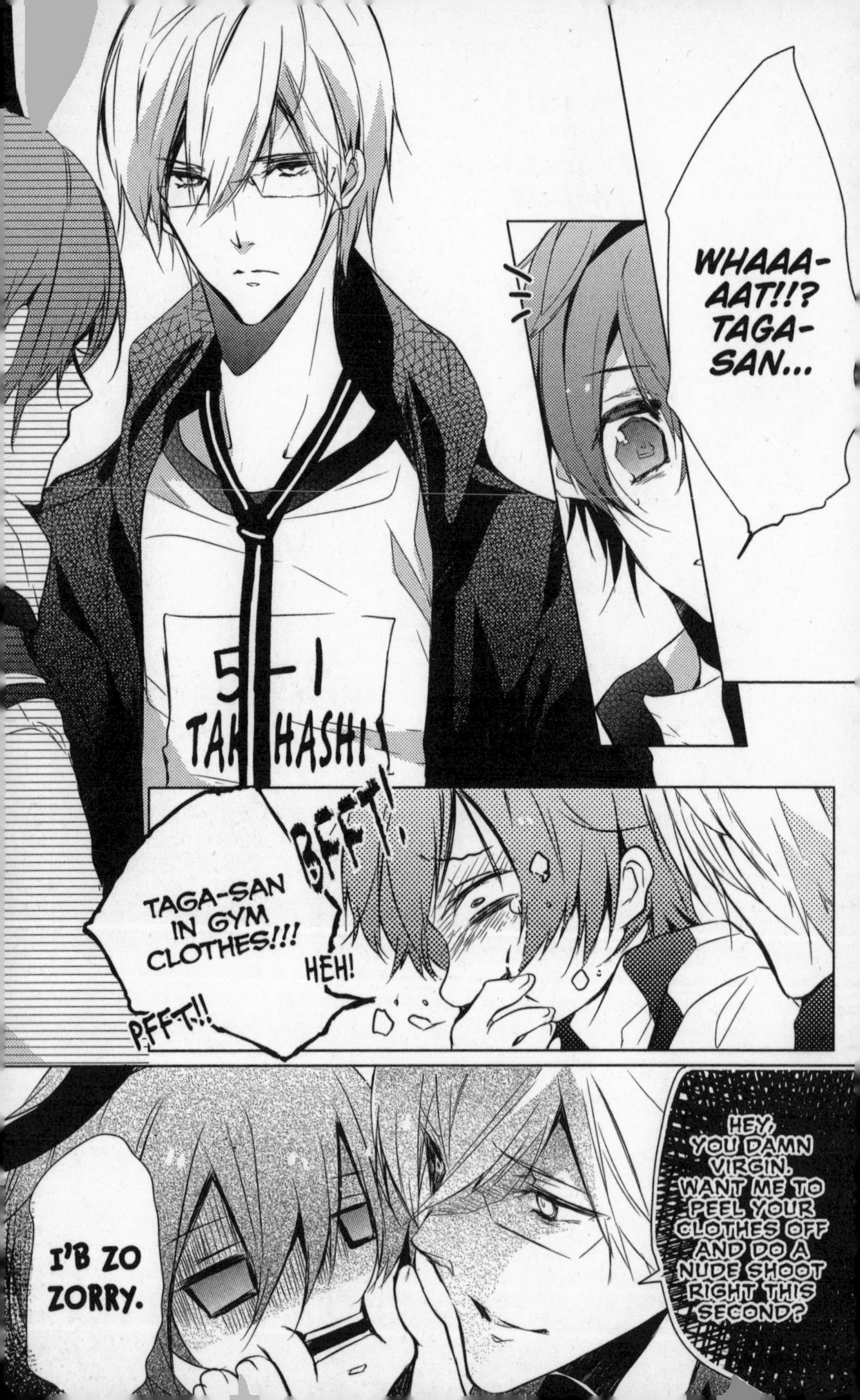
WHAAAA-AAT!!? TAGA-SAN...
5-1 TAKAHASHI
BFFT!
TAGA-SAN IN GYM CLOTHES!!!
HEH!
PFFT!!
HEY, YOU DAMN VIRGIN. WANT ME TO PEEL YOUR CLOTHES OFF AND DO A NUDE SHOOT RIGHT THIS SECOND?
I'B ZO ZORRY.

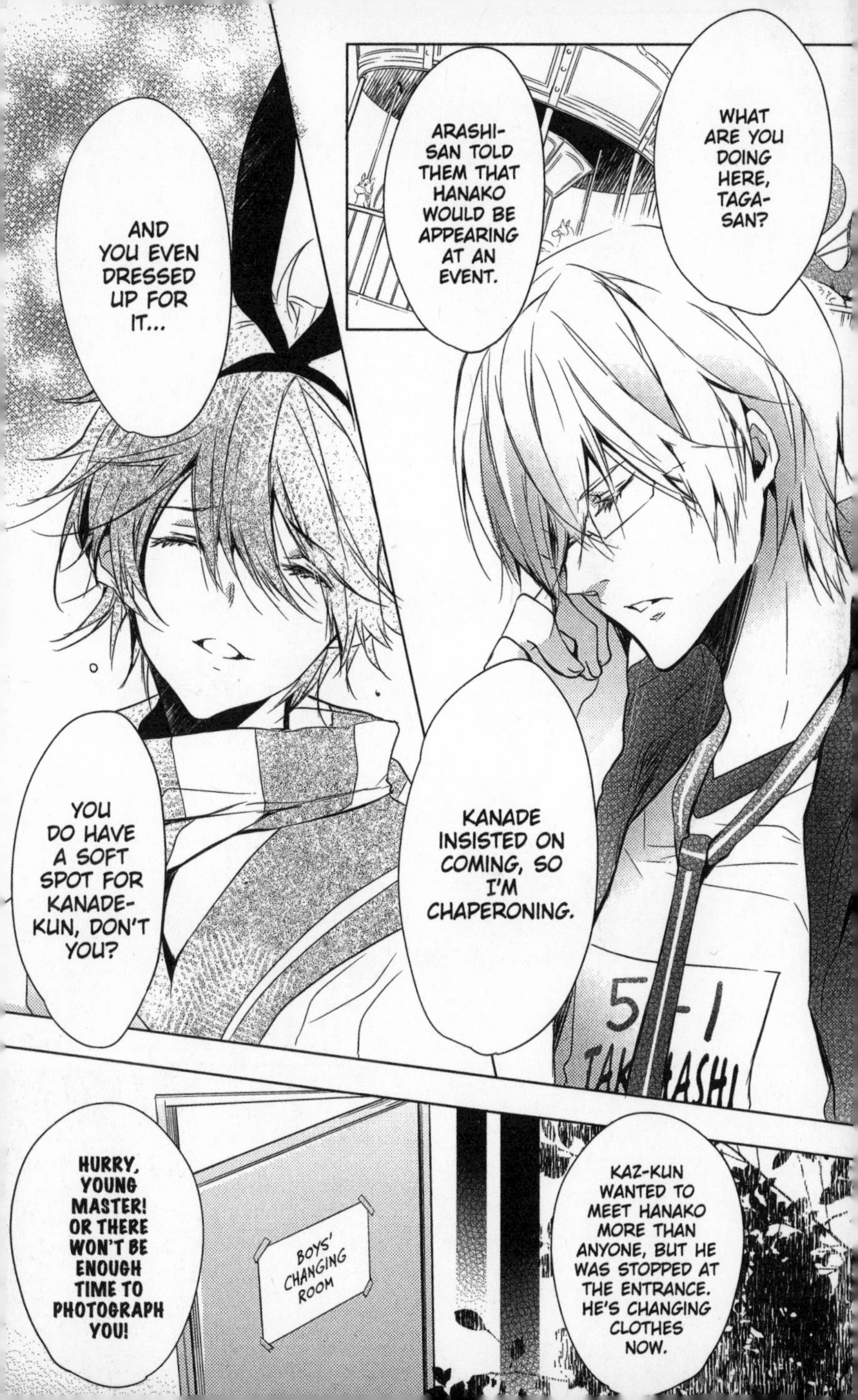
WHAT ARE YOU DOING HERE, TAGA-SAN?
ARASHI-SAN TOLD THEM THAT HANAKO WOULD BE APPEARING AT AN EVENT.
KANADE INSISTED ON COMING, SO I'M CHAPERONING.
AND YOU EVEN DRESSED UP FOR IT...
YOU DO HAVE A SOFT SPOT FOR KANADE-KUN, DON'T YOU?
KAZ-KUN WANTED TO MEET HANAKO MORE THAN ANYONE, BUT HE WAS STOPPED AT THE ENTRANCE. HE'S CHANGING CLOTHES NOW.
BOYS' CHANGING ROOM
HURRY, YOUNG MASTER! OR THERE WON'T BE ENOUGH TIME TO PHOTOGRAPH YOU!

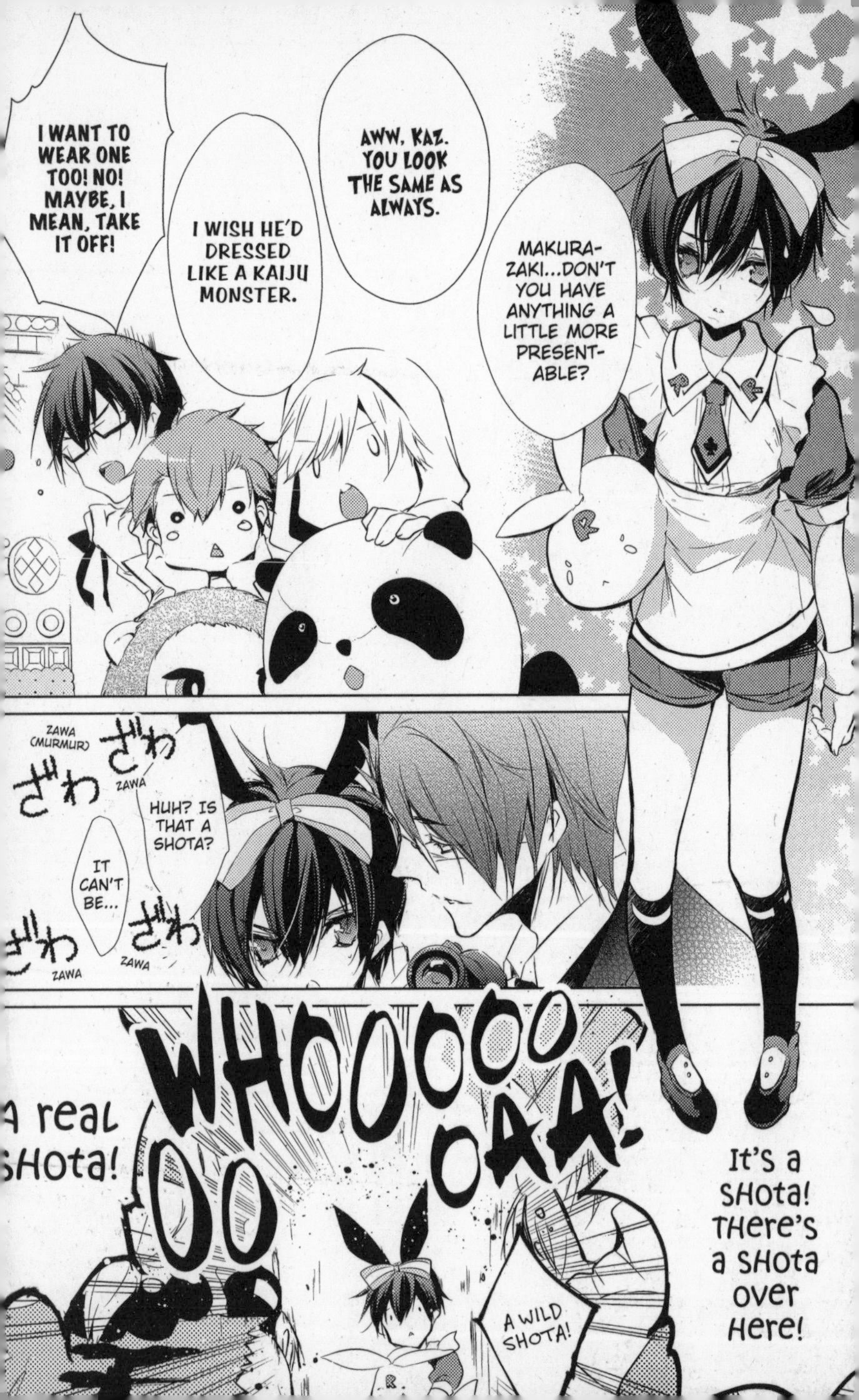
MAKURAZAKI...DON'T YOU HAVE ANYTHING A LITTLE MORE PRESENTABLE?
AWW, KAZ. YOU LOOK THE SAME AS ALWAYS.
I WISH HE'D DRESSED LIKE A KAIJU MONSTER.
I WANT TO WEAR ONE TOO! NO! MAYBE, I MEAN, TAKE IT OFF!
HUH? IS THAT A SHOTA?
ざわ ZAWA (MURMUR)
ざわ ZAWA
IT CAN'T BE...
ざわ ZAWA
ざわ ZAWA
WHOOOOOOOAA!
It's a shota! There's a shota over here!
A WILD SHOTA!
A real shota!

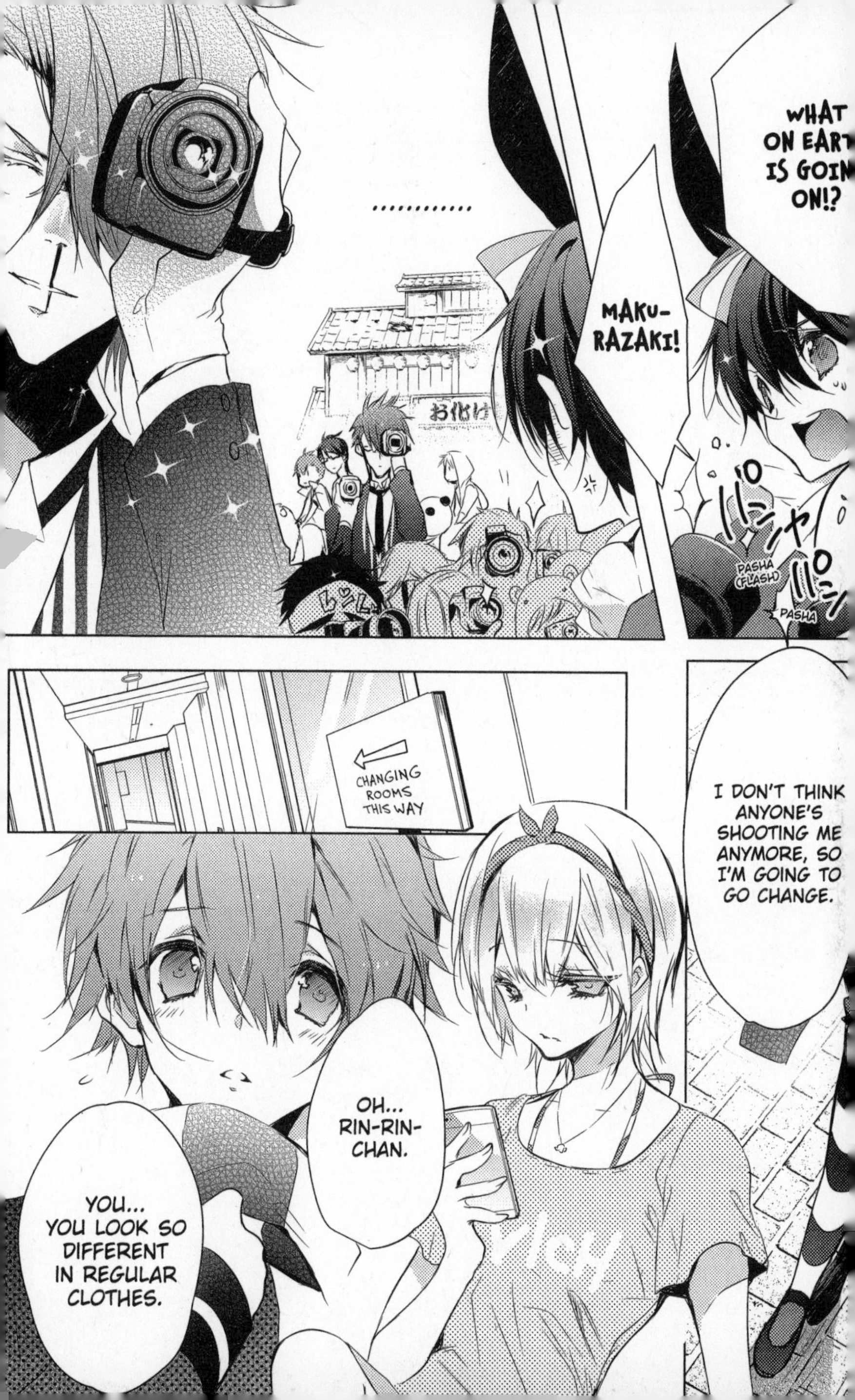

WHAT ON EART IS GOIN ON!?
MAKU-RAZAKI!
PASHA (FLASH)
PASHA
お化け
....
I DON'T THINK ANYONE'S SHOOTING ME ANYMORE, SO I'M GOING TO GO CHANGE.
CHANGING ROOMS THIS WAY
OH... RIN-RIN-CHAN.
YOU... YOU LOOK SO DIFFERENT IN REGULAR CLOTHES.

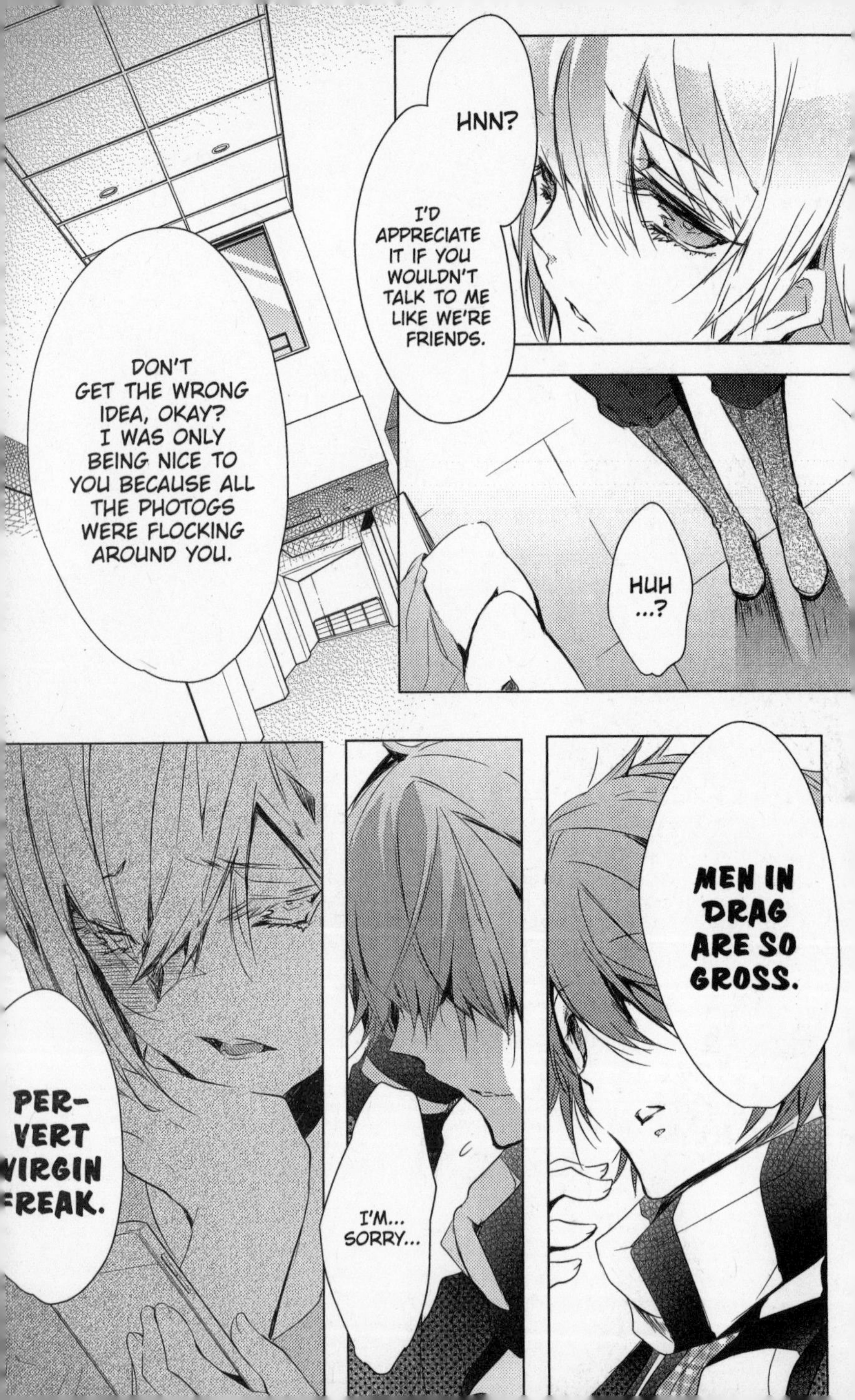
HNN?
I'D APPRECIATE IT IF YOU WOULDN'T TALK TO ME LIKE WE'RE FRIENDS.
HUH ...?
DON'T GET THE WRONG IDEA, OKAY? I WAS ONLY BEING NICE TO YOU BECAUSE ALL THE PHOTOGS WERE FLOCKING AROUND YOU.
MEN IN DRAG ARE SO GROSS.
I'M... SORRY...
PER-VERT VIRGIN FREAK.

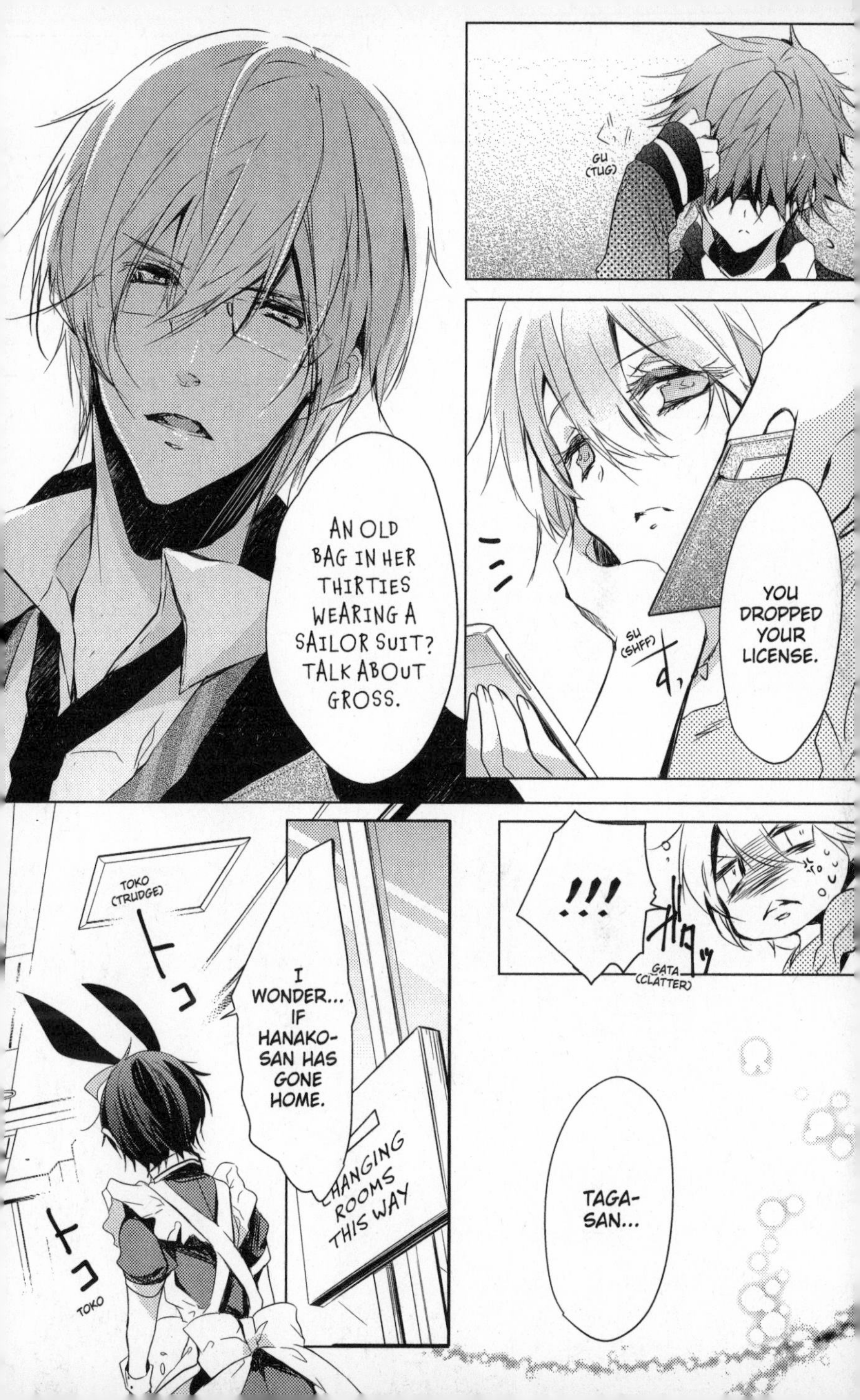
GU (TUG)
SU (SHFF)
YOU DROPPED YOUR LICENSE.
AN OLD BAG IN HER THIRTIES WEARING A SAILOR SUIT? TALK ABOUT GROSS.
!!!
GATA (CLATTER)
TAGA-SAN...
TOKO (TRUDGE)
I WONDER... IF HANAKO-SAN HAS GONE HOME.
CHANGING ROOMS THIS WAY
TOKO

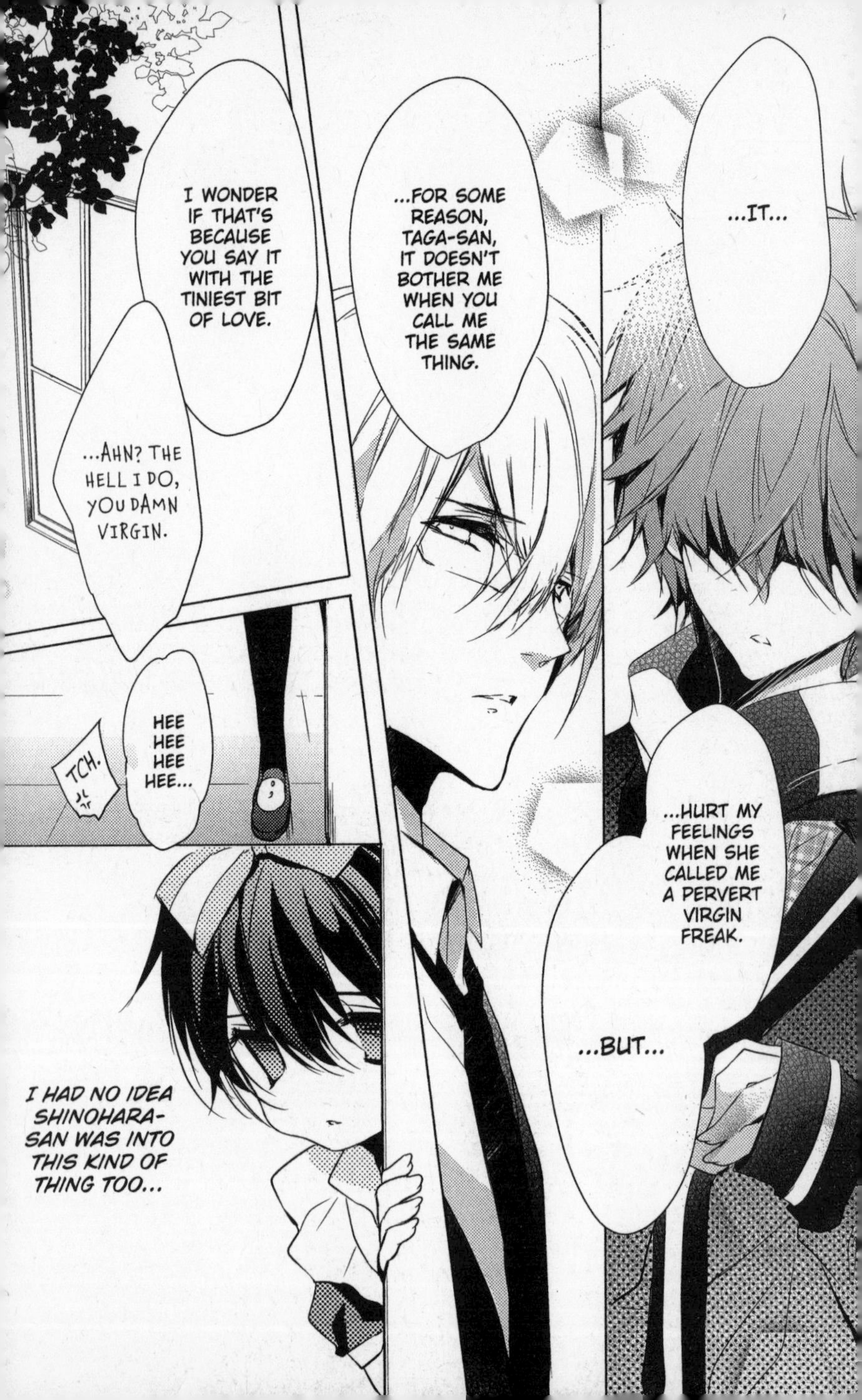
...IT...
...HURT MY FEELINGS WHEN SHE CALLED ME A PERVERT VIRGIN FREAK.
...BUT...
...FOR SOME REASON, TAGA-SAN, IT DOESN'T BOTHER ME WHEN YOU CALL ME THE SAME THING.
I WONDER IF THAT'S BECAUSE YOU SAY IT WITH THE TINIEST BIT OF LOVE.
...AHN? THE HELL I DO, YOU DAMN VIRGIN.
HEE HEE HEE HEE...
TCH.
I HAD NO IDEA SHINOHARA-SAN WAS INTO THIS KIND OF THING TOO...

Extra Episode 10
From the Land of Chiba ~First Love~

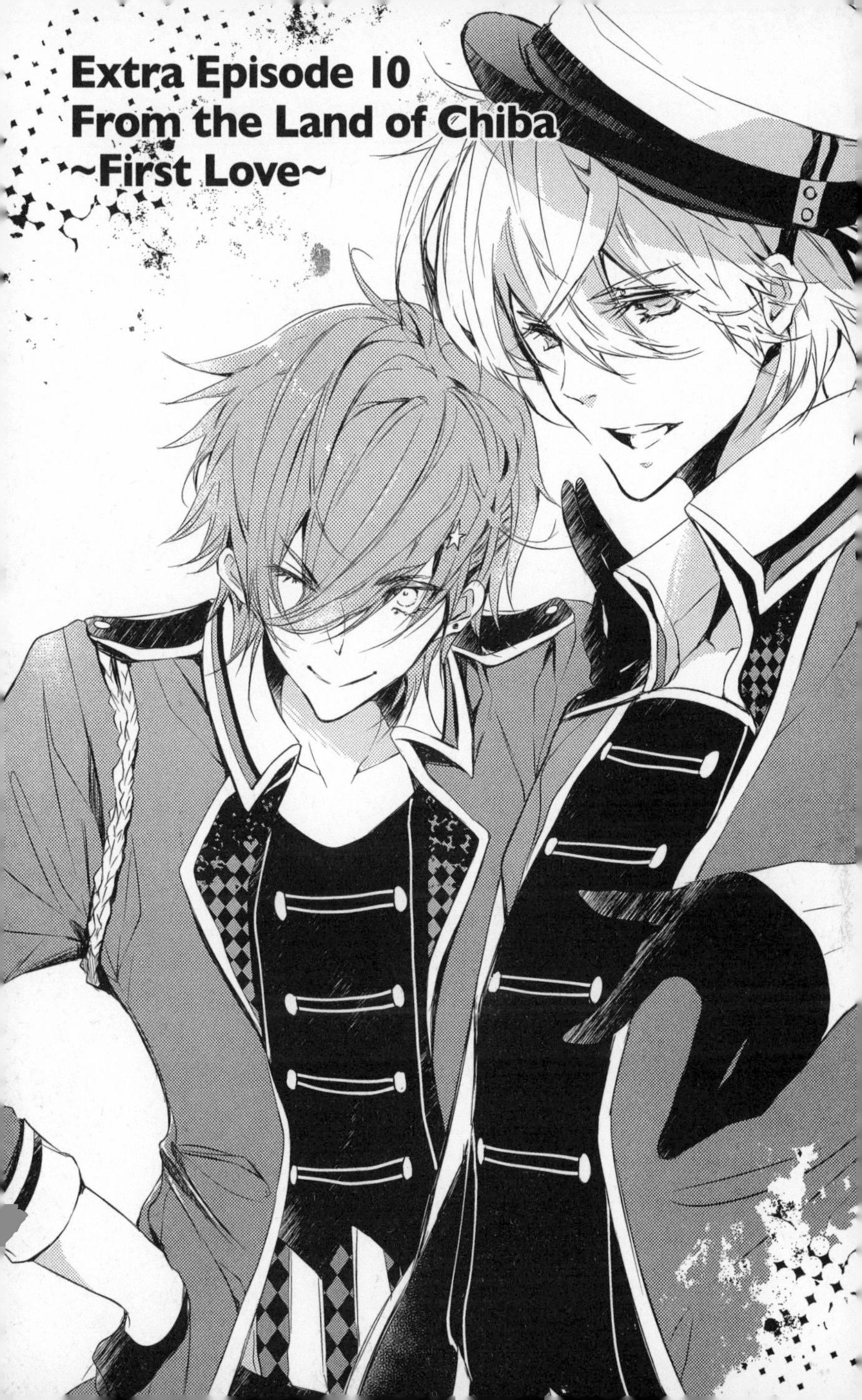

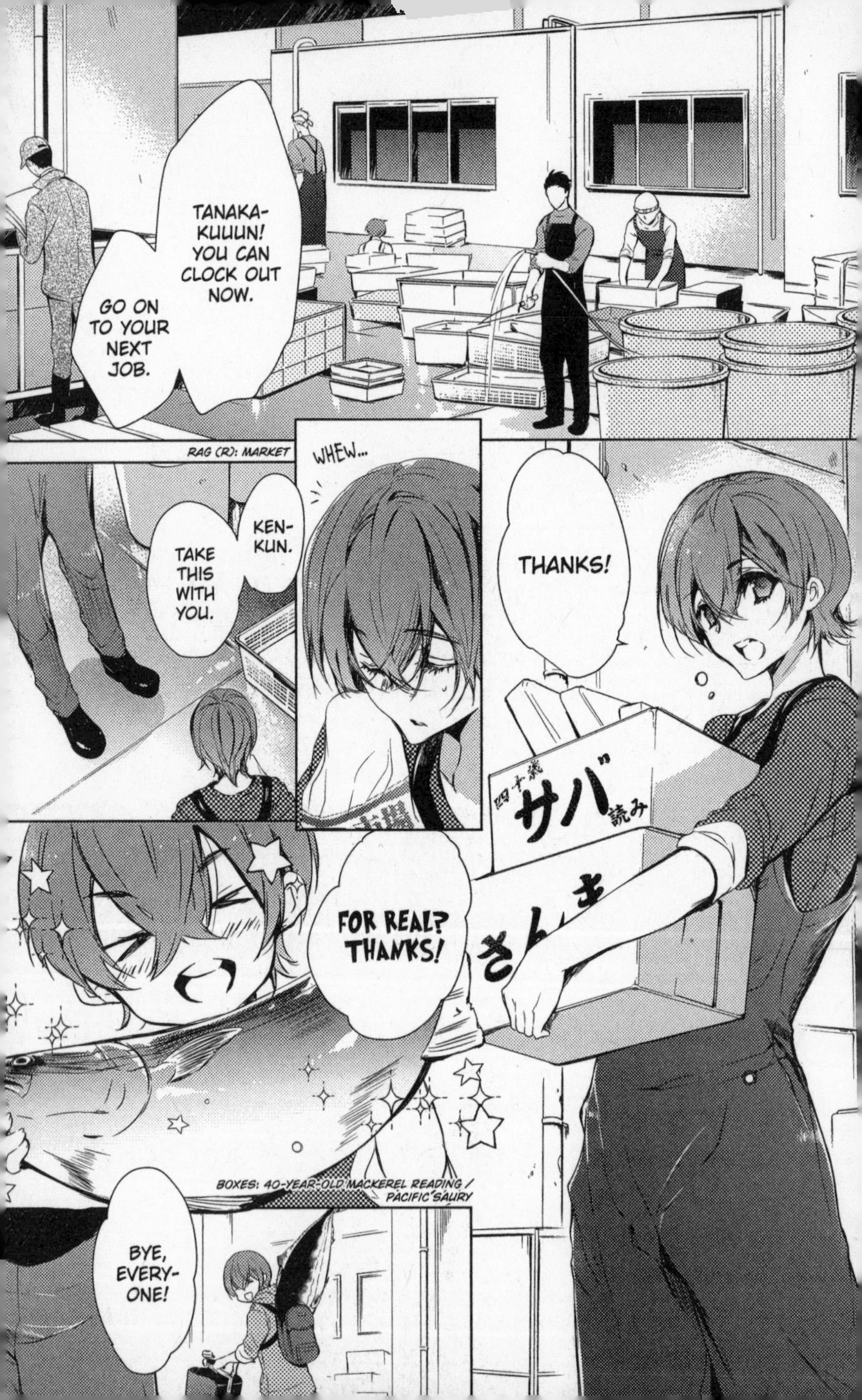
TANAKA-KUUUN! YOU CAN CLOCK OUT NOW.
GO ON TO YOUR NEXT JOB.
RAG (R): MARKET
THANKS!
四十歳サバ読み
WHEW...
KEN-KUN.
TAKE THIS WITH YOU.
FOR REAL? THANKS!
BOXES: 40-YEAR-OLD MACKEREL READING / PACIFIC SAURY
BYE, EVERY-ONE!

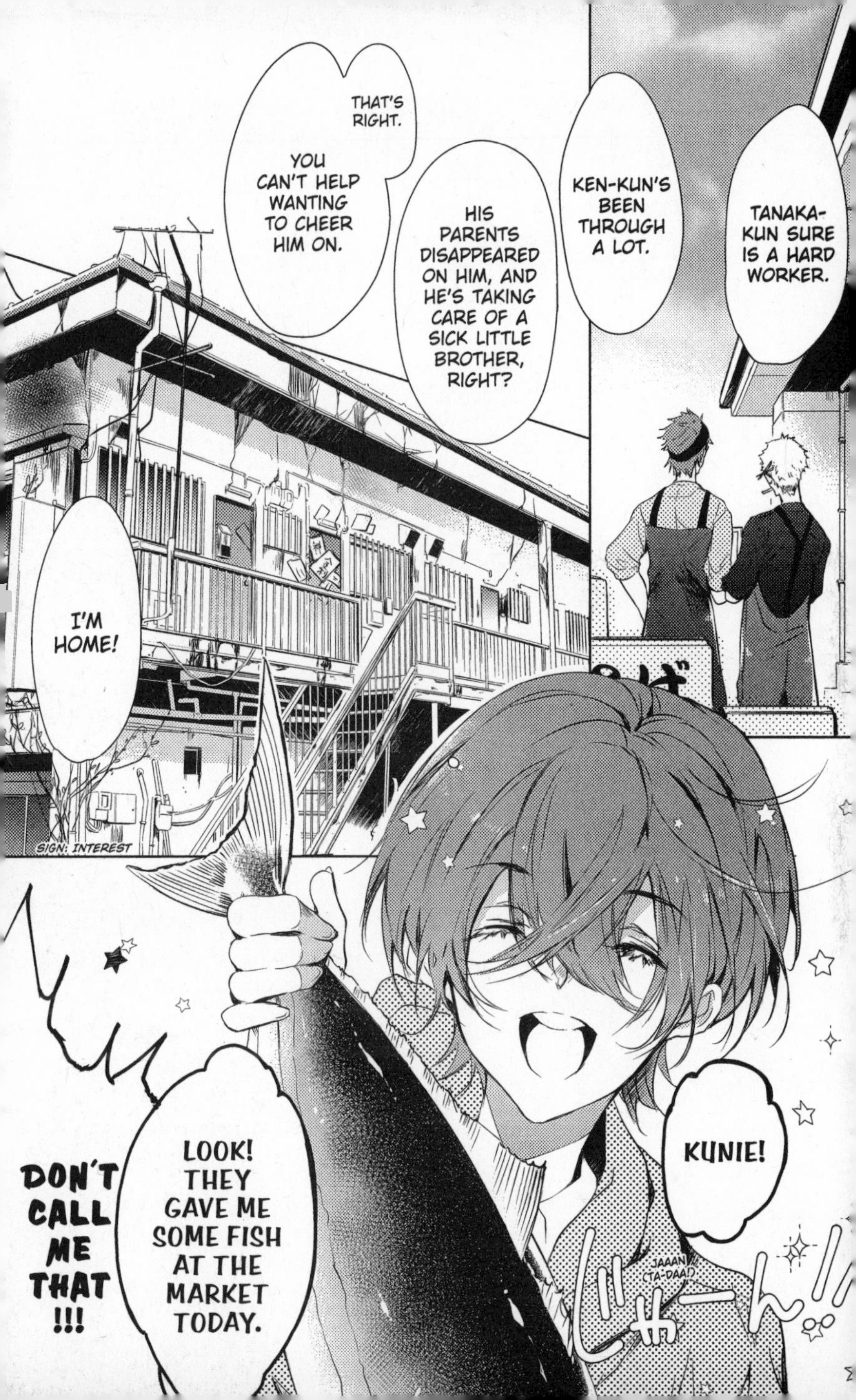
TANAKA-KUN SURE IS A HARD WORKER.
KEN-KUN'S BEEN THROUGH A LOT.
HIS PARENTS DISAPPEARED ON HIM, AND HE'S TAKING CARE OF A SICK LITTLE BROTHER, RIGHT?
THAT'S RIGHT.
YOU CAN'T HELP WANTING TO CHEER HIM ON.
I'M HOME!
SIGN: INTEREST
KUNIE!
JAAAN (TA-DAA!)
LOOK! THEY GAVE ME SOME FISH AT THE MARKET TODAY.
DON'T CALL ME THAT!!!

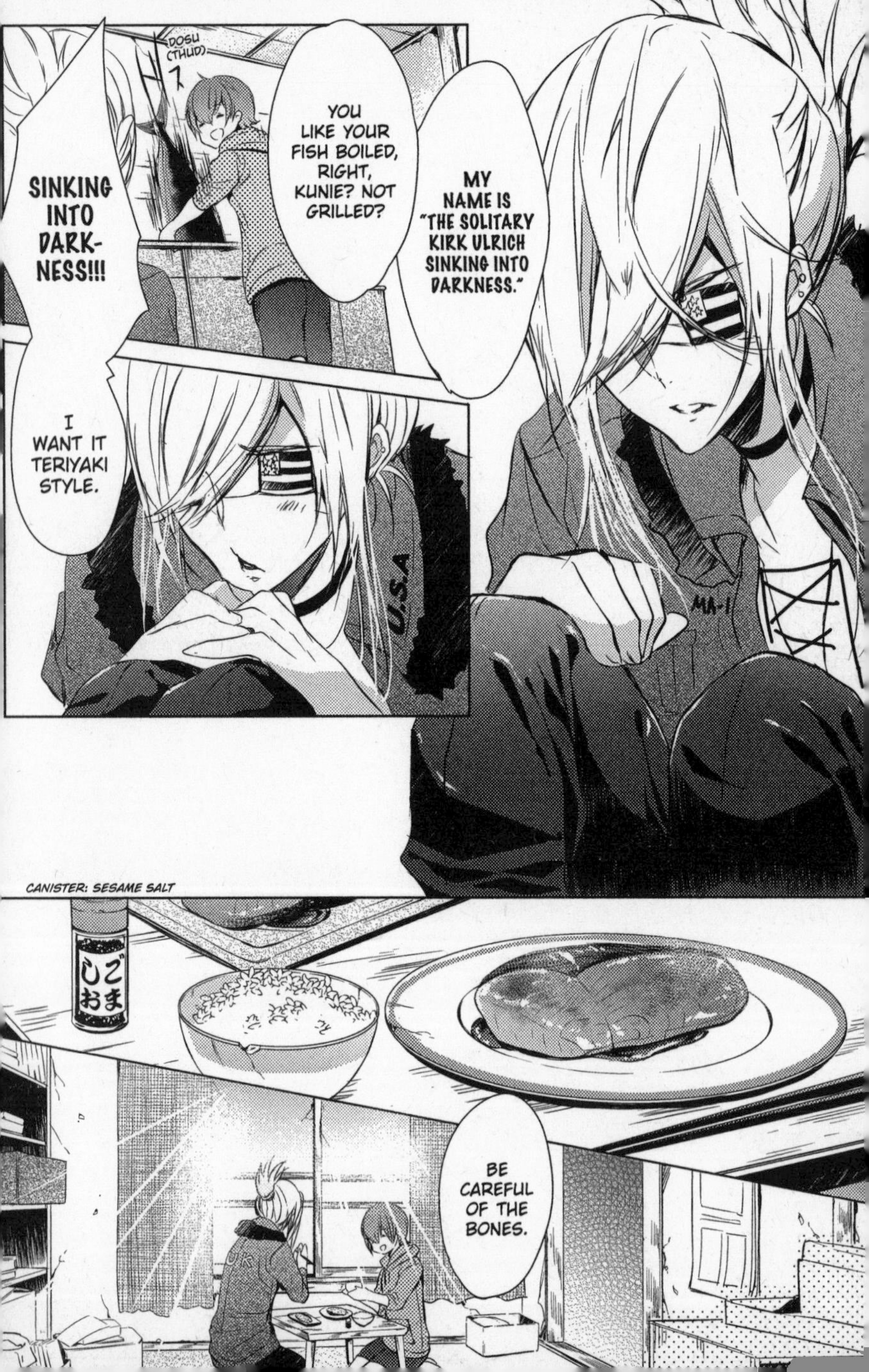
MY NAME IS "THE SOLITARY KIRK ULRICH SINKING INTO DARKNESS."
YOU LIKE YOUR FISH BOILED, RIGHT, KUNIE? NOT GRILLED?
DOSU (THUD)
SINKING INTO DARK-NESS!!!
I WANT IT TERIYAKI STYLE.
MA-1
U.S.A
CANISTER: SESAME SALT
ごましお
BE CAREFUL OF THE BONES.

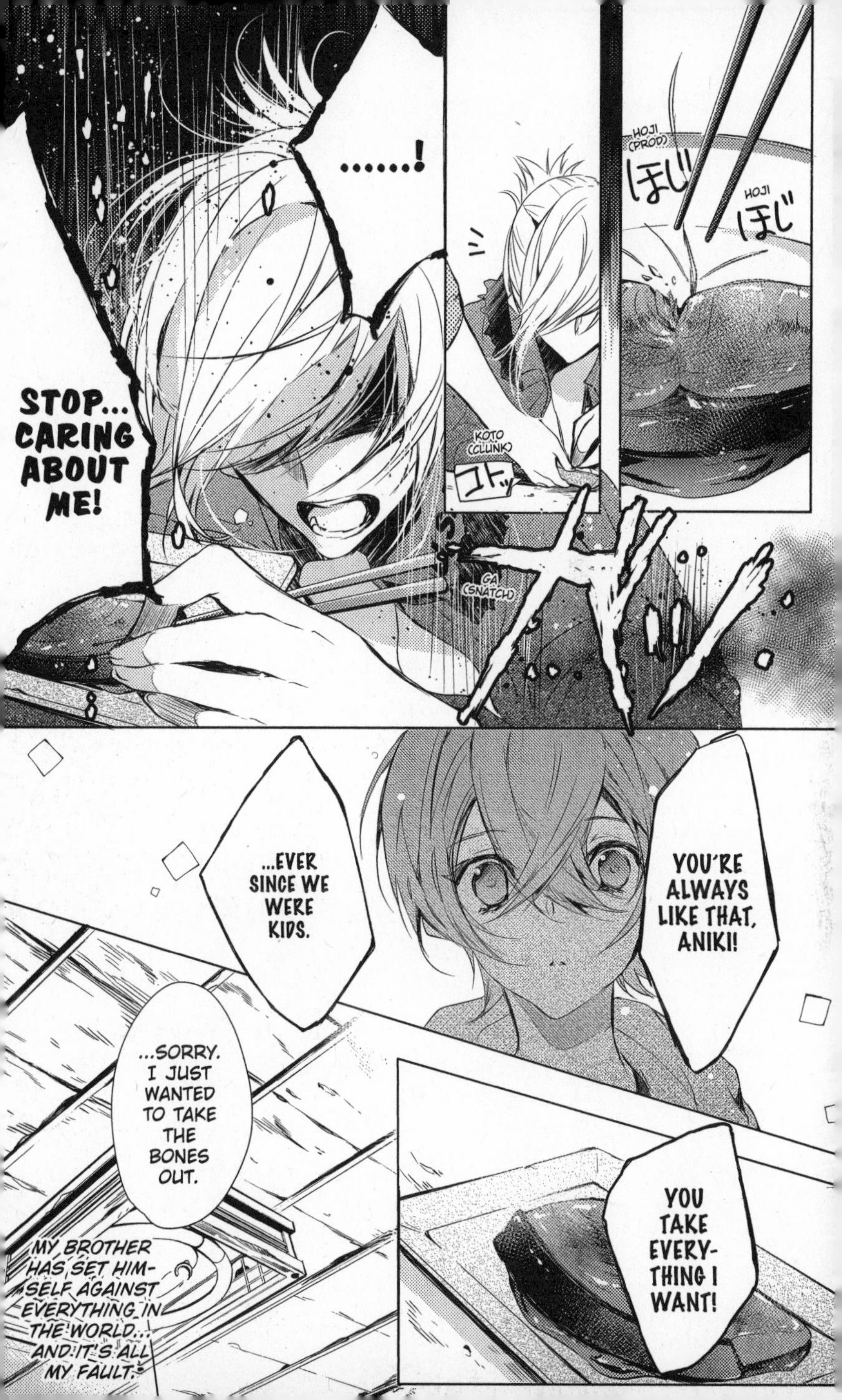

HOJI (PROD)
ほじ
HOJI
ほじ
KOTO (CLUNK)
コトッ
......!
STOP... CARING ABOUT ME!
GA (SNATCH)
YOU'RE ALWAYS LIKE THAT, ANIKI!
...EVER SINCE WE WERE KIDS.
YOU TAKE EVERY-THING I WANT!
...SORRY. I JUST WANTED TO TAKE THE BONES OUT.
MY BROTHER HAS SET HIM-SELF AGAINST EVERYTHING IN THE WORLD... AND IT'S ALL MY FAULT.

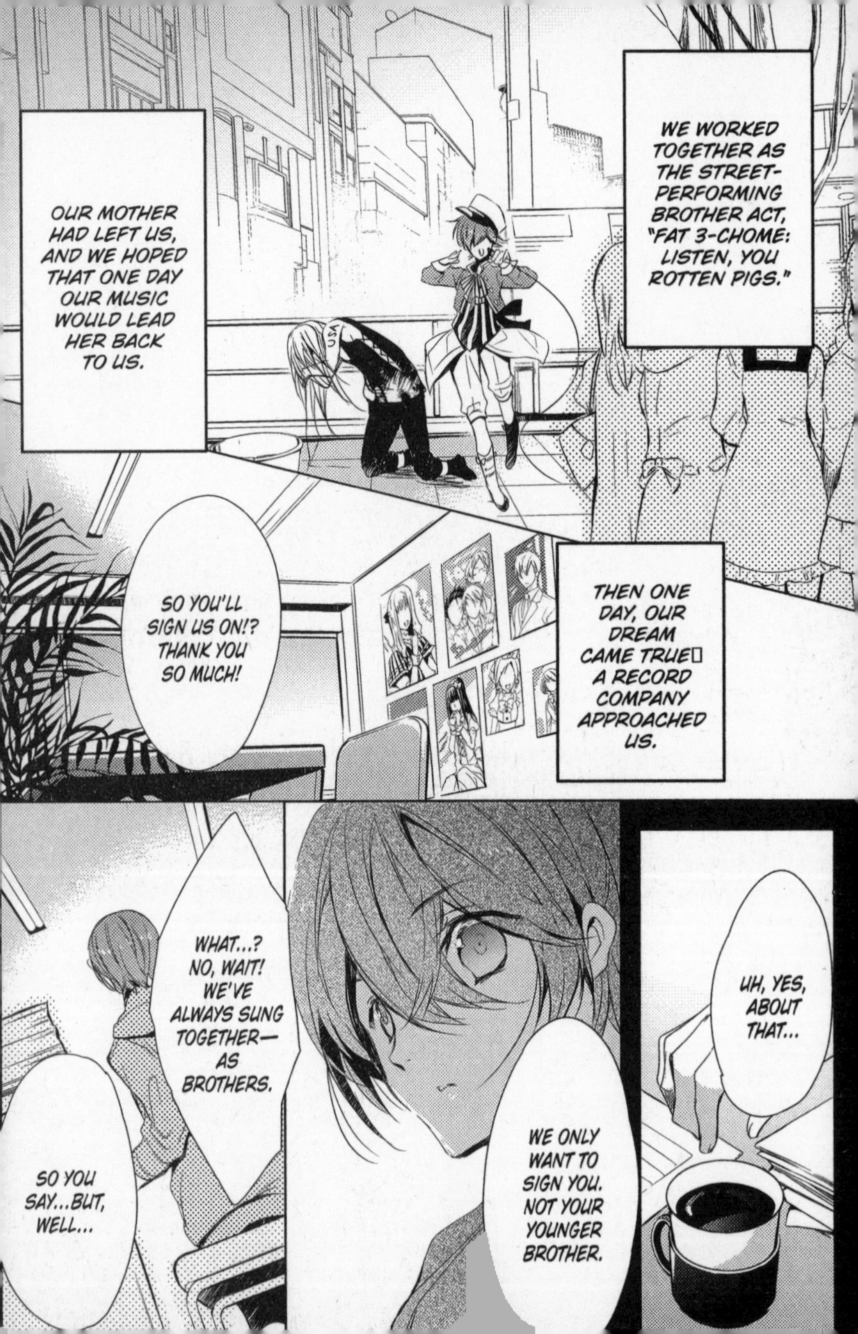

WE WORKED TOGETHER AS THE STREET-PERFORMING BROTHER ACT, "FAT 3-CHOME: LISTEN, YOU ROTTEN PIGS."
OUR MOTHER HAD LEFT US, AND WE HOPED THAT ONE DAY OUR MUSIC WOULD LEAD HER BACK TO US.
USA
THEN ONE DAY, OUR DREAM CAME TRUE— A RECORD COMPANY APPROACHED US.
SO YOU'LL SIGN US ON!? THANK YOU SO MUCH!
UH, YES, ABOUT THAT...
WE ONLY WANT TO SIGN YOU. NOT YOUR YOUNGER BROTHER.
WHAT...? NO, WAIT! WE'VE ALWAYS SUNG TOGETHER— AS BROTHERS.
SO YOU SAY...BUT, WELL...

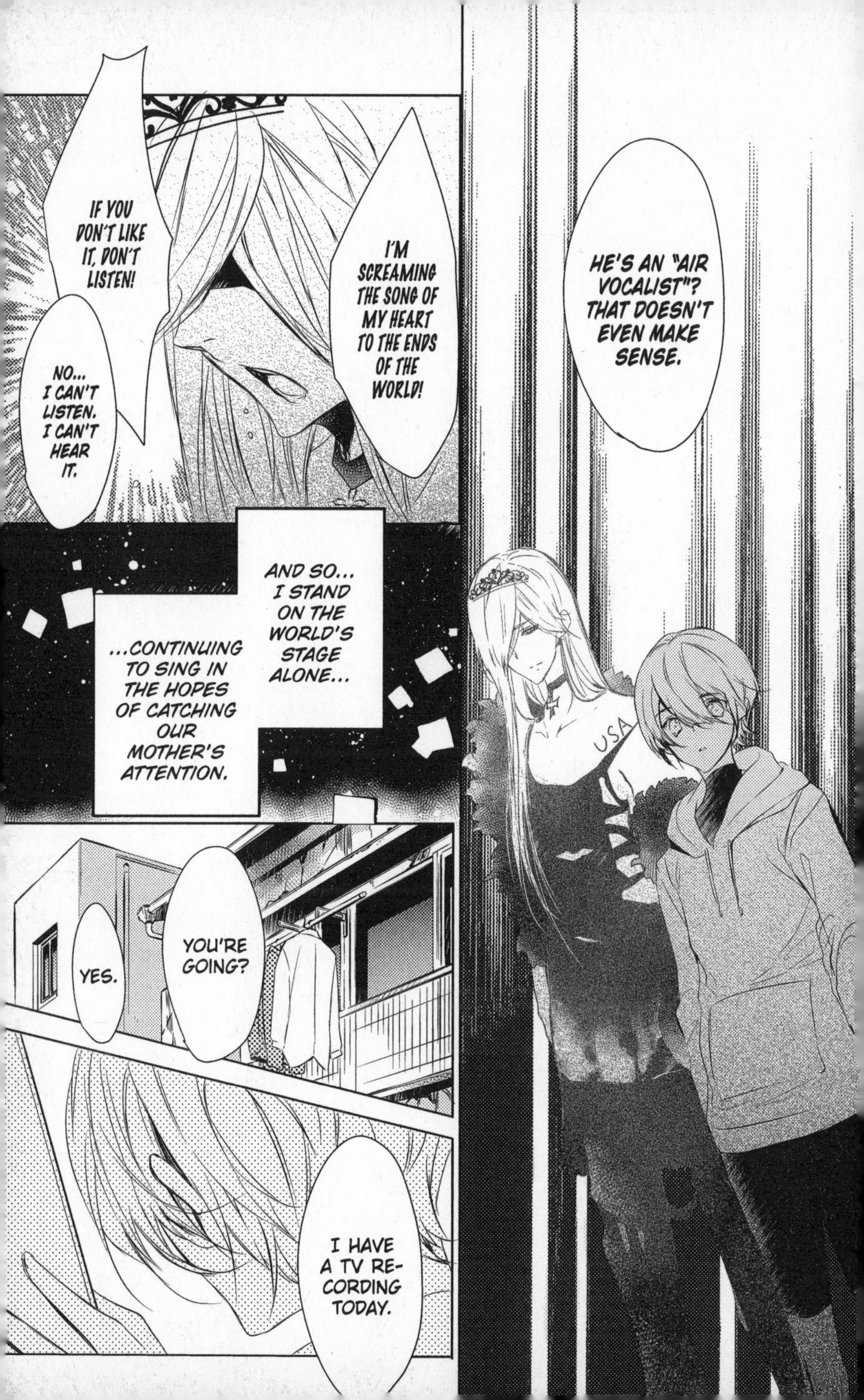
HE'S AN "AIR VOCALIST"? THAT DOESN'T EVEN MAKE SENSE.
I'M SCREAMING THE SONG OF MY HEART TO THE ENDS OF THE WORLD!
IF YOU DON'T LIKE IT, DON'T LISTEN!
NO... I CAN'T LISTEN. I CAN'T HEAR IT.
AND SO... I STAND ON THE WORLD'S STAGE ALONE...
...CONTINUING TO SING IN THE HOPES OF CATCHING OUR MOTHER'S ATTENTION.
YOU'RE GOING?
YES.
I HAVE A TV RE-CORDING TODAY.

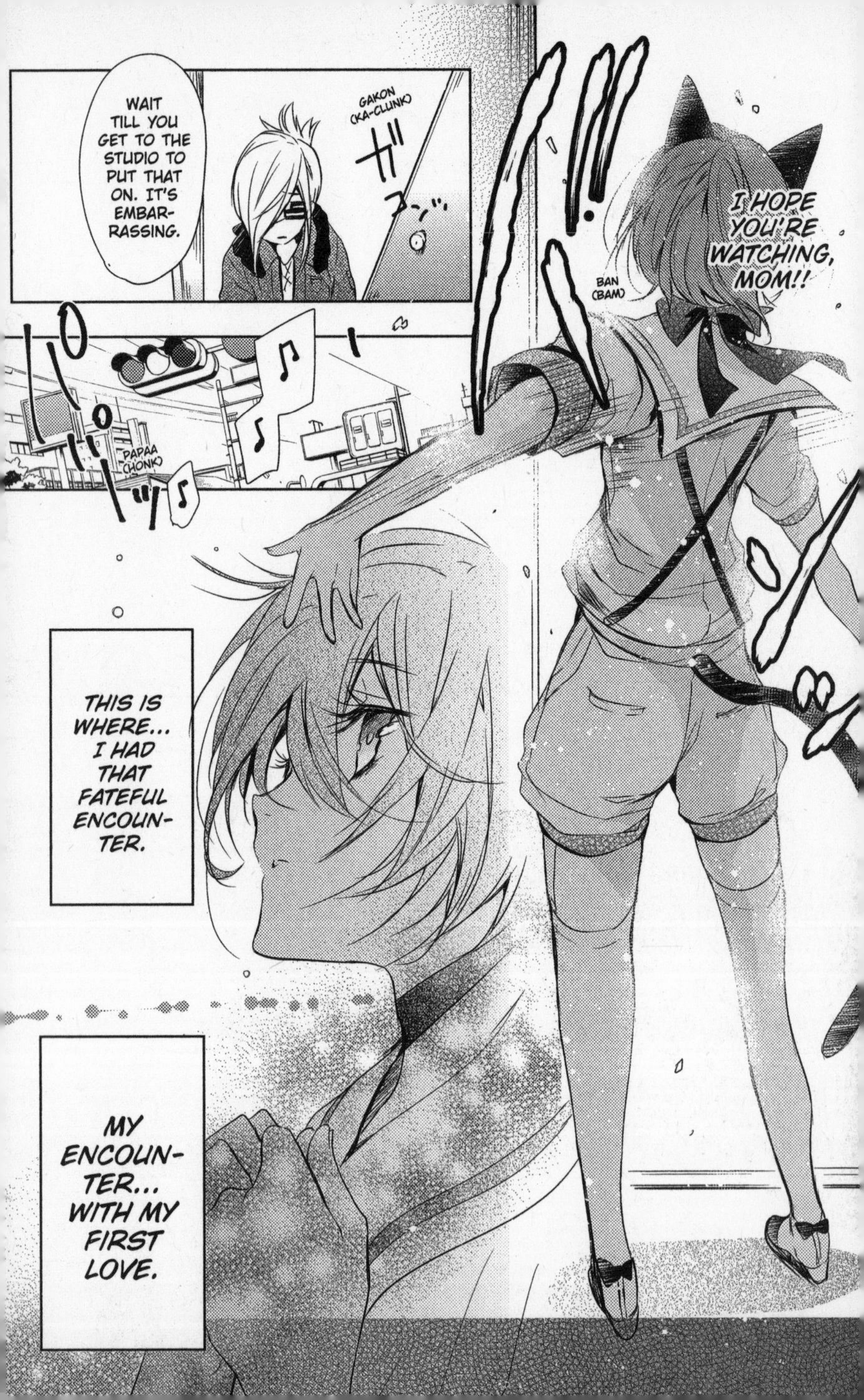
I HOPE YOU'RE WATCHING, MOM!!
BAN (BAM)
GAKON (KA-CLUNK)
WAIT TILL YOU GET TO THE STUDIO TO PUT THAT ON. IT'S EMBARRASSING.
PAPAA (CHONK)
THIS IS WHERE... I HAD THAT FATEFUL ENCOUNTER.
MY ENCOUNTER... WITH MY FIRST LOVE.

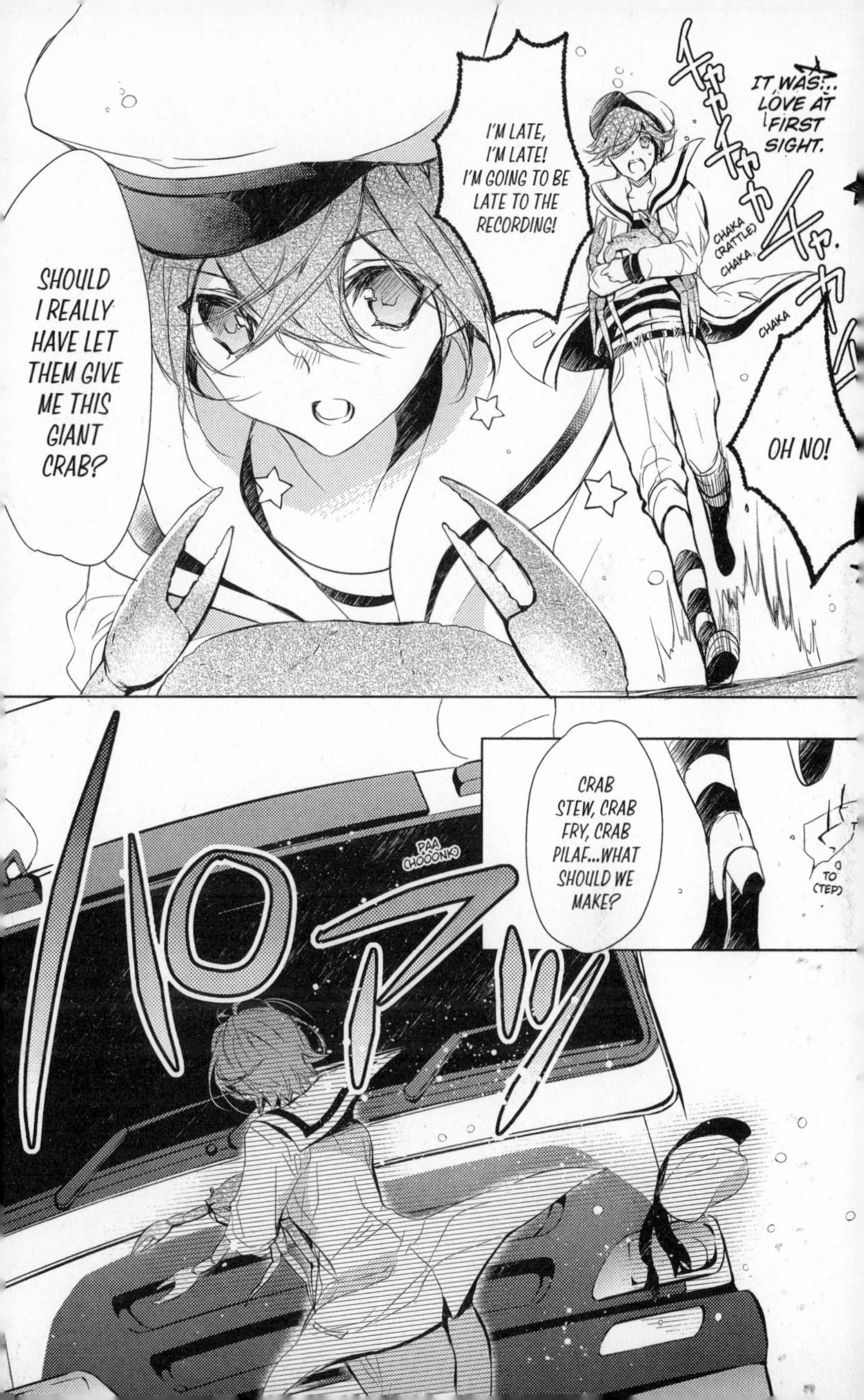
IT WAS... LOVE AT FIRST SIGHT.
CHAKA (RATTLE) CHAKA
CHAKA
OH NO!
I'M LATE, I'M LATE! I'M GOING TO BE LATE TO THE RECORDING!
SHOULD I REALLY HAVE LET THEM GIVE ME THIS GIANT CRAB?
TO (TEP)
CRAB STEW, CRAB FRY, CRAB PILAF...WHAT SHOULD WE MAKE?
PAA (HOOONK)

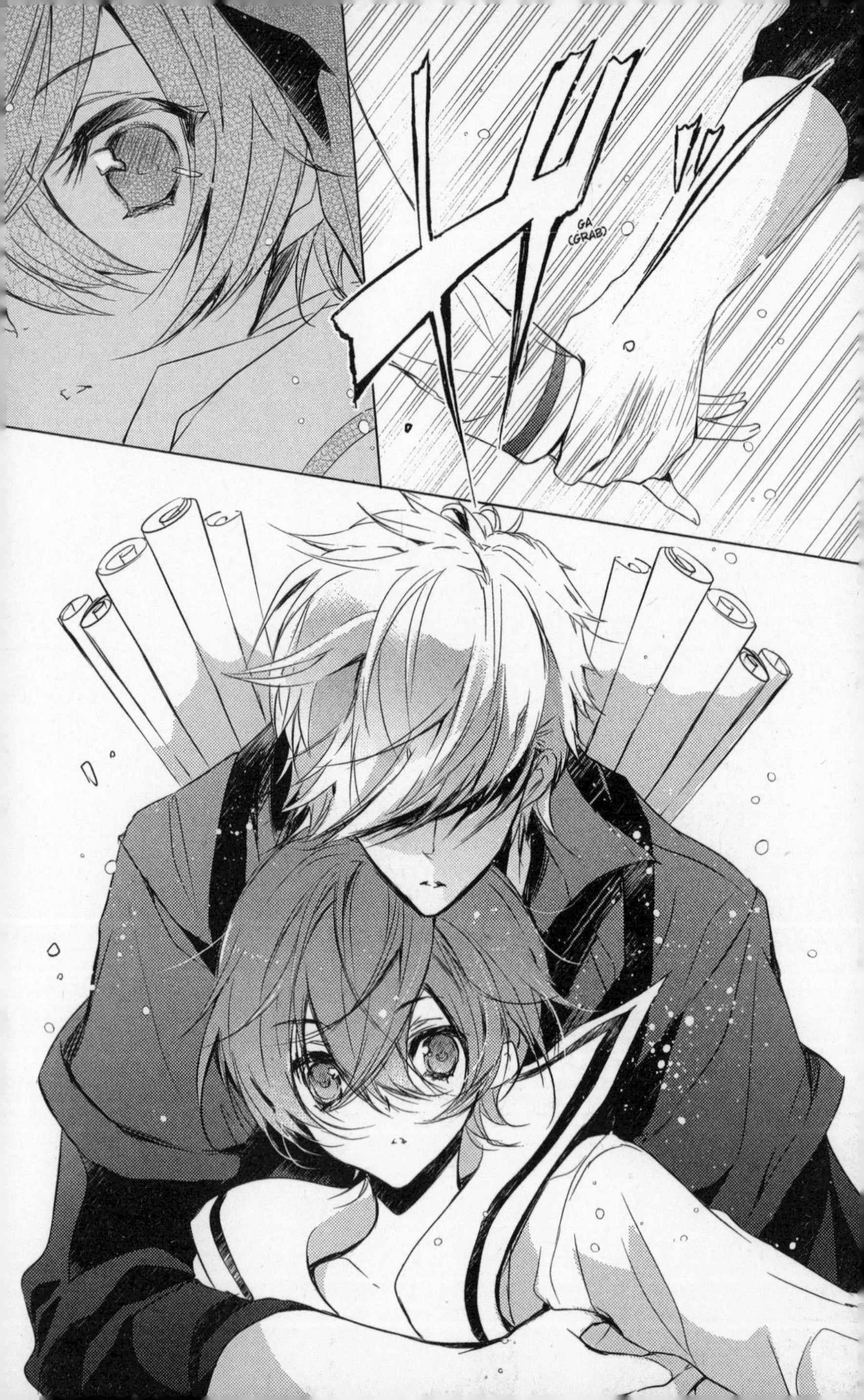
GA
(GRAB)

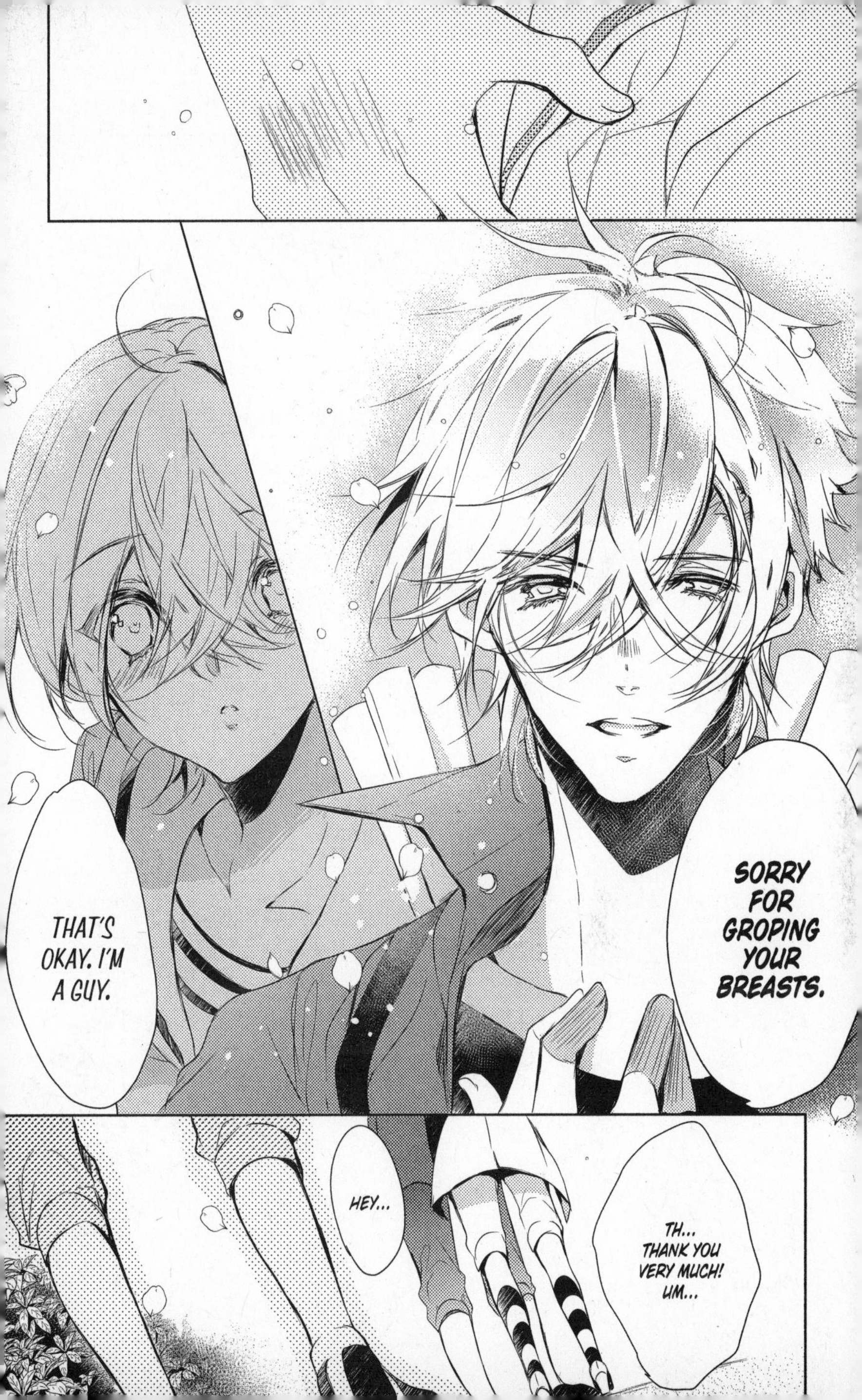
SORRY FOR GROPING YOUR BREASTS.
THAT'S OKAY. I'M A GUY.
TH... THANK YOU VERY MUCH! UM...
HEY...

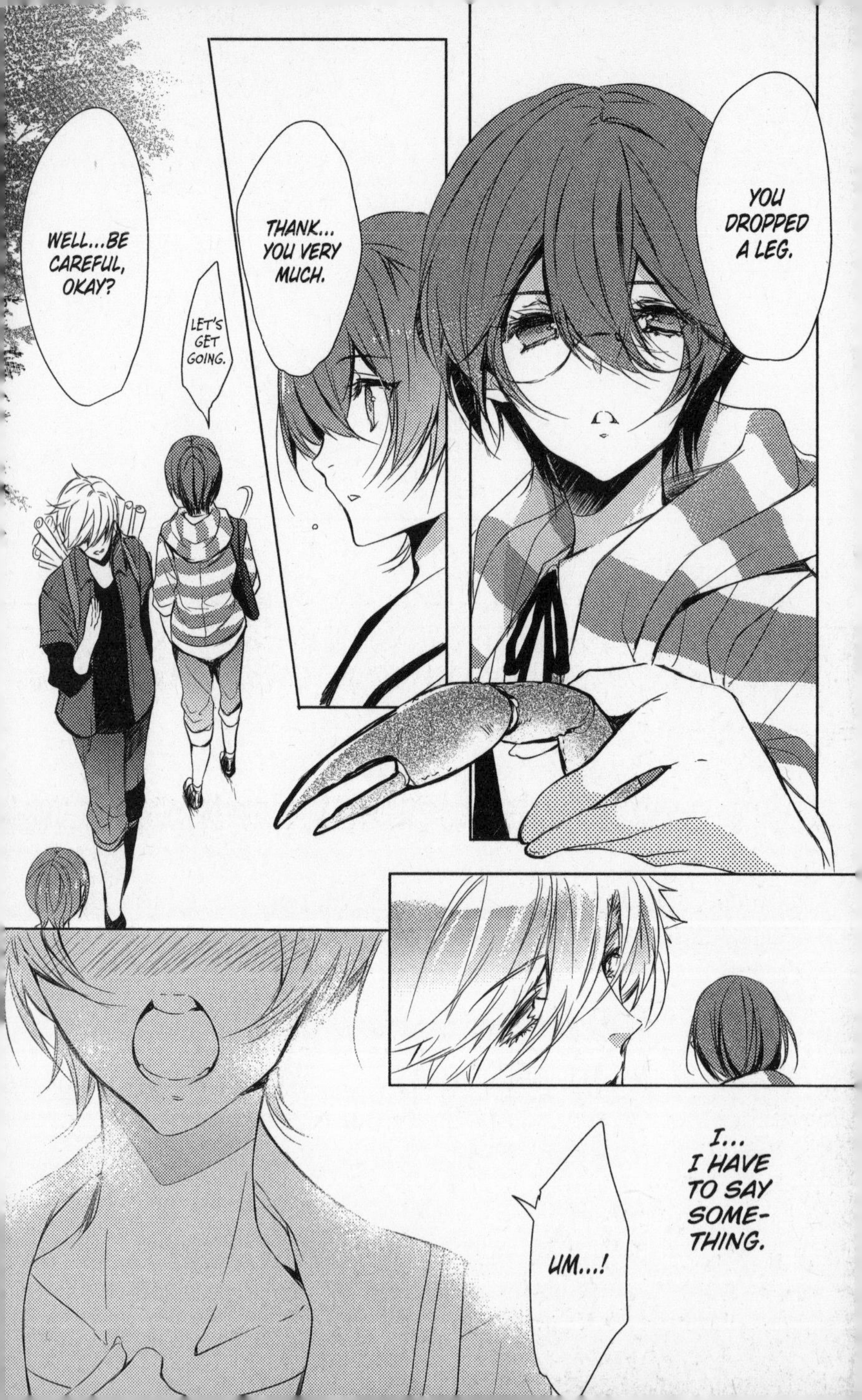
YOU DROPPED A LEG.
THANK... YOU VERY MUCH.
WELL...BE CAREFUL, OKAY?
LET'S GET GOING.
I... I HAVE TO SAY SOME-THING.
UM...!

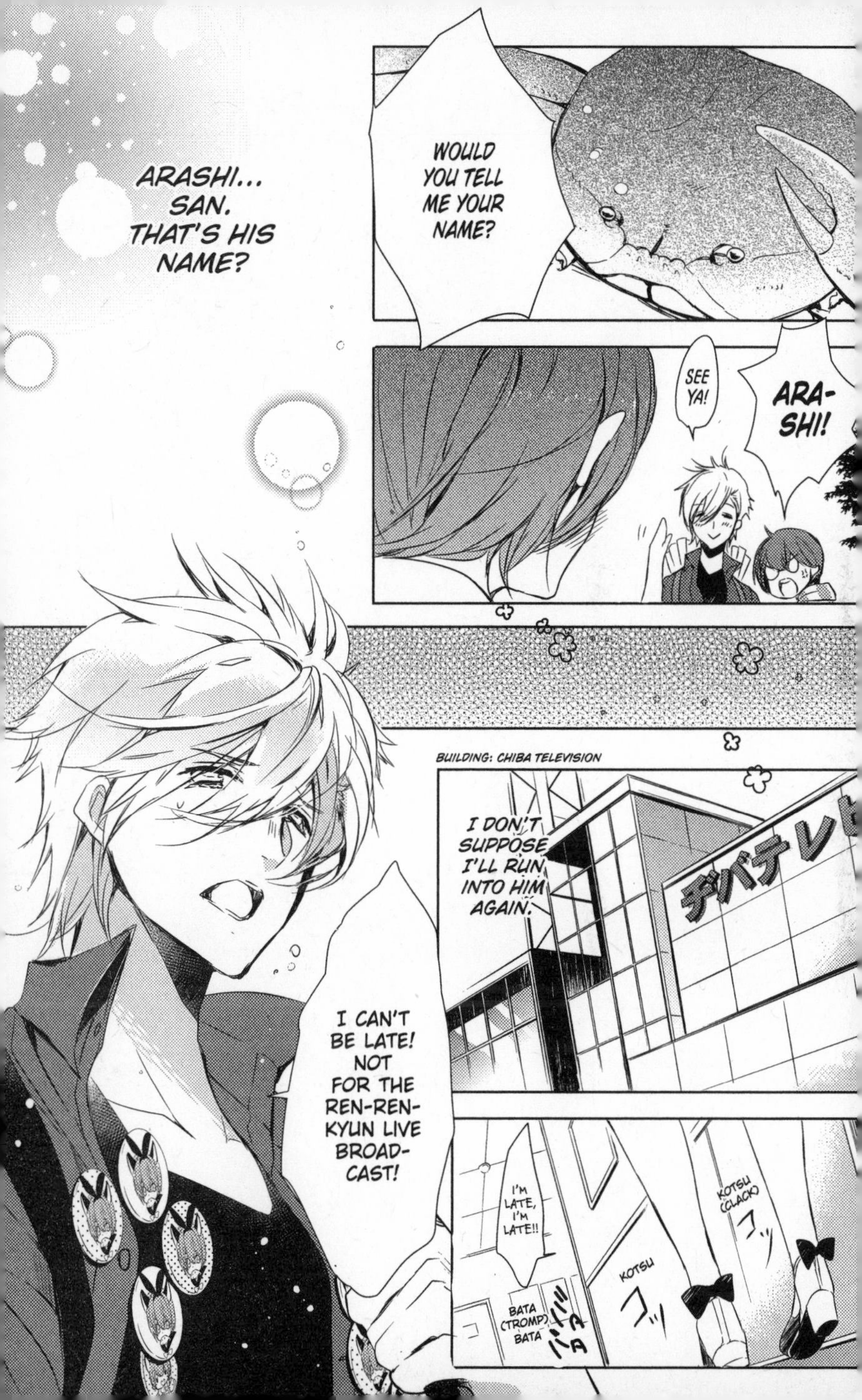
WOULD YOU TELL ME YOUR NAME?
ARA-SHI!
SEE YA!
ARASHI... SAN. THAT'S HIS NAME?
BUILDING: CHIBA TELEVISION
I DON'T SUPPOSE I'LL RUN INTO HIM AGAIN.
KOTSU (CLACK)
KOTSU
I'M LATE, I'M LATE!!
BATA (TROMP) BATA
I CAN'T BE LATE! NOT FOR THE REN-REN-KYUN LIVE BROAD-CAST!

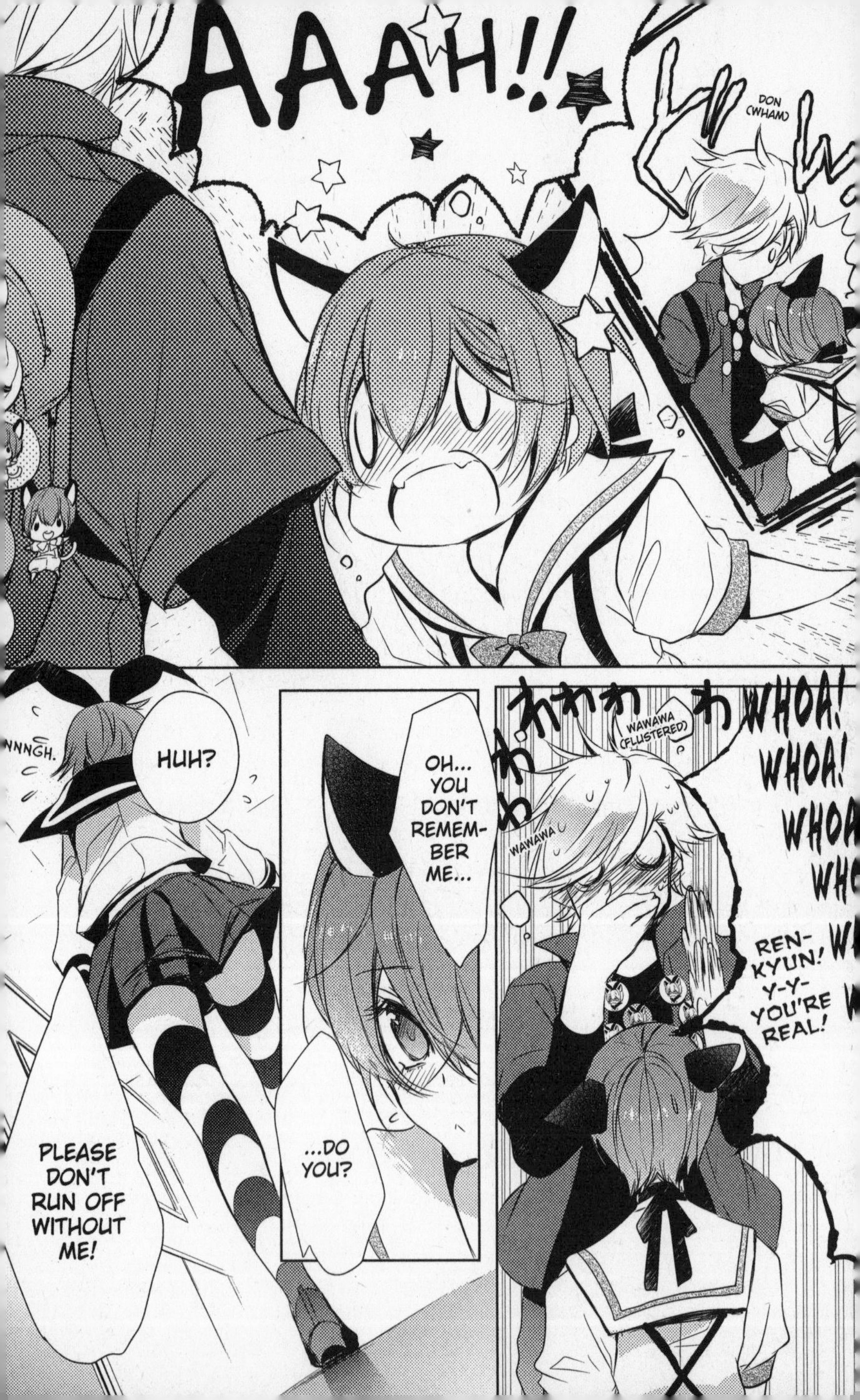
DON (WHAM)
AAAH!!
WHOA! WHOA! WHOA! WHO
わわわ わ
WAWAWA (FLUSTERED)
WAWAWA
REN-KYUN! Y-Y-YOU'RE REAL!
OH... YOU DON'T REMEM-BER ME...
...DO YOU?
HUH?
NNNGH.
PLEASE DON'T RUN OFF WITHOUT ME!

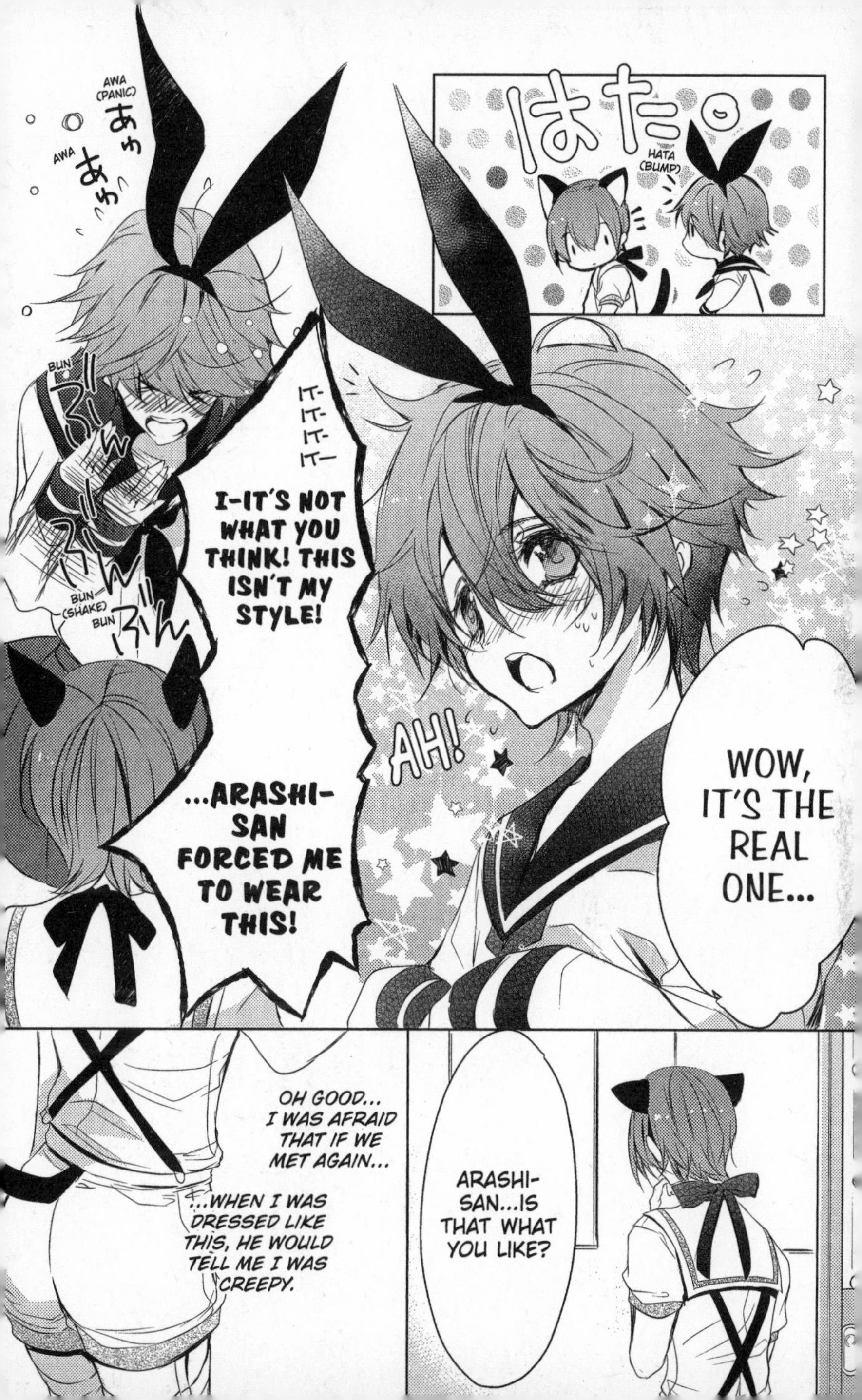

はた。
HATA (BUMP)
WOW, IT'S THE REAL ONE...
AH!
I-IT'S NOT WHAT YOU THINK! THIS ISN'T MY STYLE!
...ARASHI-SAN FORCED ME TO WEAR THIS!
AWA (PANIC)
AWA
BUN
BUN (SHAKE) BUN
ARASHI-SAN...IS THAT WHAT YOU LIKE?
OH GOOD... I WAS AFRAID THAT IF WE MET AGAIN...
...WHEN I WAS DRESSED LIKE THIS, HE WOULD TELL ME I WAS CREEPY.

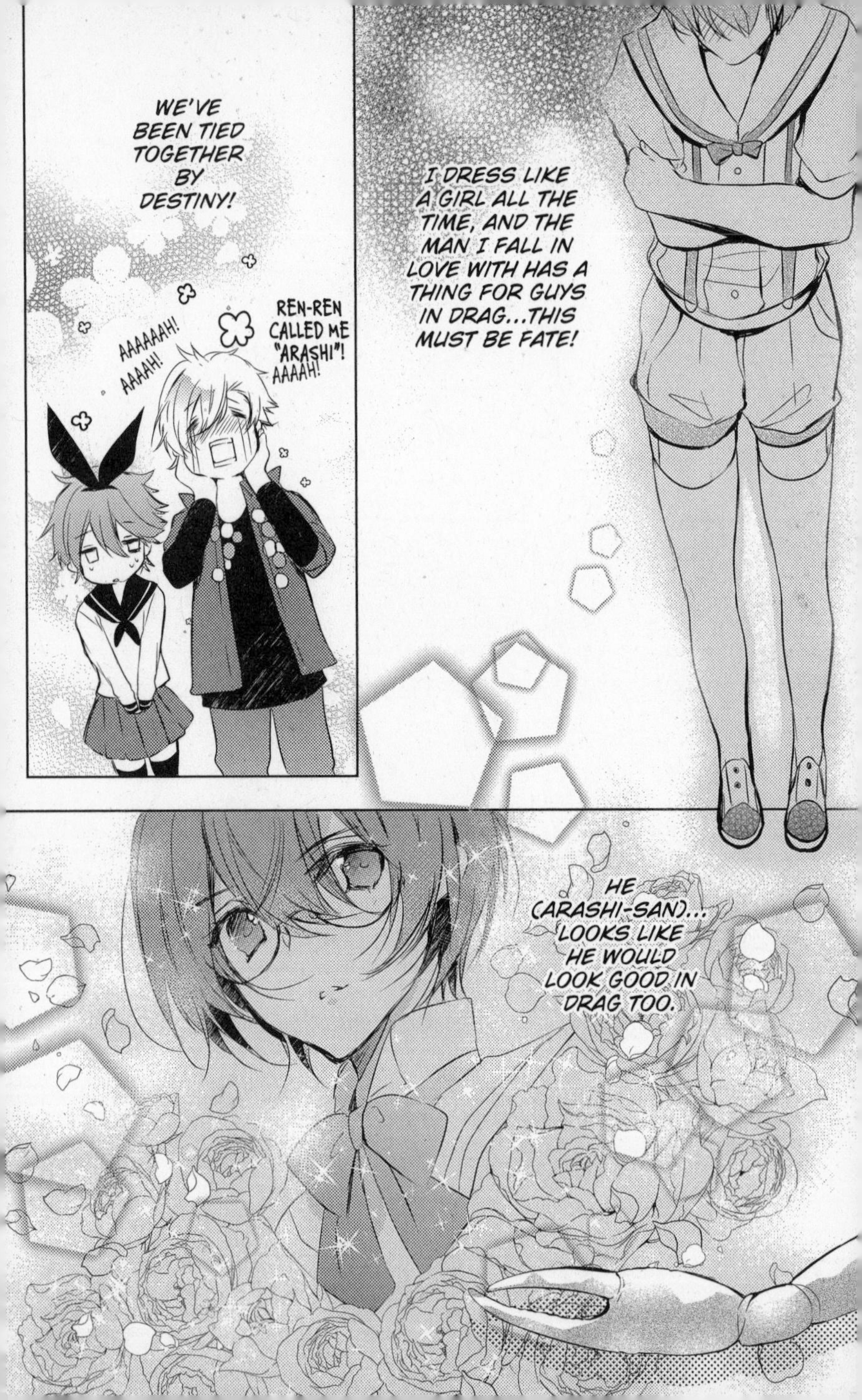
I DRESS LIKE A GIRL ALL THE TIME, AND THE MAN I FALL IN LOVE WITH HAS A THING FOR GUYS IN DRAG...THIS MUST BE FATE!
WE'VE BEEN TIED TOGETHER BY DESTINY!
REN-REN CALLED ME "ARASHI"! AAAAH!
AAAAAAH! AAAAH!
HE (ARASHI-SAN)... LOOKS LIKE HE WOULD LOOK GOOD IN DRAG TOO.

f
i
r
s
t

l
o
v
e

m
o
n
s
t
e
r

NOW INTRODUCING A NEW FRIEND FROM CLASS 5-1...

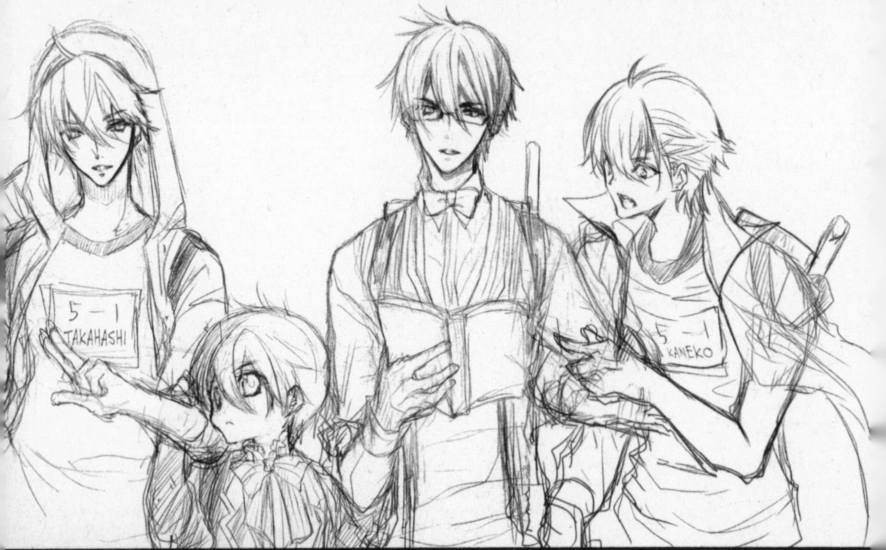
5-1
TAKAHASHI
5-1
KANEKO

I never introduced Shigeru-sensei when he showed up in Volume 5.

Why didn't I introduce him...? He's a mysterious presence on the grown-up team. In college he and Daikoku-oniichan were close enough that they would regularly eat lunch together (neither of them had any friends), and they spent their college years behind a Noh mask and a cardboard box. I don't think I'll get a chance to draw their fun campus life, but they have now been reunited.

(They absolutely did not stay in touch after graduation.)

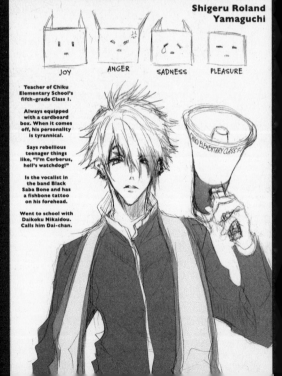

Shigeru Roland Yamaguchi

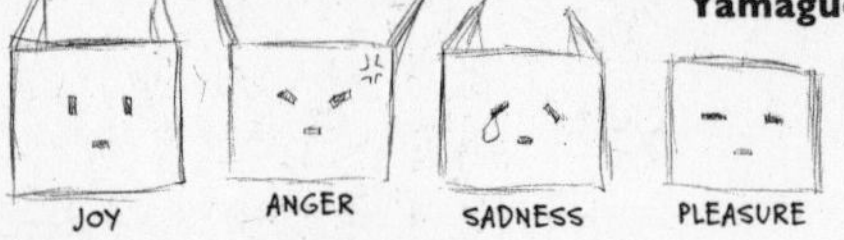
JOY
ANGER
SADNESS
PLEASURE

Teacher of Chiku Elementary School's fifth-grade Class 1.

Always equipped with a cardboard box. When it comes off, his personality is tyrannical.

Says rebellious teenager things like, "I'm Cerberus, hell's watchdog!"

Is the vocalist in the band Black Saba Bone and has a fishbone tattoo on his forehead.

Went to school with Daikoku Nikaidou. Calls him Dai-chan.

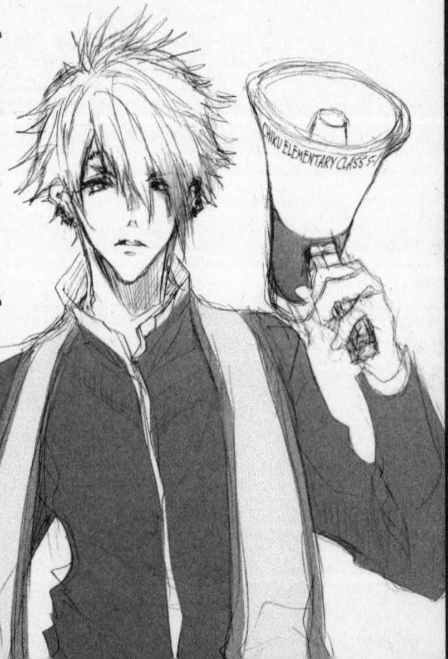
CHIKU ELEMENTARY CLASS 5-1

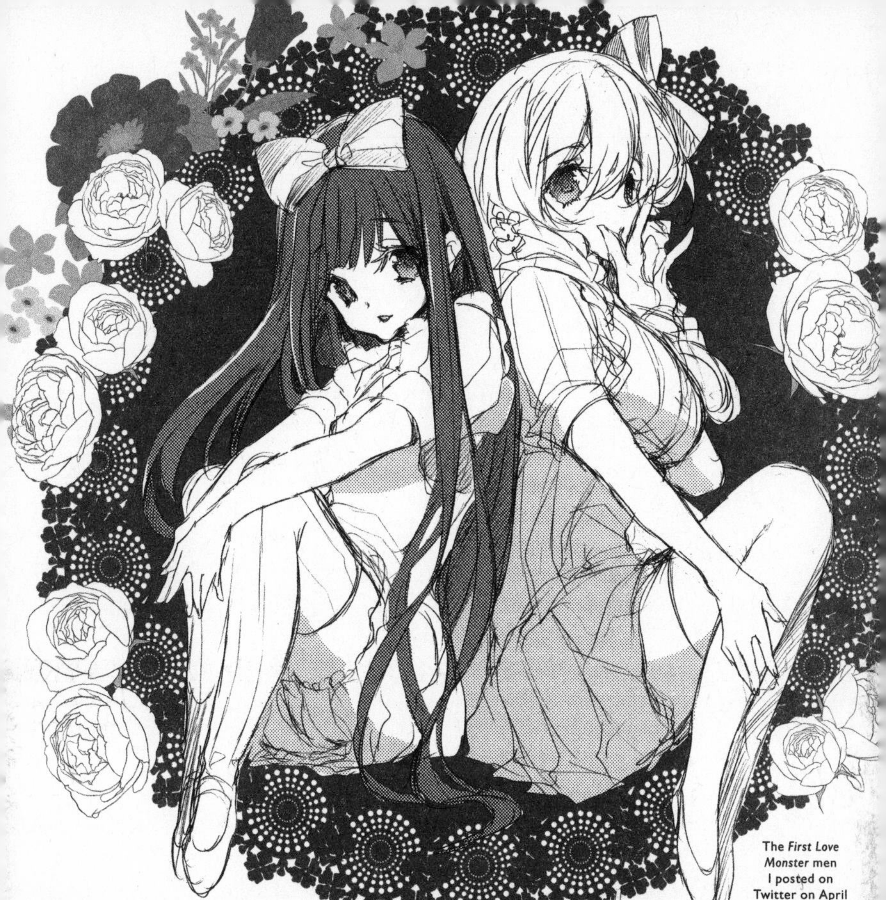

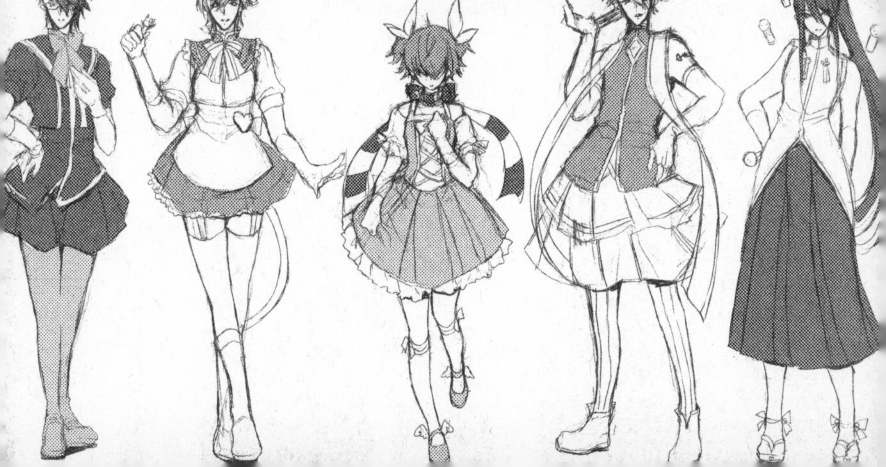

The *First Love Monster* men I posted on Twitter on April Fool's Day.

I don't know if I should say *First Love Monster* is already at Volume 6 or that it's only at Volume 6. I've been working on this series a lot longer than I'd expected, and I thought the characters would grow, but... The fifth-grade team may still be in fifth grade, but Kanade and Kaz have experienced romance(?) and will continue to climb the stairway to adulthood... So what about Gin and Tom? Will Gin actually be able to fall in love with a human being? That is an issue for a future chapter of *First Love Monster*.

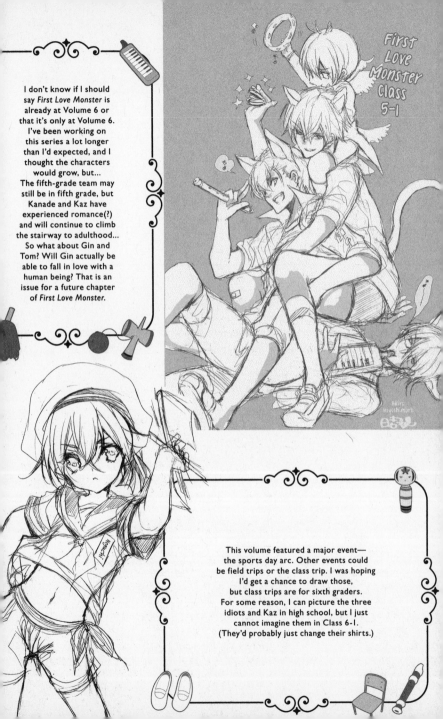

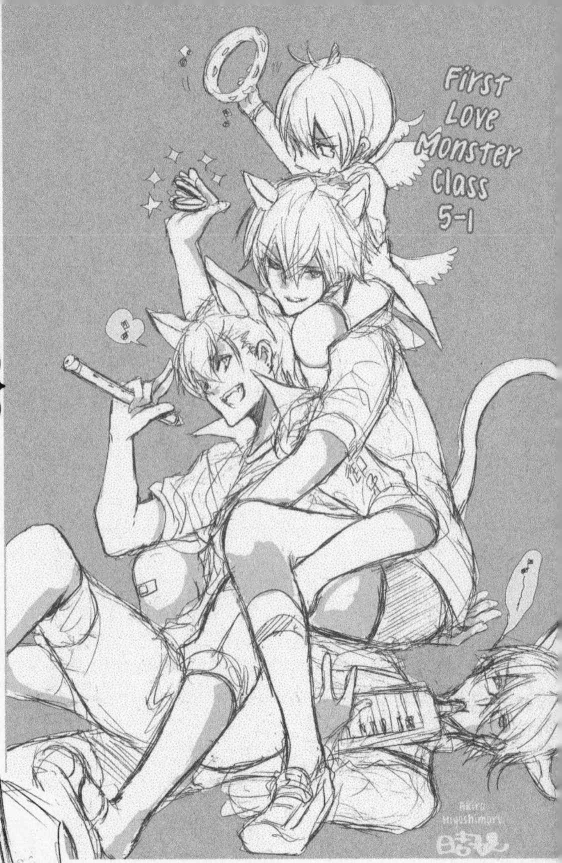
First Love Monster Class 5-1
Akira Hiyoshimaru

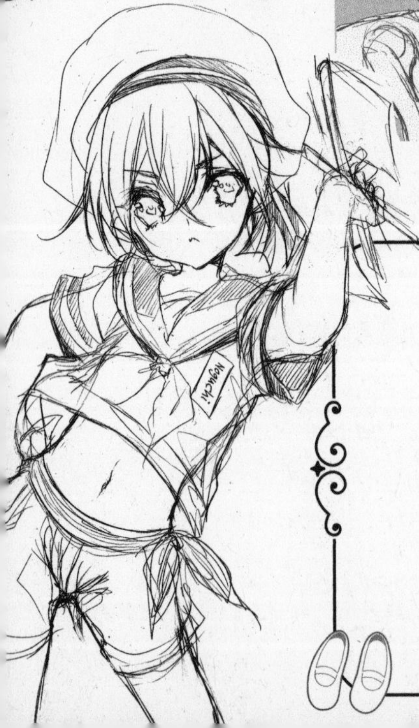
Noguchi

This volume featured a major event—the sports day arc. Other events could be field trips or the class trip. I was hoping I'd get a chance to draw those, but class trips are for sixth graders. For some reason, I can picture the three idiots and Kaz in high school, but I just cannot imagine them in Class 6-1. (They'd probably just change their shirts.)

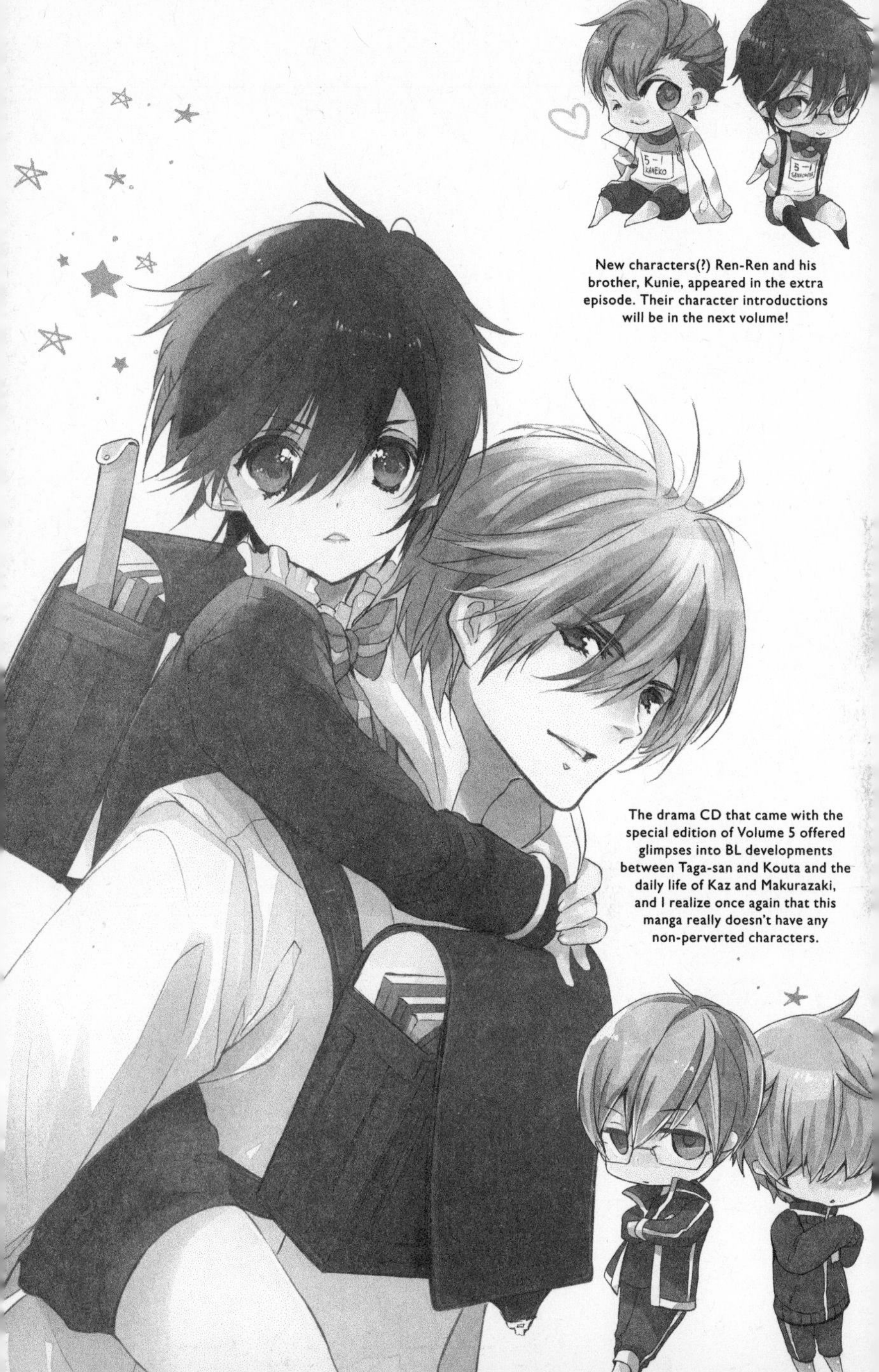

New characters(?) Ren-Ren and his brother, Kunie, appeared in the extra episode. Their character introductions will be in the next volume!

The drama CD that came with the special edition of Volume 5 offered glimpses into BL developments between Taga-san and Kouta and the daily life of Kaz and Makurazaki, and I realize once again that this manga really doesn't have any non-perverted characters.

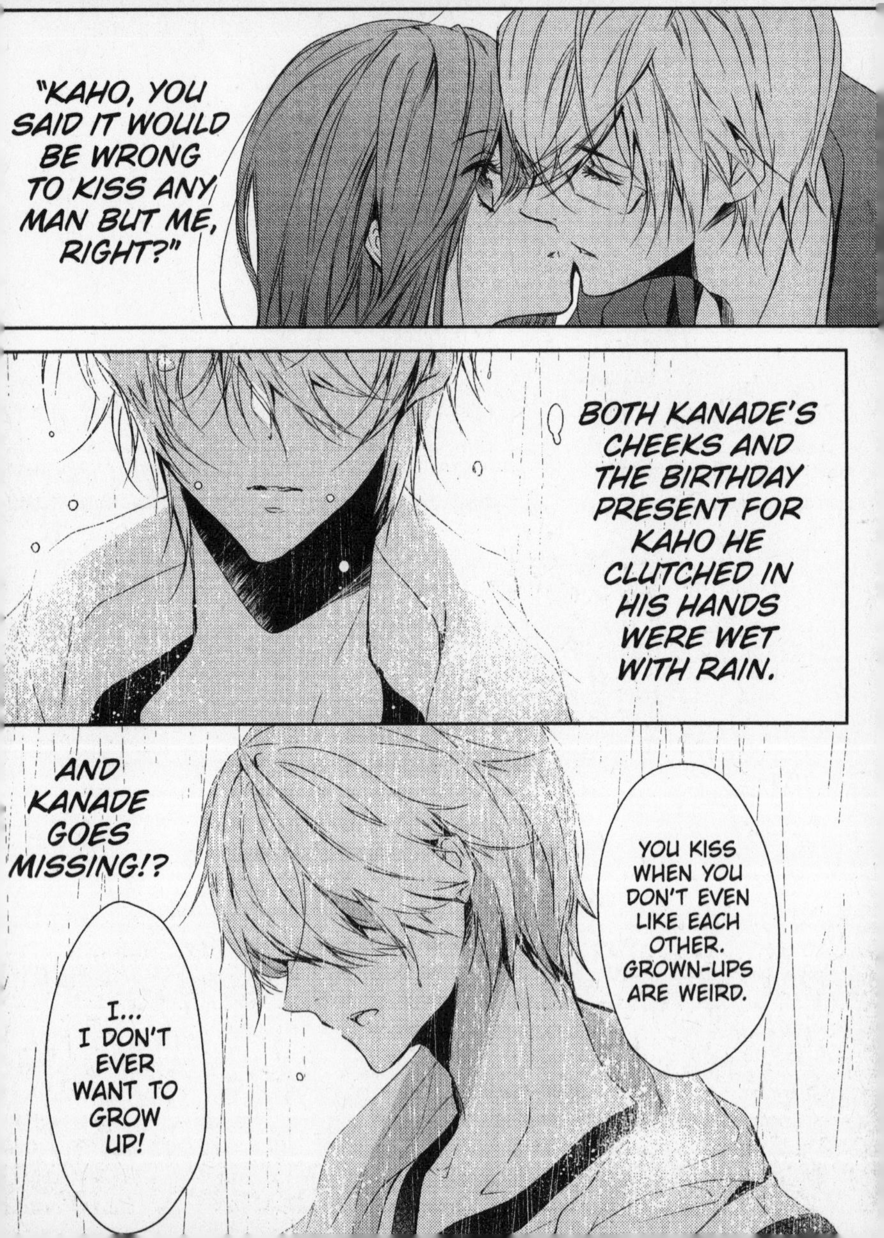
"KAHO, YOU SAID IT WOULD BE WRONG TO KISS ANY MAN BUT ME, RIGHT?"
BOTH KANADE'S CHEEKS AND THE BIRTHDAY PRESENT FOR KAHO HE CLUTCHED IN HIS HANDS WERE WET WITH RAIN.
YOU KISS WHEN YOU DON'T EVEN LIKE EACH OTHER. GROWN-UPS ARE WEIRD.
AND KANADE GOES MISSING!?
I... I DON'T EVER WANT TO GROW UP!

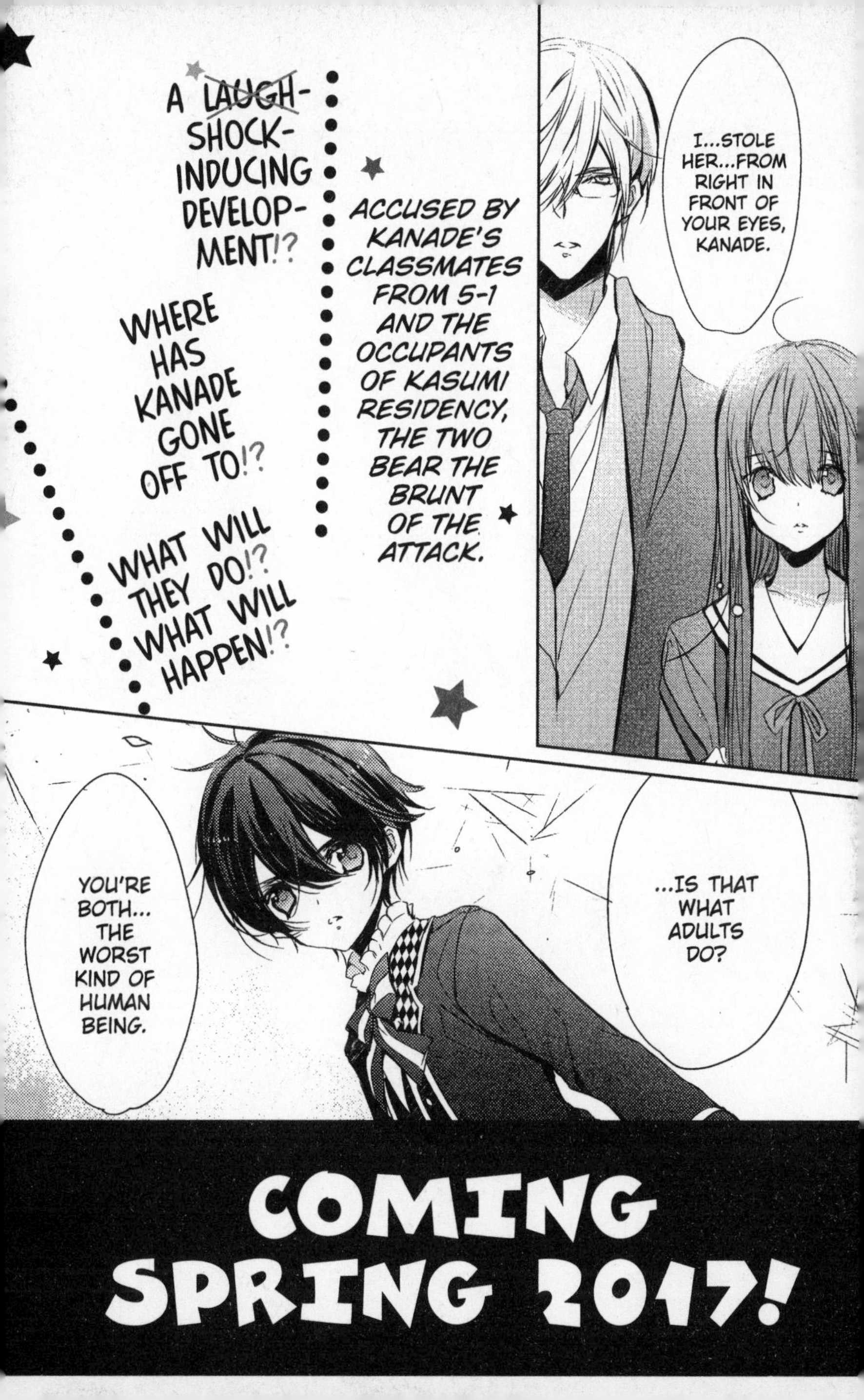
I...STOLE HER...FROM RIGHT IN FRONT OF YOUR EYES, KANADE.
ACCUSED BY KANADE'S CLASSMATES FROM 5-1 AND THE OCCUPANTS OF KASUMI RESIDENCY, THE TWO BEAR THE BRUNT OF THE ATTACK.
A ~~LAUGH~~- SHOCK-INDUCING DEVELOPMENT!?
WHERE HAS KANADE GONE OFF TO!?
WHAT WILL THEY DO!? WHAT WILL HAPPEN!?
...IS THAT WHAT ADULTS DO?
YOU'RE BOTH... THE WORST KIND OF HUMAN BEING.
COMING SPRING 2017!

What do you mean, "virgin boy"!?

As a Young Master lover, as a Young Master enthusiast, as a Young Master collector...

I have recorded every moment of my nonstop 24-hour vigil over you since the day you were weaned

I must identify this woman!!!

Please, humble Makurazaki needs your assistance!

Kazuo-sama enters his rebellious phase. (from his diary)

Find the young master's beloved.

Do you understand me now?

You seem to be enjoying yourself, Young Master.

Please, take a look at humble Makurazaki's secret 24-hour surveillance memorial DVD set and photo collection!

Please excuse my intruding upon you at such an early hour!

Young Master Kaz's welfare is at stake!

Is that so?

My Young Masterrrrrrr!

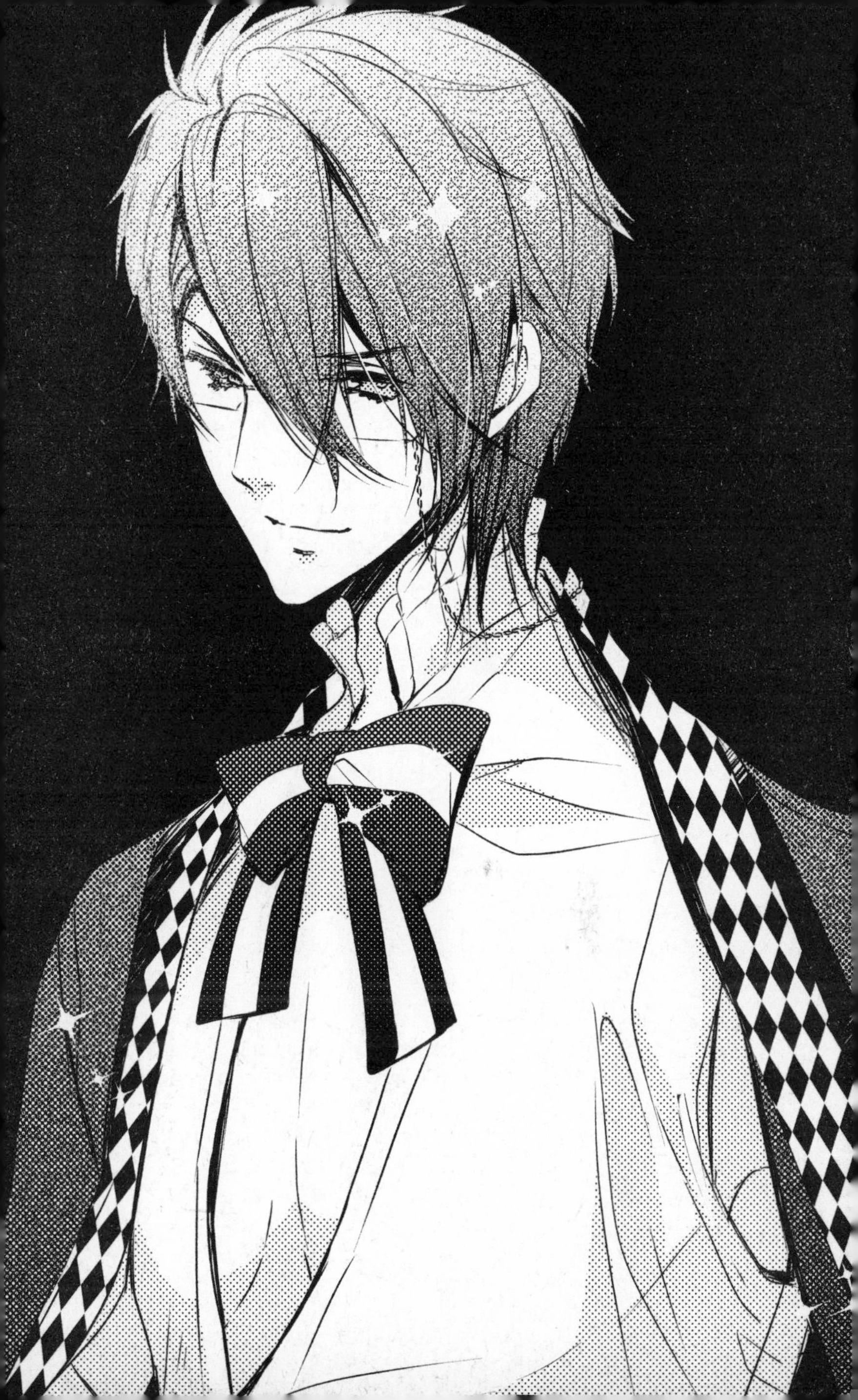

TRANSLATION NOTES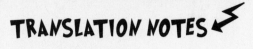

Page 12, three years of death
"Three years of death" is a loose translation of *sannen-goroshi*, which refers to poking someone between the buttocks. A more precise translation would be "three-year murder," and the action is so called because supposedly it will cause the victim to die in three years.

Page 15, Sadako's bib
The bib Sadako is wearing is called a *kintaro*, and its name comes from the name of a folklore hero who was known for wearing one just like it. The "*kin*" in Kintaro means "gold," and he wore the bib because that was what young children wore back in his time—Kintaro was still a child when he performed many of his exploits.

Page 17, human-faced dog
Japanese urban legends include rumors of *jinmenken*—dogs with human faces that can talk and run very fast. They are considered bad omens, but unlike other folkloric creatures, they're not known for killing anyone unlucky enough to encounter them. This does not stop Kanade and his friends from putting their own werewolf-like spin on the human-faced dog myth.

Page 23, Chiku Elementary School Anthem
The Japanese for "Chiku Elementary" is *chikushou*, which can also be a mild swear word, often translated as "dammit."

Pages 55–56, nuts and rice
In the original Japanese, Ginjirou hears Jouji say "Venus" (*Viinasu*) and thinks he's saying *bei nasu*, a type of eggplant. Tomu's real hatred is directed at eggplants. Incidentally, the puns that follow read like this in the original: The word for "love at first sight" is *hitomebore*, which is also a type of rice (*kome*), as is *lapha*. The kanji for the "*bei*" in *bei nasu* also means rice, so Ginjirou puts them together to come up with *kome kome bei bei*, the latter half sounding like "baby." Tomu, hearing "rice and eggplant," thinks of *mabo nasu*, which is an eggplant stir-fry dish.

Page 56, "This is a love story."
The reason this phrase is in quotes is because the phrase is also the title of a manga series that ran in *Aria*, the same magazine as *First Love Monster*. It's about the romance between characters more than twenty years apart in age.

Page 62, Mitsuko Thirtinuma-san
In Japanese, Kaminuma-sensei demands that the children call her *Kaminuma Mitsuko San Jussai*, which could either mean "Kaminuma Mitsuko, age thirty" or "Kaminuma Mitsuko-san, age ten." The translators attempted to replicate this effect by rendering it as "Mitsuko Thirtinuma-san," where it could be 30-numa or 13-uma.

Page 106, Tatsuo Umemiya
Tatsuo Umemiya is an actor who debuted in the late '50s. American movie buffs might recognize him from the 1959 film *Prince of Space*.

Page 110, "forgot my bag"
Specifically, Kanade forgot his *kyuushoku-bukuro*, which is a small drawstring bag that contains some necessities for eating his school-provided lunch. These necessities include napkins, chopsticks, spoon, etc.

Page 125, I-Cuss
Idolcustomers, or *I-Cuss*, is likely a parody of the *Idolmaster* franchise, or *I-Mas*. This could be a play on "master" being the opposite of "customer," but more importantly, in the abbreviated version, *ai-kasu*, *kasu* is Japanese for "dregs" or "scum."

Page 136, forty-year-old mackerel reading
The word *sabayomi*, literally "mackerel reading," is a Japanese idiom for lying about numbers, usually one's age or weight. Specifically, *sabayomi* refers to giving a larger number than is truthful, so it may be safe to assume that Ken Tanaka has fudged his age in order to gain employment.

FIRST LOVE MONSTER 6

AKIRA HIYOSHIMARU

Translation: Alethea and Athena Nibley

Lettering: Abigail Blackman

FIRST LOVE MONSTER Volume 6
© 2016 Akira Hiyoshimaru. All rights reserved.
First published in Japan in 2016 by Kodansha, Ltd., Tokyo.
Publication rights for this English edition arranged through Kodansha Ltd., Tokyo.

English translation © 2017 by Yen Press, LLC

Yen Press
1290 Avenue of the Americas
New York, NY 10104

Visit us at yenpress.com
facebook.com/yenpress
twitter.com/yenpress
yenpress.tumblr.com
instagram.com/yenpress

Yen Press is an imprint of Yen Press, LLC.
The Yen Press name and logo are trademarks of Yen Press, LLC.

Library of Congress Control Number: 2015952581

First Yen Press Edition: January 2017

ISBN: 978-0-316-50461-4

10 9 8 7 6 5 4 3 2 1

BVG

Printed in the United States of America